W. B. YEATS: THE CRITICAL HERITAGE

THE CRITICAL HERITAGE SERIES

GENERAL EDITOR: B. C. SOUTHAM, M.A., B.LITT. (OXON.)

Formerly Department of English, Westfield College, University of London

For a list of books in the series see the back end paper

The Editor

A. Norman Jeffares is Professor of English Studies at the University of Stirling. In addition to various works on Yeats, including *W. B. Yeats* (RKP, 1971) he has also written and edited books and articles on Restoration and eighteenth-century drama and poetry and on Anglo-Irish, Commonwealth and American literature.

W. B. YEATS

THE CRITICAL HERITAGE

Edited by

A. NORMAN JEFFARES
Professor of English, University of Stirling

ROUTLEDGE & KEGAN PAUL
LONDON, HENLEY AND BOSTON

First published in 1977
by Routledge & Kegan Paul Ltd
39 Store Street,
London WC1E 7DD,
Broadway House,
Newtown Road,
Henley-on-Thames,
Oxon RG9 1EN and
9 Park Street,
Boston, Mass. 02108, USA
Printed in Great Britain by
Redwood Burn Limited
Trowbridge & Esher

British Library Cataloguing in Publication Data

W. B. Yeats, the critical heritage. – (The critical
heritage series).

1. Yeats, William Butler – Criticism and
interpretation
I. Jeffares, Alexander Norman II. Series
821'.8   PR5907   77-30043

ISBN 0 7100 8480 3

General Editor's Preface

The reception given to a writer by his contemporaries and near-contemporaries is evidence of considerable value to the student of literature. On one side, we learn a great deal about the state of criticism at large and in particular about the development of critical attitudes towards a single writer; at the same time, through private comments in letters, journals or marginalia, we gain an insight upon the tastes and literary thought of individual readers of the period. Evidence of this kind helps us to understand the writer's historical situation, the nature of his immediate reading-public, and his response to these pressures.

The separate volumes in *The Critical Heritage Series* present a record of this early criticism. Clearly, for many of the highly-productive and lengthily-reviewed nineteenth- and twentieth-century writers, there exists an enormous body of material; and in these cases the volume editors have made a selection of the most important views, significant for their intrinsic critical worth or for their representative quality.

For writers of the eighteenth century and earlier, the materials are much scarcer and the historical period has been extended, sometimes far beyond the writer's lifetime, in order to show the inception and growth of critical views which were initially slow to appear.

In each volume the documents are headed by an Introduction, discussing the material assembled and relating the early stages of the author's reception to what we have come to identify as the critical tradition. The volumes will make available much material which would otherwise be difficult of access and it is hoped that the modern reader will be thereby helped towards an informed understanding of the ways in which literature has been read and judged.

B.C.S.

Contents

CONTENTS

ix

CONTENTS

x

Acknowledgments

The editor and publishers would like to thank the following
for permission to reprint the material cited, which is
within their copyright or control:

From 'J.B. Yeats Letters to his Son W.B. Yeats and Others';
reprinted by permission of Christy and Moore Ltd and Dutton
& Co. From 'Further Letters of Gerard Manley Hopkins',
edited by Claude Colleer Abbott, 1938; published by
Oxford University Press by arrangement with the Society
of Jesus; reprinted by permission of the publisher.
Katharine Tynan, Three Young Poets, 'Irish Monthly', March
1887; reprinted by permission of the Editor of 'Studies'.
Sir William Watson, review in 'Illustrated London News',
10 September 1892; reprinted by permission of Illustrated
London News and Sketch Ltd. Anonymous review, 'The
Athenaeum', 6 April 1895; reprinted by permission of the
'New Statesman'. Anonymous review, 'The Athenaeum', 22
May 1897; reprinted by permission of the 'New Statesman'.
Fiona Macleod, A group of Celtic writers, 'Fortnightly
Review', 1 January 1899; reprinted by permission of the
Editor of the 'Contemporary Review' (incorporating 'The
Fortnightly'). From Arthur Symons, 'Studies in Prose and
Verse', 1904; reprinted by permission of J.M. Dent & Sons
Ltd. Leading article, 'Irish Times', 9 May 1899; re-
printed by permission of the Editor, 'Irish Times'. From
'The Critical Writings of James Joyce', edited by Ellsworth
Mason and Richard Ellmann, 1959; all rights reserved; re-
printed by permission of the Viking Press, Inc. and Faber
& Faber. J.M. Synge, Le Mouvement intellectuel irlandais,
'Collected Works, II, Prose', edited by Alan Price, 1966;
reprinted by permission of Oxford University Press. From
'Letters from A E', selected and edited by Alan Denson,
1961; reprinted by permission of Alan Denson and Diarmuid
Russell (and M. Thomas, A.M. Heath & Co., George Russell's

executor). Anonymous review, 'Manchester Guardian', 12 June 1903; reprinted by permission of the Editor, the 'Guardian'. Anonymous review, 'The Athenaeum', 27 June 1903; reprinted by permission of the 'New Statesman'. Sir Max Beerbohm, Some Irish Plays and Players, 'Around Theatres', 1953; reprinted by permission of Mrs Eva Reichmann and Hart Davis Ltd. Edward Thomas, 'Letters of Edward Thomas to Gordon Bottomley', edited George Thomas, 1968; reprinted by permission of Oxford University Press. Oliver St John Gogarty, 'Many Lines to Thee', edited James F. Carens, 1971; reprinted by permission of The Dolmen Press. George A. Birmingham, The Literary Movement in Ireland, 'Fortnightly Review', December 1907; reprinted by permission of Miss A.C. Hannay and the Editor of 'The Contemporary Review' (incorporating 'The Fortnightly'). Anonymous review [Lytton Strachey], 'The Spectator', 17 October 1908; reprinted by permission of 'The Spectator'. E.M.D[owden]., review, 'The Fortnightly Review', 1 February 1909; reprinted by permission of the Editor of 'The Contemporary Review' (incorporating 'The Fortnightly'). From George Moore, 'Hail and Farewell. Ave', 1911; reprinted by permission of J.C. Medley and R.C. Medley. From Katharine Tynan, 'Twenty-five Years: Reminiscences', 1913; reprinted by permission of John Murray (Publishers) Ltd. From Lady Gregory, 'Our Irish Theatre: A Chapter of Autobiography', 1913; reprinted by permission of Colin Smythe Limited, publishers. [This work was published in enlarged form in 1972, as volume IV of the Coole Edition of Lady Gregory's 'Works'.] From Cornelius Weygandt, 'Irish Plays and Playwrights', 1913; reprinted by permission of Constable Publishers. Ezra Pound, The Later Yeats, 'Poetry IV', 11 May 1914; reprinted by permission of Faber & Faber Limited and New Directions Publishing Corporation. From J.M. Hone, 'The Life of George Moore', 1936; reprinted by permission of Victor Gollancz Ltd. From Forrest Reid, 'W.B. Yeats: a Critical Study', 1915; reprinted from the edition published by Martin Secker and Warburg Limited. From Thomas MacDonagh, 'Literature in Ireland. Studies Irish and Anglo-Irish', 1916; reprinted by permission of the Talbot Press. Various reviews and articles, the 'Times Literary Supplement'; reprinted by permission of the 'Times Literary Supplement'. Marianne Moore, review, 'Poetry' (Chicago) XII, October 1918; reprinted by permission of Clive E. Driver, literary executor of the estate of Marianne C. Moore, and of the Modern Poetry Association. From Robert Lynd, 'Old and New Masters', 1919; reprinted by permission of J.M. Dent & Sons Ltd. T.S. Eliot, A Foreign Mind, 'The Athenaeum', 4 July 1919; reprinted by permission of Mrs Valerie Eliot,

the owner of the copyright, and Faber & Faber Limited.
J. Middleton Murry, The Yeats's Swan Song, 'The Athenaeum',
4 April 1919; reprinted by permission of the Society of
Authors as the literary representative of the Estate of
John Middleton Murry. From C.L. Wrenn, W.B. Yeats. A
Literary Study, 'Durham University Journal', 1920; re-
printed by permission of the University of Durham. From
Frank O'Connor, Two friends - Yeats and AE, 'Yale Review',
September 1939; reprinted by permission of A.D. Peters &
Company, 'Yale Review' and Cyrilly Abels. A E (George
Russell), review, 'Irish Statesman', 13 February 1926;
reprinted by permission of Diarmuid Russell (and M. Thomas,
A.M. Heath & Co. Ltd as executor of G.W. Russell). Lady
Gregory, 'Journals', edited Lennox Robinson, 1946; re-
printed by permission of the Bodley Head. From I.A.
Richards, Some Contemporary Poets, 'Science and Poetry',
1927; reprinted by permission of Professor I.A. Richards.
From 'F.P. Sturm, His Life, Letters and Collected Work',
edited Richard Taylor, 1969; reprinted by permission of
Granada Publishing Limited and the University of Illinois
Press. From Charles Williams, 'Poetry at Present', 1930;
reprinted by permission of the Clarendon Press. From
William Empson, 'Seven Types of Ambiguity', 1930; reprinted
by permission of Chatto & Windus Ltd. Monk Gibbon, Yeats's
earlier Poems, 'Irish Statesman', 29 March 1930; reprinted
by permission of Mr Monk Gibbon. [This poem can also be
found in Monk Gibbon, 'The Velvet Bow and other Poems',
1972.] From Edmund Wilson, 'Axel's Castle: a Study in
the Imaginative Literature of 1870-1930', 1931; reprinted
by permission of Farrar, Straus and Giroux, Inc. and
Charles Scribner's Sons (copyright 1931, Charles Scribner's
Sons). From F.R. Leavis, 'New Bearings in English Poetry',
1932; reprinted by permission of Chatto & Windus, and the
University of Michigan Press. From Ivor Winter, T. Sturge
Moore, 'Hound and Horn', April-June 1933; reprinted by
permission of the Swallow Press. Sir Desmond MacCarthy,
article on Yeats's 'Collected Poems', 'Sunday Times',
February 1934; reprinted by permission of the 'Sunday
Times' and Mrs Chloe MacCarthy and Mr R.M. Ritchie. From
Sir Herbert Read, The Later Yeats, 'A Coat of Many Colours.
Occasional Essays', 1934; reprinted by permission of
Benedict Read and David Higham Associates Ltd. From H.G.
Porteous, review, 'The Criterion', January 1934; re-
printed by permission of Barnes & Noble Inc. From
Priscilla Thouless, 'Modern Poetic Drama', 1934; reprinted
by permission of Mrs P. Thouless. From Dame Edith Sitwell,
'Aspects of Modern Poetry', 1934; reprinted by permission
of David Higham Associates Ltd and Gerald Duckworth & Co.
Ltd. From Geoffrey Bullough, 'The Trend of Modern Poetry',

1934; reprinted by permission of Oliver & Boyd. Denis
Johnston, Mr Yeats as dramatist, 'The Spectator', 30
November 1934; reprinted by permission of 'The Spectator'.
From J.H. Pollock, 'William Butler Yeats', 1935; re-
printed by permission of Mrs Anna Y. Pollock. Michael
Roberts, The Moon and the Savage, Sunlit Heart, 'The
Spectator', 27 December 1935; reprinted by permission of
'The Spectator'. From R.P. Blackmur, The Later Poetry of
W.B. Yeats, 'Southern Review', II, 2, Autumn 1936; re-
printed by permission of the 'Southern Review'. From
Stephen Gwynn, 'Irish Literature and Drama in the English
Language: A Short Story', 1936; reprinted by permission
of Thomas Nelson & Sons Limited. John Hayward, Mr. Yeats's
Book of Modern Verse, 'The Spectator', 20 November 1936;
reprinted by permission of 'The Spectator'. H.A. Mason,
Yeats and the English Tradition, 'Scrutiny', March 1937;
reprinted by permission of Cambridge University Press.
From Austin Clarke, Irish Poets, 'New Statesman and Nation',
29 January 1938; reprinted by permission of 'New Statesman'.
Janet Adam Smith, review, 'The Criterion', April 1938;
reprinted by permission of Janet Adam Smith. Stephen
Spender, review, 'The Criterion', April 1938; reprinted
by permission of Professor Stephen Spender. From Archi-
bald MacLeish, 'Poetry and Experience', 1961; reprinted
by permission of Houghton Mifflin Company and The Bodley
Head. From Una Ellis Fermor, The Abbey Theatre Festival,
'English' II, 9, Autumn 1938; reprinted by permission of
Mrs Elaine Weston. From F.R. Higgins, lecture, 'The
Irish Theatre: Lectures delivered during the Abbey Theatre
Festival held in Dublin in August 1938', edited Lennox
Robinson, 1939; reprinted by permission of Mrs D.S.
Robinson. L.A.G. Strong, W.B. Yeats, 'The Spectator',
18 November 1938; reprinted by permission of 'The Spec-
tator'. From Cleanth Brooks, 'Modern Poetry and the
Tradition', 1939; reprinted by permission of the Uni-
versity of North Carolina Press. From Louise Bogan,
William Butler Yeats, 'A Poet's Alphabet', 1970; copy-
right 1970 by Ruth Limmer as trustee; reprinted by per-
mission of McGraw-Hill Book Company. From A.D.M. Hoare,
'The Works of Morris and Yeats in relation to Early Saga
Literature', 1939; 1971; reprinted by permission of
Mrs D.M. de Navarro and Cambridge University Press. From
Philip Henderson, 'The Poet and Society', 1939; reprinted
by permission of Martin Secker and Warburg Limited. W.H.
Auden, In Memory of W.B. Yeats, 'Collected Shorter Poems
1927-1957'; reprinted by permission of Faber & Faber
and Random House, Inc.

Introduction

I

To read through the critical reception given to Yeats's
work during his lifetime is to realise what a vast change
has taken place in criticism itself. Many of the early
reviews are descriptive. That would not be a cause for
complaint in itself; but the description does not always
have a very clear critical basis. Yeats aroused strong
positive and negative reactions in reviewers and critics:
he still does. But these were based initially on a
relatively small body of work (and from time to time
reviewers said he should write more), and on what now
seem relatively superficial attitudes. Inevitably
Yeats's involvement with the creation of a literary
movement produced political responses within Ireland and
England; equally inevitably his 'Celtic' material caused
problems for reviewers, and the level of discussion of
the Celtic material was not high, for few reviewers knew
much of the Gaelic material Yeats had found in translation.
The issue was also obscured by what was meant by mystic
and magic, and in addition there was the problem of de-
fining symbolism.

The reviewing, then, was not generally very helpful,
for criticism, as we understand it, hardly existed,
except in Yeats's own writings which were concerned to
explain and expound his views of what a national literature should be, and how it could escape being provincial.
In his earlier prose work he was hindered by the fact
that he was discussing the work of others which did not
match up to his own writing, which he was naturally, at
that period, inhibited from discussing. Some of Yeats's
close friends were aware of his aims. John Todhunter,
Lionel Johnson, Arthur Symons and A.E. were sympathetic,
knew him and knew his ideas. Of the early reviewers,

William Sharp, as 'Fiona MacLeod', wrote intelligently about Celticism, but for many the subject was cocooned in vague adjectives rather than discussed for its sources, nature and effectiveness.

By the time Yeats's 'Collected Works' appeared it was easier for reviewers to attempt assessments, but the shift in his development, the stripping of decoration, the reaction against earlier escapism and idealism was not appreciated at once, although Yeats's greater self-revelation in the poems of 'Responsibilities' virtually coincided with the first of his autobiographical accounts in prose. It is significant that Ezra Pound in his review of 'Responsibilities and Other Poems' ('Poetry (Chicago)', May 1914) was quick to hail the new style, which suited his own imperative of making it new. Forrest Reid, who wrote a book on Yeats in 1915, had been more concerned with what had been achieved (and his assessment of the prose was particularly good). The next step was to recognise the flowering of Yeats's new manner: this did not seem to become generally accepted until some of the reviewers of 'The Tower', notably John Gould Fletcher, Theodore Spencer and the 'Times Literary Supplement' reviewer, began to assess the importance of his changed style and poetic authority.

A landmark in Yeatsian criticism was Edmund Wilson's 'Axel's Castle' (1931). Sufficiently at a distance from the work of the late nineteenth-century poets (as, perhaps, Arthur Symons in 'The Symbolist Movement in Literature' (1899) was not), Wilson was able to survey Yeats's work as a whole, disliking yet undeterred by Yeats's interest in magic and the occult. He showed an appreciative awareness of what Yeats was trying to do, and a sympathetic summing up of his success. Other critics to consider in this connection are R.P. Blackmur, who wrote a somewhat overlong and heavy piece in 'The Southern Review' in 1936, and Louise Bogan, who gave a good appreciative account of what Yeats had done in the 'Atlantic Monthly' in 1938.

These American writers seem to have been better able to assess the totality of Yeats's work while he was still living. Many critics, however, tended to concentrate on particular aspects of his writing, particularly towards the end of his life. For instance, a year before the poet's death in 1939, F.R. Higgins dealt well with his dramatic work in a lecture given at a Festival in Dublin in 1938, and L.A.G. Strong paid a generous tribute to Yeats's personality in an article in 'The Spectator' in 1938.

The Yeats industry was yet to come. Joseph Hone's
biography of 1942 was followed by other studies which
examined the relationship of the poet's life and work
closely. The existence of what might now be termed an
archive, and Mrs Yeats's generous willingness to give
scholars access to it — the poet's library, what survived
of his manuscripts and his letters, all supplemented by
her memories and acute comments — allowed expository work
in the tradition of Livingstone Lowes's 'Road to Xanadu'
(1929) to proceed apace. The intellectual or biographical
sources, the starting points of poems, plays and prose
(even including 'A Vision') have been suggested or proved,
allusions teased out, meanings interpreted, biographical
problems solved (though many remain unsolved and probably
will stay so), the Variorum editions and the Concordances
completed, and bibliographical studies rounded off. A
flood of critical comment has swept remorselessly over
the reader from all quarters of the world. By about 1980
(perhaps in the hundredth year after Yeats's published
work first appeared?) we are told, there will be an official edition of the Letters and an official biography is
now being written by the Provost of Trinity College,
Dublin. It would no doubt have gratified Yeats, and
possibly the power of modern scholarship (as well as its
frequent complexity and ponderosity) might well have surprised him. He told his wife two things which are amusing
in the light of it all: that he had spent his life saying
the same thing in different ways; and that he didn't
want 'them' to know everything about him. So many, in
effect, now say the same thing by devoting so much energy
and time to him: that he is a great poet. And so many
have found out — and continue to find out — so much
about him.
    There is, then, a watershed. What we see of the recep-
tion of Yeats's work up to his death is largely reviewing.
It was limited in scope by space, by the usual difficulties
of giving virtually instantaneous progress reports on
such a changing, developing writer, and by the existing
critical tradition, which was just beginning to try out
occasional prototypes of the machinery now mass-produced
in universities throughout the world.

II

Two very early comments on Yeats's work represent different points of view which were often echoed afterwards.
Gerard Manley Hopkins wrote to Coventry Patmore on
7 November 1886 to tell him of 'a young Mr Yeats who has

written in a Trinity College publication some striking
verses'. He was presented with 'Mosada: a Dramatic Poem'
by Yeats's father, and as he could not think highly of it
praised another piece. This was 'The Two Titans: A
Political Poem', 'The Dublin University Review', March
1885, which he called 'a strained and unworkable allegory
about a young man and a sphinx on a rock in the sea (how
did they get there? what did they eat? and so on: people
think such criticisms very prosaic; but common-sense is
never out of place . . .)'. Yeats's friend, the Irish
novelist and poetess Katharine Tynan, was more enthusiastic; writing of 'a new voice' in the 'Irish Monthly',
March 1887, she described 'Mosada' as 'wonderfully clear,
rich and soft in its minor tones'. The 'stately measure'
of its blank verse was praised ('The Dublin University
Review' in which it had first been published described it
as 'powerful and pathetic'), and she thought it created
beauty which was 'rapt and exalted, the very spirit of
poetry'.

Edward Dowden's comment of 1886 that Willie Yeats
'hangs in the balance between genius and (to speak rudely)
fool' put the two views dramatically, in extreme terms.
It was difficult to decide on the status of a young man's
work, and this problem affected the reviewers of Yeats's
first volume, 'The Wanderings of Oisin, and Other Poems'
(1889). Those critics who were appreciative recognised
his originality. W.E. Henley ('Scots Observer', 7 March
1889) praised the poetic inspiration of the volume and
Francis Thompson ('Weekly Register', 27 September 1890)
regarded it as 'the work of a genuine poet', stressing
Shelley's strong influence (and warning him — unneces-
sarily as it turned out — not to take his art too
lightly). John Todhunter, in a balanced review ('The
Academy', 30 March 1889) called it a remarkable first
volume, paying tribute to Yeats's poetic gift and wondering what the poet would make of it. While recognising that
there were flaws in the execution, he commented on the
young man's instinct for imaginative diction and the
music of the verse: he realised that Yeats's rhythms
were incalculable and unexpected.

Those critics who were unenthusiastic found fault with
the technique. William Watson, for instance, reviewing
'The Countess Kathleen and Various Legends and Lyrics'
(1892) stated baldly that Yeats 'had no idea of versification', that while his artistic means were ambitious
he failed to produce any effect and the disaster was
considerable. Yeats's making the second foot of a blank
verse line trochaic was an 'excruciating trick'. (This
was a complaint made later by William Archer in 'Poets of

the Younger Generation', 1902.) Did Watson want to put
down a rival? The tone of his criticism is perhaps
meant to be funny, to treat Yeats as a stage Irishman,
with his 'grotesque machinery of sowlths and tevishes
and sheogues . . . his fantasies [were] . . . stage
properties'.

Some critics found the poetry over-remote. The Dublin
'Evening Mail', reviewing 'The Wanderings of Oisin' on
13 February 1889, had recommended him to devote his powers
to creating works of the imagination which had for ex-
clusive subject 'the joys and sorrows, hopes and fears,
of humanity'. Many criticisms of 'The Countess Kathleen'
followed this line. The 'National Observer' complained on
3 September 1892 that his drama was too remote, and 'The
Spectator' of 29 July 1893 thought his verse lacked
human interest. But these attitudes were based perhaps
on Yeats's interest in the supernatural. Two other comments — sometimes united, sometimes not — emerged at
this early stage of his career. Oscar Wilde, for
instance, regarded him as 'essentially Celtic' and
possessing 'the romantic temper'. By this time most of
the characteristics of his verse had been distinguished
by critics, though they did not agree about them. The
debate about the nature of Celticism was to continue,
notably in the writings of Fiona MacLeod, for many
reviewers found it a convenient label to attach without
much thought about what the term might mean. They also
found it convenient to describe him as writing in the
mode of very different writers. He was said to be like
Dante, Wordsworth, Shelley, Keats, Swinburne.

The general reception of 'The Countess Kathleen and
Various Legends and Lyrics' (1892), indeed, offered
much the same critical response as had been evoked by
'The Wanderings of Oisin'. Its poems were restrained
in language, the subject matter of the Gaelic sources
was, in the words of 'The Times', 'fantastic and outlandish', and the remoteness from human reality and
interest disturbed both those who liked the poetry and
those who did not. The mystery could seem mystic and
that was an easy way out. Perhaps Lionel Johnson was one
of the few to realise the essential problem — which
Yeats later put forward himself — for the Irish writer
who wrote of Irish matter: how to avoid being provincial?
Johnson saw that Yeats could write Celtic poetry 'in a
classical manner', by which he meant Yeats sought discipline in order to produce 'poems rational and thoughtful, yet beautiful with the beauty that comes of thought
about imagination'. In general, Yeats was accepted as
an able minor poet offering genuine, if quaint and

fanciful, Celtic material.

'The Celtic Twilight' (1893) reinforced Yeats's standing, particularly with British and American critics,
although Irish critics had reservations, wondering whether
some of Yeats's folklore *was* folklore, and whether
occultism was not a London literary fashion which might
lead Yeats to embroider. Melancholy was matched by
merriness now, the stories were full of romance; they
were charming and Celtic and welcome.

By 'Poems' (1895) the reception was more predictable.
Yeats was now thirty, and his reputation was becoming
firmly established. (In 'A Bibliography of the Writings
of W.B. Yeats' Wade lists over 150 signed contributions
by Yeats in verse and prose by the end of 1894.) He
was seen by British and American critics as continuing
traditional English poetry: 'more than any of the younger
men' remarked 'The Speaker' (4 January 1896). Richard
Garnett thought he wrote the kind of poetry William Morris
might have produced if he had been born and brought up
in the west of Ireland ('Illustrated London News', 21
December 1895). The 'Atlantic Monthly' (May 1896)
regarded him as 'sharing the chief honours of the "new
school" in British poetry'. To English reviewers Yeats's
Celticism was mysterious and beautiful and that was,
generally speaking, enough. Annie Macdonnel, who anticipated Fiona MacLeod's Scottish interest in Yeats's
Celticism, and twice reviewed 'Poems' (1895), enthusiastically regarded Yeats not as a man 'who finds
fairyland convenient' but as someone who believed in two
worlds balancing against each other ('The Bookman',
December 1895). He was interested, she added, in human
nature which lived near the soil and roots of things (many
critics were apt to remark that Yeats had the root of the
matter in him). But even she shied away from any search
into his deeper meanings, being content to remark that
his later 'perhaps wiser' poetry was 'more mystic, more
elusive' ('English Illustrated', December 1895).

Irish reviewers, however, were beginning to realise —
aided no doubt by Yeats's own articles and speeches — that
he was not writing entirely in the tradition into which
British and American reviewers naturally placed him,
mentioning as they did Shakespeare, Coleridge and Keats,
as well as such contemporary poets as John Davidson,
Francis Thompson and William Watson, in their descriptions
of this Irish poet's work. Yeats's friend George Russell,
A.E., wrote a lofty panegyric on Yeats's regal imagination, something not known in Ireland 'since the days of
the mystic Da Danaan races' ('Irish Weekly Independent',
26 October 1895), but John McGrath saw his poetry in terms

of his Irish predecessors of the nineteenth century, and regarded him as lifting Irish poetry out of 'the ruck of Young Ireland rhetoric', a view-point which echoed Yeats's own propaganda for new Irish literature which would arise from craftsmanship as well as a devotion to the destiny of the country.(1) And Richard Ashe King, himself an Irish writer, emphasised Yeats's love of the Irish soil and the strength he got from the Gaelic legends, seeing in his pursuit of poetry free from practical or moral ends and in his visionary dreaming nature his Irish qualities ('The Bookman', September 1897).

The stories of 'The Secret Rose' (1897) — notably those of Hanrahan — were praised by some critics for their Irish qualities, the peasant humour of 'Hanrahan the Red' appealing to the reviewer in 'The Speaker' (8 May 1897), the Irish character and manners to the reviewer in the 'Glasgow Herald' (15 April 1897), and the 'Irish prose' to the reviewer in 'United Ireland' (1 May 1897). Annie Macdonnel's views in 'The Bookman' (May 1897) were intelligent; she praised the humour and she also realised the ultimate other-worldliness of the stories, while Francis Thompson praised their visual appeal and distinctness — a movement away from the mists of the twilight. 'The Athenaeum' was somewhat para- doxical in praising the concrete beauty of the pictures, yet thinking the Celticism did not anchor the stories in time or locate them in place, or indeed in race (22 May 1897).

The melancholy of the Celtic twilight began to trouble some reviewers when 'The Wind among the Reeds' was pub- lished in 1899: the 'Irish Daily Independent' (8 May 1899) wanted 'Wind upon the hill tops' instead of the mistiness and melancholia. But the main worry of reviewers — apart from several critics feeling that he should produce more and longer poems — was not the question of obscurity. Yeats's notes to the poems seemed unnecessary to some, including Arthur Symons. The fact that he wrote notes prompted 'The Spectator' (8 July 1899) to complain that Yeats seemed not always able to interpret his own poems, that he was giving his readers dreams not thought. The mixture of Gaelic material with Yeats's own brand of occultism in the symbolism was too much for some, notably Francis Thompson, who was as strict as a schoolmaster when commenting on Yeats's use in his notes of the phrase 'I use this to signify so and so' ('The Academy', 6 May 1899): indeed, in the view of W.P. Ryan, reviewing the volume in 'The Bookman' (February 1899), the symbolism was arbitrary and obscure. Others, however, found compensation for obscurity in the remote strange melancholy music of the

verse. Arthur Symons, while he paid tribute to this
remote and strange beauty of Yeats's verse, thought the
poet had managed through his concentration to make the
personal ecstasy of his lyrics become part of the universal consciousness ('The Saturday Review', 6 May 1899).
   In the same piece Arthur Symons was enthusiastic about
Yeats's play 'The Countess Cathleen'. The production of
'The Land of Heart's Desire' (1894) had encouraged Yeats,
and 'The Countess Cathleen', published first in 1892, then
in 'Poems' (1895; the title was first spelled as Cathleen
rather than Kathleen in this edition) and again in 'Poems'
(1899), was in rehearsal when Symons saw it. He thought
it not only splendid poetry but a fine acting play.
Katharine Tynan had realised earlier that Yeats was making
a significant contribution to poetic drama; even if its
characters were shadowy they had 'a delicate human touch'
('United Ireland', 3 September 1892).
   The provincialism of much Irish criticism emerged at
the time of the play's production in Dublin, and the theological issues occupied many local critics. Max Beerbohm,
reporting on these first performances of the Irish Literary
Theatre (Martyn's 'The Heather Field' was staged as well
as 'The Countess Cathleen') in 'The Saturday Review' (13
May 1899) expressed his surprise at the furore the play
caused in Dublin. He had gone to Dublin, he wrote, on a
romantic errand, to see and to describe the revival of a
certain form of beauty in a land known to be a land of
tears and dreams. After disembarking from the night
boat, he realised, on reading his morning papers, that
he was 'in a land where tears and dreams have always a
supplement of wigs on the green':

   Here was a furious protest from the 'Catholic students
   of the Royal University' against 'Mr. Yeats' slanderous
   caricature of the Irish peasant. . . . We do not seek
   the goodwill of England, but we object to be made the
   butt of her bitter contempt.' Here was Cardinal Logue,
   who, 'judging by these extracts', had 'no hesitation
   in saying that an Irish Catholic audience which could
   sit out such a play must have sadly degenerated, both
   in religion and patriotism'. (Pleasant, to find that
   Irish Cardinals and English Bishops have one habit
   in common, at least!) Here, too, was a vitriolic
   telegram from Mr. Frank Hugh O'Donnell. (Strange, that
   Mr. Yeats in luring down the Sheogue from the hill-side,
   had also evoked a fiery spirit from the shades of
   1880!) I confess that I was altogether startled. A
   little play, written by a poet for no sake but that of
   beauty, with no aim in history or theology — and then,

in a jiffy, the green covered with wigs! Dublin
resounding with protests that no Irish peasant was
ever so degraded as to barter his soul for bread, and
that it is impious to suggest that 'the Virgin has
dropped asleep' in time of famine!

He raised the tone of the discussion. Yeats's aim was to
see 'whether beauty be not, after all, possible on the
stage'. Beerbohm thought that the beauty of Maeterlinck's
work resulted from his treatment of his characters from
a standpoint of beauty:

The fact is that it is impossible for an artist to
create beauty if he takes so ugly an age as this for
his background; nay, that it is impossible even for
an artist living in a beautiful age to create beauty
if he take his own age for background. Athens was
not ugly, nor was London in the time of Elizabeth;
yet both Shakespeare and Æschylus, in quest of beauty,
put their puppets into an age either fabulous or bygone.
Beauty seems always something remote from the stress
of common life. Though it may exist in such life, it
can be conceived only as at a distance. The greater
the distance, the clearlier can it be conceived. And
it is for this reason that Maeterlinck billets his
figures on some castle that never existed or perhaps
existed 'nowhere once'. And it is for that reason,
also, Mr. Yeats has laid his play 'in Ireland, and in
old times'. It was inevitable that Mr. Yeats should
choose Ireland as the scene, even had he known that
Irishmen would be so foolish as to treat the play as
a contribution to history. But, so far as his play
is concerned, I see no essential reason why the scene
should have been laid anywhere really on the map.
Perhaps that is because I am not an Irishman? To
an Irishman, perhaps, Mr. Yeats' play may seem steeped
in national character. To me it seems merely a beautiful poem about some men and women.

And then he modified this comment, remarking that he should
have said it was a play about a woman. After giving a
brief résumé of the plot, he complained that the conclusion of the play could not be defended. The beauty of
the Countess's sacrifice is inevitably cheapened by the
knowledge that she was saved from its consequences. It
was a matter of deep irony that Yeats had invented a happy
ending for the play.

However, it is the only fault I find with him. For
the rest, he has written a poem of exquisite and moving
beauty. I do not suggest that he is a dramatist in
the sense in which Maeterlinck is a dramatist. He
is so far a dramatist that he can tell things simply
and clearly in dramatic form. But he is, pre-eminently,
a poet; and for him words, and the ordering of words,
are always the chief care and delight. His verses,
more than the verses of any other modern poet, seem
made to be chanted; and it is, I fancy, this peculiar
vocal quality of his work, rather than any keen sense
of drama, that has drawn him into writing for the stage.

How very intelligent also was the criticism of William
Sharp, who could be severe at times with Yeats's work,
but none the less realised his purposes. He discussed
what Yeats wrote rather than giving general views of
what Celticism might mean, or indeed merely suggest in
its mysteriousness. Sharp felt something was lacking in
'The Countess Cathleen', despite its beauty and the
pleasure it gave its audiences. And he argued correctly
in the light of his view that Yeats seemed 'not primarily
a dramatist'. But he argued his point generously ('North
American Review', October 1902). 'The Shadowy Waters' was
a beautiful 'poetic drama'; and 'The Land of Heart's
Desire' showed the reflective spirit of reverie transmuted into dramatic form. He hoped Yeats would find a
compromise that would be almost a new art, a new art
perhaps. He realised Yeats's desire to escape outworn
conventions, to turn 'from the scenic musings of the stage-
carpenter and the palpable illusions of the playwright' to

> dramas of the mind there are
> Best seen against imagined tapestries.

'The Shadowy Waters' drew longer reviews. The 'Manchester Guardian' regarded it as a 'great poem', because
it was universal. The man who thirsts for the infinite,
and the woman with her earthly love seemed 'cast in the
most general mould' (4 March 1901). This was an acceptance of Yeats as human and able to speak with an accent
'clear, entrancing and his own'. G.K. Chesterton's review
in 'The Speaker' (19 January 1901) generally welcomed
the play, and regarded the symbolism as 'arbitrary but
haunting'. Summing up the limitations of this 'drama of
mood' he thought it would be admirably suited to a toy
theatre. All that was needed to bring out its charm was
'exquisite scenery, stately and motionless figures, a
certain amount of blue and green fire, and Mr. Yeats

himself under the table to intone the words in the proper
manner.'(2)   He recognised the play as part of a revival
of spiritual hypothesis, a revolt against the erection
of the rationalists into the position of universal school-
masters.   Faith they had made a sin, and thus a pleasure
for the modern aesthetes who 'instead of being "dragooned
into heaven" like the subjects of Louis XIV creep into
heaven with all the delight of trespassers'.   Foremost
of these wild boys, he remarked, was Mr Yeats 'who plucks,
in his own beautiful words

>   The silver apples of the moon,
>   The golden apples of the sun

with all the ecstasy of an urchin robbing an orchard.'
    After showing that there is no change of sentiment in
the play, the hero being just as dismal before the number
of melancholy events which happen to him as after them,
Chesterton delivered a mild reproof, balanced by his
opening remarks which compared Yeats to Blake, hoping
people would pay him the tribute of ceasing to discover
him.   Blake had been kept out of his throne by his
admirers refusing to pay him the supreme compliment of
criticism.   Yeats had outlived cheap jokes about mysticism;   he had achieved 'the first place among poets now
working worthily'.   Chesterton's criticism was directed
against Yeats's non-Christian melancholia:

> But the truth is that the whole of this beautiful
> poem is dominated by one conception, very native to
> Mr. Yeats' work and connecting it not only with the
> mythological but even more with the mediaeval spirit —
> the conception of the finite character of all things,
> even of heaven and earth.   Superficially it might be
> said that the imaginative man would have to do with
> eternity, but it is not so.   Imagination has to do with
> images — that is to say, with shapes — and eternity
> has no shape.   Here the finite note is perpetually
> struck: the whole ship of Forgael is drifting to the
> last seas, where
>
>> Time and the world and all things dwindle out.
>
> In this poem Mr. Yeats treats this finality of all
> things with an even deeper melancholy than is his
> wont.   We must admit that to us there seems nothing so
> unsupportable in these boundaries and that to complain
> that youth, for example, has a beginning and an end is
> like complaining that a cow has a head and tail.   An

outline must be a limit. Above all we can have no
sympathy whatever with that far older and idler
pessimism which makes capital out of the dispropor-
tions of the Cosmos. The size of the fixed stars no
more makes us insignificant than the size of the
animalculae makes us divine. The beauty of life is
in itself and is as indestructible whether it lasts
as long as a planet or as long as a violin solo. If
it be true that to the gods

   Armies on white roads
 And unforgotten names and the cold stars
 That have made all are dust on a moth's wing,

if we are to adopt this magnificent image of Mr. Yeats
and conceive of the whole Cosmos as a moth, its wings
coruscating with moons and stars, fluttering in the
dark void, the only thing to say of the moth is that
it is a very fine specimen. It is at least better
than an endless caterpillar.

The account in 'The Saturday Review' (29 December 1900)
commented on Yeats's 'more remote and yet essentially
more human wisdom'. It is hard to see how this was
assessed: it was possibly a way of accepting Yeats as
possessing some mystical vision, as a careful painstaking
writer who 'makes his visible pictures out of what has
come to him invisibly, in dreams, in the energetic
abandonment of meditation'. He did not render his
visions 'literally into that other language of ordinary
life, instead of translating them freely, idiom for idiom'.
Yeats wrote of his contemporaries and himself that at
the turn of the century 'everybody got down off his
stilts' ('The Oxford Book of Modern Verse 1892-1935',
1936, p.xi). Not all the critics did, but some, such as
William Archer in 'Poets of the Younger Generation' (1902),
appreciated Yeats's desire to blend primitive and cultivated elements in poetry. Archer thought Yeats's touch
had improved, though he criticised his prosody, objecting
strongly to a trochee in the second foot of a line (the
crooning rhythm of 'The Countess Cathleen', however,
appealed to him). But he raised a serious point about the
symbolism of the poems in 'The Wind among the Reeds' which
seemed to him a petrified symbolism, 'a system of hiero-
glyphs', which may have had 'some inherent significance
for their inventors, but which have now become matters
for research, of speculation, of convention'. This
objection to obscurity was echoed in reviews of 'Poems
1899-1905'. The Gaelic material was too local ('The

Saturday Review', 16 February 1907), and too unclear ('The Athenaeum', 15 December 1906). The latter review, by Mrs Bland, took exception to the notes:

> This thin blue book holds between its beautiful covers some forty poems, none of them long, and many very brief, so that the forty live in spacious ease in some sixty loosely printed pages. Beyond their dwelling lies a wide, pleasant wilderness of notes, filling the rest of the book. To us this placing seems an error. It is rare that any modern poem should need notes so copious; but if they be needed, surely it were better to set them as an introduction to the poems rather than as a supplement. Having read the notes, one might go on to the poems with an added interest. When one has read the poems the notes do but confuse and annoy. For the poems stand alone as poems, having each its own grace and its own meaning; and to the mind satisfied with these the mass of legend collected in the notes does but darken counsel, vexing and bewildering not only by a thicket of folk-lore, but by mists of modern symbolism obscuring the green mazes of the old tales. Some of the notes, beside, are superfluous, an insult to the reader and to the poems themselves — a prosy insistence on the density of the one, and a confession of the inadequacy of the other. For instance,
>
>> The North unfolds above them clinging, creeping
>>   night,
>> The East her hidden joy before the morning
>>   break,
>> The West weeps in pale dew and sighs passing
>>   away,
>> The South is pouring down roses of crimson fire.
>
> That is surely enough. What need for the note in which Mr. Yeats tells us that he 'follows much Irish and other mythology, and the magical tradition, in associating the North with night and sleep, and the East, the place of the sunrise, with hope, and the South, the place of the sun when at its height, with passion and desire, and the West, the place of sunset, with fading and dreaming things'?

The notes are mainly intended to explain the mythological allusions which occur throughout the poems, and some such explanation is certainly desirable, for Irish mythology is little known, except among the

Irish, and even among these Mr. Yeats's special brand
of metaphysical mythology must be quite a novelty;
but if these notes had to be, we repeat that they
should have been as a preface, not an afterword.

Horatio F. Krans, 'W.B. Yeats and the Irish Literary
Revival' (1904), however, did not seem to find the
symbolism causing a difficulty: a little acquaintance
with the symbolism of the old literature, assisted by
a little familiarity with Yeats's philosophy, was his
optimistic recipe for giving more wattage to the twilight.
   In his approach to Yeats's love poetry — a stepping
stone to a philosophical conception — Krans was more
reserved, and in this he was somewhat similar to those few
who reviewed 'In The Seven Woods' (1903). The poems in
this volume which marked the signs of a turning point in
Yeats's style did not then, as later, receive very
understanding comment. The reviewer in the 'Daily
Chronicle' (1 September 1903) regarded Yeats as drawing
the readers towards the parting of the ways between the
common joys of life and the lonely path winding away among
the stars; but that Yeats himself was moving into a more
practical life — managing the Abbey, coming to terms
with Maud Gonne's marriage, with his own disillusion about
nationalism — and thus to his own awareness of change
in his own life and art, was not obvious to contemporary
commentators. The note by Yeats which separated the
lyrics in this volume from the play ('On Baile's Strand')
did foreshadow 'a change that may bring a less dream-
burdened will into my verses'. Later he put the situation
in terms of the Abbey Theatre, apostrophising Douglas
Hyde, 'most popular of men':

When we are high and airy hundreds say
That if we hold that flight they'll leave the place,
While those same hundreds mock another day
Because we have made our art of common things . . . (3)

This attitude of discontent with his earlier work was not
fully realised at the time. Poems such as 'The Arrow',
'The Folly of being Comforted', 'Old Memory', 'Never
give all the heart', 'O Do not love too long' and 'Adam's
Curse' now seem to have a finality about them, a retro-
spective view of the earlier love poetry and the poet's
earlier reactions to Maud Gonne. But Yeats himself took
some time to realise how much his life had changed. It
was 1934 before he looked back on this period with cold
clarity and wrote to Mrs Shakespear (27 February 1934):
'It is curious how one's life falls into definite sections.

In 1897 a new scene was set, new actors appeared.'
   Yeats's prose began to be treated with more seriousness. In reviewing 'The Celtic Twilight' (2nd edition,
1902) W. Burkitt Dalby made a valiant effort to relate
Yeats's work to mysticism as it appeared in the nineteenth century, and showed wide reading as well as a
capacity to detect a 'mystical' reaction against materialism deriving from Neo-Platonism and fourteenth-century
German mystics. ('London Quarterly Review', October
1903). Some of the contents of Yeats's 'Ideas of Good
and Evil' (1903) had first appeared eight years earlier,
and the volume of essays contained *inter alia* Yeats's
views on symbolism, nationalism, and what he called 'The
Autumn of the Body'. The questions raised by Yeats which
took the critics' interest were the larger views of
poetry and its origins, symbolism and the spiritual or
religious element, particularly in relation to the
'Celtic' tradition. The 'Times Literary Supplement' (12
June 1903) rightly saw the path traced by Platonism
through the writings of Blake and Shelley to Yeats and
liked his contempt for material success and popularity.
But these theories could seem decadent. 'The Autumn of
the Body' appeared to the reviewer in the 'Manchester
Guardian' to have a sinister significance (12 June 1903).
The dreamy trance was exploited with skill by modern
symbolists, but there were the intellectual and phenomenal worlds which they sought to evade or transfigure,
and these worlds were a portion of reality. The reviewer
saw the 'exultations and agonies of thought' as a factor
in the eternal epic of humanity which poetry could not
ignore and which no great poet had ignored. This criticism was more subtle than that of the 'Irish Times (22
May 1903), which found a 'persistent affectation' in
Yeats; and it was echoed by A. Clutton-Brock in 'The
Academy' (20 June 1903) when he praised will and reason.
Reveries, he thought, could leave the mind a prey to
unreason and disordered physical stimuli. This was a
reply to a review in the issue of 13 June 1903, which
praised Yeats, who brought his readers to the brink of
despair, compelling them to be aware of the naked awakened
soul, as he moved poetry further away from the practical
bargains and contracts of life. The time lag was inevitable: not till 'The Fascination of What's Difficult',
written in September 1909, did Yeats give voice to the
personal exasperation caused him, after the creation of
the Abbey Theatre, and his becoming manager of it in 1904,
by his own immersion in

   . . . the day's war with every knave and dolt,
   Theatre business, management of men.

The essays of 'Discoveries' (1907) seemed to the
reviewer in 'The Bookman' to show Yeats had come out of
his land of dreams and discovered life, and the style
seemed to Edward Thomas ('Daily Chronicle', 18 May 1908)
'serious, imaginative, flexible and most sweet'. This
praise of Yeats's prose style, which seemed to 'The
Academy's' reviewer to possess 'somewhat of the grave
music of Jeremy Taylor' (28 March 1908) had also greeted
'The Tables of the Law' and 'The Adoration of the Magi'
(1904; they were previously privately printed in 1897)
and 'Stories of Red Hanrahan' (1905; they were rewritten
versions of those stories which had appeared in 'The
Secret Rose', 1897). Yeats described the earlier versions
as written 'in literary English', and praised Lady
Gregory's help in the rewriting: 'They are but half mine
now and often her beautiful idiom is the better half.'
(Note in Allan Wade, 'A Bibliography of the Writings of
W.B. Yeats', 3rd ed. 1968, p. 74.) A reviewer in 'Black
and White' (10 June 1905), who saw the beauty of art as
a kind of Platonic idea of beauty, stressed that morals
had an aesthetic value and that the worship of beauty
led men into the moralist's own tabernacle: he realised
that the strength and sweetness of Yeats's stories came
from 'the redolent earth'.

This view of art leading to morality would probably
not have appealed to Paul Elmer More, who made his protest about the direction Yeats was taking in his first
series of 'Shelburne Essays' (1904). Like Clutton-
Brock, he distrusted the effects of loose reverie (which
Yeats seemed to him to indulge when striving after exalted
mysticism), disliked Yeats's decadent habit of depicting
women's hair, notably in 'The Wind among the Reeds', and
described Yeats's sense of failure and decay. Nothing he
thought, correctly, could be further from the virile
passion and pathos, the action and interaction of strong
characters in Gaelic literature. Some other American
criticism was captious also: H.W. Boynton in the
'Atlantic Monthly' (January 1904), for instance, J.R.
Taylor in the 'Methodist Review' (March 1905), and Louise
Collier Willcox in the 'North American Review' (May 1906).
A subsequent review by the last critic of Yeats's drama,
however, was generous in its praise. This appeared in the
'North American Review' (September 1907). Mary K. Ford
in the 'North American Review' (October 1906) found him
entirely without humour.

Yeats's plays, which occupied so much of his time and
energy in the first decade of the century, were, on the
whole, well received. 'The Countess Cathleen' caused
William Archer some anxiety in 'Poets of the Younger

Generation' (1902) over whether Yeats or Maeterlinck
came first. He decided Yeats did not owe anything to
the Belgian dramatist in the matter of conception and
plan; the parallels were part of the general sympathy
of spirit. 'The Land of Heart's Desire' was generally
praised, though briefly. 'The Shadowy Waters' (1900) was
praised too, for a talent equal to that of Maeterlinck
('Glasgow Herald', 20 November 1906) and, in the revised
version of 'Poems 1899-1905' (1905), reviewed by H.C.
Burling in 'The Bookman' (November 1906), for an improvement in its dramatic effectiveness. Arthur Symons in
his 'Studies in Prose and Verse' (1904) praised this
passage in the play which he called one of its most
beautiful and imaginative passages:

> The love of all under the light of the sun
> Is but brief longing, and deceiving hope,
> And bodily tenderness; but love is made
> Imperishable fire under the boughs
> Of chrysoberyl and beryl and chrysolite
> And chrysoprase and ruby and sardonyx.

Is there a word or cadence in these lines which could
not have been used equally well in prose, or in conversation; and yet, can it be denied that those lines
are exquisite verse, moving finely to their own
music? To get as far from prose, or from conversation,
as possible: that is the aim of most writers of verse.
But really, the finest verse is that verse which, in
outward form and vocal quality, is nearest to dignified prose or serious conversation.

The performance of 'Cathleen ni Houlihan' (1902, 1904
and subsequent editions) received a percipient review by
Stephen Gwynn. He wrote of this performance later (see
p. 557) in his 'Irish Literature and Drama' (1936):

> The effect of 'Cathleen ni Houlihan' on me was that
> I went home asking myself if such plays should be
> produced unless one was prepared for people to go
> out to shoot and be shot (p. 158).

And possibly Yeats had read Gwynn's book before writing
'The Man and the Echo' ('Collected Poems', p. 393) in
1938 with its record of self-questioning in the sleepless
hours of night:

> Did that play of mine send out
> Certain men the English shot?

Some critics had reservations about the dramatic qualities
of the play; and while others recognised Ibsen and
Maeterlinck in 'Where there is Nothing' (1902), the
'Manchester Guardian's' reviewer was uncertain whether
Yeats overcame the difficulties of presenting in dramatic
form the theme of a hero working out his version of
mystic Nihilism (11 June 1903). The absence of conventional dramatic effects and trappings was praised in
comments on this play and 'The Hour Glass' (1903). A.B.
Walkley, commenting in 'The Irish National Theatre' (May
1903; included in his 'Drama and Life', 1907), on
Yeats's seriousness — 'the mood is uniformly sad' —
thought that for anything of the kind one would have to
go to some of Maeterlinck's earlier plays. This, however,
was an imperfect comparison, he added, for the Irish
theatre had an unique 'note of subdued gravity with here
and there faint harmonies of weird elfish freakishness'.
He analysed the subtlety of 'The Hour Glass' wittily,
asking his readers to imagine how an ordinary dramatist
would deal with the situation where an angel gives a man
a few moments within which to try to find means of salvation before he dies with the last running out of the sand.
He enthused over 'the whole tone of the thing' which was
grave and subdued, its 'whole texture such stuff as dreams
are made of' and it haunted the mind long afterwards.
(He also saw the note of 'L'Intruse' and other early-
manner Maeterlinck plays in 'Cathleen ni Houlihan', where
an uncomfortable feeling creeps over the family gathering
that something, they know not what, is going to happen.
There is a Maeterlinck-like fear of something impending.
This is the same dream-feeling as in 'The Hour Glass':
'The people move about silently as fearing to break the
dream, and speak with bated breath.')
     'The Pot of Broth' (1904) made little demand on
critical sensibilities. Most critics welcomed it for its
amusing foolery. Among them was E.K. Chambers, whose
account of 'The Experiments of Mr. Yeats' ('The Academy
and Literature', 9 May 1903) praised the play's humorous
observation. He criticised Yeats's attempt in 'Cathleen
ni Houlihan' to create a dramatic illusion of the presence
of an unearthly or allegorical personage amongst human
beings, regarding this as 'an almost impossible one to
secure upon the stage where all the parts have to be
played by obviously living and breathing men and women'.
He saw the play at the Queen's Gate Hall in London, not,
like Stephen Gwynn, in a Dublin audience with decidedly
different attitudes. In this article Chambers dealt with
Yeats's experiments with the Psaltery. He sympathised
with Yeats's view that the Irish theatre should speak to

the people, mirror national life and voice national ideals,
though with the caveat that art should always be cosmo-
politan. Part of Yeats's theories, he realised, was that
future Irish drama should not only be founded on national
sentiment but also on folk-art appealing to a society
which has either never attained to or has discarded the
printed book:

> Herein it is to take rank with Mr. Yeats's other 'new
> art', that of spoken poetry, about which he lectured
> in Clifford's Inn on Tuesday, while Miss Florence Farr
> illustrated the lecture by speaking and chanting
> beautiful ditties to the accompaniment of one of Mr.
> Arnold Dolmetsch's psalteries. It was a very charm-
> ing performance, and if the dramatic recitation would
> give way to the musical recitation one would have
> reason to be grateful, even if one did not altogether
> give up the printed book. In insisting that the
> musical accompaniment of verse must bring out and not
> obscure the expressiveness of the words Mr. Yeats is
> on thoroughly firm ground. He will, of course, be
> the first to admit that his so-called 'new art' is a
> very old art indeed. Thus and no otherwise did the
> mediaeval minstrel use his singing voice and his
> *vielle*, to support the interminable *laisses* of his
> *romans* and *dits* and *contes*. If Mr. Yeats will look
> at the musical notation printed in Mr. Bourdillon's
> edition of 'Aucassin et Nicolete', he will find that
> the *viel caitif* who tells that story did precisely
> the sort of thing which Miss Farr does. He chanted
> his metrical passages to two simple musical phrases,
> which he repeated over and over again, and brought in
> a third phrase, slightly more cadenced, for the con-
> cluding line of each passage, before he went back to
> his prose.

A year earlier Arthur Symons had tilted with Yeats over
an aspect of his methods of speaking verse to musical
notes. Yeats had written Speaking to the Psaltery in
'The Monthly Review', 1902 (later included in 'Ideas of
Good and Evil', 1903), to which Symons replied with The
Speaking of Verse ('The Academy and Literature', 31 May
1902). He asserted that Yeats's methods would almost
certainly drift into intoning. Yeats wrote a letter to
the Editor ('The Academy', 7 June, 1902; later reprinted
in 'The Letters of W.B. Yeats', 1954), in which he argued
for fixing the pitch by notation in the speaking of poetry
to musical notes.
   'The King's Threshold' (1904) aroused mixed feelings,

the 'Manchester Guardian' querying the likelihood of
highly symbolistic writing achieving the intended effect,
but Max Beerbohm welcomed its difference from the usual
drawing-room comedy ('The Saturday Review', 9 April 1904).
The dramatic qualities of 'On Baile's Strand' (1904) did
seem to several critics to be more viable, notably to
reviewers in 'The Spectator' (25 June 1904) and 'The
Saturday Review' (28 May 1904), the latter seeing character in action for perhaps the first time in Yeats's work.
The 'Times Literary Supplement' thought the tragic conflict a little unreal (14 December 1906), and Maurice
Joy, who praised the play's presentation of great primary
passions in 'The Speaker' (7 January 1905) had reservations about the mixture of comedy and tragedy in such a
short play.
    'Deirdre' (1907) seemed to reach a high level of
attainment, Edward Thomas praising its rich simplicity and
melody, its magic realism, in his piece in 'The Bookman'
(October 1907), and the 'Manchester Guardian's'
reviewer its easier and more various verse (3 September
1907).
    Yeats was seen as in the mood of Maeterlinck, and his
plays seemed to some to be out of touch with life (for
example, Stephen Gwynn, 'Fortnightly Review', December
1901; 'Glasgow Herald', 2 April 1904; George O'Neill,
'New Ireland Review', March 1906; 'The Athenaeum', 5
December 1908; 'Edinburgh Review', January 1909). Arthur
Symons, however, in 'Studies in Prose and Verse' (1904)
defended Yeats strongly. Though his plays might seem to
lack something of the warmth of life they were splendidly
centred upon ideas of life; at their best they spoke
an heroic language, the language of the soul. He praised
Yeats's capacity to create great dramatic speech 'in which
poetry is content to seem simpler than prose'. He complained of having to read poetical plays where often the
poetry was an ornament, not an inherent part of the play's
dramatic structure: but in Yeats's plays both poetry
and drama seemed to him to grow together like bones and
flesh. Yeats carried condensation as far as it could be
carried without becoming mere baldness:

> Each thing said is a thing which had to be said, and
> it is said as if the words flowered up out of a deep
> and obscure soil, where they had been germinating for
> a long time in the darkness. The silences of these
> plays are like the pauses in music; we have the
> consciousness, under all the beauty and clearness
> and precision of the words we hear, of something unsaid,
> something which the soul broods over in silence. The

people who speak seem to think or dream long before speaking and after speaking; and though they have legendary names, and meet fantastically on a remoter sea than that which the Flying Dutchman sails over, or starve on the threshold of king's palaces that poetry may be honoured, or fight and die ignorantly and passionately among disasters which it is their fate to bring upon themselves, they are human as a disembodied passion is human, before it has made a home or a prison for itself among circumstances and within time.

In a passage which Yeats himself might have written before the turn of the century, he remarked that the characters' words were all sighs, that they were full of weariness and ecstasy:

. . . remembering human things, and mortality, and that dreams are certainly immortal, and that perhaps there may be a love which is also immortal. They speak to one another not out of the heart or out of the mind, but out of a deeper consciousness than either heart or mind, which is perhaps what we call the soul. There is wisdom in these plays as well as beauty; but indeed beauty is but half beauty when it is not the cloak of wisdom, and wisdom, if it is not beautiful, is but a dusty sign-post, pointing the way ungraciously.

Reviews of the plays continued, of 'Plays for an Irish Theatre' (1911) and various performances and editions of 'The Land of Heart's Desire', 'The Countess Cathleen', 'Cathleen ni Houlihan', 'Deirdre' and 'The Green Helmet'. (The latter was first published in 1910 and apparently only reviewed in 'The Athenaeum', 18 February 1911, which thought the farce in this 'haunting piece of work' kept the poet's allegory from soaring too high. The New York edition published by Paget in 1911 had the same contents as the original Cuala Press edition of 1910; the Macmillan edition of 1912 contained six more poems. It is referred to on p. 310 and p. 312) Such reviews culminated in criticism which judged the value of Yeats's work rather than just giving impressionistic or generalised reactions to it. But there was a fairly common belief that while the plays contained good poetry they did not provide the stuff of drama. Yet various stagings of 'Cathleen ni Houlihan' and 'The Countess Cathleen' now received almost surprised recognition for their dramatic qualities, 'The Countess Cathleen' seeming to one critic 'a real play',

to another 'a modern morality', to another as a play
possessing 'a curiously moving' drama, to yet another a
little piece already enjoying 'something of the fame of a
classic'. Charles Tennyson ('Contemporary Review', June
1912) thought Yeats's best plays were those most removed
from human life: thus Yeats at his most characteristic,
was at his best in 'The Land of Heart's Desire', 'The
Countess Cathleen', 'Deirdre', and 'The Shadowy Waters'.
The 'Times Literary Supplement' reviewer (28 December
1911) examined the dramatist's skill in creating reverie,
in alluring his audience almost to the intensity of trance:
there was a sense of coming doom in 'Deirdre', the setting
of 'The Shadowy Waters' was vivid.(4) But the critic
seemed mesmerised. The tragic poet, he wrote, used to
reveal the actions of men's souls through external
action. Yeats, it seemed to him, had gone further.
Using the old puppets of the romantic drama — 'Kings,
and the Sons of Kings, Queens, heroes, fools and bards' —
he made men's souls the glasses through which 'we see
what words cannot tell'. The poet has put a spell on the
eyes of his audience until the audience sees in these
puppet-characters their own passing selves 'and in ourselves the powers that endure'. This echoes Yeats's
earlier view in 'Reconciliation' ('Collected Poems',
p. 102):

> I could find
> Nothing to make a song about but Kings,
> Helmets, and swords, and half forgotten things
> That were like memories of you.

It does not, however, contain Yeats's reaction to these
romantic trappings (the poem was written in February
1909, first published in 'The Green Helmet and Other
Poems', 1910):

> . . . but now
> We'll out, for the world lives as long ago;
> And while we're in our laughing, weeping fit,
> Hurl helmets, crowns, and swords into the pit.

The publication of Yeats's 'Collected Works' in the
sumptuous eight-volume Shakespeare Head Press edition of
1908 led to a certain feeling that Yeats now must be
appraised for the totality of his very considerable
achievement. Edward Dowden thought that the handsome
volumes represented Yeats's life-work, that he had chosen
to be judged by them and that whatever his future work
might be these were his title deeds to honour. His own

review, however, was not much more than a survey of the
contents of the volumes and his tribute generous in view
of the strained relations between Yeats and himself.
Edward Thomas probably took the largest view of the
'Collected Works' ('Daily Chronicle', 6 March 1909), for
he recognised Yeats's poetry as blending the simplicity
of folk art with sophisticated artistry in a virtually
religious functioning of art; he praised Yeats's aiding
'the movement of this age towards a finer and deeper
spirit'. The subtlety of Yeats's feeling was new: 'he
looked forward as well as backwards; he hankered for an
earlier age, yet he realised the need for craftsmanship'.
Thomas appreciated Yeats's awareness, 'even so far back
as Shakespeare', of a separation of the artist from the
common man. He was more attuned to Yeats's aims than
Lytton Strachey, who in his review in 'The Spectator' (17
October 1908) praised the gold in the poetry, seeing it
as part of the romantic tradition stemming from Coleridge,
and showing — in the lyrics — proof of inspiration. He
was reserved about the plays and narrative poems, but he
allowed himself the praise of the lyrics, because lyrics
could dispense with clarity of thought and construction.
Yeats would have seemed too unreasonable to Johnson and
Voltaire — and to Strachey — to be a good poet. To
Charles Tennyson he echoed the inhumanity of the Irish
sagas ('English Review', April 1909). But to Edward
Garnett it seemed that Yeats's Celtic imagination created
a dangerous wizard art ('English Review', April 1909).
Walter de la Mare in 'The Bookman' (January 1909) had,
however, a different and generous view. He traced Yeats's
intense absorption and intense confidence in his destiny.
He showed Yeats deliberately setting himself aside in
thought and reverie, pursuing one path, rejecting lures,
following only clues that deepened his insight. Yeats
had pulled his dreams to pieces, watched his own methods,
enriched and simplified his verse. De la Mare recognised
that Yeats was working, with a wider purpose than most
men, to find a national drama:

> In his own striving after perfection of style, his
> aim is to hark back through the written tradition, the
> poetry that is of the artist and of the narrow culti-
> vated class, to the unwritten tradition, the poetry of
> the people: to return to the vivid and simple sin-
> cerity of the one through the culture and art of the
> other: to win back to innocence by way of experience.
> It is a hard task enough; but he has set himself also
> a task far harder even than this. For he wishes to
> take all the scholars of Ireland along with him.

> His whole heart is in the legendary and traditional
> history of his own people. Like an old and
> tarnished but still enchanted lantern, it has lain
> half-hidden for centuries. Mr. Yeats has dedicated
> all his energies to evoking its genie.

He realised Yeats repudiated old ideas about Celtic influences in literature, and he reassured readers that they
need not concern themselves with the actual sources and
inspiration of the Celtic school of poetry. Before taking
off into an *O Altitudo* over the power of poetic imagination, he questioned Yeats as to whether he can point to

> any beauty of strangeness, or of homeliness, or of
> mystery; any character of humour, or of royalty, or
> of divinity; any delicacy of rhythm or charm of
> idiom; any restraint and purity in art, or loveli-
> ness of imagination — can he point to anything in
> his plays or poetry that the English mind and taste
> are incapable of appreciating?

It was an American mind which first fully realised the
significance of what was occurring in Yeats's poetry in
'The Green Helmet' and, particularly,'Responsibilities'.
Ezra Pound, in an essay in 'Poetry' (January 1913)
regarded Yeats's theory as dangerous and his achievement
as limited; this was notwithstanding his view that
Yeats was 'the greatest of living poets who use English'.
He had put nearly every man who writes English verse in
his debt, but while he had stripped English poetry of
many of its faults his own art had not broadened much
in the decade. But in a subsequent review of the first
Cuala Press edition of 'Responsibilities' (1914) in
'Poetry' (May 1914) Pound recognised that Yeats's
vitality was quite unimpaired, that though he had created
a new music and had no need to recast this style, there
was nevertheless a manifestly new note in his later work.
He realised Yeats was at a crossroads in 'The Green
Helmet and Other Poems'; since then his work had become
gaunter, seeking greater hardness of outline. He drew
on Yeats's own rejection of his 'Celtic' imitators in
'A Coat' and in a speech made by Yeats at a presentation
to Wilfrid Scawen Blunt. And hard light was welcome,
and present in 'The Magi'. This is good, lively forth-
right criticism and it brings a similar freshness, a
new hard light into criticism itself. Pound's confident
remarks need only be contrasted with the tentative
approach (allowing for differences of transatlantic
temperament) of the reviewer in the 'English Review'

(April 1911) who found the poems wavering between a flame and illumination (poetry of meaning and significance) 'extremely puzzling to locate'. 'The Times' (17 March 1913) was pleased that Yeats was calling down wrath upon his pupils, though it came perhaps near a sneer at his detachment 'now less that of the mystic than of the court poet'. Irish Nationalist opinion was at times hostile, as in the case of George O'Neill, who thought Yeats a poor patriot ('Irish Catholic', 23 December 1911). It was often argued that he did not represent the Irish mind. Some Irish critics realised that Yeats's work was not receiving much attention in Irish papers, among them 'George A. Birmingham' (J.O. Hannay) writing in the Fortnightly Review' (December 1907) and Katharine Tynan writing in the 'Catholic World' (April 1908).

Ezra Pound's concentration upon the literary rather than the philosophical elements in Yeats marked a new beginning of criticism. The descriptions 'Celtic' and 'mystical' would no longer be sufficient. Forrest Reid's book 'W.B. Yeats: A Critical Study' (1915), though it has the easy-going, almost self-indulgent prose of the Edwardians, possessed also a northern Irish toughness of mind. He praised and blamed, and conveyed his appreciation with sensitivity as well as sturdy forthrightness. This book was a sign that the corpus of Yeats's work already offered enough material for fuller discussion than could be accommodated in the journals. It was followed by a technical discussion of Yeats's verse and how he caught the rhythms of Irish prose in Thomas MacDonagh's 'Literature in Ireland, Studies Irish and Anglo-Irish' (1916).

Ernest Boyd's study in 'Ireland's Literary Renaissance' (1916), while not particularly stimulating to a modern reader, fully recognised Yeats's role in the literary movement and provided an intelligent, balanced account of his work. This is the work of a good literary historian, who gives his critical comments directly, and uses quotation intelligently. He insisted that Yeats was an artist rather than a thinker, notably in 'The Wind among the Reeds' and 'The Secret Rose': his mysticism in them was decorative or at best symbolic. He preferred the simpler stories of 'The Celtic Twilight' to those of 'The Secret Rose', because he thought that whatever Yeats possessed of mysticism was far more closely related to the fairy beliefs of the people than to the intellectual doctrines of the great mystics. To a certain extent his account of Yeats suffers inevitably from the fact that he wrote it when he did. He alludes, for instance, to the over-ornamentation of his middle period;

and we would now see that period as part of Yeats's early
work.

To Forrest Reid, Thomas MacDonagh and Ernest Boyd
Yeats was a fellow-countryman and therefore there was
no difference between his world — however symbolistic,
however slanted in the earlier poetry towards the supernatural (5) — and theirs; but to T.S. Eliot, reviewing
'The Cutting of an Agate' under the heading 'A Foreign
Mind' in 'The Athenaeum' (4 July 1919), 'Mr Yeats on any
subject is a cause of bewilderment and distress'. Yeats's
mind was 'a mind in which perception of fact, and feeling
and thinking are all a little different from ours'. And
the reviewer in the 'Times Literary Supplement' (1 May
1919) regarded Yeats in these essays as an ineffable
rather than an affable expounder, remarking that he had
ever seemed to regard Englishmen as dunces. This review
was probably coloured by contemporary political resent-
ments, judging by its reference to 'extreme Sinn Feiners',
but both Eliot and this reviewer obviously thought they
were making discoveries when they sensed something alien
to the English tradition in Yeats. It was as if all the
attitudes of surprise at the strangeness which fill the
reviewing of the 'Celtic' period had now to be fitted —
because, no doubt, of the bitterness and the savage
fighting in Ireland, the 'dragon-ridden' days of 'Nineteen
Hundred and Nineteen' — into an equally surprised awareness of the strangeness of the 'Irish' element. The
point was made clearly in another 'Times Literary Supplement' review, of 'Per Amica Silentia Lunae' (1918), where
the reviewer, while still using the 'Celtic' terminology,
remarks that Yeats sees not reality, but a show of
reality, something not merely that we deceive ourselves
about, but which deceives us. 'Into that "Celtic twilight",' he says, 'we cannot follow him' and he continues
in somewhat baffled vein:

> but we are the more curious about his habit of passing
> into it because of his wisdom and subtlety before he
> has passed into it. Where we can follow him, he is a
> guide to be trusted; and then suddenly he leaves us
> in a cloud. Suddenly he talks a language we do not
> understand; we do not know whether it is a language
> at all or gibberish. Is that but one instance of the
> eternal difficulty between the Irishman and the English-
> man? Always they seem to understand each other up to
> a point; and then suddenly there is an end of under-
> standing. We do not know what they mean or why they
> act; they seem to have a different notion of the
> nature of reality. We believe that the thing itself

will show itself to us if we try hard enough; for
we believe that the thing itself is there. But they
seem to believe that it is not there at all, that all
reality wears masks, that in all things there is an
anti-self. And so we are bewildered by their curious
coldness behind all their surface passion, the coldness
of moonlight and make-believe. And yet, with it all,
Mr. Yeats is a poet, as moonlight is beautiful. The
beauty that we see is the only thing common between
his mind and ours. There may not be sense to us, but
there is music; and in that there is a common
language, though we cannot translate it into words.
The Irishman speaks to us still only in his art, but
when shall we understand his actions?

How far had Yeats influenced these writers in their
awareness of his difference from them, from the 'Times
Literary Supplement' reviewer, whom one can presume to be
an Englishman, and from an expatriate American, himself
apparently striving to be assimilated into English life
(with his feeling that Yeats's sensibility is different
from 'ours')? It is possible that Yeats's first volume
of autobiography, 'Reveries over Childhood and Youth'
(1915-16), which made clear his own sense of being different, sharpened by his youthful consciousness of the
contrasts between life in Sligo and London, between his
English school and Irish family life, had already had
its effect on critics. In this volume he had shown how
he differed from his contemporaries in England, and in
Ireland, because of his unusual upbringing and background.

In the revised edition of 'Ireland's Literary Renaissance' (1922) Ernest Boyd commented on 'Reveries over
Childhood and Youth' and 'Four Years' (1921):

The former in its evocation of the child's life in his
Western Irish home is indispensable to an understanding
of the early stories and poems which he is too ready
to disown. His memories of the years from 1887 to
1891 will explain, in his elusive and allusive fashion,
that first period in London which turned his genius
definitely in a new direction, and impressed upon the
mould of his mind all those influences, occult,
symbolic and aesthetic, which have marked off his
work from that of his contemporaries who remained in
Ireland.

Although never inhuman in the sense which that term
implies in criticism of conventional biography,
these chapters from the life of W.B. Yeats have a

curious discarnate air, as though the mind of the
writer had been emptied of all common preoccupations,
and had retained only those memories that touched the
mind and spirit.   The result is to give a peculiar
dignity and beauty to the prose in which they are
written.

Lawrence Binyon paid similar tribute ('The Bookman',
January 1923) to 'The Trembling of the Veil' (1922),
finding the prose fascinating, more like beautiful talk
than writing:

You do not think of style or beauty, but you surrender
yourself to the flowing of the words which stream so
transparently over the matter within them.   And how
rich are these pages in thought and image!   If anyone
wants a commentary to the Poems, here it is.   For no
one has more sedulously directed his life to a chosen
aim that Mr. Yeats;   no poet has more chastened himself
or been at more exacting pains to clear his art of
'impurities' and perfect it from within.   And in these
pages we can read of the ideas which possessed the
poet, and how certain poems came to be written and
what men and what books influenced him.

He realised that the pages were memorable because Yeats
drew out of his memory not mere facts nor mere impressions
but 'images' which acquired a symbolic significance.
While recording some disappointment in the dramatic work,
he was generous in his assessment of Yeats's whole achievement:

I marvel at what Mr. Yeats has done, through others as
well as through his own work;   at the creative power
which has achieved so much and defeated so many
obstacles.   Is there not more of the man of action in
him than ever was in Wilde?   How much energy must have
gone out of him in this creative Irish effort!
Yet it is not this spending of energy in action which
has limited his poetical production, but rather a
restless and scrupulous self-criticism, an ever-
increasing fastidiousness and perhaps a haunting distrust of the Irish facility in words.   He has lived
to see would-be poets imitating the imagery and the
music of his earlier poems, and experienced the same
irritation and disgust that Ruskin felt when he saw
houses built in the Gothic he had advocated.

He appreciated the naked poetry, seeing in 'Baile and
Ailinn' an attainment of style which was exquisite in
simplicity and ease of movement. Intimacy and natural-
ness had been his aim in such poems as 'The Folly of Being
Comforted', and this aim had been achieved more successfully than by Shelley in 'Julian and Maddalo':

> But in his latest verse the style is grown more tenuous
> and austere, it seems to rely on gesture, so to speak,
> and tone of voice rather than on the verse itself or
> what it carries. In old days Mr. Yeats reacted from
> the Victorians, who he thought mingled in their poetry
> too many curiosities about public affairs, or science,
> or social reform. He was determined that his verse
> should be pure from such immixtures. And all through
> the years he has been writing, I think he has been
> little concerned to absorb new elements, new material,
> but much concerned to cast out any elements that had
> become not quite real to him, or that might prove
> corrupting.

Quoting 'The Fascination of What's Difficult' he wondered
whether Yeats might not have considered and brooded over
his art too much and attenuated the volume of his inspiration thereby; and very reasonably answered himself
with a question: 'But who can tell? He is one of the
great poets, and that suffices.'
     The unusual in Yeats had been stressed by 'Reveries'
and by the strange contents of 'Per Amica Silentia Lunae';
the apparent negativity of 'Responsibilities' (in such
poems as 'September 1913' and 'To a Shade') put some
critics into a state of mind where they could see the
poetry in 'The Wild Swans at Coole' as failing. The
earlier enterprise, indeed the challenge of 'A Coat' —
'In walking naked' — was not realised for what it was,
and J. Middleton Murry, for example, regarded 'The Wild
Swans at Coole' as Yeats's swan song, and the reviewer in
the 'Times Literary Supplement' thought he seemed to be
living on memories. Padraic Colum, however, did recognise that 'A Woman Homer Sung', 'The Cold Heaven' and
'The Wild Swans at Coole' were thrilling in their
austerity, in their renunciation of what was merely
emotional. The use of dreams as a quarry for symbols
disturbed the 'Times Literary Supplement' review of
'Plays in Prose and Verse' (1922); another review in
that journal, of 'Essays' (1924), thought Yeats had over-
cultivated his subconscious.
     The publication in February 1921 of 'Michael Robartes
and the Dancer' in a Cuala Press edition (dated

1920) seems to have gone virtually unnoticed. Among its
fifteen poems are contained 'Easter 1916' and 'The
Second Coming'. This volume was included in 'Later
Poems' (1922); this was Volume II of the Macmillan
'Collected Edition' of the 'Works' (1922-26), and even
this was probably not fully valued for the significance
of these two poems, in particular. It is as though there
was a time lag before criticism generally caught up with
Yeats's new kind of creativity. John Squire, for instance,
in his review ('London Mercury', February 1923) quotes
poems from earlier volumes — 'The Fascination of What's
Difficult' from 'The Green Helmet' (1910) and 'To a
Young Beauty' from 'The Wild Swans at Coole' (1919) —
and these are selected for their naked, natural statement.
True, Squire was ready for a further change in Yeats — he
was 'still capable of producing something totally unlike
anything he has ever produced before' — but did not seem
to have realised it was there to see in the 'Michael
Robertes' poems. He knew how Yeats assimilated and used
experience; he was, he said, certainly capable of dis-
covering

> aspects of life, images and manifestations which have
> never yet entered his verse. What he takes, however,
> he transmutes after his own fashion; change as he
> may, he remains himself; there has been no more
> honest, laborious and consistent craftsman in our
> time, and none whose work loses less with the passage
> of years.

The first edition of 'A Vision' did not arouse much
critical response, four reviews only being listed by
Cross and Dunlop in their 'Bibliography of Yeats Criticism'.
Edmund Wilson discussed it intelligently in the 'New
Republic' (16 January 1929). He described the work (published in a private edition) 'so far as that is possible',
realising the importance Yeats attached to it, and firmly
asserted that, as in the case of Poe's 'Eureka', we
should, if we were to extract from 'A Vision' such truth
as it contains, regard it, 'for all its abstract language
and its geometrical diagrams as primarily the production
of a poet'. He pondered whether Yeats was wanting to have
his cake and eat it: would the poet be glad to be taken
at his face value and have 'A Vision' swallowed entire
while he had 'protected himself with a devil to pass the
whole thing off as a fantasy'. His comments on the
phases of the moon are common-sensical:

Yeats has worked all this out with great care and with
considerable ingenuity. He has described each of the
twenty-eight phases and supplied us with typical
examples. What we find in this part of the book is
Yeats's familiar preoccupation with the conflict between action and philosophy, reality and imagination.
(It is amusing and characteristic that, according to
his system, the part of humanity closest to the sun —
that is, closest the objective nature — should be the
part that is bathed in darkness, whereas the part
which is furthest from the sun — that is, nearest the
subjective nature — should be the part that is
brightest!) His sense of this conflict is profound,
and it has usually inspired him well in his poetry and
his essays. But in spite of the admirable poem,
already published some time ago, from which I have
quoted above and with which he has prefaced 'A Vision',
we rebel against the 'Great Wheel': we decide that it
and its accompanying wheels have ended by grinding to
bits both Yeats's intelligence and his taste. We
contrast with his turbid horoscopes the clear and distinguished outline of the portraiture of his memoirs.

He praised the brilliance of some passages, notably the
phases of the 'Receptive Man' (Rembrandt and Synge) and
the 'Obsessed Man' (Giorgione and Keats); and he selected
for quotation the subsequent description of Helen, 'perhaps
the most eloquent passage in the book'. He objected to
Yeats's antithesis between objective and subjective:

One feels that Yeats has been aware of these objections, and has invented, in order to meet them, an
apparatus so complex that it entirely fails to impose
itself by convincing us of its inevitability, because
it could apparently be used to justify almost anything.

While he argued that the same kind of criticism could be
applied to Yeats's philosophy of history, he found the
summary of European history 'by reason of the brilliance
of his style and the excitement of his imagination' the
most readable part of the book. And he ended by contrasting the careers of Shaw and Yeats, noting that Yeats
had placed Shaw 'at a phase which I calculate is removed
from Yeats's own by about a quarter of the circumference
and which is headed straight for the deformity of seeking,
not the soul, but the world.' And he concluded, rather
wryly:

Shaw accepted the technique of science and set himself
to master the problems of industrial democratic society.
Yeats rejected the methods of naturalism and applied
himself to the problems of the individual mind.   And
while Shaw lives in the Middle of London, Yeats has
secluded himself in a tower on the farthest Irish
coast.   Their respective literary testaments, published
almost at the same time, mark as it were the final
points of their divergence: in his 'Intelligent
Woman's Guide', Shaw bases all human hope and happiness
on an equal distribution of income, which he says will
finally make impossible even the pessimism of a Swift
or a Voltaire; while Yeats, a Protestant like Shaw, has,
in 'A Vision', made the life of humanity contingent on
the movement of the stars.   'The day is far off,' he
concludes, 'when the two halves of man can define each
its own unity in the other as in a mirror, Sun in Moon,
Moon in Sun, and so escape out of the Wheel.'
    The misapplication on this scale in the field of
psychology and history of one of the first intellects
of our time is probably the price that our time has
to pay for the possession of a great poet.

A.E. wrote a review in 'The Irish Statesman' expressing
honest doubt as to whether the book would be regarded
as the greatest of Yeats's works or as his greatest
erring from the way of his natural genius (see p. 269).
But A.E. was glad he had written it, and, unlike many
subsequent commentators, suspected the author was 'animated not only by a desire to elucidate the system but
by an impish humour'.
    A.E. produced another interesting review, of Yeats's
'Autobiographies' (1926), later the same year ('The
Irish Statesman', 4 December 1926).   This stems from his
long friendship with Yeats, dating from their days at the
School of Art in Dublin.   He had some reservations, for
into Yeats's river of beautiful prose there hardly fell
an image of the imagination which was then wandering in
'The Island of Statues' (1885) or with 'Usheen in
Tirnanoge' ('The Wanderings of Oisin and Other Poems',
1889).   He thought Yeats's mirror reflected almost everything his eye had seen:

    but nothing of the imagination which was to make so
    rare a beauty and which must then have been in its
    rich springtime.   The external world evolves its
    patterns before his eye, but of the involution of the
    spirit into the bodily nature bringing with it its own
    images and memories of another nature, there is but

little, and I read this biography as I would look at
some many-coloured shell, from which the creature
inhabiting it, who might have told us about its manner
of being, had slipped away leaving us only the miracle
of form to wonder at.

He found unusual distinction in the mirroring of notable
personalities, though he said that he did not recognise
himself or his friends in the chapter Yeats had devoted
to them, while understanding how they might have 'appeared
like this to one another'. He saw a chasm between their
inner lives and the outer lives which Yeats described in
his 'Autobiographies'. He praised the cool luminous flow
of the prose and part of him surrendered to the spell,
admiring the precision with which Yeats drew the characters
or incidents he selected. And he speculated upon the
reasons for Yeats's liking for William Morris:

> I find it curious that the poet who so often speaks of
> the virtues of passionate literature when he is
> generalising, loves in fact the romances of William
> Morris, the least passionate inventions in English
> literature, more perhaps than any other imaginative
> work. He, himself, is endlessly speculative, while
> the works of Morris are without speculation. He,
> himself, writes a poetry which at times is broken in
> its intellectual coherence by the invasion of some
> factor from what I might call a fourth dimension of
> life, while Morris's romances have rarely more than two
> dimensions, and are conceived on the flat as much almost
> as a tapestry. I suppose an intellect, which is so
> restless, must be envious of a spirit which is content
> with its vision. It is rare to find any imagination
> dreaming contentedly in the mid-world as Morris does.
> If he had reached higher than the beauty of the mid-
> world, he must inevitably have developed a clair-
> voyance into the depths, which is the price we pay
> for vision on the heights, and all that placid beauty
> would have become distorted and it would have been no
> longer a resting place for an imagination like that of
> Yeats, who is insecurely in the mid-world, which his
> nature really loves, because he has seen things both
> higher and lower than Morris ever saw.

Andrew E. Malone (the pseudonym of Laurence Patrick
Byrne, 1890-1939) had some sensible things to say in
his book 'The Irish Drama' (1926). He firmly stressed
the oral nature of the Irish literary tradition, remarking
that audiences would be found 'for ballad-singers, story-

tellers, and political orators; for the circus, the
concert or the drama; for anything with action and speech
in it'. He dealt sympathetically with Yeats's efforts
on behalf of verse speaking, but pointed out that musical
emphasis and rhythm were not in themselves enough for a
theatre audience that demanded above all else plain
English. He quoted Yeats's remark of 1899 ('Essays'
(1924), p. 206) that the theatre began in ritual 'and it
cannot come to its greatness again without recalling words
to their ancient sovereignty'. Malone saw the reason
underlying the remark:

> Such a theatre, in the conditions of the late nine-
> teenth and early twentieth centuries, could appeal
> to only a few people, and Mr. Yeats often seems to be
> contradictory when he speaks of an art for the people
> which is to be so elaborate and so sophisticated that
> it could only appeal to a very small and highly
> cultured section of a highly cultured community. It
> was an attempt to elaborate the 'folk' in terms of the
> pre-Raphaelite teaching; an attempt to say that the
> gestures of the uncultivated were 'grave and decora-
> tive', while those of the cultivated urbanities were
> crude and gauche. In a word, it was the reaction of
> a very sensitive nature against the mechanisation of
> society, a mechanisation which threatened the arts and
> all the gracious things of life, but what everyone
> thought of as 'civilisation' and 'progress'. But
> time and tide have been against Mr. Yeats, as they
> were against the pre-Raphaelites, and the mechanisation
> has not only gone on, it has gone much farther and
> much faster.

The first full and forceful critical realisation of
what had been achieved in Yeats's poetry since his own early
pre-Raphaelite period came with the publication of 'The
Tower' (1928). The 'Times Literary Supplement' (1 March
1928) recognised a quality in these poems which was at
variance with their personal disquiet, 'a freedom of the
poetic elements, an imaginative and prosodic beauty that
brings one the pure and impersonal joy of art'. Other
reviewers also saw the strength of this highly personal
poetry. John Gould Fletcher, for instance, in his review
in 'The Criterion' (September 1928) bravely called Yeats
'What we moderns mean by a great poet', and Theodore
Spencer, reviewing 'The Tower' for the 'New Republic' (10
October 1928, stressed the authority, and the richness of
tone in the volume which makes the poems echo and re-echo
in the mind. Here, he proclaimed, was a proper marriage of
thought and emotion.

It is worth remembering that 1928 was also the year
when Laura Riding and Robert Graves produced their witty
'Pamphlet Against Anthologies' and enjoyed themselves with
the 'Lake Isle of Innisfree', their close attention to
the text being echoed, but differently, in William Empson's
'Seven Types of Ambiguity' (1930) where 'Fergus and the
Druid' is given another close examination.

In the same year Sean O'Faolain, reviewing 'Selected
Poems, Lyrical and Narrative', (1929) for 'The Criterion',
April 1930, was severe upon the poet for making 'a cheap
compromise between his art and his experience'. He
attacked Yeats's browsing among the alchemical writers,
which 'has never once helped his art and has constantly
deceived it'. He saw Yeats as having fluctuated all his
life between 'what his will might do and what his destiny
would do'. He praised the vibrant quality in his verse,
his precision of word and phrase, regarding his obscurity
as a betrayal of himself. Yeats's own defence of
obscurity — 'even poetry which mingles something of
illegitimate with legitimate obscurity is often very
powerful and desirable, for poetry is not an amusement
and a rest, but a fountain of ardour and peace whither
we must force our way even through the brambles and the
thicket' — seemed to him unsatisfactory; and he argued
that this was a defence which might serve for a lesser
craftsman:

> but it will not do for Mr. Yeats, who has more than
> most the faculty of making himself understood in poetry
> when he really knows what he wishes to convey. Often
> he does not know, and so often his verse is obscure
> to a fault, and so often he ceases to be true to the
> one image that actually releases him from himself —
> his lyric genius with which he wrote the 'Wanderings
> of Usheen', the only genius he has or ever could have.
> As one reads through this book one finds hints of its
> nature in the words he loves to repeat, the images
> that recur from early to late. In the 'Wanderings of
> Usheen' he had foam-pale and pearl-pale; in 'Medita-
> tions on Civil War' he has cloud-pale, and repeatedly
> we meet the word in pale stars, pale shell, pale
> strand, pale nightgown, pale rose, and the brother of
> these in such darling pictures as of the

> > 'fish that swim
> > Scale rubbing scale where night is dim
> > By a broad water-lily leaf.

And so with things that glimmer and gyre and pern,
things dim, and murmuring: in his most recent changes

he twice uses the adjective ravelled to describe
water.
     A poet of sweet words, of soft, dew-dropping music.
What more can one ask seeing that he is in his class —
whether he has chosen it or accepted it from fate —
Perfection? As for the class, the law De Gustibus
precludes arguing.

What Mr O'Faolain called the inevitable poet's fight
in his own consciousness between personality and genius
was also discussed by George Russell (A.E.) in his book
'Song and its Foundations' (1932). Tracking back the
congregation of desires in himself to their fountains in
childhood he began to see that each of his friends had
some governing myth, that a germinal mood had been born
somewhere in their past which had grown to dominion over
everything else in them:

> I can see to-day the central idea I surmised forty-five
> years ago in the young Yeats grown to full self-con-
> sciousness. I remember as a boy showing the poet some
> drawings I had made and wondering why he was interested
> most of all in a drawing of a man on a hill-top, a
> man amazed at his own shadow cast gigantically on a
> mountain mist, for this drawing had not seemed to me
> the best. But I soon found his imagination was domi-
> nated by his own myth of a duality in self, of being
> and shadow. I think somewhere in his boyhood at the
> first contact of inner and outer he became aware of
> a duality in his being. In his earlier poetry one
> could pick out twenty lines showing how he was obsessed
> with this myth, how frequently and almost unconsciously
> the same idea recurs.

> Never with us where the wild fowl chases
> Its shadow along in the evening blaze.

or

> A parrot swaying on a tree
> Rages at its own image in the enamelled sea.

or

> Nought they heard for they were ever listening
> The dewdrops to the sound of their own dropping.

or

> The boy who chases lizards in the grass,
> The sage who deep in central nature delves,
> The preacher waiting the ill hour to pass,
> All these are souls who fly from their dread selves.
>
> There are many such images in his early poetry.
> Then the mood ceased to haunt individual lines but
> became the subject of a long poem ['The Shadowy Waters'].

He recalled Yeats's telling him of the first conception of the play, and he thought that Yeats altered 'the
noble imaginative logic of its first conception' when he
fell in love. In the original the hero sought the world
of the Immortals alone, having previously cast a magical
spell on Dectora to make her fall in love with him, and
then unmade the spell. In the later ending the love won
by the magic art had become an immortal love. 'Concealed
or unconcealed', he commented, 'this preoccupation of the
poet with that dualism of being and shadow is in much that
he has written, until at last it becomes self-conscious in
'A Vision', a gigantic philosophy of self and anti-self.'
  A landmark in Yeatsian criticism was provided by Edmund
Wilson's account of Yeats in 'Axel's Castle' (1931). He
was able to survey Yeats's work with a panoptic glance,
allowing for the matter of 'A Vision' (to use a condensed
term for some of Yeats's ideas), for the Gaelic material,
for the symbolism, and not least, for Yeats's own development and his achievement. To a certain extent Wilson's
article on W.B. Yeats ('New Republic', 15 April 1925) had
been a rehearsal for this survey. In the article he
praised Yeats as 'one of the only men living' who had taken
poetry with thoroughgoing seriousness and who had achieved
success of the highest order. He examined the 'comprehensive and resolute rejections' that Yeats had been
obliged to make in order to preserve his dignity as a
poet: a turning of his back upon the whole scientific,
democratic world, a standing apart from the questions
which agitated it. He found Yeats's seeming feeling that
a belief in the supernatural was bound up with faith in
the poet's vision difficult, even ridiculous; and he
remarked that Yeats himself appeared unsatisfied. He
did not, however, want to suggest that Yeats

> would have got any further if he had occupied himself
> with legitimate science. His writings on mysticism are
> full of great intelligence and great imaginative in-
> sight and his theories — such as that which postulates
> a sea of racial images rolling to and fro through the
> mind of humanity — are often impressive, despite the

fact that they have been arrived at mystically
instead of through the methods of modern psychology.

He saw that Yeats had been related to contemporary consciousness, as the 'greatest representative in English
of the modern literary movement known as symbolism'.   He
analysed Yeats's differences from most later practitioners
of symbolism, citing the tragi-comic vein of Corbière and
Laforgue, imported into English by T.S. Eliot.   Yeats,
however, had never exploited, like Flaubert in 'Trois
Contes' or Joyce in 'Ulysses' (who were contrasting their
own lives unfavourably with some other kind of life of
which they believed men were once capable), the contrast
between a poetic 'conviction of nobility and the universal
banality of modern man'.

He moved from a consideration of Yeats in relation to
the ideas and influences of his time to a comment on his
individual genius, perhaps being one of the first critics
to make the point that if Yeats had never written anything
but 'The Wanderings of Oisin' and such lyrics as 'The
Lake Isle of Innisfree' and 'The Man Who Dreamed of
Fairyland', 'he would have still, as the creator of a new
sort of strangeness, been a considerable poet'.   But
Wilson thought the unbending of 'youth's dreamy load' had
made Yeats a better poet.   He intensified into poetry
the circumstances of his life and the events of the life
about him 'not by vulgarising his style, but by dignifying
his subjects'.   He was 'one of the few genuine masters
alive — perhaps the only poet of the first magnitude'.

In 'Axel's Castle' he lavishly praised Yeats's ability
to write poetry which charged with the emotion of a great
lyric poet 'that profound and subtle criticism of life'
which Wilson also discussed in connection with his prose.
This largeness of view, this relatively unreserved generosity of attitude was lacking in the conclusion of F.R.
Leavis's account of Yeats in 'New Bearings in English
Poetry' (1932).   Here, after an appreciative account of the
achievement of the poems both early and late, which includes
such things as his remark that 'to pass from the earlier
to the later work is "something like passing from Campion
to Donne"' and the general comment that Yeats 'achieved
a difficult and delicate sincerity and extraordinary
subtle poise', he writes that 'Symbol' (as Yeats used it,
drawn from magic and the Hermetic sciences) 'is commonly
felt to be an unsatisfactory element in his later verse
and to come from an unfortunate habit of mind'.   His
review of 'The Winding Stair' ('Scrutiny', December 1933)
has a strain of snide comment:

Those admirers of Yeats who found 'Words for Music
Perhaps' disappointing will not find this new and
larger collection, which includes the earlier, less
so. One had, of course, no right to set the standards
of one's expectations by 'The Tower', but, naturally,
one did.

Professor Leavis found nowhere in this volume 'that vital
tension between counter-attracting presences which makes
the finest poetry of "The Tower"'. What Professor Leavis
thought characteristic of 'The Winding Stair' was 'something (see, for instance, "At Algeciras — A Meditation
upon Death") on which our first comment, "this is too
elliptical", amplifies itself immediately with "and too
passive"; the constituents are inert'. But by the end of
the review a need seems to have been felt to make some
kind of amend for the strictures:

There is, of course, a great deal in the book that
is both good and characteristic, even if the kind of
critical attention that is Mr. Yeats's due yields a
report that may seem ungracious. Need it be said that
'The Winding Stair' is, in any case, one of the very
few literary events of the year? To be reminded that
we have still in this age, honouring the English
language, a spirit so austere and fine is an occasion
for gratitude.

No sniping but rather a barrage occurred when Yvor
Winters, in a piece on T. Sturge Moore ('Hound and Horn',
April-June 1933), accused Yeats of the intellectual
confusion he shared with the entire generation subsequent
to him — an attack continued by Winters after Yeats's
death. But the 'Times Literary Supplement' (5 October
1933) weighed up Yeats's lonely achievement with a question when it reviewed 'The Winding Stair and Other Poems'
(1933), and asked whether any other poet in the line of the
past had known such an event, to have reviewed a fading
fame with a fresh one, quite dissimilar? Yeats had earned
the right to be applauded a second time by the discerning.
Among them was Hugh Gordon Porteous, whose review in 'The
Criterion' (January 1934), while it carried a Leavis-like
recognition that the volume was not as 'The Tower' (it
lacked its 'fine sweep of passion'), did none the less
realise that Yeats's use of symbols was both emotionally
and intellectually felt, and that a weight of experience
was behind them. Yeats seemed to him 'the most outstanding, the most consistent, the most romantic figure' in
poetry and he realised that the 'magic' was not *all* nonsense.

'Sense and Poetry' (1934), by John Sparrow, contained some common-sensical writing about readers trying to read too much into a poem. He quoted Yeats's note on 'The Cap and Bells': 'I dreamed this story exactly as I have written it, and dreamed another long dream after it, trying to make out its meaning, and whether I was to write it in prose or verse. . . . The poem has always meant a great deal to me, though, as is the way with symbolic poems, it has not always meant quite the same thing.' Mr Sparrow argued that when the reader is told this he must accept the poem for what it is, a description in verse of something its author dreamed. But he asked why the poem meant many things to Yeats and why readers were tempted to call it difficult, searching for a further meaning, and answered his queries thus:

> Chiefly, it seems, because the story told in it, its obvious meaning, is simple, and the elements of which it is composed are suggestive; they are so richly suggestive, they so much overburden the simplicity of the story, that the reader is tempted to suppose that the poem is intended to convey a hidden meaning by the use of symbols. We are strongly conscious, as we read, of something beyond the meaning, and we therefore suspect a mysterious or inner meaning, and when our efforts to discover it are apparently confronted with impenetrable symbols, we think the poem obscure. In fact, there is nothing hidden, and therefore there is no obscurity. What is intelligible in the poem is easily understood. It only seems obscure if we try to interpret what we should be content to enjoy.

And he added, 'It is precisely this desire to interpret instead of to feel, to look for a meaning which is not there, that leads the critics to call symbolist poetry obscure.'

Sir Desmond MacCarthy wrote The Forerunner, a percipient piece, in 'The Sunday Times'(4 February 1934),which stressed the continuity of Yeats's work. There are not, he said, 'two poets, Yeats I and Yeats II; one whose poetry the most modern poet can afford to ignore, the other one whom they recognise as a master'. He insisted that from the first Yeats wrote out of the basis of his nature, the Celtic poems not to be regarded as poems of a youthful novitiate but an integral part of his genius. He saw that in the earlier poems there were many passages marred by a 'compression and sudden finality in suggestion' which later became the sole aim of imagists and vorticists. The method

arose from symbolism, the symbols different, but the poetic
method the same as that of the French, and notably
Mallarmé. He recognised the same indifference in both the
French symbolists and Yeats to the objective reality of
the symbols. Yeats related his symbols more closely to
experience as he developed, he relied more on phrase than
rhythmic pattern. The content of the later poems, 'more
philosophic and perceptive', stimulates the reader; there
is less reliance on incantation. And one of the lasting
ingredients was 'the solitude of the poetic mind'.

To this Herbert Read replied (with a dash of anti-
bourgeois anarchy?) in his review of Yeats's 'Collected
Poems' ('The Criterion', April 1934):

> In the last number of 'The Criterion' Mr. Hugh Gordon
> Porteus, in reviewing 'The Winding Stair', paid a
> tribute to the later style of Mr. Yeats which I have
> no desire to controvert. There is no doubt that Mr.
> Yeats has been influenced, and influenced for the good,
> by the technique of some of his juniors, notably by
> Mr. Pound; and if I have any desire to controvert
> anybody it is one of those critics who make the Sunday
> morning in bed safe for democracy; he recently made
> out that actually there had been little change in the
> poet's development. The Yeats of to-day, he compla-
> cently assured his tousled readers, was still the good
> old Yeats of Innisfree, and that what is 'modernist' in
> him was there before the days of the horrid 'vorticists'
> and 'imagists' (but was there, incidentally, ever a
> vorticist poet?). There is no need to argue this
> particular point, for Mr. Yeats has fully admitted the
> change in his poetic outlook and technique.

In the 'English Review', June 1935, Sean O'Faolain
reverted to his earlier interest in and distrust of
Yeats's conflicts. After writing appreciatively of 'The
Tower' and 'The Winding Stair', 'where his verse becomes
so powerful and so evocative and so tragic that one who
did not know the sequence of his work, or the sequence of
his life, or have the key to his internal conflict, could
never have thought it possible for the rather feminine
poet of 'The Wanderings of Oisin' to write [section III
of 'The Tower'. He quoted from 'It is time that I wrote
my will' to 'Dream and so create / Translunar Paradise'].'
Yeats had not unified himself, he thought, but neither
had he corroded within himself:

> I am a young man, and my generation in Ireland some-
> times finds it hard to make a bridge across to the

generation of Yeats. We find a lack of wisdom in it,
of humanity, and of sincerity. We feel we are of the
age of steel and that these last romantics are of the
age of gold, to use his imagery again. Though what
one really means by 'lack of sincerity' is, no doubt,
that our values differ, and our insistence on intellectual sincerity and his insistence on emotional
sincerity must both of them be tested by time; since
there is, no doubt, in both, equal room for self-
deceit.

   That preoccupation of Yeats with his own conflicts
is, I think, dangerous and seductive, and I feel that
wherever, in that poetry of conflict, one is aware,
not of the conflict, but of Yeats, as in a drama one
might suddenly become aware not of the theme but the
author, his poetry is at its weakest.

He quoted from 'Vacillation' the section beginning 'Between
extremities man runs his course . . .' before remarking
that Yeats was born seventy years ago and had been wavering ever since 'between that romanticism and this realism,
between that traditionalism and this revolt, that prettiness and this ugliness, that loyalty to the *moi* and this
loyalty to the *nous*, that inwardness and this outwardness,
that picturesque Ireland and this raw Ireland, that kind
of truth and this'. And he concluded his peroration with
a kind of baffled admiration:

   He has lived long enough to see a world go and a world
   come, and he is so vigorous and so alive and so emotionally intact that he cannot deny the validity of
   either of them. Which may explain why neither generation trusts him, and each claims him, and both give him
   the fullness of their admiration for the loveliness
   he has taken — I might even say, robbed without pay-
   ment from each time.

   R.P. Blackmur's essay in 'The Southern Review' (Autumn
1936) carried understanding and tolerance further. He
realised that poetry needs a literal or an imaginative
faith or a mind full of many provisional faiths. He
weighed up the price Yeats paid for his poetry and remarked perspicaciously that this was a price most readers
'simply do not know how to pay and an expense, in time
and labour and willingness to understand, beyond any
notion of adequate reward'. With this awareness he
proceeded to a very sensible discussion of Yeats's later
work, relating it to its magical convention.

In 1936 Yeats's selection of poems for the 'Oxford Book of Modern Verse 1892-1935' (1936) caused much critical comment. He wrote to Dorothy Wellesley on 15 November 1936 about the reception of the book (some typical reactions are included in this volume, see pp. 378-85) with characteristic *brio*:

> My anthology continues to sell and the critics get more and more angry. When I excluded Wilfred Owen, whom I consider unworthy of the poets' corner of a county newspaper, I did not know I was excluding a revered sandwich-board man of the revolution, and that somebody has put his worst and most famous poem in a glass-case in the British Museum — however, if I had known it, I would have excluded him just the same.

A more pleasing reaction to his work was that of the American critic Archibald MacLeish, whose terms delighted Yeats because in an article in 'The Yale Review' (Spring 1938) he praised Yeats's public speech. MacLeish was arguing that modern poetry was a return to public speech, a revolt against the private speech which, he thought, turned poetry into a minor art. Private speech he defined as special, formalised and poeticised, 'suitable only to the private communication of certain special, formalised, and poeticised emotions, . . . incapable of the communication of anything else'. Public speech he described as human, living, national and informalised, capable of the public communication of common experience. It is, he said, poetry as action. Yeats, whom he described as the best of modern poets, represented the way the best of modern poetry belonged to the world we live in. Yeats had refused the customary costume; not, he added, in his capacity as a man of politics nor as director of a theatre, but as a poet:

> He is no self-conscious genius exploiting his dif-ference from other men — and inventing differences where none exist. He is quite simply a man who is a poet. And his poetry is no escape from time and place and life and death but, on the contrary, the acceptance of these things and their embodiment.
> How great his present stature is and how greatly we owe that present stature to the revolution in his art, any man may see by looking at the record of his work. Between the faint, vague, lovely wandering of his first romantic poems and the strong presentness, the urgent voice, of such a poem as 'Byzantium', is not only the distance between mediocrity and greatness but the dis-

tance also between a poet of private speech and the
satin salons and a poet of public speech and the world.
Yeats's later poetry is poetry of the world. It is
the first English poetry in a century which has dared
to re-enter the world. It is the first poetry in
English in more than a century in which the poem is
again an act upon the world. It is the first poetry
in generations which can cast a shadow in the sun of
actual things — men's lives, men's wills, men's
future. With Yeats, poetry becomes an engine capable
of employing all the mind, all the knowledge, all the
strength. With Yeats, poetry ceases to be a closet
avocation to the practice of which a man could bring
only nostalgia, only melancholy, only fantasy, only
arts and doubtings of escape. Writing as Yeats writes,
a man need not pretend an ignorance of the world, need
not affect a strangeness from his time, need not go
mooning through an endless attic with the starlight
clicking on the roof.

The later poetry of Yeats is, then, the measure of
the actual achievement of the poetic revolution known
as modern poetry.

Cleanth Brooks's view of Yeats as a mythmaker, put
forward in his 'Modern Poetry and the Tradition' (1939),
treated Yeats's views in 'A Vision' with careful attention.
He commented that Edmund Wilson had been the only critic
thus far to deal with 'A Vision' in any detail. The 1926
edition had been privately printed and not widely reviewed;
the 1937 Macmillan edition received over thirty reviews,
among them Stephen Spender's discerning response to the
book in 'The Criterion' (April 1938). The adverse comment
on Fascism with which this ends was anticipated in Austin
Clarke's review of 'A Full Moon in March' ('London Mercury',
January 1936) with its wry comment on the marching songs
for the short-lived Irish Blueshirt movement; it was
taken up later by Philip Henderson in 'The Poet and
Society' (1939) and has occupied many critics since Yeats's
death (the main complaint being that of Conor Cruise
O'Brien, writing on Passion and Cunning: An Essay on the
Politics of W.B. Yeats, 'In Excited Reverie'(edited by
Jeffares and Cross, 1965), very ably answered in a little-
known reply by Patrick Cosgrave ('The London Magazine,
9 April 1967).

A portent of the increasingly specialised criticism of
Yeats to follow came in 1937 with Dorothy M. Hoare's book,
'Yeats and Morris in relation to Early Saga Literature'.
She realised what Yeats had done to the Gaelic material
which he had used so much in his early and into his middle

ms make amends for his
egends with phrases such as
stressed his tendency to
ation or dream, his interest
n ideal life which is linked
with   She showed, for instance,
how 'On Bai   based on an original Irish
tale of conflict and   , the events 'given for their
own sake; there is practically no reflection on them'.
And she demonstrated that this reality was precisely what
Yeats was not concerned with. She saw his delight in the
embroidery of the situation instead of direct management of it. The play, she remarked, was 'full of talk,
of the reflection of an outsider on the poetic value of
the situation. Neither the vigour, the tenderness, the
fierceness of the original has crept into these pictured
phrases.'

As Yeats had grown older, so attempts had been made to
see the totality of what he had done in and with his life.
These now became more frequent. His friends, many of
them younger writers, paid him tributes which were
balanced and just. The 'Irish Times' had collected a number of essays in honour of his seventieth birthday in
1935, but while by 1938 there was even more to assess,
Yeats was now indeed old and ill. F.R. Higgins in a
lecture delivered in Dublin in 1938 (see p. 405)was able
to see Yeats's poetic drama clearly in terms of its
achievement while L.A.G. Strong, in an article in 'The
Spectator' in November 1938, described Yeats as a sociable
man, a wit, and a brilliant talker, writing enthusiastically
of his integrity, and his aristocracy of mind. The
achievement of the life and work were simply and ably
summed up with great dignity in 'The Sunday Times' by
Desmond MacCarthy after Yeats died in February 1939, and
this selection closes with W.H. Auden's poetic tribute to
him.

III

A volume of essays entitled 'Scattering Branches: Tributes
to the Memory of W.B. Yeats', edited by Stephen Gwynn, was
published in 1940. It contained contributions by Stephen
Gwynn, Sir William Rothenstein, Lennox Robinson, W.G. Fay,
Edmund Dulac, F.R. Higgins, C. Day Lewis and L.A.G. Strong.
The essayists, many of whom had been close friends of
Yeats, had more space at their disposal than the authors
of the earlier 'Irish Times' essays published in honour of
Yeats's seventieth birthday. These essays in 'Scattering

Branches' offered readers fresh insights and information
about the poet, and F.R. Higgins, stressing Yeats's Irish
qualities, remarked that he had 'only two commingling
states of verse, One, simple bucolic, or rabelaisian;
the other, intellectual, erotic or visionary'. John
Masefield paid an eloquent tribute in 'Some Memories of
W.B. Yeats' (1940), David Daiches gave a good brief
account of his work in 'Poetry and the Modern World: A
Study of Poetry in England between 1900 and 1939' (1940)
and V.K. Narayana Menon devoted a book, 'The Development
of William Butler Yeats' (Edinburgh, 1940), to examining
Yeats's changing work. Louis MacNeice's 'The Poetry of
W.B. Yeats' (1941) offered a lively general view of the
poetry, very much seen from the point of view of a
'thirties' poet, and regarded it as being somewhat escapist.
His view, as expressed in Yeats's Epitaph ('New Republic',
24 June 1940) was that it was an insult to ignore Yeats's
deficiencies and peculiarities, while believing in his
genius. Yeats possessed the miracle of artistic integrity,
'though as a man he may sometimes have been a fraud'. He
praised 'a self-centred old man' for rising above his own
personality (in 'The Circus Animals' Desertion') 'by
pinning it down for what it is'. W.H. Auden's article
on Yeats: Master of Diction ('The Saturday Review', June
1940) stressed the value of the lyrics — 'the first thing
that strikes one about Yeats is that he really enjoyed
writing poetry'. He thought Yeats was always more concerned with whether or not a phrase sounded effective 'than
with the truth of its idea in the honesty of its emotion'.
  In the Memorial Lecture he delivered in the Abbey
Theatre in Dublin in 1940, T.S. Eliot described Yeats as
'an unquestionably great poet', yet spent much of the
lecture recounting what disturbed him in Yeats's thought
and writings. This unease, which had appeared earlier in
some of F.R. Leavis's criticism, marked Orwell's reactions,
in a review in 'Horizon' (January, 1943), to Yeats's
'artificiality' and 'hatred of democracy', as well as those
of D.S. Savage, who complained in 'The Personal Principle'
(1945) of the static universe of Yeats's vision, which
lacked inner dynamism. He thought Yeats's aestheticism was
lacking in sympathy towards himan and religious hopes. The
winter issue of 'The Southern Review', vol. 7, 1942, was
devoted to Yeats, and this contained an article by L.C.
Knights, who wrote off Yeats's poetic career as 'an heroic
failure', seeing defects of 'character' and the literary
tradition of the nineteenth century as contributory
causes, representative of our 'divided and distracted
civilization, in which the "passionate intensity" of partial
men offers itself as a substitute for the vitality that

springs from the whole consciousness'. Other articles in
this issue showed critics somewhat defensive in their
attitudes to Yeats's work. Arthur Mizener, for instance,
defended Yeats's romanticism as a fact that had to be
faced, while Allen Tate thought the poet's romanticism
would be created by his critics. Kenneth Burke, like
many others, complained of the ambiguous nature of 'A
Vision', while Austin Warren remarked that if the earlier
Yeats was whimsical or otherwise evasive on the subject
of the occult the later Yeats 'cut himself off from such
ambiguity'.

What was lacking was a fully factual basis from which
criticism could operate. The 'New Critics' wanted to
interpret only from the printed texts of the poems; but
Yeats's self-dramatisation and increasingly overt personal
poetry had meant there was a need to draw upon the events
of his life and his reading in order to aid a fuller
understanding of his aims as well as his actual achievement of them in his writing. Joseph Hone's biography
'W.B. Yeats 1865-1939' (1942) was a most helpful development. It offered a view of Yeats's life founded on personal knowledge of the poet and his times. In it he
related the poet's writings to Irish affairs. He had
the advantage of being able to use Yeats's papers and
library and to discuss with the poet's widow many aspects
of Yeats's life and writing. Others had this same privilege. The present writer, for instance, in several
articles, (for example, W.B. Yeats and his Methods of
Writing Verse, in 'The Nineteenth Century and After',
March 1946; and The Byzantine Poems of W.B. Yeats in
'Review of English Studies', January 1946) used early MS.
and TS. versions of the poems and facts about Yeats's
reading and conversations to show that some of the meanings
of the poems could be clarified by going beyond their
printed texts.

Sir Maurice Bowra's 'The Heritage of Symbolism' (1943)
and Peter Ure's 'Towards a Mythology: Studies in the
Poetry of W.B. Yeats' (1946) drew attention to Yeats's
use of symbolism and mythology; an earlier book by D.J.
O'Donnell, 'Sailing to Byzantium' (Cambridge, Mass., 1939)
had discussed the development of the later style and symbolism, but not at very great depth. There followed
several books based in part on work in Yeats's papers
and books and on conversations with his friends which
related Yeats's work to his life and thought. These were
Richard Ellmann, 'The Man and the Masks'(1948; rev. ed.
1962); A. Norman Jeffares, 'Yeats: Man and Poet' (1949;
rev. ed. 1962); and T.R. Henn, 'The Lonely Tower' (1950;
rev. ed. 1965).

Two other studies, Donald Stauffer's 'The Golden
Nightingale' (1949) and Graham Hough's 'The Last Romantics'
(1949), added to an increasing acceptance by academic
critics of Yeats's stature, one becoming less hedged in
by provisos and reservations. So much was this the case
that James Hall and Martin Steinmann, the editors of a
collection of essays published in 1950, felt able to en-
title their volume 'The Permanence of Yeats'.

In the ten years after Yeats's death several volumes
of his work had appeared. 'Last Poems and Two Plays'
(1939) and 'On the Boiler' (1939) were published by the
Cuala Press, 'Last Poems and Two Plays' appearing in
Macmillan editions in the UK and USA in 1940. 'Pages
from a Diary written in nineteen hundred and thirty' (1940)
was another Cuala publication. The definitive edition of
the 'Poems' in two volumes was issued by Macmillan in
1949.

The years since 1939 have seen a large increase in
the publication of Yeats's work. The 'Collected Poems'
(2nd edition) appeared in 1950 (US edition in 1951);   the
'Collected Plays' in 1952 (with five plays added to the
contents of the 1939 edition). In 1951 the first edition
of Allan Wade's 'A Bibliography of the Writings of W.B.
Yeats' appeared, and this, now in its third edition,
revised and edited by Russell K. Alspach (1968), is a
most valuable work for those who wish to trace the pro-
venance of poems, plays and prose. Allan Wade's edition
of 'The Letters of W.B. Yeats' was published in 1954.
This followed 'Letters or Poetry from W.B. Yeats to
Dorothy Wellesley' (1940), the letters of 'Florence Farr,
Bernard Snaw and W.B. Yeats' (Dublin, 1941: New York,
1942; and London, 1946), 'J.B. Yeats's Letters to his
Son W.B. Yeats and others' (edited by Joseph Hone, 1944),
'W.B. Yeats and Sturge Moore: Their Correspondence 1907-
1937' (1953) and 'W.B. Yeats: Letters to Katharine Tynan'
(1953).   'Ah, Sweet Dancer: W.B. Yeats, Margot Ruddock,
A Correspondence' (edited by Roger McHugh, 1970) gave the
story of Yeats's friendship with Margot Ruddock. 'Beltaine'
(1899-1900) and 'Samhain' (1901-1908) were both reprinted,
edited by B.C. Bloomfield, in 1970. In this year Routledge & Kegan Paul reissued Yeats's 'Poems of William
Blake' (first published in a Muses Library edition in 1905).
The first draft of Yeats's 'Autobiography' and the 'Journal' were included in 'Memoirs' (1972), transcribed and
edited by Denis Donoghue. Two books edited by Yeats in 1888
and 1892 make up 'Fairy and Folk Tales of Ireland' (1973),
with a Foreword by Kathleen Raine. 'Yeats and the Theatre'
(1975) in the 'Yeats Studies' series edited by Robert
O'Driscoll and Lorna Reynolds, included three unpublished

lectures and lecture notes.

The effect of the publication of these titles is re-
inforced by the massive 'Variorum Edition of the Poems of
W.B. Yeats' (1957), edited by Peter [G.D.P.] Allt and
Russell K. Alspach (this was followed in 1966 by General
Alspach's 'Variorum Edition of the Plays of W.B. Yeats').
Macmillan produced a uniform edition of some of Yeats's
prose, 'Autobiographies' (1959), 'Mythologies' (1959),
'Essays and Introductions' (1961) and 'Explorations' (1962).
'The Senate Speeches of W.B. Yeats' appeared in 1960.   'A
Concordance to the Poems of W.B. Yeats' was published in
1963, to be followed by a two-volume 'Concordance to the
Plays' in 1972.   There was also a reissue of 'Selected
Poems' in the Golden Treasury Series in 1951 (repeating
the text of the 1929 edition), and an annotated edition
by the present author in Macmillan's Scholars Library
series (1962).   'Selected Poems and Two Plays' were edited
by M.L. Rosenthal (New York, 1962), and a selection of
early poems was included in an edition of 'The Celtic
Twilight' edited by Walter Starkie (New York, 1962).   The
present author also selected and edited 'Selected Poetry'
(1962), 'Selected Plays' (1964), 'Selected Prose' (1964)
and 'Selected Criticism' (1964).   J.P. Frayne edited the
first volume of Yeats's 'Uncollected Prose' in 1970, the
second, with Colton Johnson, in 1975.   An edition of 'John
Sherman and Dhoya' edited by Richard J. Finneran was
published in 1969.

The effect of the books by Ellmann, Henn and Jeffares,
and the availability of texts of Yeats's work (it was
extremely difficult to obtain second-hand copies of, say,
'Collected Poems' (1934), 'Collected Plays' (1934),
'Autobiographies' (1926; New York, 1938) or 'Essays' (1924)
in the 1940s: 'Collected Poems' was not reprinted in a
second edition until 1950, 'Collected Plays' until 1952,
and 'Autobiographies' until 1955, the new Macmillan editions of the prose volumes appearing in 1959, 1961 and
1962) was that research tended to eventuate in specialised
studies which began to appear at an increasing tempo.   For
instance, whereas the work of Dorothy M. Hoare in 1937
had dealt with both Yeats's and Morris's work in relation
to early Gaelic material (for the two poets' relationship,
see Peter Faulkner, 'William Morris and W.B. Yeats', 1962),
in 1950 Brigit Bjersby's research was more concentrated,
as is indicated by the title of her book 'The Cuchulain
Legend in the Works of W.B. Yeats'.   Morton Irving Seiden
dealt largely with the mythology of 'A Vision' in his
long book 'William Butler Yeats: The Poet as a Mythmaker
1865-1939' (1962), while in 1967 Daniel Hoffman's
'Barbarous Knowledge: Myth in the Poetry of Yeats,

Graves and Muir' explored lines between and the use made
of folk beliefs, ballads, fable and folk lore by three
poets.

Austin Clarke applied his knowledge of the Gaelic
background to a study of 'The Celtic Twilight and the
Nineties' (1969), which included two chapters on Yeats's
plays. Daniel Albright continued studies on Yeats's use
of mythology in 'The Myth against Myth' (1972), which
showed Yeats altering his mythology. This book reinter-
prets the early poetry. The latest work on the influence
of what can be termed folk mythology is Colin Meir's
'The Ballads and Songs of W.B. Yeats' (1974).

Appreciation of Yeats has spread through the world, and
Shotaro Oshima's beautiful 'W.B. Yeats and Japan' (1965)
contained letters of Yeats, essays on some eastern
aspects of his work, as well as interviews and a valuable —
and large — bibliography of books and periodicals on
Yeats in Japan, where there is a flourishing Yeats
Society. Corinna Salvadori in 'Yeats and Castiglione:
Poet and Courtier' (1965) illustrated Yeats's attitude to
the Italian renaissance. Among European studies of Yeats
may be mentioned Johannes Kleinstück's 'W.B. Yeats oder
Der Dichter in der modernen Welt' (1965), and Isolde
von Bülow, 'Der Tanz in Drama: Untersuchungen zu W.B.
Yeats', Dramatischer Theorie und Praxis (1969). There
have been several books on Yeats by Indian critics, and
Naresh Guha's 'W.B. Yeats: An Indian Approach' (1968)
provided a useful detailed account of Yeats's friendships
with Mohini Chatterjee and Purohit Swami as well as dealing with his interest in Theosophy. Translations include
'Gedichte' (1958) translated by Herberth E. Herlitska,
'Quaranta Poesie' (1965) by Giorgio Melchiori, and 'Yeats:
choix de poèmes' (1974) by René Frechet.

Yeats's drama has interested many critics, notably
B.L. Reid, in 'William Butler Yeats: The Lyric of
Tragedy' (1961); Peter Ure, in 'Yeats the Playwright'
(1963), which provided a very careful examination of the
content of Yeats's plays and of his technique as a
dramatist, stressing the importance of character and
design; S.B. Bushrui, in 'Yeats's Verse Plays: The
Revisions 1900-1910' (1964); David R. Clark, in 'W.B.
Yeats and the Theatre of Desolate Reality' (1965); and
Leonard E. Nathan, in 'The Tragic Drama of William Butler
Yeats: Figures in a Dance' (1965), which analysed the
cosmic conflict brought out by Yeats's division between
spiritual aspirations and the natural order. A recent
study by Reg Skene, 'The Cuchulain Plays of W.B. Yeats'
(1974), draws upon the author's experience in the production of some of Yeats's dramatic work. Akhtar Qamber, in

'Yeats and the Noh' (1974), discussed Yeats's use of the
Noh material, but less successfully than Richard Taylor
in 'The Drama of W.B. Yeats: Irish Myth and the Japanese
Nō' (1976) which is a masterly handling of a difficult
and complex subject.
   Margot Rudd's 'Divided Image: A Study of William Blake
and Yeats' (1953) contained some unpublished marginalia
and notes by Yeats. It was followed by a more useful
book, Hazard Adams's 'Blake and Yeats: The Contrary
Vision' (1955). T.R. Henn's exploration of the inter-
relationships between Yeats's poems and particular pictures was followed by Frank Kermode's 'Romantic Image'
(1959), which described Yeats as committed to the image,
and expressed some reservations about the effect of this
theory upon poets. This book viewed Yeats in relation to
the ideas of Pater, Symons and late nineteenth-century
European literary and artistic tradition. Henn's posthumous volume 'Last Essays' (1976) contains some of the
excellent, highly personal and stimulating lectures he
delivered at the Sligo Yeats International Summer School,
over which he presided so effectively for many years.
Arland Ussher's admirable pamphlet, 'Yeats at the Municipal
Gallery' (1959), gave a detailed exposition of the pictures
there that attracted Yeats's interest and delight. Ussher's
capacity for stimulating, original comment can be found in
the essays of his 'Three Great Irishmen: Shaw, Yeats,
Joyce' (1952), a book which should be read in conjunction
with the enlightening generalisations of his 'The Face
and Mind of Ireland' (1949). A brilliant and elegant book
by Giorgio Melchiori, 'The Whole Mystery of Art: Pattern
into Poetry in the Work of W.B. Yeats' (1960) brought an
Italian sensibility and an acute intelligence to bear upon
the effect of the visual arts on Yeats's writing. A later
study, Edward Engelberg's 'The Vast Design: Patterns in
W.B. Yeats's Aesthetic' (1964) also examined the importance
of painting and sculpture to Yeats, and looked at his
links with European patterns of thought and aesthetics.
D.J. Gordon's 'W.B. Yeats: Images of a Poet' (1961),
a book issued to accompany an exhibition in Manchester
University in 1961 (earlier mounted on a smaller scale in
Reading in 1957, with a smaller catalogue), provided comment
on and illustrations of Yeats's images. Sheelah Kirby's
'The Yeats Country' (1962) with maps and drawings by Ruth
Brandt provides a useful guide to what is now known as the
Yeats country, mainly County Sligo.
   Three books which give excellent visual background to
Yeats's life and work are 'Images and Memoirs: A Pictorial
Record of the Life and Work of W.B. Yeats' (1970),
selected and edited by S.B. Bushrui and J.M. Munro, 'W.B.

Yeats and his World' (1971) by Micháel MacLiammóir and
Eavan Boland, and 'Yeats' (1976) by Frank Tuohy.

Yeats's interest in the occult was explored by Virginia
Moore in 'The Unicorn: William Butler Yeats's Search for
Reality' (1954), the first detailed study of Yeats's
attitudes to such matters as Cabalism, Neo-Platonism,
Rosicrucianism and Hermetic lore in general. In 1958
appeared the first of F.A.C. Wilson's books, 'Yeats and
Tradition', in which he pursued Yeats's use of occult
symbolism in a study dealing with the allegorical meanings of the five last plays. In his next book, 'Yeats's
Iconography' (1960) Wilson discussed the 'Four Plays for
Dancers', 'The Cat and the Moon', and some lyrics. He
insisted that Yeats's work needs to be related to esoteric knowledge. Emphasis upon the influence, particularly, of 'An Indian Monk' and the 'Upanishads' upon
Yeats's 'Supernatural Songs' and 'The Herne's Egg' came
in Harbans Rai Bachchan's 'W.B. Yeats and Occultism. A
Study of his Works in relation to Indian Lore, the Cabbala,
Swedenborg, Boehme, and Theology' (1965; revised edn.
1974). Further work on this subject has come from
Kathleen Raine, 'Yeats, the Tarot and the Golden Dawn'
(1972). While Ellic Howe's 'The Magicians of the Golden
Dawn' (1972) gave a general documentary history of this
magical order from 1887 to 1923, George Mills Harper's
'Yeats's Golden Dawn' (1974) discussed Yeats's participation in the order in detail, notably in the period from
April 1900 to February 1901. This study is useful for the
light it throws on the composition of 'The Shadowy
Waters' and 'The Speckled Bird', Yeats's unpublished
novel, announced as about to be published in 1976. The
editor, W.H. O'Donnell, has already edited a version for
the Cuala Press (1974), but the forthcoming edition will
give all the MS and TS versions of what is largely an
autobiographical document found useful by Yeats's bio-
graphers. Mr Howe and Professor Harper bring out the
importance to Yeats of the Order of the Golden Dawn, of
which he was an active member for thirty-two years.
Kathleen Raine has stressed his indebtedness to Plotinus
(as he found him in Stephen MacKenna's translation) in
'Death-in-Life and Life-in-Death' (1974). And 'Yeats and
the Occult' (1975) edited by George Mills Harper, another
volume in the 'Yeats Studies' series, contained sixteen
essays on this aspect of Yeats's life.

These detailed investigations into Yeats's interest
in mystical experience were matched by closer study of
'A Vision'. Helen Hennessy Vendler, in 'Yeats's Vision
and the Later Plays' (1963) examined the relationship of
the plays to Yeats's 'sacred book'. Thomas R. Whitaker,

in 'Swan and Shadow: Yeats's Dialogue with History'
(1964), also studied Yeats's attitudes, so eloquently
put in 'A Vision'.   Yeats's theories of poetry were
dealt with by Frank Lentricchia in 'The Gaiety of Language:
an Essay on the Radical Poetics of W.B. Yeats and Wallace
Stevens' (1968) especially as seen in the Byzantine poems,
while Arra M. Garab, 'Beyond Byzantium.   The Last Phase
of Yeats's Career' (1969) concentrated on Yeats's poetic
methods in his old age.   Richard J. Finneran collected
seventeen critical essays together (as well as two passages
from Yeats's prose) for 'William Butler Yeats, the Byzantine Poems' (1970).   A book by Bernard Levine entitled
'The Dissolving Image.   The Spiritual and Esthetic
Development of W.B. Yeats' (1970) examined the poems 'as
manifestations of their narrator's evolving state of mind'.
Robert Snukal in 'High Talk: The Philosophical Poetry
of W.B. Yeats' (1973) deals with history as well as
placing Yeats in a tradition within an idealistic framework.   Mr Snukal sees him as rejecting transcendental
answers to questions about the nature of human experience
and believ ing that reality is a human creation.   James
Land Jones in 'Adam's Dream' (1975) has explored mythic
consciousness in Keats and Yeats.
    Another line of investigation has concentrated upon
Yeats's methods of composition, illuminating the meanings of plays and poems in the process.   G.D.P. (Peter)
Allt's article on Yeats and the Revision of his Early
Verse ('Hermathena', November 1946) and various articles
by Jeffares published in the 1940s were followed by
Thomas Parkinson's book 'W.B. Yeats, Self Critic: A
Study of his Early Verse' (1951), which traced the in-
fluence of Yeats's work for the Abbey Theatre in a chap-
ter on 'The Shadowy Waters', later exhaustively explored
by Michael J. Sidnell, George P. Mayhew and David R.
Clark in 'Druid Craft: The Writing of The Shadowy
Waters' (1971).   Parkinson continued his work in 'W.B.
Yeats: The Later Poetry' (1964).   Jon Stallworthy's
scholarship is noteworthy in this kind of investigation.
His book 'Between the Lines: Yeats's Poetry in the
Making' (1963) traced the history of poems from initial
drafts to printed texts.   This careful, meticulous work
was continued in his second study, 'Vision and Revision
in Yeats's Last Poems' (1969), a similar examination of the
history of thirteen of the 'Last Poems' from their genesis
to final printed version.   S.B. Bushrui's book on the
revisions of the verse plays (1900-10) has been mentioned; another book published in 1965 was Curtis Bradford's 'Yeats at Work', another account of how a study of
Yeats's manuscripts and revisions can illuminate not only

his methods of work but add meaning to some of the poems
and plays. Marjorie Perlott's 'Rhyme and Meaning in the
Poetry of Yeats' analyses his metrics statistically and
shows the function of rhyme in typical Yeats poems.
    The question of the meaning - and indeed at times the
significance — of Yeats's work was re-questioned by Yvor
Winters, a non-recanting New Critic, who remarked in 'The
Poetry of W.B. Yeats' (1960), apropos the great deal of
scholarly work recently done on Yeats, 'unfortunately,
the better one understands him, the harder it is to take
him seriously'. The New Critics' wish to keep to a study
of the texts alone without accepting glosses from the poet
or biographical commentators inspired Vivienne Koch in
'W.B. Yeats: The Tragic Phrase' (1951), a book which revealed the inadequacy of this approach. Frank Hughes
Murphy in a misnamed study 'Yeats's Early Poetry' (1975),
also pursued this purist line but did not add very much
to an understanding of the poems. This was also demonstrated in John Wain's article Among School Children
('Interpretations', 1957), where Mr Wain was too eager
'to brush aside the reading of his [Yeats's] own words',
out of impatience with Yeats's 'personal fandago of
mysticism and superstition'. William Empson, in gayer
vein, mocked some of F.A.C. Wilson's conclusions, in
Mr Wilson on the Byzantine Poems ('A Review of English
Literature I', III, July 1960), regarding 'Byzantium's
clockwork bird with a built in tweet-tweet' as pathetically ludicrous. Robert Graves also enjoyed tilting at
Yeats in his Clark Lectures of 1954-5, which he published
in 'The Crowning Privilege' (1955): he was developing the
light-hearted view he and Laura Riding had taken of 'The
Lake Isle of Innisfree' many years before.
    'The Identity of Yeats' (1954), a second book on Yeats
by Richard Ellmann, showed inter alia that the early
poetry contained elements foreshadowing later developments, that there was a consistent attitude and approach
on the part of the poet. By 1968 Harold Orel in 'The
Development of William Butler Yeats, 1885-1900' was
stressing the importance of the early work per se. In
1969 Allen R. Grossman examined the effect of Yeats's
cabalistic interests upon his early poetry in 'Poetic
Knowledge in the Early Yeats. A Study of "The Wind among
the Reeds"'.
    More attention was paid to biographical material in
the 1960s. For instance, the complexities of Yeats's
relationship to the Anglo-Irish tradition which he began
to explore with excitement and enthusiasm during the
period of the Civil War, and which inspired much of his
work as a Senator of the Irish Free State, were ably

investigated by Donald T. Torchiana in 'Yeats and
Georgian Ireland' (1968). A less satisfactory though
lively study of this element in Yeats is contained in
Dudley Young, 'Out of Ireland. The Poetry of W.B.
Yeats' (1975) which dealt with particular poems. Various
biographical points were discussed by Richard Ellmann in
an essay in 'Eminent Domain' (1967), and some points
added in parts of his 'Golden Codgers' (1973). A.
Norman Jeffares discussed, in some of the essays of 'The
Circus Animals' (1970), Yeats's role as a public man,
his friendship with Oliver St John Gogarty, and his
father's character. Yeats wrote in 1910 that he had no
sympathy with the mid-Victorian thought that a poet's
life concerned nobody but himself.

> A poet is by the very nature of things a man who lives
> with entire sincerity, or rather the better his
> poetry the more sincere his life; his life is an
> experiment in living and those that come after have
> a right to know it, above all it is necessary that the
> lyric poet's life should be known that we should
> understand that his poetry is no rootless flower but
> the speech of a man.

This quotation from a lecture entitled Friends of my
Youth was used by Joseph Ronsley in his book 'Yeats's
Autobiography - Life as Symbolic Pattern' (1968), which
showed how Yeats ordered his experiences artistically.
Daniel A. Harris, in 'Yeats, Coole Park and Ballylee'
(1974) examined the body of poetry Yeats wrote about
Coole Park and his own tower, seeing these places in
terms of Celtic, medieval, Renaissance and Anglo-Irish
mythology. Phillip L. Marcus, in 'Yeats and the Beginning of the Irish Renaissance' (1970) was concerned
with Yeats's work for the literary movement, while Dwight
Eddins in 'Yeats: The Nineteenth Century Matrix' (1971)
sought to set him in both Irish and English backgrounds.
Von Wulf Kunne also discussed Yeats's autobiographical
writings in his 'Konzeption und Stil im Yeats' Autobiographies' (Bonn, 1972). Something of his character
had been brought out in Alex Zwerdling's 'Yeats and the
Heroic Ideal' (1965), the anti-heroic view of Yeats
having been put forward earlier in Monk Gibbon's 'The
Masterpiece and the Man: Yeats As I Knew Him' (1959), a
book which reflected the relationship between the older
established literary figure and a younger, highly critical iconoclast. The effect of Shelley on Yeats as
poet was stressed by Harold Bloom, in his 'Yeats' (1970),
a theme explored by George Bornstein also, in his 'Yeats

and Shelley' (1976) which showed the impact of Shelley
on Yeats, and how Yeats developed alternatives to Shelley's
views. Brenda S. Webster in 'Yeats: A Psychoanalytic
Study' (1974) imagines the effect of incidents in Yeats's
childhood upon him, drawing, at times, somewhat ludicrous
conclusions as a result, perhaps, of seeing him as if
he had grown up in New York and succumbed to psycho-
analysis. This book demonstrates how far critics will
push a specialised thesis, and it is time to consider
some of the recent general views of Yeats.

In 1954 G.S. Fraser wrote an admirably balanced brief
account of Yeats for the Writers and their Work series,
and Herbert Howarth in 'The Irish Writers: Literature
and Nationalism, 1880-1940' (New York, 1959) placed Yeats
well in the political and cultural background of his time.
In 1961 the present author published a brief study, 'The
Poetry of W.B. Yeats', and in the same year A.G. Stock's
'W.B. Yeats: His Poetry and Thought' was issued. Her
knowledge of Yeats benefited not only from her being
Irish but also from her experience of India, and she wrote
with sympathetic understanding of Yeats's poetry in this
excellent book. Peter Ure's 'Yeats' (1963) in the Writers
and Critics series was marked by this critic's usual
depth of thought and reflection, qualities which inform
his posthumous essays 'Yeats and Anglo-Irish Literature'
(edited by C.J. Rawson, 1974). J.I.M. Stewart's essay
in 'Eight Modern Writers' (1963) was a polished and confident piece of work. An Indian view of 'The Poetry
of W.B. Yeats' was written by Bhabatosh Chatterjee in
1962; and C.K. Stead's 'The New Poetic' (1964), a highly
influential work of the 1960s, recorded a lively response
to Yeats from New Zealand. Other general studies were
Raymond Cowell's 'Yeats' (1969), in the Literature in
Perspective series; B. Rajan's 'Yeats' (1965), in the
Hutchinson Home University Library series; Denis Donoghue's
'Yeats' (1971) in the Fontana Modern Masters Series; and
the present writer's 'W.B. Yeats' in the Profiles in
Literature series (1971).

Detailed comments on the texts of Yeats's poems and
plays have included George Brandon Saul's 'Prolegomena
to the Study of Yeats's Poems' (1957). This was followed
by John Unterecker's 'A Reader's Guide to W.B. Yeats'
(1959) and the present author's 'Commentary on the Collected
Poems of W.B. Yeats' (1968). George Brandon Saul's
'Prolegomena to the Study of Yeats's Plays' was published
in 1958, Edward Malins's 'A Preface to Yeats' in 1974 and
'A Commentary on the Collected Plays of W.B. Yeats', by
A. Norman Jeffares and A.S. Knowland, in 1975.

Articles continue to be written about Yeats in profusion
in critical journals, and there have been some collections,
among them John Unterecker's 'Yeats: A Collection of
Critical Essays' (New Jersey, 1963).   The centenary year,
1965, was greeted by several collections: 'An Honoured
Guest: New Essays on W.B. Yeats', edited by Denis
Donoghue and J.R. Mulryne;   'In Excited Reverie: A
Centenary Tribute', edited by A. Norman Jeffares and G.F.
Cross;   'W.B. Yeats 1865-1939.   Centenary Essays' (edited
by D.E.S. Maxwell and S.B. Bushrui, Ibadan);   'The World
of W.B. Yeats: Essays in Perspective' (edited by Robin
Skelton and Ann Saddlemyer, Dublin).   The Dolmen Press
issued a set of centenary papers (1968-) edited by Liam
Miller, and followed this with 'New Yeats Papers' of
which the first was William M. Murphy's 'The Yeats Family
and the Pollexfens of Sligo' which contained drawings by
John Butler Yeats (1971).   Various journals have devoted
issues to Yeats.   And now the business of Yeats scholarship has so increased that the specialised journal 'Yeats
Studies', edited by Lorna Reynolds and Robert O'Driscoll,
has evolved into book form.

NOTES

1 Cf. the article on Hopes and Fears for Irish Literature,
  'United Ireland', 15 October 1892, where he preaches
  giving to art the devotion the crusaders of old gave
  to their cause.   The poet must be content to be alone
  among men, ready to give days to a few lines and (like
  Yeats himself) ready to pay for his work 'with certain
  other days of dire exhaustion and depression'.   There
  was an inevitable paradox: literature should be as
  national as possible, but those who wrote it and criticised it should be deeply educated by international
  standards of literature.
2 Cf. a comment made by Edward Marsh (24 April 1900) on
  Yeats's reading 'something out of a new volume of his
  poems' which 'seemed most beautiful in sound, tho' I
  never can understand poetry read out.   He read them in
  an extremely monotonous voice, with very strong
  emphasis on all the accents — it was rather effective,
  but I think it's possible to read in a more natural way
  without sacrificing the music of the verse.'   From
  Christopher Hassall, 'Edward Marsh, Patron of the Arts:
  A Biography' (1959).
3 W.B. Yeats, 'At the Abbey Theatre', 'Collected Poems',
  (Macmillan, 1961 edn), p. 107.

4 Synge's view was decidedly different;   he commented 'I do
  not believe in the possibility of "a purely fantastic,
  unmodern, ideal, breezy, spring-dayish, Cuchulanoid
  National Theatre". We had "The Shadowy Waters" on
  that stage last week, and it was the most *distressing*
  failure the mind can imagine — a half-empty room, with
  growling men and tittering females. Of course, it is
  possible to write drama that fulfils your description
  and yet it is fitter for the stage than "The Shadowy
  Waters", but no drama can grow out of anything other
  than the fundamental realities of life which are never
  fantastic, are neither modern nor unmodern, and, as I
  see them, rarely spring-dayish, or breezy or Cuchulanoid.'
  (From David H. Greene and Edward M. Stephens, 'J.M.
  Synge 1871-1909', New York, 1959, p. 157.)
5 But James Stephens (?1882-1950) the Irish poet,
  dramatist, essayist, critic and broadcaster, (best
  known for 'The Crock of Gold', 1912), was worried about
  the direction Yeats was taking, as can be seen in his
  comment on Yeats's play 'The Dreaming of the Bones'
  (1919). This was written in Dublin on 7 July 1917 in a
  letter to Oliver St John Gogarty:
  > The play Yeats read us last night is marvellous. I
  > can't help thinking it is a pity he should put so
  > much artifice between the play & the audience. The
  > drum, that is, & the unwinding cloth, & the little
  > journeys round the stage. The play is so beautiful
  > that these first aids to the feeble are not needed
  > — When a convention is native & belongs to a
  > country it is understood & takes its proper sub-
  > ordinate position; but in these cases it can
  > easily be the play which is subordinate. Of
  > course this play is such that it requires to be
  > elongated from the world of the audience. Maybe
  > he is right. It was good last night in your house,
  > but it always is.
  >
  > *Mise*
  > JAMES STEPHENS

Note on the text

The order of the contents in this volume follows the chronological order of Yeats's publications where possible; the period covered corresponds to W.B. Yeats's literary career. Where criticism is general and not based upon a particular work of Yeats the piece has been placed chronologically unless otherwise stated (as, for example, in the case of Frank O'Connor's comments on Yeats made in 1939, but here contrasted with those made by St John Ervine in 1920, the two pieces are contained in item 59, placed chronologically as 1920). The sources of the items are indicated in the head notes. Because of the high fees asked by some authors, publishers or agents it has not been possible to include some criticism which the editor would have liked to make available in this selection.

The Youthful Poet

1. JOHN BUTLER YEATS ON HIS SON'S YOUTHFUL POETRY

1884

Extract from a letter dated 7 January 1884 to Edward
Dowden (see note on p.62). From John Butler Yeats,
'Letters to his son W.B. Yeats and others, 1869-1922'
(1944), edited with a memoir by Joseph Hone. The letter
was written from Howth, outside Dublin, where the Yeats
family was living at the time.

John Butler Yeats (1839-1922), artist, essayist,
letter-writer and conversationalist, was educated at
Trinity College, Dublin. He married Susan Pollexfen of
Sligo, was called to the Irish bar but never practised,
deciding instead to become an artist. He lived in London
but was not successful financially, returning to Ireland
in 1881 when the small income from family lands in Kildare
dried up as a result of the Land War. In 1887, having
painted many fine portraits (his pencil sketches are more
attractive than his portraits, on which he often worked
too long), and contributed to Dublin's intellectual life
with his brilliant conversation, he returned to London.
After his wife's death he settled in Dublin again in
1900, and found a munificent patron in the Irish-American
lawyer John Quinn in 1902. In 1907 he went on a visit to
New York, where he stayed till his death in 1922. His
letters convey something of his lively intellect, his
capacity for criticism and for arresting generalisations,
and his wit. Quantities of these letters remain as yet
unpublished.

Yeats's relationship with his son, who supported him
financially in his latter years, was close; he never
ceased to write to him with a ceaseless outpouring of

ideas, advice and appreciation. By marrying a Pollexfen, he said, 'I have given a tongue to the sea-cliffs.'

Could you send me Willie's MS. His railway ticket is up so that he is a prisoner at Howth and cannot go for it. If you rolled it up and put a stamp on it would it not come safely. He wants it for a rehearsal which is to come off immediately. . . .

Of course I never dreamed of publishing the effort of a youth of eighteen. The only passage in it which seems to me finally to decide the question as to his poetic faculty is the dialogue between Time and the Queen.(1) There was evidence in it of some power (however rudimentary) of thinking, as if some day he might have something to tell.

I tell him prose and verse are alike in one thing — the best is that to which went the hardest thoughts. This also is the secret of originality, also the secret of sincerity. So far I have his confidence. That he is a poet I have long believed, where he may reach is another matter. . . .

His bad metres arise very much from his composing in a loud voice manipulating of course the quantities to his taste.

Note

1 W.B. Yeats wrote his first poems in 1882, just before he was seventeen. Much of his early work, which included a number of plays, remained unpublished.

2. PROFESSOR DOWDEN ON THE YOUTHFUL YEATS

1885, 1886

Extract from William M. Murphy, The Yeatses and the Dowdens, a paper delivered at the conference held by the International Association for the Study of Anglo-Irish Literature, Cork, Ireland, August 1973. The first extract was dated 1885, the second 1886.

Edward Dowden (1843-1913), educated at Trinity College, Dublin, was the first Professor of English Literature in the University of Dublin, from 1867. His books include 'Shakespeare: His Mind and Art' (1875); 'Life of Shelley'

(1886); 'The French Revolution and English Literature'
(1897); 'Puritan and Anglican' (1900). A friend and
contemporary of John Butler Yeats (who thought less of his
abilities in later life) he encouraged W.B. in his youth —
'for perhaps a couple of years he was an image of
romance' — but later they became estranged. Dowden was
President of the Irish Unionist Alliance. Maurice
Elliott, Yeats and the Professors, 'Ariel', III, 3, July
1972, also examines Yeats's relations with him.

(a) Willie Yeats is an interesting bow of hope in the
clouds — an interesting boy whether he turn out much of
a poet or not. The sap in him is all so green and young
that I cannot guess what his fibre may afterwards be.
So I shall only prophesy that he is to be a poet after
the event.

(b) Willie Yeats . . . hangs in the balance between
genius and (to speak rudely) fool. I shall rejoice if
it be the first. But it remains doubtful.

Mosada (1886)

3. GERARD MANLEY HOPKINS ON 'MOSADA', A YOUNG MAN'S
PAMPHLET

1886

Extract from a letter, dated 7 November 1886, to Coventry
Patmore. From 'Further Letters of Gerard Manley Hopkins
including his Correspondence with Coventry Patmore'
(1938), edited by C.C. Abbott.

Gerard Manley Hopkins (1844-89), was educated at
Balliol College, Oxford. A pupil of Jowett and Pater,
he came under the influence of Pusey and Newman, entering
the Roman Catholic church in 1886, and joining the Jesuit
order in 1868. He was a parish priest before becoming
Professor of Greek at University College, Dublin in 1884.
His poems were not published until 1918, edited by his
friend Robert Bridges, since Hopkins thought their publication would have been contrary to his duty as a Jesuit.
His works include 'Letters and Correspondence' (2 vols,
1935; revised, 1956); 'Notebooks and Papers' (1937);
'Journals and Papers' (1959); 'Sermons and Devotional
Writings' (1959). The fourth edition of the 'Poems',
edited by W.H. Gardner and N.H. Mackenzie (1967), is
the best text.

. . . I seem to have been among odds and ends of poets and
poetesses of late. . . . There is a young Mr. Yeats who
has written in a Trinity College publication some striking
verses (1) and who has been perhaps unduly pushed by the
late Sir Samuel Ferguson (I do not know if you have read
or heard of him: he was a learned antiquary, a Protestant
but once an ally of Thomas Davis and the Young Ireland

Party, but he withdrew from them and even suppressed
some of his best poems for fear they, or he, shd. be
claimed by the Nationalists of later days; for he was a
poet; the 'Forging of the Anchor' is, I believe, his
most famous poem; he was a poet as the Irish are — to
judge by the little of his I have seen — full of feeling,
high thoughts, flow of verse, point, often fine imagery
and other virtues, but the essential and only lasting
thing left out — what I call *inscape*, that is species or
individually-distinctive beauty of style: on this point
I believe we quite agree, as on most: but this is a
serious parenthesis). I called on his, young Yeats's,
father by desire lately; he is a painter; and with some
emphasis of manner he presented me with 'Mosada: A
Dramatic Poem' by W.B. Yeats,(2) with a portrait of the
author by J.B. Yeats,(3) himself; the young man having
finely cut intellectual features and his father being a
fine draughtsman. For a young man's pamphlet this was
something too much; but you will understand a father's
feeling. Now this 'Mosada' I cannot think highly of, but
I was happily not required then to praise what presumably
I had not then read, and I had read and could praise
another piece. It was a strained and unworkable allegory
about a young man and a sphinx on a rock in the sea (how
did they get there? what did they eat? and so on:
people think such criticisms very prosaic; but common-
sense is never out of place anywhere, neither on Parnassus
nor on Tabor nor on the Mount where our Lord preached;
and, not to quote Christ's parables all taken from real
life but in the frankly impossible, as in the 'Tempest',
with what consummate and penetrating imagination is
Ariel's 'spiriting' put before us! all that led up and
that must follow the scenes in the play is realised and
suggested and you cannot lay your finger on the point
where it breaks down), but still containing fine lines and
vivid imagery. . . . Give my kind regards to your circle
and believe me your sincere friend

                                        GERARD HOPKINS, S.J.

Notes

1 Twelve verse contributions by W.B. Yeats were included
  in 'The Dublin University Review' in 1885 and 1886.
  Most of them were reprinted in 'The Wanderings of Oisin',
  1889.
2 W.B. Yeats's first separate publication, 'Mosada',
  originally appeared in 'The Dublin University Review'
  for June, 1886.
3 John Butler Yeats, R.H.A. (1839-1922).

4.   KATHARINE TYNAN ON THE NEW VOICE IN 'MOSADA'

1887

Extract from a review of 'Mosada' (1886) by Katharine
Tynan, Three Young Poets, 'Irish Monthly', March 1887.
   Katharine Tynan (1861-1931), poet and novelist, was
educated at Drogheda. Like her father, a farmer who lived
at Clondalkin, Co. Dublin, she was a Parnellite; but
her main interest was in literature. Yeats became a
friend of hers in 1885, frequently visiting the Clondalkin
farm and writing many letters to her. (These have been
edited by Professor Roger McHugh, 1955). Her book of
poems, 'Louise de la Vallière' (1885) was the first of the
hundred books she wrote. Her autobiographical writings,
notably 'Twenty-five Years: Reminiscences' (1913) and
'Memories' (1924), give her impressions of many figures of
the Irish literary movement. She was a friend of the
Rossettis and the Meynells. She married H.A. Hinkson in
1883: he was also an author who became a resident
magistrate in Mayo, and died in 1919. Her portrait was
painted by Yeats's father in 1887, by his brother in 1986;
both are in the National Gallery, Dublin.

We are glad to welcome in its less perishable form Mr. W.B.
Yeats' beautiful poem, 'Mosada', which attracted the
attention of all poetry-lovers at the time of its appearance in the 'Dublin University Review', and which now
Messrs. Sealy, Bryers, and Walker have reproduced in
pamphlet form, with a stiff paper cover. We hope it will
soon form an item of the poet's first book, the advent of
which may be well awaited with high hopes and expectations. The voice in the poem seems to us a new voice,
wonderfully clear, rich, and soft in its minor tones, for
it has this one point of agreement with modern music that
it is pitched in a minor key. We are glad to welcome a
new singer in Erin, one who will take high place among
the world's future singers if the promise of this early
work be fulfilled, or if, indeed, the performance of the
future be equal to that of to-day. The young poet follows
no master, and reminds us of no elder poet. This poem is
rich with colour, alive with dramatic feeling, and the
stately measure of the blank verse never halts or is
disconcerted. Here is a beautiful picture. The Moorish
girl, Mosada, is drawing, by burning her magic-endowed
herbs, pictures from the smoke wherein she shall find her

lost lover's whereabouts; waving her arms, she cries:

> Thus, thus I beckon from her viewless fields,
> Thus beckon to our aid a phantom fair
> And calm, robed all in raiment moony white.
> She was a great enchantress once of yore,
> Whose dwelling was a tree-wrapt island, lulled
> Far out upon the water-world and ringed
> With wonderful white sand, where never yet
> Were furled the wings of ships. There in a dell
> A lily-blanchèd place, she sat and sang,
> And in her singing wove around her head
> White lilies, and her song flew forth afar
> Along the sea; and many a man grew hushed
> In his own house or 'mong the merchants grey,
> Hearing the far-off singing guile, and groaned,
> And manned an argosy and sailing died.
> In the far isle she sang herself to sleep
> At last. But now I wave her to my side.

> COLA *(a little lame boy.)* — Stay, stay, or I will hold
>   your white arms down.
> Ah me! I cannot reach them, here and there
> Darting you wave them, darting in the smoke,
> Heard you? Your lute upon the wall has sounded,
> I feel a finger drawn across my cheek.

> MOSADA.   The phantoms come; ha! ha! they come,
>   they come,
> I wave them hither, my breast heaves with joy.
> Ah, now I'm eastern-hearted once again,
> And while they gather round my beckoning arms
> I'll sing the songs the dusky lovers sing,
> Wandering in the sultry palaces of Ind,
> A lotus in their hands.

It is full of such beauty as this — beauty rapt and
exalted, the very spirit of poetry; it is strong and joyful with the consciousness of power. If it were the work
of an old poet, it would be beautiful work; being the work
of a very young one, it has far greater value. Of Mr.
Yeats' future position as a poet, great things may be
prophesied; we to whom he belongs by blood and birth,
will watch his career with especial trust and pride. A
portrait of him by his father makes a most interesting
frontispiece to the little book.

The Wanderings of Oisin and Other Poems (1889)

5. JOHN TODHUNTER ON A REMARKABLE FIRST VOLUME

1889

A review of 'The Wanderings of Oisin and other Poems'
(1889) by John Todhunter, 'The Academy', January-June
1889.

John Todhunter (1839-1916), playwright, poet, biographer, and translator, was born in Dublin, educated
at Trinity College, Dublin (where he and John Butler
Yeats became friends), Vienna and Paris. He practised
medicine in Dublin up to 1874 then abandoned it for
literature and moved to Bedford Park, London. His best-
known poem 'Aghadoe' was included in 'The Banshee'
(1888).His plays 'Helena in Troas' (1886) and 'A
Sicilian Idyll' (1890), favourably reviewed by W.B.
Yeats, were succeeded by 'The Black Cat' (1893), one
of the first Ibsenite plays produced in England. His
other plays include 'Mary Queen of Scots' and 'The
Poison Flower'. 'Selected Poems' appeared in 1929.

This is a remarkable first volume; not merely full of
promise in the aggregate, but containing a few poems of
distinct achievement, which deserve a more than ephemeral
recognition. Every poet must finally be judged by the
quality of his verse; and Mr. Yeats's is not the fashionable verse of the day — smooth, cultured, elegant, not
without a certain intellectual charm, but wanting in
spontaneous music. A poem with the true breath of life
in it is rhythmical with an incalculable and unexpected
rhythm, following the natural ebb and flow of the emotion.
It is not too self-conscious to dare some breach of the

fashionable canon in its adventurous sallies after fuller
expression. Mr. Yeats's verse is of this adventurous
kind, and is not without its wood-notes wild of originality. The supercilious critic-of-all-work could, no
doubt, in the natural exercise of his functions, easily
quote from these poems lines and passages which, apart
from their context, might be made to seem ridiculous.
There are even real flaws of execution — slovenly lines,
awkward and uncouth constructions, exuberances which are
not beauties, concentrations of expression which are
crude and stiff rather than powerful. But in the main,
Mr. Yeats has the true poet's instinct for imaginative
diction and musical verse, musical both in rhythm and
sound. Many passages pleasantly haunt the ear and the
imagination.

There is a good deal of variety in this little volume —
narrative poems, short dramatic sketches, meditative and
fanciful lyrics, ballads, songs, and quatrains. 'The
Wanderings of Oisin', which gives its title to the book,
is a long narrative poem, founded on the old Irish
tradition that the Fenian hero Oisin (the Ossian of
Macpherson) was lured away by a fair enchantress to
Tir-nan-oge, the Land of Youth; and that, having so-
journed there for three hundred years, he longed for the
old human life, and returned, to find the Fenians gone
and the Christians in possession. His foot having accidentally touched mortal soil, the enchanted steed which
had carried him back vanished, old age fell upon him,
and he became the unwilling disciple of St. Patrick.
Mr. Yeats makes him tell St. Patrick the story of his
adventures in the three islands — of the Living, of
Victories, and of Forgetfulness; and the narrative is
agreeably varied by good bits of dramatic dialogue between
the heathen and the saint. The poem is in three parts,
each in a metre appropriate to the subject — the first
in free octo-syllabics, the second in Keatsian deca-
syllabic couplets, the third in quatrains of long-lined
anapaestic and dactylic verse. The first and third of
these metres are managed with considerable mastery,
especially the third, which is distinctly original in its
music. In the Keatsian verse Mr. Yeats is evidently much
less at ease. There are good bits of imaginative description in all three sections, perhaps the finest being
that of the enchanted heroes lying asleep in the Island
of Forgetfulness with great owls sidling about their
prostrate bodies and nestling in their beards and hair.
Here the long, sleepy gallop of the heavy-footed anapests
is most effective. The whole poem is drenched in youthful
fantasy, pleasant and winning; and the reader is borne

easily along from vision to vision.

Mr. Yeats is seen at his best in his shorter pieces, which have that spontaneous singing quality so rare in our self-conscious modern verse. Here is the first stanza of 'The Stolen Child,' a charming little poem which has already found admirers in the collection of new 'Young Ireland Ballads' published last year:

> Where dips the rocky highland
>   Of Slewth Wood in the lake,
> There lies a leafy island
>   Where flapping herons wake
> The drowsy water-rats:
> There we've hid our fairy vats,
> Full of berries,
> And of reddest, stolen cherries.
> Come away, O human child!
> To the woods and waters wild,
> With a fairy, hand in hand,
> For the world's more full of weeping than you
>   can understand.

This last beautiful line forms the refrain of all the stanzas. Here also is a dainty little song from the fantastic pastoral, 'The Island of Statues,' which ends the volume:

> What do you weave so fair and bright?
> The cloak I weave of Sorrow.
>   Oh, lovely to see in all men's sight
> Shall be the cloak of Sorrow,
>   In all men's sight.
>
> What do you build with sails for flight?
> A boat I build for Sorrow.
>   Oh, swift on the seas all day and night
> Saileth the rover Sorrow,
>   All day and night.
>
> What do you weave with wool so white?
> The sandals these of Sorrow.
>   Soundless shall be the footfall light,
> In each man's ears, of Sorrow,
>   Sudden and light.

The short group of Indian poems contains some of Mr. Yeats's most felicitous work. 'Kanva on God' and 'Kanva on Himself' are each admirable in its way; and the dramatic idyll 'Jealousy' has caught something of the

delicate spirit of the Sakuntala.
   Of the other dramatic sketches 'Mosada' is the most
ambitious. Ebremor, the Grand Inquisitor, has condemned
Mosada, a Moorish sorceress, to the stake. In an inter-
view in her dungeon he discovers that she is the love of
his youth; but she, having taken poison, dies, like
Gretchen, delirious, dreaming of her lover but not recognising him. There are some touches of true pathos in
this scene. In 'Time and the Witch Vivien' Vivien stakes
her life against Time's hour-glass. They play at dice
and chess, she is beaten, and dies exclaiming: 'Chance
hath a skill.' In 'The Seeker' an aged knight comes at
last into the presence of a phantom he has been all his
life pursuing, and finds a bearded witch whose name is
Infamy. In 'The Island of Statues,' a dramatic pastoral
chiefly in rhymed verse, Naschina, an Areadian maiden,
rescues her lover and many other youths who had been
transformed into statues by an enchantress. In all
these poems an idea underlies the fantastic imagination —
more is meant than meets the ear. 'The Seeker,' in
particular, arrests the reader with the strange challenge
of its symbolic meaning.
   Many passages in these dramatic sketches show that Mr.
Yeats can write graceful and delicate blank verse; and
in the short idyllic poem, 'Ephemera,' he also handles it
very skilfully. Here a pair of lovers, in an autumn
wood, discourse of passion and its inevitable waning. The
man pleads for new adventure in love, the woman for
constancy. The poem ends thus:

   Then he: 'Let us not mourn
   That we are tired, for other loves await us.
   Hate on and love through unrepining hours.
   Before us lies eternity; our souls
   Are love, and a continual farewell.'
   He spoke once more and fondled on his lips
   That word of the soul's peace — 'Eternity.'
   The little waves that walked in evening whiteness,
   Glimmering in her drooped eyes, saw her lips move
   And whisper, 'The innumerable reeds
   I know the word they cry, "Eternity!"
   And sing from shore to shore, and every year
   They pine away and yellow and wear out,
   And ah, they know not, as they pine and cease,
   Not they are the eternal — 'tis the cry.'

There is no immaturity in these lines. The sentiment
finds its expression easily and perfectly. Another
meditative poem, one of the most perfectly beautiful of

the many beautiful things in the book is 'Miserrimus.'
It tells how 'the man whom sorrow named his friend'
sought for a sympathetic hearer of his 'piteous story,'
and, finding none, breathed it into a shell, hoping to
have comfort from hearing it re-worded in the hollows of
the shell's heart.

> Then sang he softly nigh the pearly rim;
>   But the sad dweller by the seaways lone
>   Changed all his words to inarticulate moan
> Within her wildering whirls — forgetting him.

Here, as a final sample of the contents of the volume,
is one of the aphoristic quatrains:

> The ghosts went by me with their lips apart
> From death's late languor as these lines I read
> On Brahma's gateway, 'They within have fed
> The soul upon the ashes of the heart.'

'The Ballad of Moll Magee' is too long to give entire, and
would be mutilated by quotation. It deserves special
mention as a successful descent from the cloudlands of
fantasy to the real world. It is a pathetic tale of an
Irish woman turned out of house by her husband for over-
laying her child, told us by herself in perfectly simple
language.
     That Mr. Yeats has a poetic gift which deserves
recognition there can be no doubt: it remains to be seen
what he will finally make of this gift.

6. OSCAR WILDE SEES NOBILITY IN YEATS'S EARLY VERSE

1889

Extract from an unsigned review [by Oscar Wilde], Three
New Poets: Yeats, Fitzgerald, Le Gallienne, 'Pall Mall
Gazette', 12 July 1889.
     Oscar Wilde (1856-1900) met Yeats at a party given by
W.E. Henley and once invited him to a Christmas dinner at
his Chelsea house. He liked Yeats's narrative skill,
though he upset the shy younger man by saying, when asked
for some literary gossip for a provincial newspaper,
that writing literary gossip was no job for a gentleman,
and by fixing his eyes on the shoes Yeats wore which were

'a little too yellow'. Yeats saw a lot of him, probably
in 1888-9, and admired his conversational skill, his
capacity to talk in perfect sentences. (See his accounts
of Wilde in 'Autobiographies'.) Wilde also praised Yeats's
story 'The Crucifixion of the Outlaw' in 1894, having
arrived at the end of a performance of Yeats's 'The Land
of Heart's Desire'. Yeats remarked that 'it was to ask
my pardon that he overwhelmed me with compliments'.
Prompted by his father, Yeats went to deliver letters of
sympathy from Dublin friends in 1895 after Wilde's
arrest; he never saw Wilde again.

Books of poetry by young writers are usually promissory
notes that are never met. Now and then, however, one
comes across a volume that is so far above the average
that one can hardly resist the fascinating temptation
of recklessly prophesying a fine future for its author.
Such a volume Mr. Yeats's 'Wanderings of Oisin' certainly
is. Here we find nobility of treatment and nobility of
subject matter, delicacy of poetic instinct, and richness
of imaginative resource. Unequal and uneven much of the
work must be admitted to be. Mr. Yeats does not try to
'out-baby' Wordsworth, we are glad to say, but he occasionally succeeds in 'out-glittering' Keats, and here and
there in his book we come across strange crudities and
irritating conceits. But when he is at his best he is
very good. If he has not the grand simplicity of epic
treatment, he has at least something of that largeness
of vision that belongs to the epical temper. He does
not rob of their stature the great heroes of Celtic
mythology. He is very naïve, and very primitive, and
speaks of his giants with the awe of a child. . . .

7. FRANCIS THOMPSON ON THE WORK OF A GENUINE POET

1890

A review of 'The Wanderings of Oisin and Other Poems'
(1889), by Francis Thompson, 'Weekly Register', 27
September 1890.
    Francis Thompson (1859-1907), a poet and critic, was
educated at Owens College, Manchester, where he studied
medicine for six years and then abandoned it. After a
spell of destitution and opium-taking which ruined his

health he was befriended by Wilfrid Meynell. His 'Poems'
(1893) contained 'The Hound of Heaven'. He was influenced
by the poetry of Richard Crashaw and of Coventry Patmore.

This is unmistakably the work of a genuine poet, if as
yet a young poet, not quite sure of his wings. It is
markedly in the Shelleian vein, or rather in one Shelleian
vein. Take the Shelley of 'The Witch of Atlas'; imagine
him piping on a fairy straw, instead of sweeping the harp
of the winds; and you have Mr. Yeats. He is a fay hopped
out of a corner of Shelley's brain. Nor do we say this in
the smallest disparaging sense; for Mr. Yeats himself
would not claim to fill the whole of Shelley's brain.
In a day when the influence of Rossetti, Swinburne, and
William Morris is so overwhelmingly dominant, it implies
no slight independence that a young poet should
hardly display the trace of an influence posterior to
Keats. Only in a very occasional phrase are we shown
that the writer has read Rossetti. And the evident
influence of Shelley is far from excluding individual
poetic power; if the image and superscription are
Shelley's, the silver is Mr. Yeats's own. Like most young
poets, he has put his longest poem foremost in this
volume; but very unlike most young poets, in this longest
poem he has written his best poem. It is an Irish legend
of supernatural wanderings; making no demand on thought,
feeling, or passion, but giving full scope for toying
with imaginative invention: and for these reasons the
theme exactly suits Mr. Yeats. He has produced a fairy
poem full of beautiful fantasies, from which we should
like to make many extracts. But we are deterred by the
feeling that no brief excerpt can convey the impression of
luxuriant fancy which the poem itself creates. Let us
merely note at random an image so individual and apt as
that regarding the stars:

> Each one woven to the other,
> Each one woven to his brother,
> Like bubbles in a frozen pond.

Or the original and admirable phrase for the sea: 'The
sound of the sea's vague drum'. Among the other poems we
would especially remark 'The Island of Statues', a
pastoral fragment with some charmingly Shelleian passages,
especially in the lyrics; and a little idyllic scene,
'Jealousy', of which the same may be said, two of its
three lyrics being especially felicitous. In his briefer
pieces Mr. Yeats is, as ever, best when they are on fairy

subjects;   then he is always dainty.   Not as an adequate
specimen of Mr. Yeats, but as the least inadequate complete poem short enough for quotation, we may cite 'Kanva,
the Indian, on God';   a happy blending of poetry and
humour.   Observe that the gentle satire is directed, not
against our theological ideas of God, but against our
inevitable human habit of clothing Him with our own
physical attributes:

I passed along the water's edge below the humid trees,
My spirit rocked in evening's hush, the rushes round my knees,
My spirit rocked in sleep and sighs; and saw the moorfowl pace,
All dripping on a grassy slope, and saw them cease to chase
Each other round in circles;   and I heard the eldest speak;
'Who holds the world between His bill, and makes us strong or weak,
Is an undying moorfowl, and He lives beyond the sky,
The rains are from His dripping wing, the moonbeams from
      His eye.'
I passed a little further on, and heard a lotus talk:
'Who made the world and ruleth it, He hangeth on a stalk,
For I am in His image made, and all this tinkling tide
Is but a sliding drop of rain between His petals wide.'
A little way within the gloom a roebuck raised his eyes,
Brimful of starlight, and he said: 'The Stamper of the Skies,
He is a gentle roebuck; for how else, I pray, could He
Conceive a thing so sad and soft, a gentle thing like me?'
I passed a little further, and I heard a peacock say:
'Who made the grass, and made the worms, and made my
      feathers gay?
He is a monstrous peacock, and He waveth all the night
His languid tail above us, lit with myriad spots of light.'

    To conclude: Mr. Yeats's range is as yet limited, but
lovely;   he moves in a narrow circle, but it is an elfin-
ring.   If he will serve his art devoutly;   if he will shun
the ruinous error, committed by so many *dilettante* poets
nowadays, of thinking that he can make his muse a toy for
idle moments, that he can take poetry comfortably;   if
he will do this, he should assume a distinct place among
our younger singers — Titania's Shelley.

The Countess Kathleen and Various Legends and Lyrics (1892)

8. SIR WILLIAM WATSON ON YEATS'S GROTESQUE MACHINERY

1892

A review of 'The Countess Kathleen and Various Legends and Lyrics' (1892), by Sir William Watson, 'Illustrated London News', 10 September 1892.

Sir William Watson (1858-1935), a Yorkshireman, was educated at Southport, his first book of poems appearing in 1880. 'Wordsworth's Grave and Other Poems' (1890) established his reputation, and was followed by several other volumes, 'Poems, Brief and New', appearing in 1925, and 'Poems 1878-1935', in 1936.

It may be laid down as an art-maxim of general application that to fail in the attainment of any given end is disastrous in direct proportion to the ambitiousness of the means employed. Mr. Yeats's artistic means are ambitious; he fails to produce any kind of effect, and the disaster is accordingly considerable. To supplement his human puppets — we cannot say his human beings, for being they have none, in the sense of life or life-likeness — he invokes the aid of all manner of supernatural and elemental agencies, spirits and fairies, and what not, together with *sowlths* and *tevishes*, whatever they may be, for we unblushingly confess our ignorance of their nature or attributes. There are also a great many *sheogues*, and we do not feel in the least called upon to know what a *sheogue* is like — in fact, we would much rather not be told. How many legs has it? There is also a peasant who nods by the fire 'telling old shannachus.' Now, we should really like to have heard a shannachu. Why

didn't Mr. Yeats let us have one? It would have been worth
a world of sheogues. The fact is — to drop into seriousness for a moment, with many apologies — the supernatural
in poetry has no excuse for itself except where, as in
'The Ancient Mariner', for instance, it bites its way
into the reader's consciousness and compels imaginative
belief by the sheer despotism of imperious genius. All
Mr. Yeats's grotesque machinery of sowlths and tevishes and
sheogues leaves us without a shudder; his fantasies are
stage-properties of the most unillusive kind. He intro-
duces to us a brace of demons in the guise of merchants,
who go about buying souls, which they put into a bag. One
of the demons succeeds in purchasing the soul of a priest.
This is the demon's account of what followed:

> And then I thrust his soul into the bag
> And hurried home. His right hand, on the way —
> The hand that blessed the poor and raised the Host —
> Tore through the leather with sharp piety,
> And he escaped me.

Could any attempt at spiritual symbolism be cruder than
this? Mr. Yeats seems to be under the delusion that imaginative belief can be compelled by the employment of
baldly material detail, as when he talks of 'Michael
looking down from Heaven's door-post'. Sometimes he certainly has a kind of extravagant picturesqueness, as when
he makes the waves of the sea clash like cymbals, but what
does 'the long-hoarding surges' mean? And he has literally
no idea of versification: witness his excruciating trick —
a favourite one with him — of making the second foot of
a blank verse line trochaic. A man who can do this could
commit — but one must not be libellous in so respectable
a journal.
    In the *motif* of his poem about Cuchullin fighting
the waves there was ready to hand a certain element of
romantic grandeur, but Mr. Yeats has made little of the
opportunity. By far the best thing in the volume — and
it is worthy to have been one of Blake's 'Songs of
Innocence' — is the cradle song on page 122. The last
stanza — the idea of which is of the nature of a bull,
an idealised and glorified bull — is as charming and
exquisite as anything of the kind we ever read —

> I kiss you and kiss you,
>   With arms round my own;
> *Ah, how I shall miss you*
>   *When, dear, you have grown!*

9.   LIONEL JOHNSON ON YEATS'S CELTIC NOTES IN A CLASSICAL
MANNER

1892

A review of 'The Countess Kathleen and Various Legends
and Lyrics' (1892), by Lionel Johnson, 'The Academy',
July-December 1892 [1 October 1892].
   Lionel Pigot Johnson (1868-1902) poet and critic, was
educated at New College, Oxford, and was influenced by
Walter Pater.   He contributed to critical journals, to the
'Yellow Book' and the 'Book of the Rhymers' Club'.   His
'Poems' (1895) and 'Ireland and other poems' (1897) were
affected by his conversion to Roman Catholicism in 1891
and his belief in the Irish literary revival.   Yeats was
impressed by his classical and medieval learning, and
regarded him as one of the tragic generation.   Johnson
was given to alcoholism.   Ezra Pound edited his 'Poetical
Works' (1915);   the 'Complete Poems' (1953) were edited
by Ian Fletcher.

Drayton, in one of his great sonnets, laments that English
is not understood all the world over, so that his mistress
might be celebrated everywhere;   but at least her praises
may be known beyond England: there are the Orcades and
there is Ireland:

> And let the *Bards* within that *Irish* isle,
> To whom my Muse with fierie Wings shall pass,
> Call back the stiffe-necked Rebels from Exile,
> And mollifie the slaught'ring *Galliglasse*.

   Let me amuse my fancy by thinking those lines prophetic,
by finding in them a prophecy of Ireland's regeneration
through the discipline of culture, education, thought.
'Young Ireland' did much to create and to foster the
imaginative and spiritual wealth of Irish minds;   and
now the Irish Literary Society has begun its work, with
Sir Charles Gavan Duffy, returned 'from Exile', for its
president;   and with more than one 'Bard', in England and
in Ireland, to charm a distressful country.   In all
seriousness, the Renaissance of literature in Ireland
seems to have begun: of literature, in the wide sense,
implying all that is disciplinary and severe in the acqui-
sition of knowledge, yet without injuring that delicate,
dreamy, Celtic spirit which Celtic races never wholly
lose.   It is the Irish bards, says Drayton, who are to

work upon the mind and sentiment of their countrymen,
but urged and prompted to use their own powers, in their
own way, by the example of another Muse. In other words,
Irish writers, eager for the cultivation of Irish arts
and letters, should themselves have caught the spirit of
true culture, real learning, disciplined taste, from all
that is best in the genius of other lands and of other
times.

Mr. Yeats has published two volumes of verse: 'The
Wanderings of Oisin' and 'The Countess Kathleen'.
Doubtless it is difficult to speak with perfect security
about the first books of a living writer; but I feel
little diffidence in speaking of these two volumes. In
the last two or three years much charming verse has been
published by many writers who may make themselves distinguished names; but nothing which seems to me, in the
most critical and dispassionate state of mind, equal in
value to the poems of Mr. Yeats. Irish of the Irish, in
the themes and sentiments of his verse, he has also no
lack of that wider sympathy with the world, without which
the finest national verse must remain provincial. Yet,
for all his interests of a general sort, his poetry has
not lost one Irish grace, one Celtic delicacy, one native
charm. It is easy to be fantastic, mystical, quaint,
full of old-world delight in myths and legends, devoted
to dreams and sentiments of a fairy antiquity; but
writers of this kind are commonly successful by fits and
starts, their charm is elusive and fugitive. They have
the vague imagination of Welsh and Irish folk: that
perpetual vision of things under enchanted lights, which
makes the thought and speech of many an old peasant
woman so graceful, so 'poetical'. But when they approach
the art of literature, they are unequal to its demands;
they cannot so master the art as to make it convey the
imagination. Many and many an Irish poem, by writers
quite obscure, startles us by the felicity of lines and
phrases here, and by the poverty of lines and phrases
there. The poet has cared more for his inward vision
than for its outward expression: so something of what he
feels be expressed, he is content. Others, again, have
so cultivated a technical excellence as to lose the
intrinsic beauty of their themes or thoughts: their work
is polite and dull.

The distinction of Mr. Yeats, as an Irish poet, is
his ability to write Celtic poetry, with all the Celtic
notes of style and imagination, in a classical manner.
Like all men of the true poetical spirit, he is not overcome by the apparent antagonism of the classical and the
romantic in art. Like the fine Greeks or Romans, he

treats his subject according to its nature. Simple as
that sounds, it is a praise not often to be bestowed.
Consider the 'Attis' of Catullus: how the monstrous,
barbaric frenzy of the theme is realised in verse of the
strictest beauty. It is not a Latin theme, congenial to
a Latin nature: it is Asiatic, insane, grotesque; its
passion is abnormal and harsh. Yet the poem, while
terrible in its intensity of life, is a masterpiece of
severe art. It is in this spirit, if I may dare so great
a comparison, that Mr. Yeats has written: his poetry
has plenty of imperfections, but it is not based upon a
fundamental mistake; he sees very clearly where success
may be found. When he takes a Celtic theme, some vast
and epic legend, or some sad and lyrical fancy, he does
not reflect the mere confused vastness of the one, the
mere flying vagueness of the other: his art is full of
reason. So he produces poems, rational and thoughtful,
yet beautiful with the beauty that comes of thought about
imagination. It is not the subjects alone, nor the
musical skill alone, nor the dominant mood alone, but all
these together that make these poems so satisfying and so
haunting. They have that natural felicity which belongs
to beautiful things in nature, but a felicity under the
control of art. . . .
     . . . The play, ['The Countess Kathleen'] while not
dramatic in the ordinary sense, as regards evolution of
design, shows a dramatic directness and severity, for
which Mr. Yeats's other poems hardly led us to look.
'The Countess Kathleen' is far more than a lyrical
episode thrown into dramatic form: the spirit of drama
is strongly felt, in the concrete, practical handling of
the scenes.
     The Legends and Lyrics of this volume are very various.
There are stories from the old Irish cycles, ballads
founded upon more modern incidents, mystical love poems,
and poems of imaginative beauty upon other things than
love. They conclude with a poem, in which Mr. Yeats
makes his profession of faith and loyalty towards Ireland, and justifies the tone of his poems, their 'druid'
quality, their care for an ideal beauty of love and an
ideal wisdom of truth: because in singing of these he
is singing of Ireland and for Ireland.

     Ah, fairies, dancing under the moon,
     A druid land, a druid time!

In these poems, the immediate charm is their haunting
music, which depends not upon any rich wealth of words,
but upon a subtile strain of music in their whole quality

of thoughts and images, some incommunicable beauty, felt
in the simplest words and verses. Collins, Blake,
Coleridge, had the secret of such music; Mr. Yeats
sings somewhat in their various ways, but with a certain
instinct of his own, definitely Irish. The verse is
stately and solemn, without any elaboration; the thought
falls into a lofty rhythm. Or the verse is wistful and
melancholy, an aërial murmur of sad things without any
affectation.

> Who dreams that beauty passes like a dream?
> For these red lips with all their mournful pride,
> Mournful that no new wonder may betide,
> Troy passed away in one high funeral gleam,
>   And Usna's children died.

From verse so stately turn to this quite humble, simple
poem, the 'Lamentation of the Old Pensioner', merely
versified from the old man's own words.

> I had a chair at every hearth,
>   When no one turned to see,
> With 'Look at that old fellow there,
>   And who may he be?'
> And therefore do I wander on,
>   And the fret lies on me.
>
> The road-side trees keep murmuring.
>   Ah, wherefore murmur ye,
> As in the old days long gone by,
>   Green oak and poplar tree?
> The well-known faces are all gone,
>   And the fret lies on me.

In all the poems, even the most mystical in thought,
there is a deep tone of sympathy with the world's for-
tunes, or with the natures of living things: a curiously
tender gladness at the thought of it all. The poet finds

> In all poor foolish things that live a day,
> Eternal beauty wandering on her way.

His ballads are full of this natural sentiment, shown
rather in their simple mention of facts and things, as
an old poet might mention them, than in any artificial
simplicity. There is humour in this verse: a sense of
the human soul in all things, a fearless treatment of
facts, a gentleness towards life, because it is all
wonderful and nothing is despicable. And through the

poems there pierces that spiritual cry, which is too rare
and fine to reach ears satisfied with the gross richness
of a material Muse. 'Le genie celtique,' says Michelet,
'sympathise profondément avec le genie grec.' Neither
Greek nor Celtic poetry has that *gravitas,* that *auctoritas,*
which belongs to the poetry of Rome and of England. In
place of it, the Greeks and Celts have the gift of simple
spirituality, a quickness and adroitness in seizing the
spiritual relations of things, a beautiful childishness
and freshness. There is much to distress some readers
in Mr. Yeats's poems. Cuchullin, to them, is less
familiar than King Arthur, and they know nothing about
the Irish symbolism of the Rose, and much fearless simplicity seems to them but odd and foolish. All writers of
distinction, who have a personal vision of life, and
thoughts of their own, and a music of unfamiliar beauty,
must lay their account with ridicule or misapprehension.
But a very little patience will overcome all difficulties.
It is impossible to read these poems without falling under
their fascination and taking them home to heart. With
Drayton I began: with Drayton let me end. He sings about
the various lands and kinds of poetry:

> The *Irish* I admire,
> And still cleave to that Lyre,
> As our Muscila's Mother,
> And thinke, till I expire,
> Apollo's such another.

10. ANDREW LANG ON YEATS AND IRISH FAIRIES

1893

A review of 'The Celtic Twilight' (1893), by Andrew Lang,
Irish Fairies, 'Illustrated London News', 23 December 1893.
    Andrew Lang (1897-1916), educated at St Andrews Uni-
versity and Balliol College, Oxford, was a man of letters,
who translated Homer's 'Iliad' (with W. Leaf and E. Myers)
and 'Odyssey' (with S.H. Butcher). He wrote on the philosophy and religion of primitive man in 'Custom and Myth'
(1884); 'Myth, Ritual, and Religion' (1877; 1899);
'Modern Mythology' (1897); and 'The Making of Religion'
(1898). He wrote poetry, a novel, various histories and
several fairy books.

For a pleasant, pathetic, charming view of Irish people
and Irish manners, no modern writer is to be matched with
Mr. Yeats. His new book . . . reminds the reader, in some
degree, of a Celtic Charles Lamb. Many of the essays are
short, but, as we wish them longer, Mr. Yeats has succeeded. 'A remonstrance with Scotsmen for having soured
the disposition of their Ghosts and Fairies' is particularly good, and, to some extent, historically true. It is not,
however, the natural disposition of the Scotch that has
reacted unfavourably on the fairies, but the Puritanism
of the Reformers and the Covenanters produced the heavy
change. Thus, in the singular and minute account of the
Fairy Commonwealth by the Rev. Mr. Kirk (1692), he speaks
of the fairies just as he might of the Antipodes. They are
a peculiar people, of course, with ways of their own,
'joquing sprites', wags; their young women are 'incon-
venient', because only too affectionate. Never a harsh
word has Mr. Kirk for his occasionally visible parish-
ioners. But then, Mr. Kirk was, apparently, an Episcopalian before the Revolution of 1638. At the very least
he must have been one of the 'indulged' or more moderately
Puritan clergy. Again, the Rev. John Frazer of Tiree and
Coll, who died ten years after Kirk, was an Episcopalian
minister, Dean of the Isles, and a Jacobite. He was made
prisoner by the English, when they attacked the little
Isle of Eigg, in 1689, and committed many acts of lust and
rapine, which had been foretold by second-sighted men,
as both Frazer and Martin, Dr. Johnson's favourite
author, gravely informs us. Mr. Frazer left a work on the
second sight and other island marvels, published three
years after his death, in 1705. He has no harsh remarks
to make on the subject — indeed, unlike Kirk, he has a
thoroughly modern and scientific theory that visions are
merely revived impressions on the brain. This kind of
minister sours the disposition of the local ghosts and
fairies, for this kind of minister was no Puritan. 'The
Catholic religion likes to keep on good terms with its
neighbours', 'the guid neebours,' as the Scotch naturally
call them, 'the people of peace'. But the Calvinism of
southern Scotland did not feel particularly anxious to
keep on good terms with anyone who would not sign the
Solemn League and Covenant. No fairy ever did anything
of the kind. Thus, when witches were tried in Scotland,
having 'nothing to fess', like Topsy, they merely told how
they had met the fairies, the Queen of Elfan, and the
fairy king and queen (in origin akin to Pluto and Pros-
erpine) were confused in Presbyterian minds with the
Devil. Presbyterianism left no middle region, nothing
analogous to purgatory. A spirit was a good spirit or a

bad spirit, bad for choice; he was condemned, and people who saw him ran a risk of being burned. John Mair, or Major, writing before the Reformation, proves that the Church was not so strict then, at least as regards Brownies.

Fairies are gay and graceful in Ireland, says Mr. Yeats; they do deeds of terror in Scotland. This sounds very well; but they do deeds of terror in Ireland too, according to Mr. Yeats's own story of 'The Three O'Byrnes and the Evil Fairies'. As for the fairy girls who killed their lovers in Glenfinlas, this they did, not because they were Scotch, but because 'it was their nature to'. The Sirens (not Scotch exactly) were of the same family, and Mr. Stevenson has found these dangerous flirts in the South Sea Isles, as he shows in 'Island Nights' Entertainment'. As for the story of the piper (M'Crimmon in Mr. Yeats's book), who got into the cave and never came out, does the story not occur in Ireland? It is told in Edinburgh of a passage between Holyrood and the Castle; at Campbeltown, in Mull, of Mackinnon's cave, and in Skyle, if a M'Crimmon, one of McLeod's hereditary pipers, is named as the hero. One expect to find the story wherever one finds a cave. The water-cow still resides in Loch-na-Bheast in spite of baits set for her and an attempt to drain her out. But the water-cow, called the Bunyip, has been seen by Europeans in Australian lakes. She is like a fresh-water seal. Probably the Irish do not set lines for their water-cows — a course of conduct which is likely to sour the water-cow's disposition. As for ghosts, the only sourness on record is that of the bogle who bowled out the Rev. Mr. Thomson, minister of Southdean and father of the author of 'The Castle of Indolence'. According to legend, Mr. Thomson went to exorcise this bogle, who slew him with a ball of fire for interfering. As a matter of fact, Mr. Thomson did die suddenly — too suddenly for his son Jamie, then in Edinburgh, to receive his last blessing. Moreover, there was, in the parish, at Wolflea, a house which had to be pulled down because it was haunted. Again, Mr. Thomson was buried two days after his death, which was unusually hasty. But there does not appear to be any evidence that he had visited Wolflea just before his decease. The country gossip probably combined a sudden death and a local bogle into the legend. Thus, it is of no great value for Mr. Yeats's argument. His Hibernian spectres in 'Village Ghosts' are not at all more genial than common. They make the usual noises, and burn people on the wrists in the habitual way. 'The great Celtic phantasmagoria' is the great world's phantasmagoria. Mr.

Yeats has found a village Blake, and a peasant Taliesin.
Perhaps Blake was Irish; when we come to think of it, the
name is common in Ireland.   It may be argued that all the
world has its visionaries — Scandinavia, Germany, Greece,
where the Nereids do duty for fairies, Finland, where the
poetry has a note usually called Celtic — and that we
only hear more of phantasmagoria in Ireland because
newspapers and education come slower up that way.   It is
an astonishing thing that, with all the poetry of the
popular Irish imagination, the country has had no great
literary poet.   It is also rather odd that there are
sorcerers in Ireland, who sacrifice black cocks, sit in
the dark over smouldering herbs, play all the old, old
game, and let Mr. Yeats view the performance.   One wonders
how these men vote.

11.   ROBERT LOUIS STEVENSON ON 'THE LAKE ISLE OF INNISFREE'

1894

A letter to W.B. Yeats dated 14 April 1894, written at
Vailima, Samoa. From R.L. Stevenson, 'Letters', vol. 5
(5 vols, 1924), edited by Sir Sidney Colvin.
     Robert Louis Balfour Stevenson (1850-94) was educated
at the University of Edinburgh;   he studied engineering
for a session, then became an advocate in 1875.   Subsequently he travelled in France.   There he met a divorcée,
Fanny Osbourne, whom he married in America in 1880.   On
his return to Europe he began his battle against tuber-
culosis.   'Treasure Island' (1883) had brought him fame as
a writer of fiction, which his subsequent books reinforced.
His essays, travel books and poems were marked by variety
— the interest in moral ambiguities and evil of 'Dr Jekyll
and Mr Hyde' (1886) matched by the nostalgia of 'A Child's
Garden of Verses' (1885).   In 1888 he and his wife,
along with his step-children, settled at Vailima, Samoa.

Dear Sir,

Long since when I was a boy I remember the emotions with
which I repeated Swinburne's poems and ballads.   Some
ten years ago, a similar spell was cast upon me by
Meredith's 'Love in a Valley';   the stanzas beginning
'When her mother tends her' haunted me and made me drunk

like wine; and I remember waking with them all the echoes
of the hills about Hyères. It may interest you to hear
that I have a third time fallen in slavery: this is to
your poem called the 'Lake Isle of Innisfree'. It is so
quaint and airy, simple, artful, and eloquent to the
heart — but I seek words in vain. Enough that 'always
night and day I hear lake water lapping with low sounds
on the shore', and am, yours gratefully,

Robert Louis Stevenson

12. APPRECIATION OF YEATS'S CRITICAL VIEW OF IRISH POETRY

1895

Extract from an unsigned review of 'A Book of Irish
Verse: Selected from Modern writers with an Introduction
and Notes by W.B. Yeats' (1895), 'The Athenaeum',
6 April 1895.

Every one knows that Mr. Yeats is Irish: his own verses
have a quality that is at once personal and national. No
other Irishman has thought or felt precisely as he thinks
and feels, yet it is impossible to conceive that just
his special note of fancy and imagination could be sounded
by any save an Irish poet. Nor is it a secret that Mr.
Yeats is a 'patriot' of the advanced school: he is, if we
mistake not, the president of various Young Ireland and
Panceltic societies of Dublin and London to whose members
he dedicates his anthology. But Irish patriot though he
be, Mr. Yeats is before all things a poet, and it is quite
beyond him to see the poetry of his fatherland through
green glasses.
   To him poetry is poetry and literature is literature,
so his patriotism is directed rather to persuade his
fellow patriots to mend the error of their literary ways
than to that uncritical and unmeasured praise of everything
Irish that has done so much to create in Ireland an admiration for verse of native manufacture, no matter of what
quality. . . .
   In the introduction to his volume he takes a critical
survey of the poetry of modern Ireland which should be
laid to heart by all who are interested in the true glory
of Ireland and in her literary laurels. No Englishman

could without offence give utterance to the salutary
truths which Mr. Yeats writes unsparingly, dispassionately,
and calmly, through his loyalty to literature and his wish
that the Irishman of the future shall be a more sincere
artist than the Irishman of the past, and shall take part
in 'building up a literature which, whether important or
unimportant, grows always more unlike others.' Although
Moore still keeps a hold on old-fashioned folk in Ireland,
few of Mr. Yeats's contemporaries will quarrel seriously
with his dictum that the 'Irish melodies are to most
cultivated ears but excellent drawing-room songs, pretty
with a prettiness that is contraband of Parnassus'; and
it is by his criticism of the writings of the sacrosanct
Young Irelanders that Mr. Yeats will bring the storm about
his ears. His book, he says, is

> intended only a little for English readers, and not
> at all for the Irish peasants, but almost wholly for
> the small beginning of that educated and national public
> which is our greatest need and perhaps our vainest hope.

Writing for such a public, it needed courage to speak
with perfect candour of the ''48' men, who

> were full of earnestness, but never understood that
> though a poet may govern his life by his enthusiasms,
> he must, when he sits down at his desk, but use them
> as a potter his clay. Their thoughts were a little
> insincere, because they lived in the half illusions of
> their admirable ideals. . . . No man was more sincere,
> no man had a less mechanical mind than Thomas Davis,
> and yet he is often a little insincere and mechanical
> in his verse. When he sat down to write he had so
> great a desire to make the peasantry courageous and
> powerful that he half believed them already the
> finest peasantry upon earth, and wrote not a few such
> verses as —

> > Lead him to fight for native land,
> > His is no courage cold and wary;
> > The troops live not that could withstand
> > The headlong charge of Tipperary,

and to-day we are paying the reckoning with such
bombast. . . . He was in the main an orator influencing
men's acts, and not a poet shaping their emotions, and
. . . the poets who gathered about Thomas Davis, and
whose work has come down to us in 'The Spirit of the
Nation', were of practical and political, not of

literary importance. Meanwhile Samuel Ferguson,
William Allingham, and Mr. Aubrey de Vere were working
quietly as men of letters. . . . They were wiser than
Young Ireland in the choice of their models, for, while
drawing not less from purely Irish sources, they turned
to the great poets of the world, Mr. de Vere owing
something of his gravity to Wordsworth, Ferguson much
of his simplicity to Homer, while Allingham had
trained an ear, too delicate to catch the tune of but
a single master, upon the lyric poetry of many lands.
Allingham was the best artist, but Ferguson had the more
ample imagination, the more epic aim.

Here follows an appreciative and most able criticism
of Ferguson, 'apart and solitary, an epic figure in a
lyric age', and of Allingham, 'who will take his place
among those minor immortals who have put their souls into
little songs to humble the proud'; but the praise is
sober and discriminate though unstinted, and Mr. Yeats
is conscious of the limitations of the poets he admires,
while of those who were produced by that Fenian movement
with which he is, politically, much in sympathy, he can
only write that they 'were,at times, very excellent'.
As for the quite recent verse, it is impossible to form
an unbiassed estimate of its value, and Mr. Yeats pru-
dently withholds a verdict, while he urges his contemporaries to 'a passion for artistic perfection' lest 'the
deluge of incoherence, vulgarity, and triviality pass over
our heads.'. . .
 . . . Modesty is a quality so charming in a youthful
editor that we ought not to upbraid Mr. Yeats for the
entire omission of his own poems, yet it is impossible
not to feel that his book has suffered by a delicacy which
has rendered an admirable selection incomplete. Yet, in
truth, wherever Mr. Yeats errs it is on the wise side of
omission; there is nothing in the volume that the most
fastidious would wish away, and one or two old favourites
that seem to be quite worthy of a place have been excluded. . . .
 . . . However, here Mr. Yeats disarms criticism by
confessing that 'the book is founded upon its editor's
likes and dislikes', a system he has justified by
results, as well as by the irrefutable plea 'that he had
only his temperament for a chart'.
We have quoted largely from Mr. Yeats's introduction
because it is unusually able, original, and courageous,
a new departure in an Irish man of letters, and one which
will, it is to be hoped, lead to a more sober and just
estimate of Irish production by Irish men. . . .

Poems (1895)

13. A REVIEWER ON YEATS'S CONSCIOUSNESS OF TWO WORLDS

1895

Extract from a review of 'Poems' (1895), signed A.M.,
Mr Yeats's Poems, 'The Bookman', December 1895.

>   Ah, leave me still
> A little space for the rose-breath to fill!
> Lest I no more hear common things that crave;
> The weak worm hiding down in its small cave,
> The field mouse running by me in the grass,
> And heavy mortal hopes that toil and pass;
> But seek alone to hear the strange things said
> By God to the bright hearts of those long dead,
> And learn to chaunt a tongue men do not know.

This is the key to all the poetry Mr. Yeats has yet
given us. The consciousness of two worlds is ever
present in his dreams, not this and that of a dim future,
but one co-existing with and invading the other, each
disputing the other's claims. Perhaps the most revealing
thing in all this volume — I am inclined to call it the
most remarkable poem — is 'The Man who Dreamed of Fairyland'. This world was not without its interests to the
man. He fell in love. But as 'he stood among a crowd at
Drumahair', he heard a Druid song, and

> The singing shook him out of his new ease.

He gathered money like a prudent man, but in the midst of
his reckonings came a song again,

89

And at that singing he was no more wise.

His hot blood was stirred with anger, but as he turned
to take vengeance, vengeance fled before a tale of a
lonely, peaceful fairy folk, and

The tale drove his fine angry mood away.

He was gathered to his fathers, and there he might have
known stillness —

Were not the worms that spired about his bones
    A-telling with their low and reedy cry,
    Of how God leans His hands out of the sky,
To bless that isle with honey in His tones;
That none may feel the power of squall and wave,
    And no one any leaf-crowned dancer miss
    Until He burn up Nature with a kiss:
The man has found no comfort in the grave.

These are not the poems of a man who finds fairyland
convenient because it provides pretty and picturesque and
romantic circumstance. They are haunted by 'the wayward
twilight companies'. For in the balance of one world
against another, it is easy to see which scale is the
more heavily weighted — in spite of Cathleen and her
sacrifice, in spite of the very human 'Ephemera', and in
spite of the rough ballads, direct translations from
humanity. The human nature, by the bye, that interests
him most lives near the soil and the roots of things.
Rudeness is not repellent to him; and such ballads as
'Moll Magee' are fashioned not after literary models,
but rather after the rough chanting chronicles that, to
this day, give recent and current affairs impressiveness,
sung by the wandering bards of Brittany.
   But the bliss of dreaming — and its ruin, too —

No maiden loves me, no man seeks my help,
Because I be not of the things I dream,

are as yet more native themes. Not many of us love
poetry very much, and a moderate lover has generally a
preference that his own life, idealised, should be the
stuff from which poetry is woven. I do not think Mr.
Yeats appeals to any moderate lovers. But there are
words for those who hanker after what is called the
'human element', even outside the poems I have named
above. Wisdom has often had a way of dwelling apart
from those it lived to help; and in the search for beauty

tenderness is a not infrequent comrade, since the searcher
finds

> In all poor foolish things that live a day
> Eternal Beauty wandering on her way.

Mr. Yeats has revised much, and not always to please
his older readers. He has cast out some poems which
deserved honourable places, and which surely will not
knock at the doors of future editions in vain. There is
a lack of finish in some of his work, quite distinguishable
from his artful love of the crude. His plays are wanting
in a dramatic sense, and there are a few mystical poems
which need a key. But there is not one commonplace line.
There is hardly a misused term. There is no exaggeration,
no eccentricity. It is the verse of a man born into the
ranks of the poets, who sees poetry and breathes it, and
who happens to have the gift of words. That indeed he
has. Listen to it in 'The Lake Isle of Inisfree', in
'The Rose of Battle', in the almost too much rewritten
'Wanderings of Usheen', in the last lament of Oona that
ends the 'Countess Cathleen':

> The years like great black oxen tread the world,
> And God the herdsman goads them on behind,
> And I am broken by their passing feet.

A.M.

14. ERNEST RHYS ON YEATS'S REVISIONS

1896

A review of 'Poems' (1895), by Ernest Rhys, 'The Academy',
22 February 1896.
    Ernest Percival Rhys (1859-1946), editor and poet, grew
up in Carmarthen and became a mining engineer. He edited
the Camelot Classics for Walter Scott's publishing firm,
and included Yeats's 'Fairy and Folk Tales of the Irish
Peasantry' (1888) in it. He was responsible for editing
the Everyman Library for Dent. His own verse was romantic; 'A London Rose' (1891) and 'Song of the Sun' (1937)
are representative volumes. His 'English Lyric Poetry'
(1913) contained good criticism, and he wrote memoirs in
'Everyman Remembers' (1931) and 'Wales England Wed' (1941).
He joined Yeats and T.W. Rolleston in founding the Rhymers'

Club. His early recollections of Yeats appeared in an
article in the 'Fortnightly Review', July 1935.

In this thrice-taking volume, with its pale buff and
gold covers of mystic design, we have the total accom-
plishment in poetry, so far, of Mr. Yeats. It contains,
he tells us, all he cares 'to preserve out of his previous volumes of verse', in some cases revised, in others
re-written; and the result is as handsome an argument
as a younger poet need wish to offer contemporary criticism. With it, in fact, so far as that criticism
goes, Mr. Yeats may be said to emerge from the coteries
and to reach the centre.
     In puttint it together Mr. Yeats has clearly sub-
jected himself to a severer criticism than any but hyper-
critics else are likely to offer. Those who have learnt
to know his poems in those slim earlier volumes, out of
which this is built, may complain, possibly, over some of
his new readings of familiar passages, and new versions of
familiar names; as in his conversion of 'Oisin' to
'Usheen'. Again, they will miss some favourite pieces,
such as more than one of the lyrics in that Shelleyan
fragment, 'The Island of Statues', and among them the
delightful song of the voices, which was well worth the
pains of revision. Thus it begins:

          A man has the fields of heaven,
            But soulless a fairy dies,
     As a leaf that is old and withered and cold,
          When the wintry vapours rise.

Again, in the curious 'Indian Song' in the same first
volume, which now reappears as 'The Indian to his Love',
and which, in shedding something of its extravagance,
loses something of its lyric fervour, the ear of many of
his readers will not sanction the practical suppression
of such a verse as this:

          Oh wanderer in the southern weather,
            Our isle awaits us: on each lea
     The pea-hens dance; in crimson feather,
            A parrot swaying on a tree
          Rages at his own image in the enamelled sea.

But, mainly, what one finds in these changes is that if
Mr. Yeats is growing rather more literary, he is, too,
more severe an artist than he used to be. In making

them it is clear that he has tried to heighten the imaginative truth of his poems, even at the cost of throwing away their fanciful trappings. His revision is,
then, generally good, if sometimes bad.

That he should have paused to go back and review himself in this way, instead of hastening on, in the fashion
of our time, to do endless new things, says much for his
artistic conscience; and it is as an artist through and
through that he is likely to impress his readers in these
collected poems. This alone makes him a notable appearance among the Irish poets, who have hitherto (with two
or three notable exceptions) showed more fervour than
poetic form, and more facility than fine art. And this,
remembering that there are others working with him, may
show that Irish literature, in its modern interpretation, has entered on a new phase. So far as one can see
now, indeed, it is to Mr. Yeats that men will point here-
after, as marking the beginning of the new period; and
this volume of his may serve as a striking landmark in a
remarkable movement. Modern criticism has cleared the
way and prepared the audience and made the standards plain;
and the new poets, if they be indeed poets born, like Mr.
Yeats, and not merely made, like Mr. ——, have an opportunity such as Keats and Shelley might have envied. . . .

To justify this belief in Mr. Yeats one is most likely
to convince the unbeliever perhaps by quoting him on his
lyric side first. What could be more touching than this?

Down by the salley gardens my love and I did meet

[Quotes following 2 stanzas of 'Down by the Salley
Gardens'·]

What more haunting, more irresistible, than his song of
'The Lake Isle of Innisfree'.

[Quotes first stanza of the poem.cf. 'Collected Poems',
p. 44·]

Such lines as these reach the ear and hold it, and through
it touch the heart. A few such songs may suffice for the
poet's immortality, and there is no younger poet of our
time in whose future fame one may feel a stronger faith.

It remains to speak of the longer poems, and particularly of 'The Countess Cathleen', whose story — how,
in time of famine, she sold her soul to the devil to save
the souls of her people — is full of openings peculiarly
suited to Mr. Yeats, and to his native feeling for the
old associations and lurking traditions of remote Irish

countrysides. He has cast the story in dramatic form;
and although one may not feel altogether certain of its
technical qualities as an acting play, it reads dramatically, as well as being imaginative and profound to a
degree. A play may not be judged by passages; but something of its charm may be gathered from these lines of the
opening scene, which is laid in an Irish wayside hostelry,
'The Inn of Shemus Rua', whose kitchen, with its hanging
shrine, is lit by a dim bog-oak fire.

> TEIG.   Hear how the dog bays, mother,
> And how the grey hen flutters in the coop.
> Strange things are going up and down the land,
> These famine times. By Tubber-vanach cross roads
> A woman met a man with ears spread out,
> And they moved up and down like wings of bats.
>
> MAIRE. Shemus stays late.
>
> TEIG.   By Carrick-orus churchyard,
> A herdsman met a man who had no mouth,
> Nor ears, nor eyes, his face a wall of flesh.
> He saw him plainly by the moon.
>
> MAIRE (going over to the little shrine).
>   White Virgin,
> Bring Shemus from the wolves - Shemus is reckless;
> And save him from the demons of the woods,
> Who have crept out and pace upon the roads,
> Deluding dim-eyed souls now newly dead,
> And these alive who have gone crazed with famine,
> Save him, White Virgin!
>
> TEIG.   And but now
> I thought I heard far-off tympans and harps.
>   (Knocking at the door.)
>
> MAIRE. Shemus has come.
>
> TEIG.   May he bring better food
> Than the lean crow he brought us yesterday.
>   (MAIRE opens the door, and SHEMUS comes in
>   with a dead wolf on his shoulder.)

Of the other two longer poems in the book, 'The
Wanderings of Usheen' and 'The Land of Heart's Desire',
there is not space to say more than that they are equally
characteristic, and equally surcharged with the imagination and the Celtic glamour which Mr. Yeats puts into his
best work, and which make this volume so perfect a thing of its
kind.

The Secret Rose (1897)

15. THE DREAMY GLAMOUR OF THE CELT

1897

An unsigned review of 'The Secret Rose' (1897), 'The Academy', 1 May 1897.

It is a hard case when the one right word for a critic to use is a word that has been so hackneyed, so bandied about in vague characterisation, that it has become rightly suspect and almost even tabooed. Yet hackneyed or not, there is only one word which describes the quality of Mr. Yeats's stories, and that is glamour — the glamour of the Celt. His tales have a good deal of talk about magic in them, more, in fact, than is to everybody's taste, for not everybody can be brought to take spirit-raising seriously; but on every page in the book there is proof given of a magic to which all lovers of literature must be submissive — the natural magic of style. Here is no artifice of haziness, no mist of words; rather, the extraordinary thing about these stories is the distinctness with which they bring present to the senses whatever is related. Take, for instance, a few words from the first one, 'The Binding of the Hair', which tells of Queen Dectira and the bard Aodh's (Hugh's) last song, upon whose prelude there broke in the alarm for battle.

> Then he took down from a pillar his shield of wicker and hide, and his bronze helmet and sword, and passed among the crowd that went shouting through the wide door; and there was no one left in the room except the queen and her women and the foolish king, who slept on, with his head against a pillar.

How that conjures up the sense of desolation and vastness
in the hall that a moment before had been crowded; one
seems to feel the noise of feet dying away. It is all
distinct, but with the distinctness of a dream; and Mr.
Yeats's utterance is, like Aodh's, 'dream-heavy'. The
thing is done partly by a singular felicity of comparison,
as in this phrase: 'A very old man, whose face was almost
as fleshless as the foot of a bird'; but chiefly by the
distinctness of the artist's own vision. Yet this constant appeal to the eye is never allowed to predominate or
to mask the central thought which each study conveys, as
for instance, 'The Heart of the Spring', which sets out the
aspiration of the alchemist and life's ironic commentary
upon it. Dreamy as the stories are, they are not fantastic;
their characters act with human coherency. Mr. Yeats is
fond of the supernatural: in 'The Curse of the Fires and
of the Shadows' he has introduced it for his own pleasure
since in the tradition it was no one of the Shee who led
the five Cromwellians to their fatal gallop over the pre-
cipice, but a simple peasant. Yet we like him best when
he does not stir outside of the human pale. 'The Crucifixion of the Outcast' is a grim tale of the way in which
respectable folk dealt with the strolling gleeman when
respectability had full power to make itself respected;
we suspect an apologue. Anyhow, this is one of the only
two stories in the book touched with the humour that made
'Celtic Twilight' so delightful. The other is by far
the best of them all, the tale or series of tales relating
to the adventures of Owen Hanrahan the Red, last of the
Gaelic singers in Ireland. Here is a splendid touch. The
poet whose power over women had been not less than his
passion for them sees a girl crying, and offers help:

> 'My father and my mother and my brothers,' she
> went on, 'are marrying me to old Paddy Doe because of
> the hundred acres he rents under the mountain, and I
> would have you put him into a rhyme as you put old
> Peter Kilmartin in the days when you were young, that
> sorrow may be over him, rising up and lying down.'
> 'I will put him into a little song that shall bring
> shame and sorrow over him; but how many years has he,
> for I would put them into a song?'
> 'Oh, he has years upon years — he is as old as you
> are, Owen Hanrahan.'
> 'As old as me,' said Hanrahan, in a broken voice.
> 'There are twenty years between him and me if there is
> a day. An evil hour has come for Owen Hanrahan when a
> colleen with a cheek like the blossom of May thinks him
> an old man. Colleen, colleen, an arrow is in my heart.'

Beautiful as is the 'Vision of Owen Hanrahan' with its
fine symbolism, there is nothing in it worth that. But
beautiful it is, a new and genuine inspiration from the
old mythology of the Gael. The old gods are no more dead
for Mr. Yeats than were Pan and Apollo for Milton. 'When
one looks into the darkness,' he says in his preface, there
is always something there.' Most of us look very little
into the dark; and we are inclined to retort that those
who look into the dark see nothing but fancies. Yet such
a book as this makes one ponder whether the light of
common day does not blind us to many starry presences.
For all that we have no patience with the last and longest
story, 'Rosa Alchemica', which is totally distinct from
the rest and resembles the recital of an opium-dream. Like
everything else in the book, however, it is beautifully
written — in long, slow, undulating sentences, easy and
sinuous in their progress as the motion of a serpent.

The illustrations are admirable. There are not many
points of likeness between Mr. Yeats and Mr. Kipling; but
each has a father who draws beautiful pictures for his
son's books. Print and paper leave nothing to be desired;
but it was a pity to use ridged not smooth material for the
binding, as it impairs the effect of Miss Gyles's intricate symbolic design for the cover — a model of decorative
work.

16. MYSTIC BYWAYS AND SYMBOLIC INTENTIONS IN YEATS'S PROSE

1897

An unsigned review of 'The Secret Rose' (1897), The
Illusion of Mystery, 'The Athenaeum', 22 May 1897.

Mr. Yeats has the courage of his Celtic imagination if he
thinks, at this wrong end of a hardened century, to arouse
our slumbering Saxon taste for allegory and symbolism. The
fashion of Cynewulf's day is a little outworn; and we have
ceased to read Guillaume de Lorris with unaffected exhi-
laration. Yet here, in an age of all the utilities, is a
young writer who invites us, with the frank confidence of
youth, to follow him through the mystic byways of a new
'Roman de la Rose'. If a fine enthusiasm for his theme
could touch our hearts, the appeal must surely strike
home. But the hearts of some of us are not in the right

place; and our heads are troubled with an intelligence a
shade too analytic. The author's heart is right enough;
but he, too, suffers from the latter-day trick of introspection. It is the snare of even the greatest artists who
imitate archaic forms or subjects. Dante Rossetti in
his ballads does not altogether escape it; still less
does Tennyson in his 'Idylls of the King'; Matthew
Arnold perhaps least of all in his avowedly Hellenic work.
Such a passage as this from Mr. Yeats's book may serve to
show how the touch of a too modern spirit may hurt the
harmony of old-world sentiment:

> 'If you come with evil thoughts and armed men,' said
> the son of Dermott, flushing, 'no matter how strong
> your hands to wrestle and to swing the sword, it shall
> go badly with you, for some of my wife's clan have
> come out of Mayo, and my three brothers and their ser-
> vants have come down from the Mountains of the Ox'; and
> while he spoke he kept his hand inside his coat as
> though upon the handle of a weapon. 'No,' answered
> Costello, 'I but come to dance a farewell dance with
> your daughter'. . . . The girl lifted her eyes and
> gazed at Costello, and in her gaze was that trust of
> the humble in the proud, the gentle in the violent,
> which has been the tragedy of woman from the beginning.

The one word 'tragedy', quite apart from the sentiment of
the conclusion, imparts a disturbing element; it has
almost the air of modern literary slang. Again:

> Costello led her among the dancers, and they were soon
> drawn into the rhythm of the Pavane . . . and while they
> danced there came over them the unutterable melancholy,
> the weariness with the world, the poignant and bitter
> pity for one another, the vague anger against common
> hopes and fears, which is the exultation of love.

The reflection, though it comes from the author and not
from his characters, is still a violation of unity, an
anachronism in sentiment.
  A fault akin to this, but less easily to be pardoned,
is seen in the absence of what, for want of a better phrase,
may be called the right local colouring. Let it be granted
that Mr. Yeats is sufficiently Irish in his nomenclature
and antiquities. We have abundant local feeling in his
names — the Steep Place of the Strangers, the Lough of
the Little Wood, the Town of the Shelly River; every page
is full of them. There are also 'boreens' and 'garrons'
and 'bodachs', and other properly unintelligible Celticisms.

But for all that we can seldom identify in his pictures
the marks either of place or time. We pass over a wide
range of seasons from early Christian times to at least the
seventeenth century with scarce any sign to mark the
change. Characters of all ages and conditions speak in
much the same manner; and, if we except a desultory
phrase or two, their racial idiosyncrasies are but faintly
revealed. On the other hand, it would be ill-natured not
to acknowledge our gratitude for being spared the local
equivalent of the Kailyard jargon.

But we must revert to the question of symbolism, for
these tales pretend to mean more than mere tales of
faerie. Mr. Yeats assures his readers in his dedication that they all 'have but one subject, the war of
spiritual with natural order'. And certainly in the
broader issues of some of these stories the symbolic
intention may be obvious; yet when, after the author's
warning, we search for esoteric interpretations in the
multifarious details of his images, the process is found to
be futile and exhausting. We are forced to give up the
task and content ourselves with the human interest of the
story itself, which is often far to seek; or with the
concrete beauty of his pictures, or with the glow and
grace of his eloquence. But unhappily the high qualities
of an eloquence which at its best has a conquering charm
are not sustained. Had Mr. Yeats brought to bear upon his
work a keener sense of negative humour (the absence of
positive humour may be excused under the circumstances) he
would never have allowed us the shock of certain occasional lapses from the ethereal range of his poetic diction.
He would never have told us that 'when they came to Dermott's
house they saw before the door *an unusually large group of
the very poor*'; or that Margaret Rooney had 'some dilapi-
dated remnants of tolerably good looks'. The bathos of
such phrases can only be appreciated by comparison with Mr.
Yeats's exalted manner. Purists, as distinct from humour-
ists, may further complain of the fatal attraction of 'and'
to the relative in many places in this book.

Finally, after putting trivial blemishes aside, all
who know anything of Mr. Yeats's exceptional ability as
a poet will feel that in these prose stories he has not
chosen the medium most suited to his remarkable powers.
Now and again, in a white heat of energy, he 'makes the
live shape at a jet'; at other times he must himself be
conscious that his material compels him to treat his
themes too clearly and too explicitly to preserve the
illusion of mystery. As a writer of imaginative prose
he takes high rank, it is true, among the men of our
younger generation; but as a poet of the school of Shelley

the author of 'The Wanderings of Usheen' stands alone.
Some of the verses scattered about the present book are
laboured in accentuation;   but he has proved sufficiently
his mastery over form as well as matter, and it is in the
sphere of poetry rather than of prose that we look for
the development of powers which promise a brilliant future.
It is to be hoped that there is no personal presage in
his comment upon the works of certain authors found by
him in the House of the Order of 'Rosa Alchemica', where
he says:

> I noted also many poets and prose writers of every
> age, but only those who were a little weary of life,
> as indeed the greatest have been everywhere, and who
> cast their imagination to us, as a something they
> needed no longer now that they were going up in their
> fiery chariots.

We know no young Elisha who is quite prepared to assume
the mantle of Mr. Yeats.

17.   FIONA MacLEOD ON YEATS AS POET, TALE-TELLER AND
CRITIC

1899

Extract from Fiona MacLeod, A Group of Celtic Writers,
'Fortnightly Review', 1 January 1899.
    Fiona MacLeod (William Sharp, 1855-1905), poet, novelist,
dramatist and essayist, was educated at the University of
Glasgow, and worked in Glasgow in a law office before becoming a literary journalist in London in 1879.   He wrote
'Celtic' tales and romances, romantic and mystic, under the
name of 'Fiona MacLeod', carefully concealing his supposed
cousin's identity.   The best known of these was 'Pharais,
a Romance of the Isles' (1894);   his verse play 'The
Immortal Hour' (1900) was very successful after the First
World War.

. . . .Beautiful as is that lyrical narrative 'The
Wanderings of Oisin', exquisite in delicate form and
aerial touch as are the poetic plays, 'The Land of Heart's
Desire' and 'Countess Cathleen', we have not here any
ultimate expression.   It is because these are so fine —

and for me, I may add, they have a beauty and a charm
beyond any other contemporary work of the kind — that
we are unwilling to accept them as other than the preliminary airs of a new and strangely beautiful music. It
is perhaps Mr. Yeats' highest distinction — rather than
that he has the most haunting sense of beauty of any of
our younger writers, or the most subtle developments of
style — that it is to him we look more than to any other
for art which shall not only be invested with the suggestion of greatness, but itself be great. He has the finest
imagination of all the younger writers; the most distinction; by far the rarest touch. But he has defects also,
and it remains to be seen whether he can transcend these
defects, or at least so control or direct them that they
run subservient to his genius. His mysticism is sometimes
mere vagueness: his symbolism sometimes mere arbitrary
imagery: and there is in his imaginative prose in particular a tendency to veil the contours of the motive
thought in a moonshine mist or in dyes of a romantic
beauty too august, too remote, for the following minds of
a cast over-mundane for such excellences to appear other
than mere rainbow-shimmer. I could wish for him that for
a year or two he might neither read nor think nor hear of
other mystics, and above all that the Rosierucian cult
and everything to do with esoteric mysticism might be put
aside from him; and that in this interval he would set
himself vigorously only to the determinable, the measurable,
the attainable. There is enough mysticism for him in the
old legends and myths of the Gael, profoundly symbolical
as much of these are, and as practically all the earliest
portion is. In the interpretation of myths such as those
of Etain and Fand, of Lu and Angus Og and Manannan, there
is enough scope for the most restless and eager mind,
there is scope even for dramatic use, as, for example, in
the beautiful 'Meave' of Mr. Edward Martyn. In these old
myths and legends is an older wisdom still, and in the
words of the Gaelic shenachie or his modern interpreter
we may hear the more ancient words of the early shepherd-
kings, 'who knew the stars', or of the white-robed
ministers of forgotten gods, who beneath their crude
symbols apprehended and interpreted the eternal mysteries.
On this ground, Mr. Yeats would be independent of confusing
influences: and whether he wrote of the ancient people,
or of the peasants of today, of the other world, or of the
earth whose pulse we are, would find naturally his own
interpretation, his own symbols, his own visionary reality.
I mistrust those medieval systems which beleaguer the
citadel of the spirit with secret avenues of thought,
occult byways of expression, and obscure passages of outworn and arbitrary symbol.

As a mere writer, Mr. Yeats interests me profoundly.
As poet, as tale-teller, as critic, he displays three
distinct avenues of approach to his own mind. Broadly,
he remembers, and as an echo of that remembrance we have
his poetry: out of dreams, he shapes realities, and we
have his strange and lovely tales, born of spiritual
vision and emotion as much as of essential observation,
and the rhythmic instinct of creation; and he ponders
the interrelation of persons, conditions, and the vast
concourse of past and present, and material and spiritual
circumstances, and writes with an acumen and a perspicacity
not less remarkable than his lyrical instinct in his verse,
or his rhythmic movement in his imaginative prose. There
is no criticism so difficult as that of oneself, for pre-
dilection and not austerity of taste is the basis of most
criticism. That Mr. Yeats has this invaluable quality is
to be inferred from internal evidence in his work; but
a notable instance obtains in the collective edition of his
poetical writings. Compare 'The Wanderings of Oisin' and
other poems in that volume with the corresponding contents
of the volume in the 'Cameo' series entitled 'The Wanderings of Oisin' — and some of these, again, with yet
earlier issues — and the lover of his poetry will detect
the scrupulous eliminative instinct of the anxious
artist. . . .
. . .I find no contemporary prose, employed in the
service of the imagination, so fine, so subtle, so seductive, as that of the author of 'The Secret Rose'. Sometimes it lacks suppleness; occasionally it lacks strength;
and too often it is obscured by a partly instinctive, but
sometimes wilful mysticism; while again and again it is
determined by arbitrary whim rather than by compelling
intuition. Mr. Yeats has, so far as I know and can
judge, failed once only in prose; for in the short
novel 'John Sherman' he simply accomplishes without
distinction what a hundred contemporaries could do as
well, and many better.
I believe his prose, fine as it is, to be transitional;
and that his maturer work will be rather towards the
simplicity of diction of 'The Celtic Twilight' than
towards the too highly wrought, often too esoteric prose
of the much-admired 'Rosa Alchemica'. At present, I
account his finest, because most appropriate prose to be
that of the 'Hanrahan the Red' series. I think, too, that
a keener sense of the incongruous would save Mr. Yeats
from some mistakes. That he has humour is evident in 'The
Celtic Twilight' and elsewhere: as, notably, in the account
of his Irish peasant-friend and visionary who, given a
large bottle of whisky, was overcome by a great enthusiasm,

and died in three days. But serious art demands the most
searching heed, not necessarily against the conventionally
incongruous, but against the inherently incongruous. Yet
even an ignoring of the conventionally incongruous may
involve disaster. There must be few, I take it, who could
read the account of the sudden cock-crowing of the old
Celtic visionary in Paris, in 'The Adoration of the Magi'
without a perilous smile, though it is only fair to add
that this story is in the privately issued volume, 'The
Tables of the Law'.

Of Mr. Yeats's critical writing I have already expressed my admiration. His danger, characteristically, is
in generalisations; perhaps also in too great a trust
in sympathetic intuitions. This, however, is surmise; and
I may well have misapprehended; and in any case I allude
to casual instance, and certainly not to a mental habit.
Of late he has done some valuable work in folk-lore
narration and exposition; and has published recently an
admirable article on the Celtic element in literature: an
exposition with which I, for one, find myself wholly in
accord, believing as I, too, do, that much of what is
specifically called Celtic is simply ancient, and that it
is only because the antique shepherd, the antique hunter,
the antique visionary in Druid woods or by sacred fires,
survive more in the dreaming and overborne Celt than in any
other modern people, and particularly in the disherited
Gael, that we have at this day a racial genius so distinct
in its outlook, in its backlook, in its inlook, so distinct in the bent of its thought and the turn of its expression, from that of our predominantly Anglo-Saxon
kindred. . . .

Poems (1899) and The Wind among the Reeds (1899)

18. FRANCIS THOMPSON ON YEATS'S DELICATE AND EVANESCENT
CHARM

1899

A review of 'Poems' (1st edition, 1895; 2nd, 1899) and
'The Wind among the Reeds' (1899), 'The Academy', 6 May
1899.
For note on Francis Thompson see pp. 73-4.

Mr. W.B. Yeats is well known as one of the most active
and prominent leaders of that movement in present literature which goes by the somewhat high-flown title of the
Celtic Renaissance. It numbers both poets and prose
writers belonging to the kindred kingdoms of Ireland and
Scotland. In Scotland it boasts Miss Fiona MacLeod.
Miss Jane Barlow represents another side of it; while
even Wales sends its contributors. Mr. Yeats has for-
warded it both with poetry and prose, and he has a number
of coadjutors. Such movements are the fashion nowadays.
In France a union of Gascon writers has broken out with
much parade and display and self-glorification, after the
way of things Gallic in general and Gascon in particular.
The Celtic movement is less self-laudatory and more work-
manlike. Our English instincts might desire even less
public emphasis; but it is the way of the hour, and it
cannot be questioned that the members are doing a needed
thing in trying to awaken the dormant literary instincts
of Ireland. For it is in Ireland that it is most noteworthy, by contrast with the long neglect of letters in
that country; and it is a plain fact, dependent on no
flourish of trumpets, that at present Ireland has a

number of workers who have made their mark in the more
refined and fastidious pursuits of literature.
    None among them has a more genuine, more distinctive
and personal note than Mr. Yeats. His first book, 'The
Wanderings of Oisin', some years ago made that evident,
and he has not receded from the promise then given. His
work has been slender in quantity. Since he collected
his previously published verse into one by no means bulky
volume of 'Poems', his total product in verse and prose
is included in five small books, counting the present one.
But it has quality; it is artistic and conscientious.
His prose inclines to a poetised style: it is good of its
kind, but not eminently good. With all its poetic in-
fusion, it has nothing tawdry. With all its self-
conscious artistry, the note is not forced: its rhythm
is a true prose-rhythm, with none of that terrible
bastard movement — like blank verse gone very much to the
bad — which makes most writing of this sort anathema.
A very good specimen is 'Dhoya', included in the volume
called 'John Sherman'. Yet it is not sufficient for a
reputation.
    That reputation must rest on Mr. Yeats's poetry. Here
he stands quite alone: a poet he is, and — to our
thinking — a poet only. In everything else which he
writes he suggests the poet. As poet he suggests nothing
outside poetry — the simple essence; not poetic embodiment of this thing or that, but just poetry. In this
respect he belongs natively to the same order as Coleridge and Spenser and Shelley — when Shelley has got
kings and priestcraft and the making of new universes off
his mind: the Shelley of the songs and the 'Skylark' and
the 'Cloud' and the 'Witch of Atlas'. Not that Mr.
Yeats is as one of these; not his a large or wide gift.
It is, in truth, an exceedingly contracted gift; but a
gift it is, authentically his and no man else's. Whether
from singular self-judgment or the good-hap of simple
sincerity, Mr. Yeats has practically recognised this. He
has known that his gift was small, he has known that his
gift was narrow; he has known that his gift was *his*
gift — or he has acted as if he knew, which comes to
the same thing; and he has held to it and within it,
unswerving and contented as the blackbird on the bough.
'O blackbird, sing me something new!' cries Tennyson.
'Always true is always new,' answers the wise blackbird
and Mr. Yeats. 'A poor thing, but mine own', he might
modestly claim with Touchstone.
    This gift of Mr. Yeats, so one and individual, is easy
to feel, not easy to state: it is not the gift of any
poet before him. Some of his earlier work, in particular,

shows close study of Shelley, and happy affinities with
Shelley's lighter fancy; but his most characteristic
work is not at all Shelleian. Nor yet can we acquiesce in
Mr. Andrew Lang's description of him — 'a Celtic Heine'.
We fail to see resemblance between the German poet and Mr.
Yeats. In connexion with this 'Celtic movement' we have
heard much of the characteristic quality belonging to that
native Celtic poetry sealed from the Saxon reader by the
language in which it is written — a quality sometimes
noted in Matthew Arnold's phrase as 'Celtic magic', sometimes in a later phrase as 'the Gaelic glamour'. The
latter has the advantage that it does 'something affect
the letter', as Holofernes says when he means to alliterate
abominably. The Saxon is disposed to be sceptical, after
much search, as to the very existence of this quality. He
looks for it amid the poems of Irish writers in the English
tongue, and finds it not. Even the strange thwarted genius
of Clarence Mangan has nothing answering to this. Still
less can one attach the phrase to the writers of the
'Celtic movement'. It may be hidden from us behind the
veil of the old Erse tongue, but it finds no way beyond
it. These young Irish writers of the movement have their
various powers, but not this. There is one exception, to
our mind, and it is Mr. Yeats. To the peculiar *aura*, the
effluence of his poetry, if we were asked to attach the
phrase 'Celtic magic' our conscience would not take
alarm. Certainly, if it be not *the* magic — on which let
Celts pronounce — it is *a* magic which merits a distinctive phrase.

It is an inhuman beauty, a haunting of something remote,
intangible, which the poet himself only feels, but cannot
trace to its source. In proportion as he becomes, or tries
to be, definite this power passes from him. It is when he
is obeying the dictates of an emotion, a sentiment, as
insubstantial and uncapturable as a gust of the night,
that he achieves this most delicate and evanescent charm.
With a true instinct of his own prevailing quality he
calls this latest book 'The Wind Among the Reeds'. No
less frail and mysterious than such a wind is the appeal
of Mr. Yeats's best verse.

The very finest examples are contained in his collected
'Poems' — namely, 'The Lake Isle of Innisfree' and 'The
Man Who Dreamed of Fairyland'. The first expresses in
most daintily sweet verse the appeal of remembered solitary water and reedy isle to a born dreamer stranded in
city streets. The second embodies in finely haunting
verse Mr. Yeats's most constant mood — the call upon
the visionary's heartstrings of the legendary country,
where is 'the light that never was on sea or land'. On

the whole, it is Mr. Yeats's best poem. And it should
be; for he is himself 'the man that dreamed of fairyland'. All his poetry is one plaintive cry for a domain
set apart from 'life's exceeding injocundity'. We are
not pronouncing whether this is a wholesome or desirable
frame of mind. Perhaps we have other views. We merely
state the case. And since every poet is best when he
expresses his dominant love, Mr. Yeats is always at his
best when he is dealing with the world of fays or
spirits. At such times his lightness of touch is exquisite. It is hard to say where the fascination lies.
It is as much in the music as the apparent words — a
true test in lyrics of this kind, which are sensitive
rather than intellectual. Take this quite incidental
lyric from the fairy play, 'The Land of Heart's Desire'
— a song sung by fairies to entice a mortal girl:

> The wind blows out of the gates of the day,
> The wind blows over the lonely of heart
> And the lonely of heart is withered away,
> While the fairies dance in a place apart.
> Shaking their milk-white feet in a ring,
> Tossing their milk-white arms in the air;
> For they hear the wind laugh, and murmur and sing
> Of a land where even the old are fair,
> And even the wise are merry of tongue;
> But I heard a reed of Coolaney say,
> 'When the wind has laughed and murmured and sung,
> The lonely of heart must wither away!'

Could anything be more airy and delicate? In this
sense Mr. Yeats has always been a mystic. He has always
'dreamed of fairyland'. But in this new volume there
are signs that he desires to be a mystic in a more recondite sense. The old Irish mythology, which always
attracted him, he has taken up the study of in its symbolic meanings, and endeavours to import it into his verse
as a vehicle for the expression of modern and personal
ideas.

Frankly, we view this development with alarm. It
would always be a perilous experiment, because, unlike
the language of Greek or Biblical religion, Irish mythology is so unknown to English readers. But Mr. Yeats's
treatment of it increases the difficulty. He frequently
uses this mythological imagery in a sense of his own, though
in his elaborate notes he acknowledges himself doubtful
about the correctness of his interpretation — that he is,
in fact, guessing at the meanings of the symbols he uses.
But how shall the reader follow this arbitrary use of

symbolism, or be certain where the poet himself is uncertain? The only road out is the clumsy expedient of
explanatory notes. This is not the true use of symbolism,
and from a purely poetical standpoint is quite inartistic.
It creates wanton difficulty. Mr. Yeats should at any
rate be clear to the few who understand the system of
mythological imagery. But his arbitrary use of it often
leaves even them in the dark. 'I use this to signify so
and so,' is the formula. But he should not 'use it to
signify' anything. He should use it, if he needs it, for
what it does signify; and if he is unsure what it sig-
nifies, he should not use it at all. It is wantonness to
darken his poetry by employing recondite imagery, which
he confesses elaborately he is doubtful about the meaning
of. Frankly, there is more ingenuity than insight in
much of it.

   This we have said with some emphasis, because it is a
feature which threatens to mar Mr. Yeats's poetry; and
his poetry is too good for us to see it marred with
equanimity. But it is the trick of an artist unduly
enamoured of a new medium for its own sake, and he will
grow out of it. There is plenty of work in this new volume
which shows the old charm. Take the 'Cap and Bells'. Mr.
Yeats confesses that the meaning varies to him. But this
is not the result of obscure expression; and a poet may
quite legitimately be doubtful about his own allegory. It
is a wise poet that knows, in this sense, his own child.

[Quotes text of 'Cap and Bells'.]

. . . We might venture an interpretation. The mistress
whom poets serve desires not a poet — a poet pure and
simple — for his wisdom, his study, let us say, of solar
mythologists — who are not even the chattering of owls,
for owls see in the dark — nor for his much service,
but just for — his cap and bells, for his sweet intuitive gift of rhyme. That is the way of knowledge and of
all else for him. Truly, if he follow that way, 'the
heart and the soul come through'. But there is much else,
besides this poem, to show that Mr. Yeats is still Mr.
Yeats.

19.   ARTHUR SYMONS ON YEATS AS LYRIC POET

1899

A review of 'Poems' (1899) and 'The Wind among the Reeds'
(1899), by Arthur Symons, Mr Yeats as a Lyric Poet, 'The
Saturday Review', 6 May 1899, later revised and included
in 'Studies in Prose and Verse' (1904).

Arthur Symons (1865-1945), poet, critic and literary
journalist, was educated at private schools abroad, and
joined the Rhymers' Club in London, becoming a friend of
Dowson, Wilde and Yeats (with whom he shared rooms in the
Temple in 1896;   they visited the west of Ireland, notably
the Aran Islands, in that year).   He introduced the work
of the French symbolists to English readers, and contributed to the 'Yellow Book' and the 'Savoy'.   He was a
disciple of Pater, published several volumes of sad
poetry, did some useful summing-up in 'The Symbolist
Movement in Literature' (1899), and wrote various critical studies as well as accounts of modern painting.   His
'Confessions: A Study in Pathology' (1930) is a poignant
account of his mental breakdown in Italy.

Mr. Yeats is the only one among the younger English poets
who has the whole poetical temperament, and nothing but
the poetical temperament.   He lives on one plane, and you
will find in the whole of his work, with its varying
degrees of artistic achievement, no unworthy or trivial
mood, no occasional concession to the fatigue of high
thinking.   It is this continuously poetical quality of
mind that seems to me to distinguish Mr. Yeats from the
many men of talent, and to place him among the few men of
genius.   A man may indeed be a poet because he has written
a single perfect lyric.   He will not be a poet of high
order, he will not be a poet in the full sense, unless
his work, however unequal it may be in actual literary
skill, presents this undeviating aspect, as of one to
whom the act of writing is no more than the occasional
flowering of a mood into speech.   And that, certainly, is
the impression which remains with one after a careful
reading of the revised edition of Mr. Yeats' collected
poems and of his new volume of lyrics, 'The Wind among
the Reeds', which have appeared almost simultaneously.
The big book, now reissued with a cover by a young artist
of subtle and delicate talent, Miss Althea Gyles, contains work of many kinds.   There is a play, 'The Countess
Cathleen', which is to be performed in Dublin next week;

and a second play, 'The Land of Heart's Desire', which
was performed in London in 1894. 'The Countess Cathleen'
is certainly Mr. Yeats' masterpiece. I have but just come
from seeing it rehearsed, and the rehearsal has taught
me, what I indeed suspected, that it is not only splendid
poetry, but, in a very serious sense, a fine acting play.
Its visionary ecstasy is firmly embodied in persons whose
action is indeed largely a spiritual action, but action
which has the lyrical movement of great drama. Here is
poetry which is not only heard, but seen; forming a
picture, not less than moving to music. And here it is
the poetry which makes the drama, or I might say equally
the drama which makes the poetry; for the finest writing
is always part of the dramatic action, not a hindrance
to it, as in almost all the poetical plays of this
century. In the long narrative poem contained in the
same volume, 'The Wanderings of Oisin', an early work,
much rewritten, a far less mature skill has squandered
lyrical poetry with a romantic prodigality. Among the
lyrics in other parts of the book there are a few which
Mr. Yeats has never excelled in a felicity which seems
almost a matter of mere luck; there is not a lyric
which has not some personal quality of beauty; but we
must turn to the new volume to find the full extent of
his capacity as a lyric poet.
    In the new volume, 'The Wind among the Reeds', in
which symbolism extends to the cover, where reeds are
woven into a net to catch the wandering sounds, Mr. Yeats
becomes completely master of himself and of his own re-
sources. Technically the verse is far in advance of anything he has ever done, and if a certain youthful freshness, as of one to whom the woods were still the only
talkers upon earth, has gone inevitably, its place has
been taken by a deeper, more passionate, and wiser
sense of the 'everlasting voices' which he has come to
apprehend, no longer quite joyously, in the crying of
birds, the tongues of flame, and the silence of the heart.
It is only gradually that Mr. Yeats has learnt to become
quite human. Life is the last thing he has learnt, and
it is life, an extraordinarily intense inner life, that I
find in this book of lyrics, which may seem also to be one
long 'hymn to intellectual beauty'.
    The poems which make up a volume apparently discon-
nected are subdivided dramatically among certain symbolical persons, familiar to the readers of 'The Secret
Rose', Aedh, Hanrahan, Robartes, each of whom, as indeed
Mr. Yeats is at the trouble to explain in his notes, is
but the pseudonym of a particular outlook of the consciousness, in its passionate, or dreaming, or intellectual

moments.   It is by means of these dramatic symbols,
refining still further upon the large mythological symbolism which he has built up into almost a system, that
Mr. Yeats weaves about the simplicity of moods that
elaborate web of atmosphere in which the illusion of love,
and the cruelty of pain, and the gross ecstasy of hope,
become changed into beauty.   Here is a poet who has
realised, as no one else, just now, seems to realise,
that the only excuse for writing a poem is the making of
a beautiful thing.   But he has come finally to realise
that, among all kinds of beauty, the beauty which rises
out of human passion is the one most proper to the lyric;
and in this volume, so full of a remote beauty of atmosphere, of a strange beauty of figure and allusion, there
is a 'lyrical cry' which has never before, in his pages,
made itself heard with so penetrating a monotony.
    There are love-poems in this book which almost give a
voice to that silence in which the lover forgets even the
terrible egoism of love.   Love, in its state of desire, can
be expressed in verse very directly;   but that 'love, which
moves the sun and the other stars', love to which the
imagination has given infinity, can but be suggested, as
it is suggested in these poems, by some image, in which
for a moment it is reflected, as a flame is reflected in
trembling water.   'Aedh hears the cry of the sedge,' for
instance;   and this is how the sedge speaks to him:

        I wander by the edge
        Of this desolate lake
        Where wind cries in the sedge
        Until the axle break
        That keeps the stars in their round
        And hands hurl in the deep
        The banners of East and West
        And the girdle of light is unbound,
        Your head will not lie on the breast
        Of your beloved in sleep.

By such little, unheard voices the great secret is
whispered, the secret, too, which the whole world is
busy with.

        O sweet everlasting Voices be still;
        Go to the guards of the heavenly fold
        And bid them wander obeying your will
        Flame under flame, till Time be no more;
        Have you not heard that our hearts are old,
        That you call in birds, in wind on the hill,

In shaken boughs, in tide on the shore?
O sweet everlasting Voices be still.

To a poet who is also a mystic there is a great simplicity in things, beauty being really one of the foundations of the world, woman a symbol of beauty, and the
visible moment, in which to love or to write love-songs
is an identical act, really as long and short as eternity.
Never, in these love-songs, concrete as they become through
the precision of their imagery, does an earthly circumstance divorce ecstasy from the impersonality of vision.
This poet cannot see beauty except as the absolute beauty,
cannot distinguish between the mortal person and the
eternal idea. Every rapture hurries him beyond the edge
of the world and beyond the end of time.
   The conception of lyric poetry which Mr. Yeats has
perfected in this volume, in which every poem is so nearly
achieved to the full extent of its intention, may be
clearly defined; for Mr. Yeats is not a poet who writes
by caprice. A lyric, then, is an embodied ecstasy, and
an ecstasy so profoundly personal that it loses the accidental qualities of personality, and becomes a part of
the universal consciousness. Itself, in its first,
merely personal stage, a symbol, it can be expressed only
by symbol; and Mr. Yeats has chosen his symbolism out
of Irish mythology, which gives him the advantage of an
elaborate poetic background, new to modern poetry. I am
not sure that he does not assume in his readers too
ready an acquaintance with Irish tradition, and I am not
sure that his notes, whose delightfully unscientific
vagueness renders them by no means out of place in a book
of poems, will do quite all that is needed in familiar-
ising people's minds with that tradition. But after all,
though Mr. Yeats will probably regret it, almost everything
in his book can be perfectly understood by any poetically
sensitive reader who has never heard of a single Irish
legend, and who does not even glance at his notes. For
he has made for himself a poetical style which is much
more simple, as it is much more concise, than any prose
style; and, in the final perfecting of his form, he has
made for himself a rhythm which is more natural, more
precise in its slow and wandering cadence, than any prose
rhythm. It is a common mistake to suppose that poetry
should be ornate and prose simple. It is prose that may
often allow itself the relief of ornament; poetry, if it
is to be of the finest quality, is bound to be simple, a
mere breathing, in which individual words almost disappear
into music. Probably, to many people, accustomed to the
artificiality which they mistake for poetical style,

and to the sing-song which they mistake for poetical
rhythm, Mr. Yeats' style, at its best, will seem a little
bare, and his rhythm, at its best, a little uncertain.
They will be astonished, perhaps not altogether pleased,
at finding a poet who uses no inversions, who says in
one line, as straightforward as prose, what most poets
would dilute into a stanza, and who, in his music, re-
places the aria by the recitative. How few, it annoys
me to think, as I read over this simple and learned
poetry, will realise the extraordinary art which has
worked these tiny poems, which seem as free as waves,
into a form at once so monumental and so alive! Here,
at last, is poetry which has found for itself a new form,
a form really modern, in its rejection of every artifice,
its return to the natural chant out of which verse was
evolved;   and it expresses, with a passionate quietude,
the elemental desires of humanity, the desire of love,
the desire of wisdom, the desire of beauty.

20.   IRISH DISLIKE OF 'THE COUNTESS CATHLEEN'

1899

Extract from leading article, 'Irish Times', 9 May 1899.
When Yeats's play 'The Countess Cathleen' was first produced, at the Antient Concert Rooms, Great Brunswick (now
Pearse) Street, Dublin on 8 May 1899 by the Irish Literary
Theatre, it aroused strong opposition, and the play was
performed with police protection and with interruptions
from a hostile section of the audience.

'The Countess Cathleen' is neither a play nor a presentment of either the ideals or actions or motives of Irish
men and women. . . . 'The Countess Cathleen' as performed
last night by a company of artists chosen by those account-
able for the movement is, in the first place, not 'The
Countess Cathleen' published by Mr. Yeats, and is consequently not a play. It is without action, without
definiteness in the characterisation and without consistency in the dramatic development, without truth in its
reflection of Celtic temperament or life, and like all
inferior plays it fails to excite the smallest genuine
interest. . . . 'The Countess Cathleen' has no action
which could seize and carry on to a climax the interest

of an audience; therefore, it is not a good play and in
as much as it offends against the tenour of Irish history
in regard to Theological connection and against the position of the Irish peasant in face of physical pain, it
cannot be considered an Irish play. . . . Still less as a
Celtic dramatic effort it was not entitled to have serious
consideration.

21. JAMES JOYCE'S RESERVED JUDGMENT

1901

Extract from The Day of the Rabblement, 'Two Essays', by
James Joyce and F.J.C. Skeffington (1901).
   James Joyce (1882-1941) was educated by the Jesuits
and at University College, Dublin. After graduating in
1902 (he also trained as a singer) he left Ireland, returning in 1903 when his mother was fatally ill. He
left permanently in 1904, having then nearly completed
the fifteen stories of 'Dubliners', which, however, were
not published until 1914 because of difficulties between
Joyce and his publishers.
   Yeats realised Joyce's ability; he also wrote an amusing
account of their meeting in a preface intended for 'Ideas of
Good and Evil' (1903), but this was not published until
after his death. In this meeting Joyce, then twenty, told
Yeats after hearing his age, 'I thought as much. I have
met you too late. You are too old.' Yeats later, in
1903, tried to get him work on 'The Academy'; in 1915 he
wrote to Gosse and the Secretary of the Royal Literary
Fund, praising him as 'the most remarkable new talent in
Ireland today' and 'a man of genius'; in 1918 he praised
a part of 'Ulysses' in 'The New Review' as 'an entirely
new thing'; in 1922 he wrote to Olivia Shakespear of
its Irish cruelty and strength and beauty, though in
1923 he told her he must conceal from Joyce the fact that
he had never finished it. In a letter to her of 9 March
1933 he commented that Joyce never escaped from his
Catholic sense of sin.

Meanwhile, what of the artists? It is equally unsafe at
present to say of Mr. Yeats that he has or has not genius.
In aim and form 'The Wind among the Reeds' is poetry of
the highest order, and 'The Adoration of the Magi' (a

story which one of the great Russians might have written)
shows what Mr. Yeats can do when he breaks with the half-
gods. But an aesthete has a floating will, and Mr.
Yeats's treacherous instinct of adaptability must be blamed for his
recent association with a platform from which even self-
respect should have urged him to refrain. Mr. Martyn
and Mr. Moore are not writers of much originality. Mr.
Martyn, disabled as he is by an incorrigible style, has
none of the fierce, hysterical power of Strindberg, whom
he suggests at times; and with him one is conscious of a
lack of breadth and distinction which outweighs the
nobility of certain passages. Mr. Moore, however, has
wonderful mimetic ability, and some years ago his books
might have entitled him to the place of honour among
English novelists. But though 'Vain Fortune' (perhaps
one should add some of 'Esther Waters') is fine, original
work, Mr. Moore is really struggling in the backwash of
that tide which has advanced from Flaubert through Jakob-
sen to D'Annunzio: for two entire eras lie between
'Madame Bovary' and 'Il Fuoco'. It is plain from
'Celibates' and the later novels that Mr. Moore is beginning to draw upon his literary account, and the quest of
a new impulse may explain his recent startling conversion.
Converts are in the movement now, and Mr. Moore and his
island have been fitly admired. But however frankly Mr.
Moore may misquote Pater and Turgenieff to defend himself,
his new impulse has no kind of relation to the future of
art.

22. J.M. SYNGE ON YEATS AND THE IRISH INTELLECTUAL
MOVEMENT

1902

Extract translated from J.M. Synge, Le Mouvement Intellectuel Irlandais, 'L'Européen', 31 May 1902, later printed
in 'Collected Works: Volume II, Prose' (1966), edited
by Alan Price.
    John Millington Synge (1871-1909), dramatist, poet and
prose writer, was educated at Trinity College, Dublin.
His desire to make music his career horrified his evan-
gelical family; he went to Paris in 1895, and in 1896 met
Yeats there. Yeats persuaded him to go to the Aran
Islands, and to write of the Irish peasantry and countryside. He had read Gaelic and Hebrew at Trinity, and there

he studied the speech and customs of the Aran Islanders.
His book 'The Aran Islands' (1907) was illustrated by
Yeats's brother, Jack B. Yeats. Yeats realised Synge's
genius, made him a director of the Abbey Theatre, fought
strenuously on behalf of 'The Playboy of the Western
World' in 1907, and wrote appreciatively of him in poems
and various essays, notably the preface to Synge's 'Poems
and Translations' (1909) and J.M. Synge and the Ireland
of his Time (1911), both included in 'The Cutting of an
Agate', 'Essays and Introductions' (1961).

. . . This state of things lasted a long time but, little
by little, an increasing knowledge of the English language
among ordinary people and a more complete assimilation of
people of English extraction gave the country a new
literary field.

    In 1798 William Carleton was born in County Tyrone and
thirty years later he published his 'Traits and Stories of
the Irish Peasantry', a book which has become famous,
which marks the definitive start of modern Irish literature. Since that moment Irish writers were many and
prolific. One finds novelists, young people who were part
littérateur, part politician (who were numerous towards
the year 1848), poets and some savants who mainly occupied themselves with national antiquities. None the less,
it must be acknowledged that all the literature produced during the first three quarters of the century does
not contain anything of very real value. The national
sentiment was too ardent, too selfconscious, if one may
say so, among these writers; their prose as a result fell
over-easily into overcharged rhetoric, whereas in poetry
it was felt that in singing the glories of ancient Ireland
one had done enough.

    Furthermore, the writers of that period wrote in a
language which a great portion of the people round them
had never fully mastered. As a result their attitude
towards the English language remained entirely without
that special intimacy which, alone, can give birth to
genuine works of literature.

    Now, as we pass to the present generation, we find that
these defects have lessened, if they have not completely
disappeared. With a rather broader culture the national
sentiment no longer is dominated by an obsession, and,
gradually, the English language has become, throughout
most of Ireland, a genuine mother tongue. We see the
scope of this amelioration especially in the works of Mr
W.B. Yeats, the genius at the head of the new school of
Irish poetry. With him, national sentiment, while re-

maining as deep as it was with his predecessors, restricts
itself to giving a distinctive character to the atmosphere in which the delicate creatures of his imagination
flourish.
       On the other hand, his rhymes, composed with a curiously
simple wisdom, bear witness to his rare knowledge of the
English language. It is not possible to criticise in a
few lines the complete works of Mr Yeats, who in any case
is not unknown in Paris. . . . I confine myself therefore
to pointing out here the strange beauty of his lyrical
poems without, however, being able to leave the names of
two books, 'The Secret Rose', in prose, and 'The Shadowy
Waters', a verse play, which has a rare distinction of
language and sentiment. . . .
       Two or three lesser-known poets have recently pub-
lished some fairly interesting work, but I will not mention them in order to go on to 'The Literary Theatre', a
literary theatre which can be taken to be the centre of
the intellectual movement. The first productions were
staged in May 1899. The first was a piece by Mr Yeats
called 'The Countess Cathleen'. In it he portrayed the
Countess Cathleen, a sort of chatelaine, who, at a moment
of scarcity in Ireland, sold her soul to demons in order
to come to the aid of the people who were dying of hunger
around her castle. This seems very innocent, but in
Dublin some of the public is still sufficiently orthodox
to find itself shocked by such an action. The clergy
expressed a certain disapprobation and, at each performance, one could see scandalised drunks shouting, from
the gallery, observations on the morals of Mr Yeats and
his colleagues.

23.   FIONA MacLEOD ON SYMBOLISM AND DRAMA

1902

Extract from Fiona MacLeod, The Later Poetry of Mr. W.B.
Yeats, 'North American Review', July-December 1902
[October 1902].
       For note on Fiona MacLeod see p.100.

. . . Mr. Yeats is assuredly of that small band of poets
and dreamers who write from no other impulse than because
they see and dream in a reality so vivid that it is called

imagination. With him the imagination is in truth the
second-sight of the mind. Thus it is that he lives with
symbols, as unimaginative natures live with facts.

A symbolist stands in some danger here. The obvious
peril is a confusion of the spiritual beauty behind the
symbol with the arbitrary expression of that spiritual
beauty through that particular symbol. There are blind
alleys and lost roads in symbolism, and few of those who
follow that loveliest trail into 'the undiscovered Edens'
of Beauty but sometimes lose themselves, and go after
shadows, and idly name the stars, and inhabit planets with
their own desires, putting their vain dreams upon these
unheeding children of eternity.

Perhaps a truer wisdom is that which would see the
symbols in the facts, and the facts translated from their
material body to their spiritual significance. It is
the constant reminder of the man who breaks stones to the
man who measures the stars, that he concerns himself with
remote unrealities; but the star-gazer is also apt to
forget that without broken stones no road would be paven.
And I cannot but think that Mr. Yeats is a star-gazer too
reluctant to listen to the plaint of those who break
stones or are spiritually dumb hewers of wood and drawers
of water. He does not always sing of things of beauty and
mystery as the things of beauty and mystery are best
sung, so that the least may understand; but rather as those
priests of Isis who, when bidden to chant the Sun-Hymn to
the people, sang, beautifully, incomprehensible alge-
braical formulae.

> The Powers whose name and shape no living creature knows
> Have pulled the Immortal Rose:
> And though the Seven Lights bowed in their dance and wept,
> The Polar Dragon slept,
> His heavy rings uncoiled from glimmering deep to deep:
> When will he wake from sleep?

Or again:

> We who still labour by the cromlech on the shore,
> The grey cairn on the hill, when day sinks drowned in dew,
> Being weary of the world's empires, bow down to you,
> Master of the still stars and of the flaming door.

Or that strange poem of love with its fantastic dream-
beauty, beginning:

> Do you not hear me calling, white deer with no horns?
> I have been changed to a hound with one red ear.

To some there is no need to explain 'the white deer with
no horns', 'the hound with one red ear', 'the boar without
bristles, out of the West': to some the symbols of the
'Polar Dragon' and the 'Immortal Rose' stand evident. But
these must be few: and though in a sense all excelling
poetry is mystical, in the wider and not less true sense
it should be as water is, or as air is, or as flame is.
For it too is an elemental, being in the spiritual life
what wind is in the natural life.

When the reader, unfamiliar with 'the signature of
symbol', shall read these and kindred lines, will he not
feel that his young priest of the Sun should translate to
a more human key his too transcendental vision? What,
he will ask, is the Immortal Rose, and what the Polar
Dragon? Who is the guardian of the flaming door, and of
what is it the portal? If a Gael, he may have heart of
the white fawn that is Love, of the white hound that is
Death. Is it this symbol that lives anew in the hound with
one red ear, in the white deer without horns?

For all who may not be able readily to follow his honey
of old wisdom, Mr. Yeats has added notes. It would be more
exact to say that one-half of the book comprises the prose
equivalent of the verse. If all notes afforded reading
such as one may read here! Mr. Yeats turns round men-
tally and shows us the other side, where the roots grow
and the fibres fill with sap, and how they grow to that
blossom we have already seen, and what the sap is. In
their kind, these notes have something of the charm of
the poems to which they stand interpreter. Yet they
should be superfluous. It is not their presence that one
objects to, but their need. Poetry is an art which should
be as rigorously aloof from the explicative as the art of
painting is, or as sculpture is, or music. When Mr.
Yeats gives us work on a larger scale, with a greater
sweep, he will, let us hope, remember that every purely
esoteric symbol is a vague image — and vagueness is the
inevitable defect against which the symbolist has to
contend.

But, when all is said that criticism is called upon to
say, what a lovely gift of music and spiritual intensity
and beauty is here. I have an incalculable pleasure in
this subtle magic which creates so much loveliness out of
a few words. If, at times, the motive has triumphed at
the expense of the manner, it is rare that music and meaning do not go in delectable harmony. What lover of
perfect verse but could take keen pleasure in a little
poem so rose-like in its intricate symmetry as this

[Quotes 'He wishes for the Cloths of Heaven', 'Collected
Poems', p. 81.]

The nobler use of symbolism — which is but an analogue
of the soul's speech — gives a strange spiritual intensity to these poems. All do indeed live with an
intense life, though of conventional actuality they have
little or nothing. Some seem to be written in accordance
with 'the magical tradition'; some conform to the
utterance of Celtic mythology; some have no other shape
or aspect than their own, as they came, like moths out
of twilight, from the twilight of the poetic imagination.
All come

> from a more dream-heavy land,
> A more dream-heavy hour than this;

and it is the infinite, because never wholly to be overtaken, charm of these breaths — breaths of the reeds of
the spirit shaken in that wind which comes out of the
past of time and the past of the heart — that, in them,
we too, as the poet himself, may hear 'white Beauty
sighing'. In no descriptive sense, but in a deeper sense,
this book is one of a small company that are pioneers in
that intimate return to nature from which we may and do
expect so profound and beautiful a revelation. For a
few come with new vision, to reveal what is so old, what
is younger than all else, and new always. . . .
    A larger note is struck in 'The Shadowy Waters'. In
this dramatic poem — in this poetic vision, told in
verse cast in a dramatic form — Mr. Yeats has forsaken
the acute moment become lyrical for the lyrical thought
become continuous. It is not an epical poem, because it
is a symbolical reflection of what is in the poet's mind,
rather than the imaginative upbuilding of what his imagination has definitely shaped. It is not, strictly, a
poetical drama, for action and speech are subservient to
the writer's entranced vision of the symbolism of the
action and of the speech. It is one of those new and
strange utterances, so perplexing to many minds, wherewith
conventional methods are used for novel, perturbing,
sometimes bewildering, at times bewildered, thought: one
of those 'dramas of the mind, best seen against imagined
tapestries', which reveal so much more to us than do the
common or familiar 'tapestries', the dramas of the
obvious, of merely spectacular life. . . .
    In his symbolical and mythological allusions, Mr.
Yeats is again, as in 'The Wind Among the Reeds', too
esoteric often, sometimes too vague. One may speak the
tongue of angels, but the accent must be human and familiar.
A still more serious literary fault is the overuse of certain words: 'winds and waters', 'the pale hound', 'heart's

desire', and others, come too facilely from Mr. Yeats's
generally so heedful art. Mannerism threatens dillusion
when it becomes a common use, as when in close conjunction
Mr. Yeats thrice uses a favorite, but at best dubious,
epithet *druid*, uses it as an adjective for 'mystic' or
kindred word: 'a druid vapor', 'druid moons', 'with
druid apple-wood'. It has a contagion, for a day or two
ago I saw in a paper an allusion to 'the druid spell of
Mr. Yeats's poetry, its druid lights and shadows'. I
can understand a druid spell, though 'druidic' is the fit
word: but not druid lights and shadows.
    'The Shadowy Waters' does not yield all its beauty at
once. It is like that flower which Moan, a dark queen
of the Hidden People, showed to Cuchulain in his madness:
a flower of a pale hue and faint fragrance, that every
day disclosed a richer hue, the color of a moment, or
loosed, passing as a moth's wing, a new fragrance. It
is the story of a dream, of a symbolic vision; but its
enchantment lies in its subtly beautiful interpretation of
a dream that is not of one mind but of many minds, of a
vision that has not sustained one heart's desire only
but the desire of many hearts in the troubled congregation of men and women.
    The miscarriage which awaits the pioneer lurks in the
probable failure between theory and fulfilment. Mr.
Yeats has written carefully concerning dramatic ideals and
the Celtic Theatre: but he has not yet seemed explicit
to the reader eager to sympathize with both, nor has his
published dramatic work fulfilled the desired end. Like
so many of us, he mistakes sometimes the gossamer drama
woven inwardly of the wind of the spirit and the light
of the imagination, for the tangible drama woven to represent adequately the things of the imagination and the
spirit. He thinks in light and dreams in shadow, but
forgets that the translation of these into thought made
visible must be as explicit as the translation of the wind's
cry on the wave or murmur among the leaves, when through
a formal and exact notation the musician would convey
the mystery of the one and the troubled deeps of the other.
Hitherto, he has stood overmuch by the inner sureties of
the loom of thought: now, if he has to achieve what he
has in aim, he must study the outward weaving of the web,
the external aspect of the woven dream, with not less
careful heed, with careful, careful art. In 'The Land of
Heart's Desire', in 'Countess Cathleen', in 'The Shadowy
Waters', he does not convince dramatically. In these he
persuades. It may be the finer way for the imagination:
to persuade by the thing seen, rather than by the thing
shown. But it is not the way of Drama, whose end is to

be achieved by methods of illusion other than those of
cadence and color. Mr. Yeats has not yet perceived that
the particular method of illusion demanded by the Drama
necessitates both an acceptance of certain conventions,
and an avoidance of certain scenic imaginative realities
inept as visible scenic actualities. 'The Countess
Cathleen' ranks first in what he has done in dramatic
form, a play of great beauty, and whose repeated public
performance delighted those who saw it. Yet it is impossible not to feel that something is wanting. This
want is not of the obvious: we do not mean that it
should be longer or shorter, swifter or slower, more
mumorous or more tragic, more wrought in poetry or sustained in prose. We take it as it is, and judge it for
its shape and color, its own life, its spirit, its aim.
It is, then, that below the charm of the verse we are
aware of a lack. It is not that the thought is slight,
though it is not strenuous or deep; or that the phrase
is inadequate in suggestion; or that unrealities wave
conflicting plumes among the ordered march of the words,
though insurgent unrealities there are at moments, and
rebel insincerities, unconscious traitors no doubt. But
something is lacking, as in a still, breathless wood we
miss the lifting airs that are the wind. And the wind
whose airs Mr. Yeats does not yet command is the wind of
the dramatic spirit. He does not think, shape, reveal
dramatically. This is as obvious in his dramatic poems
as in his tales. A dramatic conception of an event or
a linked sequence of events is not enough: there must be
a dramatic vision of the coherent and actual congregation
of the 'symbols' in which that conception is to be made
unique and visible: there must, further, be that faculty
of mental economy which can use the few words only, the
slight detail, which can relinquish the literary idea for
the visible actuality: and there must be the power to
distinguish between the method of illusion that lies with
reverie and inward vision, and the method of illusion that
lies with concentrated thought and its immediate expression, with their demonstration in the visible.

The flaw in Mr. Yeats's dramatic work seems to me to be
just this, that he is not primarily a dramatist. That he
can write a beautiful dramatic poem is evident in 'The
Shadowy Waters': that he can write a beautiful 'poetic
drama' is evident in 'The Countess Cathleen': that he can
transmute into dramatic form the reflective spirit of
reverie is evident in 'The Land of Heart's Desire'. But
these are not dramas in the sense that they are the outward and actual representation, through men and women and
the actual world, of the dreams and thoughts and ideas of

which men and women and the actual world are the shadows
and vivid phantoms. It is not the visible, the dramatic
interpretation that Mr. Yeats gives us, but the woven
shape and color of his dreams. 'The Shadowy Waters' is a
vision related as a dramatic poem: it could have been
related in dramatic prose, or in the continuous linked
prose of reverie, or in the deftly entangled prose of
dialogue, or in the mirroring lucidities of the prose of
narrative. We are glad of it as it stands: we may consider that it could not appeal to us more finely in
another form. But it has not inevitableness. Even in
the one drama more nearly suited for external representation which Mr. Yeats has written, there are spiritual
truths, symbols, images which are as foreign voices crying
for interpretation: images, symbols, and truths which, in
their reality to him, he has forgotten are, to others,
unrelated voices, wandering shapes, the idle signature of
falling stars in the abyss.

And yet since I have re-read 'The Shadowy Waters' I
believe that Mr. Yeats may give us a wonderful compromise
that shall be almost a new art, a new art perhaps. He
may find the way where the dreaming spirit and the shaping
mind are not two companions but one traveller: he may
stoop by a well we have not seen, and hear the forgotten
voice of Connla, and out of old wisdom fashion newly a new
thing. In words already quoted,

> dramas of the mind there are,
> Best seen against imagined tapestries,

and it may well be that, in a day of outworn conventions,
many of us may turn gladly from the scenic illusions of the
stage-carpenter, and the palpable illusions of the playwright, to the ever-new illusions of the dreaming mind,
woven in a new intense dramatic reality against 'imagined
tapestries', against revealing shadows and tragic glooms
and radiances as real, and as near, as the crude symbols of
painted boards and stereotyped phrase in which we still
have a receding pleasure.

24. WILLIAM ARCHER'S VIEW OF YEATS AS DRAMATIST

1902

Extract from William Archer, 'Poets of the Younger Generation' (1902).

William Archer (1856-1924), dramatist and critic, was
a graduate of the University of Edinburgh, who moved to
London in 1878 and became dramatic critic of 'The World',
a post he held for twenty-one years. He was a propa-
gandist for the New Drama, official translator of Ibsen,
and an advocate of a National Theatre. He interested
Shaw in writing plays, his own play 'The Green Goddess'
(1921) being a successful example of the well-made play.
His most influential criticism was 'The Old Drama and
the New' (1921). He was a member of the Rationalist
Free Association and a convinced Spiritualist.

It is not easy to determine the precise relation between
Mr. Yeats and M. Maurice Maeterlinck. Their affinity of
spirit is obvious. Both are mystics; both regard the
visible world as little more than a hampering veil between them and the far more real and momentous unseen
universe; both are full of pity for the blindness and
helplessness of man, encompassed, in all his goings out
and comings in, by capricious, vaguely divined, and
generally malevolent powers. M. Maeterlinck, no less
than Mr. Yeats, goes to folklore, to nursery legend one
might say, for his material; though his folklore is
generalised, not local or even racial. The Flemish
poet has, to my thinking, a less melodious, less lyrical,
but more specifically dramatic genius, and he is certainly the more penetrating and accomplished psycholo-
gist. But the true problem for criticism is not to
balance the merits of the two writers, but to determine
whether their curious similarity of method is due to
independent development along parallel lines, or is partly attributable to the direct influence of the one upon
the other. In 'The Countess Cathleen' we recognise
some of the most original features of M. Maeterlinck's
dramatic method: the indeterminate time and place, the
almost childlike simplicity of speech, the art of
eliminating even the illusion of free-will, and representing human beings as the passive, plaintive puppets
of dominions and powers unseen. Now, 'The Countess
Cathleen' was published in the autumn of 1892, and
Maeterlinck's early works, 'La Princess Maleine',
'L'Intruse', and 'Les Aveugles', had been read and discussed in England for at least a year previously.(1)
Thus it is probable enough that Mr. Yeats was acquainted
with these plays of Maeterlinck's before his own play was
published. But in dedicating it to Miss Maud Gonne, he
stated that it was 'planned out and begun some three
years ago' — that is to say, before any of M. Maeter-

linck's works were published, or at all events before
the first rumour of them had crossed the Channel. The
original conception and plan, then, which are quite as
Maeterlinckian as any of the details, cannot owe anything to M. Maeterlinck. Unknown to each other, and
almost simultaneously, the two poets must have sought
and found a similar vehicle for expression. M. Maeterlinck, possessing, as I have said, the more distinctively
dramatic talent, was the first to perfect his vehicle;
and his example may very likely have been of assistance
to Mr. Yeats. But it may with confidence be said that
the similarity between them is much more truly attributable to general sympathy of spirit than to conscious,
or even unconscious, imitation on Mr. Yeats's part.

A melancholy theme indeed is that of 'The Countess
Cathleen'. It can be told in a few words: The land is
famine-stricken; Satan sends two demons in the guise
of merchants to buy the souls of the starving peasants;
the Countess Cathleen will sacrifice all her vast wealth,
her 'gold and green forests', to save the people; but
the emissaries of hell (the heavenly powers being apparently asleep) steal her treasure, becalm her ships,
delay the passage of her flocks and herds; so that at
last there is nothing for her to do but to sell her own
soul and feed the people with the proceeds. The absolute impotence, the practical non-existence, of the powers
of good, and the perfect ease with which the powers of
evil execute their plots, render the play depressing
almost to the point of exasperation. It is true that at
the end an Angel intervenes, and gives us to understand
that Cathleen's soul is safe, because

> The Light of Lights
> Looks always on the motive, not the deed,
> The Shadow of Shadows on the deed alone.

But this tardy consolation to the reader, who feels,
moreover, that Satan is not quite fairly dealt with,
being baulked by a quibble, not openly encountered and
vanquished. Oppressive melancholy, however, is the note
of the folklore from which Mr. Yeats draws his inspiration; though in his delightful little book of prose, 'The
Celtic Twilight', he seems inclined to contest the fact.
Be this as it may, 'The Countess Cathleen' (especially
in its revised form) is as beautiful as it is sad. The
blank verse has a monotonous, insinuating melody which is
all its own, arising not only from the dainty simplicity
of the diction, but from the preponderance of final
monosyllables and of what the professors of Shakespearo-

metry call 'end-stopped' lines. Mr. Yeats eschews all
attempt to get dramatic force and variety into his verse
by aid of the well-known tricks of frequent elisions,
feminine endings, periodic structure, and all the rest of
it. And herein he does well. No rush and tumult of
versification could suit his mournful fantasies so perfectly as this crooning rhythm, this limpid melody,
which seems, as Cyrano de Bergerac would say, to have a
touch of the brogue in it.

Let me now note a few passages in which the resemblance
to Maeterlinck is most apparent. The first scene takes
place in the famine-stricken cabin of Shemus Rua, the
personages being Shemus, his wife Maire, and their son
Teig:

> MAIRE.   Why did the house-dog bay?
>
> SHEMUS. He heard me coming and smelt food — what else?
>
> TEIG. We will not starve awhile.
>
> SHEMUS.   What food is within?
>
> TEIG. There is a bag half full of meal, a pan
> Half full of milk.
>
> SHEMUS.   And we have Maive the hen.
>
> TEIG. The pinewood were less hard.
>
> MAIRE.   Before you came
> She made a great noise in the hencoop, Shemus.
> What fluttered in the window?
>
> TEIG.   Two horned owls
> Have blinked and fluttered on the window sill
> From when the dog began to bay.
>
> SHEMUS.   Hush, hush.

Who can fail to be reminded here of M. Maeterlinck's fond-
ness for extracting eerie effects from the (alleged)
sensitiveness of the animal kingdom to spiritual presences? The baying of the dog and the fluttering of the
hen are eminently Maeterlinckian — only that in Maeterlinck the hen would be a swan. Think, for example, of
the part played by the swans in 'L'Intruse', or of the
fight of the dogs and the swans in 'Pelléas et Mélisande'.
The two owls, I should add, are not on the same plane as

the dog and the hen, for they are the demons in disguise. They are first-cousins, not of M. Maeterlinck's
swans, but of the poodle in 'Faust'. Nevertheless, the
passage is absolutely Maeterlinckian in effect; and so
is the following:

> MAIRE. Who knows what evil you have brought to us?
> I fear the wood things, Shemus.
>> *(A knock at the door.*
>> *Do not open.*
>
> SHEMUS. A crown and twenty pennies are not enough
> To stop the hole that lets the famine in.
>
>> *(The little shrine falls.*
> MAIRE. Look! Look!
>
> SHEMUS *(crushing it underfoot).* The Mother of God has
>> dropped asleep,
> And all her household things have gone to wrack.
>
> MAIRE. O Mary, Mother of God, be pitiful.
>
>> (SHEMUS *opens the door. Two* MERCHANTS
>> *stand without. They have bands of gold*
>> *round their foreheads, and each carries*
>> *a bag upon his shoulder.*

The two Merchants are the owls of the previous
passage, in another disguise; and the falling of the
shrine at their approach is a piece of pure Maeterlinck.
Take, again, the following:

> COUNTESS CATHLEEN. We must find out this castle in the
>> wood
> Before the chill o' the night.
>
>> *(The* MUSICIANS *begin to tune their*
>> *instruments.*
>
>> Do not blame me,
> Good woman, for the tympan and the harp:
> I was bid fly the terror of the times
> And wrap me round with music and sweet song
> Or else pine to my grave. I have lost my way;
> Aleel, the poet who should know these woods,
> Because we met him on their border but now
> Wandering and singing like the foam of the sea,
> Is so wrapped up in dreams of terrors to come
> That he can give no help.

MAIRE *(Going to the door with her)*.   Beyond the hazel
Is a green shadowed pathway, and it goes
To your great castle in malevolent woods.

Here the style is not at all that of Maeterlinck; but the
concluding phrase — the 'great castle in malevolent
woods' — depicts in five words the scene of half of
Mr. Maeterlinck's dramas. The old nurse Oona, too, is
entirely in the spirit of the author of 'Les Aveugles'
and the creator of so many weird embodiments of pallid
eld. Take this for an example:

OONA. Now lay your head once more upon my knees.
I'll sing how Fergus drove his brazen cars.
                    (She chaunts with the thin voice of age.

  Who will go drive with Fergus now,
    And pierce the deep wood's woven shade,
    And dance upon the level shore?
Young man, lift up your russet brow,
    And lift your tender eyelids, maid,
    And brood on hopes and fears no more.

You have dropped down again into your trouble.
You do not hear me.

CATHLEEN.   Ah, sing on, old Oona,
I hear the horn of Fergus in my heart.

OONA. I do not know the meaning of the song.
I am too old.

CATHLEEN.   The horn is calling, calling.

OONA.
  And no more turn aside and brood
    Upon Love's bitter mystery;
      For Fergus rules the brazen cars,
  And rules the shadows of the wood,
    And the white breast of the dim sea
      And all dishevelled wandering stars.

. . .

Why, you are weeping — and such tears! Such tears!
Look, child, how big they are. Your shadow falls,
O Weeping Willow of the World, O Eri,
On this the loveliest daughter of your race,
Your leaves blow round her. I give God great thanks
That I am old — lost in the sleep of age.(2)

Like Oona, 'I do not know the meaning of the song', but
I know that it is beautiful; and I know that Oona
speaks with the tongue of her aged sisters in the dramas
of M. Maeterlinck.
And here I am tempted to return for a moment to the
question of race-influence, suggested in the opening
paragraph of this essay. M. Maeterlinck's swans and Mr.
Yeats's hen may stand in the relation of cause and
effect, or (as I rather believe) may be co-ordinate
effects of similar psychological causes; but in any case
there can be no possible doubt of the strong spiritual
affinity between the two poets. Now mark the difficulty
with which we are brought face to face. Mr. Maeterlinck,
as a Fleming, is presumably of Teutonic race; while
Mr. Yeats, as we know, is a Kelt ofthe Kelts. How do
the critics who found their faith (like the lady in
Dickens) upon 'blood', account for this close brotherhood between men of two races which it is the fashion to
regard as diametrically antagonistic to each other in the
structure of their sould? Observe, too, that it is precisely in his most Keltic qualities that Mr. Yeats approxi-
mates most closely to M. Maeterlinck. The Teuton is, if
possible, more Keltic than the Kelt. Are we to assume
that some single far-off Keltic ancestor (perhaps one of
the Irish soldiers in the army which 'swore terribly in
Flanders') lives again, by a freak of atavism, in
M. Maeterlinck? There is nothing impossible in such a
conjecture; but if we admit it in this case, we can
scarcely exclude a similar conjecture in any other case.(3)
And thus we strike at the root of all race-theorising by
owning it impossible to assert, of any Western European,
that the blood of any one of the great races flows un-
tainted in his veins. Wherefore I suggest that, as a
foundation for theories of the artistic temperament,
blood is very little thicker than water.

Notes

1 An article by me entitled A Pessimist Playwright
  appeared in the 'Fortnightly Review' for September
  1891, and I believe Mr. George Moore had published an
  appreciation of Maeterlinck even earlier.
2 The last six lines quoted do not appear in the 1901
  edition of the play.
3 It is suggested that M. Maeterlinck may be a Walloon,
  and so of Keltic stock.

25. A.E. (GEORGE RUSSELL)'S PRACTICAL CRITICISM

1903

A letter from A.E. [written in ?March 1903] included in
'Letters from AE' (1961), selected and edited by Alan
Denson. 'The Hour Glass' to which he refers was first
performed in the Molesworth Hall by the Irish National
Theatre Company on 14 March 1903.
    George William Russell (1867-1935), poet, editor and
economist, born in Co. Armagh, was employed as a clerk in
Pim's drapery store in Dublin and in his spare time
attended classes at the Metropolitan School of Art, where
he met Yeats, with whom he formed a close friendship. He
became a Theosophist and his mystical paintings led on
to his poems, the first volume of which was 'Homeward:
Songs by the Way' (1894). He became an official of the
Irish Agricultural Organisation in 1899. He exercised a
stimulus on many younger writers, and his home became a
centre of good conversation in Dublin.
    He edited the 'Irish Homestead' (1906-23) and was a
brilliant editor of 'The Irish Statesman' (1923-30).
His play 'Deirdre' was staged in 1902, and he wrote
several volumes of verse; his 'Candle of Vision' (1918)
expresses much of his philosophy. His pen name A.E.
was a shortening of a former pseudonym, Aeon.

Dear W.B.Y.,
I was looking at a couple of rehearsals of the 'Hour
Glass' and it struck me that it was a little difficult
to understand why the Wise Man remains lamenting in his
room though there are crowds without. He has only a few
moments to find his believer and he sends messengers and
remains himself. It is a little hard to believe and is
not quite convincing as I saw it. Could you invent some
reason for his remaining? This point is not observable
when reading but is to my mind noticeable when it is
acted.
    Another point which of course you might justify to
some extent by the only half developed materialism of
your wise man, but which I think is somewhat out of keeping with his character as a despiser of all spiritual
influences, is his references to the planetary influences.
Of course in astrology the planets are gods, and when he
speaks of the 'amorous star' he speaks of the spiritual
power which it symbolises. I do not think it is logical
to disbelieve in God and the angels and to believe in the

divine influence of the planets. I think he should be
sceptic of these things also and tell how men before he
came believed in love coming from the 'amorous star' but
that now it is simply a comely presence and the promise
of bodily beauty which awakens love. I just jot these
points down for your consideration; a line here and
there would make it right if you think the criticism is
correct. Kind regards to Lady Gregory.
Yours ever, Geo. W. Russell.

Ideas of Good and Evil (1903)

26. A.E. (GEORGE RUSSELL) ON YEATS MAKING A RELIGION
OF BEAUTY

1903

A letter written by George Russell in May 1903, included
in 'Letters from AE' (1961), selected and edited by
Alan Denson.
For note on George Russell, see p. 130.

My dear Yeats,
It is a good many years since I have read a book which
pleases me more than your 'Ideas of Good and Evil'. I
like it better than the 'Celtic Twilight' or 'The Secret
Rose'. I think it will do more than anything you have
yet written to bring the mystical interpretation of life
into literature, not because your prose is as good as
your verse, but because it shows the long meditation out
of which your verse springs. The lightest lyrics will
lose their isolation and gather a unity from the background of philosophy which will glimmer behind them for
all readers of this book. I have been away and have not
yet had time to read it all but just write this to con-
gratulate you unreservedly. I did not think I would like
the book so well as I do for I had only read one or two of
the essays before, but read together they throw a
reflected light on each other and the book has a perfect
unity. I have seen one or two glowing reviews and
gather that it will be a great success. But better than
a wide circulation in England will be it will give aims
to the few here who are making ready for Armageddon. I
wish you would think when writing new essays of making

them a criticism of orthodox religion from the standpoint
of an artist and mystic and lover of beauty. The orthodox priest or parson has survived science because his
religion is too woolly to be hurt by a club, and has survived materialism because he is on the right side though
with wrong weapons, but to attack him with the scorn of
the artist and mystic would, I think, do much more. You
might make a new religion of beauty, and the more arrogance and contempt you display in your references to the
churches the better. The religions of the grocer and the
counting house must be killed. I think I would like to
write something on this myself, but the devil having
appeared to me in the form of a wife and family it would
so far as I see have to be a posthumous book, though if
someone put me in a rage I would do it. . . .

Yours ever,
Geo. W. Russell

27. WAS YEATS'S AESTHETIC EXPERIENCE TOO LIMITED?

1903

An unsigned review of 'Ideas of Good and Evil' (1903),
'Manchester Guardian', 12 June 1903. Dr M. Napier has
suggested that this review may have been by Professor
George Saintsbury.

In England the Symbolist movement has been an immediate
outgrowth of what we know as the 'Celtic Renascence'; but
in France and Belgium it has other sources; and Mr Yeats
has urged, quite logically, that the so-called 'Celtic
element' in literature ought rather to be regarded as an
influx, or survival, of primeval poetry and religion, once
current in the legend lore of many nationalities, of
which the Celtic alone has remained for centuries close
to the main river of European literature.

When Matthew Arnold wrote it was not easy to know as
much as we know now of folk-song and folk-belief, and
I do not think that he understood that our 'natural
magic' is but the ancient religion of the world, the
ancient worship of Nature and that troubled ecstasy
before her, that certainty of all beautiful places
being haunted, which it brought to men's minds.

The poetry of 'natural magic', Mr Yeats allows, the
Finns and Scandinavians share with the Celts, and he even
thinks that the old Irish and Welsh, though they had more
of 'the old way' than the makers of the Sagas, had less
of it than the Finnish makers of the 'Kalevala'.

Ethnologically it is an undoubted gain to have the
rigour of the 'Celtic' claim to all that is magical in
English poetry thus far relaxed. On the side of criticism, however, Mr Yeats seems to us still to judge and
legislate for poetry under a too exclusively Celtic - or
Finnish - bias. No one has shown with greater penetra-
tion, by example as by precept, how an 'irrational' and
fantastic phrase may carry ineffable suggestion to the
heart; no one has climbed with more assured and brilliant
audacity that 'ladder of the impossible' which he has
elsewhere declared to be the true highway of poetry. The
fine irrationality of myth may, it is true, touch
strange hidden chords in us which no perfectly articulate
thought can compass. Nevertheless, what gives myth this
potency is not its irrationality or its inarticulateness,
but a subtlety of association which conveys a sense of
affinities too fine for explicit speech. But speech
which is itself quite articulate may have this power of
suggestion too; assuming that poetry must always suggest,
the condition is as fully complied with when 'more is
meant than meets the ear' as when something apparently
quite different is meant. In other words, poetic expression may as easily be an elementary or shadowy yet
so far as it goes veracious utterance of the reality it
conveys as an 'irrational' symbol of it. When Dante
makes Piccarda in Paradise say 'And in His will is our
peace', or when Wordsworth tells that his Michael 'never
lifted up a single stone', the profound simplicity we
feel in these lines arises from their being, so to speak,
included in all that they convey. And by far the greater
part of Dante's poetic form is of this kind. The 'Divine
Comedy' itself has doubtless, as he tells us, a secondary
sense — the rewards and penalties incurred by Man in the
exercise of his free will; but its 'literal' sense is
not for Dante mere figure, far less irrational figure,
but a vision of reality wrought out with the utmost
power of an imagination fed by all the learning of his
time and guided and controlled by its thought. The world
of imagination was true for Dante, but so was the world of
the senses and the world of the intellect. Modern
symbolism, on the other hand, is rooted in a profound
distrust of both. Reality, for its exponents, is veiled
by 'things', and mutilated and maligned by 'thought'.
The one gate they recognise to it is the dreamy trance,

poised between ecstasy and slumber. And that gate they
have opened with marvellous skill. But after all the
phenomenal and intellectual worlds which they seek to
transfigure or evade are for us portions of reality,
whatever elements of illusion they may contain; 'the
splendour of the grass, the glory of the flower', which
Mr Yeats would subtilise into faint and nervous imagery,
'wild and wintry' in its dread of light and glow, make a
part of the pageant of Nature by which we live; and the
exultations and agonies of thought, baffled as it may
be in the effort to lay bare the secret of things, are
for us an element of that secret, a factor in the eternal
epic of humanity which the poetry of man cannot with
impunity ignore. And no great poet has yet in the long
run ignored it.

Hence we cannot but find a somewhat sinister significance for Mr Yeats in the picture he draws in the paper
called 'The Autumn of the Body' of the 'stairway' down
which Dante and Shakespeare took the first fatal steps,
while Goethe and Wordsworth and Browning had reached the
bottom of the descent, inasmuch as with all, in varying
degrees, 'poetry gave up the right to consider all things
in the world as a dictionary of types and symbols and
began to call itself a critic of life and an interpreter
of things as they are'. We rather think that a closer
study of Goethe would induce Mr Yeats, whose culture
strikes us as unequal on the Germanic side, to qualify
some of the extreme symbolist positions. It would certainly have helped him to the conception of the 'Popular
Poetry' which he expounds, as a startling innovation, in
the opening paper — a conception worked out by Herder more
than a century ago, and since then a commonplace of German
criticism.

28. POET WITH A PHILOSOPHY

1903

Extract from an unsigned review of 'Ideas of Good and
Evil' (1903), 'The Athenaeum', 27 June 1903.

. . . Mr. Yeats, though his best verse has an air of
singular spontaneity, and is, indeed, finished to that
point where art at last attains nature, is by no means a

merely instinctive writer. Much has 'come to him in his
sleep', but nothing has been set down without the very
conscious co-operation of an exacting mind. As he confesses, with not a little interesting and curious detail,
in the paper on 'Magic', he believes in 'the visions of
truth in the depths of the mind when the eyes are closed'.
But he has not followed the flickering guidance of the
moods without trying to make his own system out of his
own glimpses of what seems to him the truth. He has
woven together a personal philosophy out of visions, and
out of mystical books, and out of unwritten traditions;
and he is, in a very definite sense, a disciple of Blake,
whose visionary and often difficult wisdom he attempted
to expound, with the help of a more capricious and light-
hearted commentator, some ten years ago, in the three
huge volumes of 'The Works of William Blake'. The influence of Blake has overshadowed the mind of Mr. Yeats
from the first, or, rather, may be said to have gone before
him, a pillar of cloud, perhaps, by day, but certainly a
pillar of fire by night. If Blake should ever come to be
recognized as an inspired teacher, it will be through the
long and eager devotion of Mr. Yeats, and through the new
and vital incarnation which he has given to the fundamental ideas of that extraordinary man.

It is, then, as a poet, but as a poet with a philosophy, that Mr. Yeats speaks throughout this book of
essays. The long essay on 'The Philosophy of Shelley's
Poetry' is the most elaborate exposition in the book, and,
though it requires careful reading, it is worth it. It
is an attempt to trace an undercurrent of symbolic meaning in what appears to many a somewhat vague and fantastic
system of ideas, and to show that what may seem no more
than metaphors and picturesque phrases

> were certainly more than metaphors and picturesque
> phrases to one who believed 'the thoughts which are
> called real or external objects' differed but in regu-
> larity of occurrence from 'hallucinations, dreams, and
> the ideas of madness'.

Much of what is essential in the ideas of Blake will be
found in the admirable essay on Blake's illustrations to
Dante, and these ideas are developed, but, it seems to
us, less convincingly, in the essay which follows, on
'Symbolism in Painting', and, with unquestionable truth,
in the essay on 'The Symbolism of Poetry', to which the
first paper in the book, 'What is Popular Poetry?' may
be added as a foot-note. . . .

One of the distinguishing characteristics of Mr.
Yeats's attitude, his religious attitude, towards literature is that he never treats a work of art in the distinctively literary way, but as the speech and embodiment
of forces that are and have been spiritually at work in
the world. In this he is in the great tradition, not
only with Blake, whose wisdom has often to be filtered
clear of prejudices that are perhaps no more than names
used upside down, but also with Coleridge, whom he has
apparently read but little, and with Rossetti, who said
many essential things about poetry, as if by accident, and
hardly anything that was not essential. It is to be
regretted that there should be a certain lack of careful
knowledge in a writer who unites spiritual ardour and
imaginative insight with sanity of judgment and delicate
accuracy of taste. Mr. Yeats shares with Coleridge a
memory of unfailing and often enlightening inaccuracy;
he rewrites his quotations, remodels the title of every
second book of which he speaks, and respells the name of
any third writer to whom he refers. To be accurate is
not necessarily to be mechanical, and there are many
persons not discriminating enough to realize that an
argument may be essentially correct, although the fact
quoted in support of it is incorrect. Again, in his
manner of writing Mr. Yeats sometimes carries monotony to
a point at which a drowsiness begins to creep into it,
and the subtle and beautiful prose, in which there is
always space and atmosphere, falls into this kind of
indolent chaos:

> Longfellow, and Campbell, and Mrs. Hemans, and Macaulay
> in his 'Lays', and Scott in his longer poems, are the
> poets of the middle class, of people who have unlearned
> the unwritten tradition which binds the unlettered,
> so long as they are masters of themselves, to the be-
> ginning of time and to the foundation of the world,
> and who have not learned the written tradition which
> has been established upon the unwritten.

That is not, like sentences here and there in this book,
actually ungrammatical; but how undistinguished, how
clumsy, it is! As in some of his verse Mr. Yeats will
allow a line to drift into unrhythmical prose through
sheer over-subtlety in experimenting upon the capabilities
of the instrument of verse, so in prose which, at its best,
has the ardent quietude of the controlling imagination,
he is capable of becoming both obscure and slipshod, in
the avoidance of one or another of the brilliant vices
of contemporary writing.

It will be because of the lulling influence of this
slow and measured and at once simple and complex style
if all that is startling and revolutionary in these 'Ideas
of Good and Evil' does not show itself in its true light
until it has found some plausible entrance-way into many
well-guarded strongholds. There is hardly an idol of the
mob or of the market-place from which it does not seek to
turn worshippers aside; yet with how insidious a courtesy! The essay on Shakspeare and his 'English Kings',
in which it is shown how Shakespearian criticism may become 'a vulgar worshipper of success', is a little sermon
against Imperialism. London is the place 'where all the
intellectual traditions gather to die'; but then
'natural magic' is not to be found only in 'the Celtic
note':

> Matthew Arnold asks how much of the Celt must one
> imagine in the ideal man of genius. I prefer to say,
> How much of the ancient hunters and fishers and of the
> ecstatic dancers among hills and woods must one imagine
> in the ideal man of genius?

29.   PAGAN MYSTICISM IN THE DRAMA OF REVOLT

1903

Extract from an unsigned review of 'Where there is Nothing'
(1902;   1903), A Drama of Revolt, 'The Academy and Literature', 4 July 1903.

When Mr. Yeats was transmuting into exquisite preter-
natural poetry the legends which lingered among the Irish
peasantry;   or rather, and more essentially, the effect
of those legends upon himself, he was most himself. We
regretted a growing and alien complexity in part of the
'Wind Among the Reeds', a symbolic pedantry. But from
that to realism is more than a return;   it is a new
departure. To abandon the lovely filmy poetry which
expresses his own temper (the temper of a cultivated
babe, if we may use that expression, drawing from the
peasant breast the 'milk of Paradise') and assimilate
with the milk of the peasant foster-mother her tongue
and even her personality — or rather painfully imitate
than assimilate them — this is a reversal of all he has

previously done, and we think a mistake.
  The aim and substance, of course, are ideal — for
Mr. Yeats under any garb must be Mr. Yeats; but the
method, the presentment, are zealously realistic — the
poet gratulates himself on having caught the peasant
speech better than ever before. And not only so, but the
atmosphere of the play is realistic. In 'The Land of
Heart's Desire', peasant characters were made subservient to a wholly ideal method. Not so here; and frankly,
we grudge Mr. Yeats to realism. Men of less rare gift can
handle the method as well, and better. But Mr. Yeats's
way was the secret of Mr. Yeats. The realism, we imagine,
is largely successful, yet does not quite persuade our
acceptance. Are these indeed Irish tinkers? Very surely
they are not English tinkers. With all the poet's emphasis, in detail, of their materiality, they are not
material, not gross enough, for one's experience of lawless, uneducated humanity. The monastery is unthinkable
to anyone with a knowledge of monasteries. But were the
realism above question, we should still mourn. For the
poet's poetry is gone. It appears in a saying here and
there; in a few passages where Mr. Yeats lets himself go,
and speaks through the hero's mouth; but even there it is
rather poetic eloquence than poetry. The whole thing
resembles a sometimes eloquent prose pamphlet, for the
dissemination of Mr. Yeats's views; a pamphlet cast in
dramatic form, but with its pamphlet purpose writ large
on it. The hero, designed for an iconoclastic genius,
comes out as a bundle of eccentricities. He does not
live. He is thinkable as a madman rather than a genius.
The eccentricities of genius are accidents; here they
become principal, so that the character is a mere
congeries of petty revolts, a bundle of minor icono-
clasms, rather than a man. The reality and sanity of
his central revolt suffers in consequence. He becomes a
mere ox (and a mythical ox) kicking against the pricks;
or rather a mule. There are scenes and parts which
interest one, for it is Mr. Yeats. The eloquence is like
this:

> The Christian's business is not reformation but reve-
> lation, and the only labours he can put his hand to
> can never be accomplished in Time. He must so live
> that all things shall pass away. Give me wine out
> of thy pitchers; oh, God, how splendid is the cup of
> my drunkenness. We must become blind, and deaf, and
> dizzy. We must get rid of everything that is not
> measureless eternal life. We must put out hope as I
> put out this candle. And memory as I put out this

candle. And thought, the master of Life, as I put out
this candle. And at last we must put out the light
of the Sun and of the Moon, and all the light of the
World and the World itself. We must destroy the
World; we must destroy everything that has Law and
Number, for where there is nothing, there is God.

That expounds also the main teaching of the play — the
teaching of pagan mysticism in general, but applied in
Mr. Yeats's own particular manner to external things. Of
the body of the play no extract would give a notion. It
is a drama of revolt, but it is not a poem. And to anything but essential (yea, and quintessential) poetry we
grudge Mr. Yeats.

30. A LACK OF DRAMA AND CHARACTERISATION

1904

An unsigned review of 'The Hour Glass and Other Plays'
(1904), 'The Academy and Literature', 2 April 1904.

Of the plays before us we may at once put aside 'The
Pot of Broth', a capital farce, and 'The Hour Glass', a
Morality, the moral teaching of which is universal and
not particular to Ireland. The tone of the other three
plays is partly mystical, partly mythical and to my mind
will do nothing at all to aid the cause of the revival
of Irish literature. Mr. Yeats, in his plays, apparently,
counts human hearts as of little worth and ignores human
emotion. In 'The King's Threshold' the motive of the play
is the banishing of the poets from the upper table in
King Guaire's hall, of Seanchan in particular, who refuses to eat or drink until his privilege is restored.
Of such material a drama cannot be made, a poem may be.
'On Baile's Strand' deals with an event in the life of
Cuchullain, King of Muirthemne, who, having unwittingly
slain his son, plunges into the waves of the sea; here,
perhaps, is tragedy, but not as Mr. Yeats has handled the
matter, the characters do not live, they talk but do not
convince, they act but we care not what they do. 'Cathleen Ni Houlihan' is sheer mysticism. These plays have
been written for 'an Irish Theatre'; there is much good
work in them, much good poetry, but no drama and no characterisation; they will not do anything in my opinion to

help the Irish stage. 'The Pot of Broth', farce though it
be, is Mr. Yeats' nearest approach to what is needed to
achieve his purpose.
    What is needed? Simply living, human dramas and
comedies of Irish life of to-day. It is scarcely too
much to say that no dramatist has ever written a fine
acting play which was not imbued with the spirit of his
own times. Shakespeare wrote of Troy, Rome, Egypt, but
his works breathed throughout of Elizabethan England;
their setting was a detail, their essence was Elizabethan. If Mr. Yeats and his fellow workers desire to
found a living Irish drama they must look to the life of
to-day, not of yesterday, and must take for their characters human beings, not abstractions. Carleton should
be their example; he wrote with power and pathos of the
lives of the peasantry amid whom he lived; let our
Irish dramatists go out into the country and write plays
dealing with the tragedies and comedies that lie so thickly
strewn over the hills and valleys of Irish life; living
hearts, not dead bones — however poetic — those are what
are needed, and if they be not given the Irish drama
cannot live. I have every sympathy with these endeavours,
and would have them succeed; but exotics will not 'do',
we want hardy plants.

31. SIR MAX BEERBOHM'S HIGH HOPES FOR IRISH POETIC DRAMA

1904

_____

This piece by Sir Max Beerbohm, Some Irish Plays and
Players, in 'The Saturday Review', 9 April 1904, was
reprinted in his 'Around Theatres' (1953). The Irish
players — the Irish National Dramatic Company — first
visited London in 1903; the visit discussed below is
that made in 1904 after the Abbey Theatre Company had
been formed (with Yeats as production-manager) and the
Abbey Theatre had opened in Dublin.
    Sir Henry Maximilian Beerbohm (1872-1956), novelist,
essayist, parodist and caricaturist, was educated at
Merton College, Oxford. He succeeded Shaw as dramatic
critic for 'The Saturday Review'. In 1910 he married an
American actress, Florence Kahn, and retired to Rapallo
except for periods during the two wars. The 'Works of
Max Beerbohm' appeared in 1896; 'The Happy Hypocrite'
in 1897, and his masterpiece, 'Zuleika Dobson', an

Oxford fantasy, in 1911. His caricatures appeared in
various volumes; his broadcast talks were excellent, as
'Mainly on the Air' (1947) demonstrates.

The other day I came to one of the rare oases that are in
the desert of our drama. For one whole afternoon my feet
were on very verdure, and there was clear cold water for
my parched throat. We plodders through this unending
commercial desert could not plod so bravely if it were
not for the oases, dear in proportion to their rarity,
offered to us by uncommercial little societies. 'The
sands are running out' somewhere, perhaps; but here, in
this desert, they run on for ever, from every point of
the horizon, down our throats. For ever and for ever we
plod through 'Lady Thingummy's drawing-room overlooking the
Green Park' (a mirage, that Green Park), and for ever and
for ever Lady Thingummy (played by Miss So-and-So with
her usual grace and sensibility) gives her husband (whose
role is sustained by the manager with even more than his
usual sincerity and conviction) reason to suppose that her
flirtation with Sir Blank Dash (Mr. Dash Blank has never
done anything better than his impersonation of Sir Blank
Dash) is a really serious affair, whereas, of course, all
the while. . . . Add a 'decimal point recurring' over
that last dot. Imagine those dots running on, like the
desert's grains of sand, for ever and for ever, and then
you will be able to enter into the feelings of a dramatic
critic, and to realise with what joy he, condemned to an
eternity and an infinity of barren drawing-room comedy or
drawing-room comedy-drama, turns aside to such accidents
as the Irish Theatre.
    The afternoon's programme included three little plays:
one by Mr. Yeats, 'The King's Threshold', and two by Mr.
J.M. Synge, 'Riders to the Sea' and 'In the Shadow of the
Glen'. Very widely though the three plays differed from
one another, from all one derived the same quality of
pleasure — the pleasure in something quite simple and
quite strange. There was in none of the plays any structural complexity, and yet none of them was not truly
dramatic. It is fashionably supposed that a playwright,
in order to compass a truly dramatic effect, must steep
himself in some kind of black art — must become a very
wizard, master of all manner of mysterious processes
whereat we outsiders dare scarcely guess. Well, of course,
dramatic effect can be produced through many complex
means. But it is a fallacy to suppose that only through
such means can it be produced. Out of a dramatic idea
you can produce a dramatic effect, even though you go

about it quite simply and straightforwardly. You must,
however, first catch your dramatic idea. That is where the
amateur often fails, afterwards attributing his failure to
his ignorance of technique. That parrot-cry 'technique'!
How many a good literary man has been scared off by it;
and of how much, therefore, dramatic literature has been
baulked by it! My advice to the terror-stricken is quite
simple, and quite sound: first catch your dramatic idea,
and then go artlessly ahead with your expression of it.
When your play is acted, you will be delighted to find
that the audience finds it quite dramatic: the idea will
have carried it through for you. Belike, your very
artlessness is an advantage. For thought dramatic effect
may be compassed through very complex and highly specialised means, the man who has mastered those means is often,
in his turn, mastered by them, insomuch that one cannot see
the wood for the trees. Mr. Pinero is an instance of a
man who shows us only trees. Fine, upstanding, thriving
trees they are, but — where is the wood? Mr. Yeats
showed me a wood quite clearly, and Mr. Synge showed me
two woods. And the sight was all the more welcome because
there was no fuss about it. Simplicity! That was, also,
the keynote of the stage-setting. I have no objection to
rich scenery and dresses — so long as the richness be
not inappropriate or excessive. But, just for a change,
how delightful to have a management which, so far from
trying to dazzle us into awed calculations of its outlay,
rather prides itself on its poverty. There is a prologue
to 'The King's Threshold', and in the printed copy of the
play, Mr. Yeats notifies that this prologue was 'not used
in Dublin, as, owing to the smallness of the company,
nobody could be spared to speak it'. Of course, the pride
of poverty is not in itself less ridiculous than the
pride of wealth. But it has, for the London playgoer, at
least, the charm of newness. Apart from that, it was
fitting that a play about legendary Ireland, and two plays
about peasants in modern Ireland, should be produced as
simply as possible. As for the acting, I am not sure
that so much simplicity as the players exemplified was
quite artistically right. Mr. Yeats' poetry, doubtless —
or any other man's poetry — gains by simple recitation.
Dramatic inflections of the voice, dramatic gestures and
so forth, do, of course, detract from sheer melody; but,
equally, their absence detracts from drama. For dramatic
poetry, therefore, the right treatment is a compromise.
And when these players, trained to heed Mr. Yeats' poetry,
and untrained to express anything dramatically, came to
interpret Mr. Synge's prose, they did seem decidedly
amiss. They, with their blank faces and their stiff

movements, taking up their cues so abruptly, and seeming
not to hear anything said by their interlocutors, certainly did impede the right effect of the play. For all
that, I would not they had been otherwise. One could not
object to them as to the ordinary amateur. They were not
floundering in the effort to do something beyond their
powers. With perfect simplicity, perfect dignity and
composure, they were just themselves, speaking a task that
they had well by heart. Just themselves; and how could
such Irish selves not be irresistible? Several of our
metropolitan players are Irish, and even they, however
thickly coated with Saxonism, have a charm for us beyond
their Saxon-blooded fellows. The Irish people, un-
spoiled, in their own island — who can resist them? But
footlights heighten every effect; and behind them un-
spoiled Irish people win us quicklier and more absolutely
than ever. And behind London footlights! There they have
not merely their own charm, but that charm also which
belongs to all exotics. Many people went many times,
lately, to 'In Dahomey', fascinated by the sight of a
strange and remote race expressing through our own
language things most strange to us and remote from us.
Well, we are as far removed from the Irish people as
from the negroes, and our spiritual distance seems all
the greater by reason of our nearness in actual mileage.
I admit that it was, in a way, more pleasant to see those
negroes than to see these Irish folk. When we contemplate
negroes, one clear impression comes through our dim bewilderment: we are assuredly in the presence of an inferior race. Whereas he must be a particularly dull
Saxon who does not discern and confess (at any rate to
himself), that the Keltic race is, spiritually and intellectually, a race much finer, and also much more attractive, than that to which he has the honour to belong.

I spoke of the Irish Theatre as 'an accident' only in
reference to myself. I did not mean to imply there was
not a good reason for the Irish Theatre, or that there
was not an expansive future for it. For a national drama,
you require dramatists and players. Acting is not a
natural art to the inexpressive Saxon; but the inex-
pressiveness of Mr. Yeats' own particular players does
not shake my conviction that to the Kelt the art of
acting will come almost as naturally as to the Latin.
Likewise, true dramatists are much likelier to crop up
in Ireland than in England. When an idea occurs to an
Englishman, his first impulse is to get it put into practice. An Irishman broods over an idea, and translates
it into some symbolic form. For instance, it has occurred
to Mr. Yeats that he is not taken seriously enough. People

buy his books and compliment him very highly; but the
State does not recognise him as a factor in public life.
No title is bestowed on him. The Royal family does not
make him its pet. He sees eminent statesmen, soldiers,
lawyers, and other men of action, being petted and decorated all the time; but he, the man of Thought, is not invited to step out of his niche and join that giddy
throng. Were Mr. Yeats an English poet, he would forth-
with have written an article for one of the monthly reviews, forcibly demonstrating how necessary a part of the
national life is Thought, and how extremely impolitic it
is, therefore, for the State to encourage and honour only
men of action. In fact, he would have done exactly what
was done, a month or two ago, by Mr. William Watson.
Were Mr. William Watson an Irishman, he would have written
'The King's Threshold', telling us, with exquisite lyric
fervour, the tale of the poet Seanchan, who, because King
Guaire refused him his right to sit at meat among the
great councillors and warriors, and thus dishonoured
through him the majesty of all bards, lay down across the
threshold of the palace, and there would have starved
himself to death, had not King Edw—— I mean King
Guaire, relenting at length, kneeled down to him and
offered to him the very crown. As it is, I admired Mr.
Watson's article very much, and I readily admit that King
Edward, a practical man, would be less quickly perturbed
by the dream-laden beauty of 'The King's Threshold' than
by the urgent and unanswerable arguments in that article.
Only, one can't have it both ways; and Mr. Yeats' way
naturally seems to me, as dramatic critic, the better
way; and, as it is also the typical Irish way, I have
high hopes of poetic drama in Ireland.

32. EDWARD THOMAS ON 'THE TABLES OF THE LAW' AND 'THE
ADORATION OF THE MAGI'

1904

Edward Thomas was reviewing 'The Tables of the Law' and
'The Adoration of the Magi' (1904). This book was originally privately printed for Yeats in 1897; the 1904
edition was published by Elkin Mathews, the second published edition of 1914 initially by the Shakespeare Head
Press, later (c.1916) by Macmillan and Co. Ltd. The
reviews are preceded by two letters: (a) of 1 July 1904

and (b) of 6 August 1904, included in 'Letters of Edward
Thomas to Gordon Bottomley'(1968), edited by George
Thomas. The first review (c) appeared in 'The Week's
Survey', 13 August 1904; the second (d) in the 'Daily
Chronicle', 15 August 1904.

Philip Edward Thomas (1878-1917), poet and prose writer,
was educated at Lincoln College, Oxford. He wrote topo-
graphical and biographical studies, then encouraged by
Robert Frost to turn to poetry in 1914, he wrote most of
his poetry on active service between 1915 and his death
at Arras in 1917. The 'Collected Poems' (1920) shows his
capacity for detailed observation and insistence on the
solitary enduring nature of man in the face of Nature's
austerity.

(a)

. . . But I am much puzzled by Yeats's 'Tables of the Law'.
Does he see the point (if any) of the two stories? Or
are they records of experiences to which he hopes that
the reader may discover a point? I like them especially
the 'Adoration of the Magi', but they seem to me full of
gaps, unless of course they are simply records of experiences. Tell me what you think— . . .

Yours ever, Edward Thomas

(b)

You are quite right (about 'The Tables of the Law & The
Adoration of the Magi'). But they have a grave & pur-
poseful look about them which does not quite suit their
real irresponsibility. And, as it stands, 'The Tables of
the Law' is not of a piece; it might easily have been
longer or shorter.

(c)   As the wings of a dove (1904)

During the last few days I have been delighted, amused,
and at length disturbed, by someone who continually
showers upon me a recitation of several passages from Mr.
W.B. Yeats' prose. He has a fine voice, at once mobile,
capable of magnificent monotone, and the prose compels
him to use all his skill and all his passion in the
utterance. The sense of complete domination by the
sentences, as of a Sybil shaken by the inspiration of a
god, is praise enough; and by way of conclusion he

remarks mysteriously, 'Yet shall ye be as the wings of a
dove'. But, in the intervals of recitation, my rhapsodist
tells me why I also should admire. The prose, he says, is
as simple as Swift's, and almost as free from decoration. It is also, he says, right through, aërated and
made keen against the palate, as Swift's never was, by
the passionate spirit of the writer entering into it. He
even tells me that if Mr. Yeats and another writer had the
same thing to say, though Mr. Yeats were as brief, and
though he used the same words as his rival, there would be
something (he says this with emphasis) in our author's
work which was lacking in the other's — *something* making
it as different as the knitted surface of water flowing
over pebbles is different from the water in a basin.
   Here is one passage: 'At first I was full of happiness',
he replied, 'for I felt a divine ecstasy, an immortal fire
in every passion, in every hope, in every desire, in
every dream; and I saw, in the shadows under leaves, in
the hollow waters, in the eyes of men and women, its
image as in a mirror; it was as though I was about to
touch the Heart of God. Then all changed and I was full
of misery, and I said to myself that I was caught in the
glittering folds of an enormous serpent, and was falling
with him through a fathomless abyss, and that henceforth
the glittering folds were my world; and in my misery it
was revealed to me that man can only come to that Heart
through the sense of separation from it which we call
sin, and I understood that I could not sin, because I had
discovered the law of my being, and could only express
or fail to express my being, and I understood that God has
made a simple and an arbitrary law that we may sin and
repent!'
   The passage describes the experience of a mystic, the
hero of 'The Tables of the Law', who had gone far in
pursuit of a theory of the thirteenth century mystic,
Joachim of Flora — that revelation in the Christian
Church was continual, that the old was for every wearing
out and the new appearing, and that, finally, the Kingdom
of the Father had passed, the Kingdom of the Son was
passing, and the Kingdom of the Holy Spirit was about to
come, and with it a life of contemplation and liberty and
love. The story has many fine qualities. But if I am to
agree with my rhapsodist's opinion, I must also agree with
his explanation. He, when he is thwarted in his eulogies
of Mr. Yeats, falls back upon the word 'soul'. And as
that is a word which is excellently fitted for describing something great, since it means not the same to any
two persons, I will fall back upon it, too. There are, as
I have hinted, things in the book that one need not

praise ambiguously, things which would be praised by any judge. But, like the rhapsodist, I see that the sum of these parts is not equal to the whole. Just as the land-scape of shaven fields and full-bosomed oaks, on which I am looking, was stilled and bemused an hour ago and gained a faculty, from neither light nor shade nor any-thing visible, which was most moving and likely to be remembered when the oaks and fields are indistinguish-able in the past: so there is an unnameable something in 'The Tables of the Law' which will survive its most melodious paragraph and aptest detail, in the memory.

My friend has equal praises for the other story in this book, 'The Adoration of the Magi'. It tell of three old men who lived an unworldly, or old worldly, life in the western islands of Ireland. And one day, in a vision, they were bidden to set out for Paris, where a dying prostitute 'would reveal to them the secret names of the gods, which can be perfectly spoken only when the mind is steeped in certain colours and certain sounds and certain odours, but at whose perfect speaking the immortals cease to be cries and shadows, and walk and talk with one like men and women.' In Paris, another vision honoured their obedience to the visionary life, and Hermes appeared and told them to bow down to the woman — 'Bow down, and understand that when they (the immortals) are about to overthrow the things that are to-day and bring the things that were yesterday, they have no one to help them, but one whom the things that are to-day have cast out. Bow down very low, for they have chosen for their priestess this woman in whose heart all follies have gathered, and in whose body all desires have awaked; this woman who has been driven out of time and has lain upon the bosom of eternity. After you have bowed down the old things shall be again, and another Argo shall carry heroes over the deep, and another Achilles beleaguer another Troy.' So the woman revealed to them 'many secret powerful names', of which the last seems to have been that of 'a symbolist painter she was fond of'. But the story itself is not one to be praised or blamed. It may actually be a dream. It is in any case as a child or a dream, which may suggest much to one and nothing to another, but is not to be criticised. If it is, it will certainly suffer, and Mr. Yeats seems to take no responsibility for it. As for me, I remember one splendid hint at a difficult truth: 'When people are good the world likes them and takes possession of them, and so Eternity comes through people who are not good or who have been forgotten.' And I remember and can still recapture the joyous sense of being, for a time, made airy-light,

independent of many laws, and floating upon the surface
of Mr. Yeats' prose, with its marvellous texture ever
beneath my feet.

(d) Back into other years (1904)

The most dangerous of heretics are those who sin by being
unable to keep back with the slow progress of the Church,
thus outstripping the steps of the orthodox, for not only
are their heresies indestructible, but they cast a reproach upon those in power, and they make it clear to the
onlooker that what is supposed to be an immobile graven
image is a living thing, whose one necessity is growth.
One of the few heretics of this class who have not
even yet been overtaken by the Church was Joachim of
Flora, whom the piety and decorum of his life saved from
condemnation and actually placed among the mystics in
Dante's Paradise. The mystic is always a heretic; once
in an age he has the doubtful good fortune to be also the
founder of a religion. Joachim, by virtue of a leading
conception, was certainly the one, and may still prove to
be the other.

Three Epochs of Religion
That idea was: that the religious history of the world
was divided into three epochs — the first under the kingdom of the Father; the second, under the Son, and that
kingdom was passing in Joachim's day; and the third, under
the Holy Spirit, and that was about to be — a kingdom of
intelligence, liberty, contemplation and love.
Joachim lived in the flourishing time of monasticism;
he held St. Benedict in extreme reverence; and it is,
therefore, not surprising that when he looked forward to
the kingdom of the Spirit he saw, as its perfect subject,
the recluse. But the kingdom was not at hand. The age
which followed upon his death was the great and notable
day of layman, as against cleric, and Joachim had forgotten the layman.
But to-day, when the sympathies of mystics float over
troubled and deep waters, and often find a haven, if at
all, in the blue calm of the middle ages, such a mystic as
Joachim is sure to attract many to his fight. And if we
should turn to other men for a just interpretation, who
is so fit among living writers to make imaginative use
of Joachim, as Mr. Yeats?
In 'The Tables of the Law' he has drawn the portrait of
one, Owen Aherne, who possessed a unique copy of a long-
concealed work of Joachim's. The original (says Mr. Yeats)

was burnt by the order of Alexander IV:

> One copy alone remained, and was in the hands of a
> lute-player of Florence, and from him it passed to
> his son, and so from generation to generation until
> it came to the lute-player who was father to Ben-
> venuto Cellini.

The Passing of a Book
So it passed from a 'student of the kabalistic heresies
of Pico' to Owen Aherne. Already Aherne was one with
'desires so unbounded that no vessel can contain them,
intuitions so immaterial that their sudden and far-off
fire leaves heavy darkness about hand and foot'. The
effect of Joachim's book — whose history alone would have
inflamed a cooler head — upon the proud, extravagant
mystic was enormous. The Kingdom of the Spirit hung upon
his horizon like a sunset so awful that all the weary
intervening hills and valleys are forgotten. He put out
his hand; he set forth, as we are sometimes tempted to
set forth, into the west. He knew himself for one of
those Children of the Holy Spirit, through whom the kingdom was to come:

> Just as poets and painters and musicians labour at
> their works, building them with lawless and lawful
> things alike, so long as they embody the beauty that
> is beyond the grave, these children of the Holy
> Spirit labour at their moments with eyes upon the
> shining substance on which Time had heaped the refuse
> of creation. For the world only exists to be a tale
> in the care of coming generations; and terror and
> content, birth and death, love and hatred, and the
> fruit of the Tree, are but instruments for that
> supreme art which is to win us from life and gather
> us into eternity like doves into their dovecotes.

So he went away, to 'know all accidents and destinies',
and prepare ordinances to supersede the outworn decalogue,
and make ready for the firmer establishment of the kingdom
on his return. But on his return he knew only misery;
for he had 'looked out of the eyes of angels' in his
spiritual adventure, and learned that he could not sin;
and 'man can only come to that Heart through the sense
of separation from it, which we call Sin.' He disappears
from the story in the midst of a vision of uncertain
import.

Style and the Man
Mr. Yeats's style is nowhere more admirable than here
and in the companion story of 'The Adoration of the Magi'.
That is to say, it has a simplicity and a subtle and
tender rhythm and a spirituality which are unequalled in
England to-day. He draws the state of the mystic as one
who knows. He illustrates the slipping and disappointment of spiritual ambition, without leaving us any doubt
but that it is better to have desired the highest than
not to have desired, though it is certainly less easy.
Nevertheless, as an invention the story seems to us among
his less successful work.

Parts of it — not, perhaps, entirely essential parts
of it — are superb. For example, the romantic history
of the mysterious book is beyond discussion. But on the
subject of Joachim and the contents of the book, he gives
much imaginary detail without being explicit, and without
giving any but the most fantastic reader a chance of
believing that Joachim of Flora could have written such
things. The language of the mediaeval mystic is left in
its old form, and unelucidated, and, much as it may
suggest to Mr. Yeats, it was surely to be expected that
he would tell us what it meant to Owen Aherne.

In short, Mr. Yeats seems to us to have committed no
slight artistic sin, by elaborating his details, and by
confining himself, in the most difficult parts of his
narrative, to airy and ambiguous suggestions, without
any of those homely touches and proofs of an ecstatic
observation of the visible world, which are characteristic of most mystical writings, and usually of his own.
His Owen Aherne was a being of flesh and blood, as well
as of clouds and stars, and in leaving out the flesh
and blood he has weakened the effect of the clouds and
stars.

33. PAUL ELMER MORE FINDS YEATS TROUBLING AND UNWHOLESOME

1904

This extract is from Paul Elmer More, Two Poets of the
Irish Movement, 'Shelburne Essays' (1904).

Paul Elmer More (1864-1937), an American author and
literary journalist, who is best known for his 'Shelburne
Essays' (1904-1921) and 'New Shelburne Essays' (3 vols,
1928-36), also wrote on Platonism, Hellenistic Philo-

sophies, and the Christ of the New Testament. He was
literary editor of 'The Independent' (1901-3), of the
'New York Evening Post' (1903-9) and of 'The Nation'
(1909-14).

If one were to ask Mr. W.B. Yeats what he considered the
chief characteristic of the movement he so ably represents,
no doubt the last word to come to him would be *defeat,* and
yet, if properly considered, this so-called Gaelic Revival,
this endeavour to resuscitate a bygone past and to temper
the needs of the present to outworn emotions, is, when
all is said, just that and nothing more — a movement of
defeat. I say this with some confidence, because the visit
of Mr. Yeats among us, to lecture as a guest of the Irish
Literary Society, has led me to look through his successive
volumes systematically, and I have been more than ever
impressed by the gradual development in them of a sense of
failure and decay rather than of mastery and growth. And
the impression has saddened me a little; for I confess to
have become somewhat wearied by the imperialistic arrogance
of Kipling the great and the lesser Kiplings, and to have
been ready to welcome the gentler Muse of the Irish poets
who are so often contrasted with him. I had expected,
indeed, 'to hear a voice of lamentation out of the Golden
Age', but what really came to my ears was more like an
imitation of the bewildered wailings of decadence which
ruled lately in France and which has swept with it not
a few Englishmen such as Mr. Arthur Symons. Nothing can
be further from the virile passion and pathos, the action
and interknitting of strong characters in the ancient
Irish literature, than this modern 'Celtic phantasmagoria',
to use Mr. Yeats's own words, 'whose meaning no man has
discovered, nor any angel revealed'. I read the tremendous story of Deirdre in Lady Gregory's version of the
Irish saga of Cuchulain, and I am filled with the sorrow
of her lamentation as with one of the unforgettable sorrows
of the world:

> 'I am Deirdre without gladness, and I at the end of my
> life; since it is grief to be without them, I myself
> will not be long after them.'
> After that complaint Deirdre loosed her hair, and
> threw herself on the body of Naoise before it was put
> in the grave and gave three kisses to him, and when her
> mouth touched his blood, the colour of burning sods
> came into her cheeks, and she rose up like one that
> had lost her wits, and she went through the night
> till she came to where the waves were breaking on the

strand. And a fisherman was there and his wife, and
they brought her into their cabin and sheltered her,
and she neither smiled nor laughed, nor took food,
drink, or sleep, nor raised her head from her knees,
but crying always after the sons of Usnach.

I read this noble adaptation of old Irish passion, and
then turn to Mr. Yeats, who attempts to express 'the
stir and tumult of defeated dreams' through the mouths
of these same heroes of ancient song, and this, for an
example, is what I find:

> Were you but lying cold and dead,
> And lights were paling out of the West,
> You would come hither, and bend your head,
> And I would lay my head on your breast;
> And you would murmur tender words,
> Forgiving me because you were dead;
> Nor would you rise and hasten away,
> Though you have the will of the wild birds,
> But know your hair was bound and wound
> About the stars and moon and sun.

Mr. Yeats has somewhere defined certain poems as an
endeavour 'to capture some high, impalpable mood in a net
of obscure images', and no little part of his own verse
might fall under the same definition. Too often he
appears to strive after an exalted mysticism by giving the
reins to loose revery, seeming, indeed, not to recognise
any distinction between these two states of mind. The
long tradition of defeat that overshadows his country
has turned him, together with most of the other singers
of a New Ireland, away from the cruel realities of their
world and from the simple passions that control the im-
pulsive energies of men into this Celtic twilight of
defeated dreams. In the silence of this retreat from
the world, in the hush that falls after the thunder and
tumult of the passing war gods, one might look to hear the
still small voice of that genuine mysticism which, alone
of all poetic moods, has scarcely come to utterance in
English poetry. This would seem to be the true field for
these poets who are so open to impressions of patriotism
and whose native land, dear in innumerable ways, has
suffered so many a sad eclipse. Something of this higher
mysticism was, perhaps, heard in Mr. Yeats's earlier
poems, but no one can read his more recent productions
without observing what may be called a defalcation of the
mind. Instead of the true voice of the spirit, we hear
the chattering of old women whose memory is troubled by

vague and foolish superstitions; we perceive a poet of
undoubted powers lending himself to the mystery mon-
gering of a circle of morbid clerks; we listen to the
revelations of wandering beggars and workhouse paupers
as if they were apocalyptic in origin; we find a man gone
out among the hills to track 'every old dream that has
been strong enough to fling the weight of the world from
its shoulders', and we get from him idle ghost stories
and babbling repetitions of old wives' tales. To me,
at least, it is all rather sad, for I should be so willing to accept this vaunted symbolism as a true message
from one who has beheld the vision. Is it too much to
say that this is the poetry of defeat? The 'fret', to
use an expressive Irish word, is over him, and too long
brooding on the sorrow of the land has brought him to a
state perilously like an absconding of the intellect.
     Were it not that Mr. Yeats stands as the leader of a
group of young poets who show undoubted talent and who
have just cause for attempting to form a school of poetry
somewhat apart from the main current of English literature, there would be no reason for taking his delinquencies
seriously. As it is, one resents this flaccid note in
what might otherwise be a concord of subtle and exquisite
music. As I have said, the real kinship of Mr. Yeats's
present style is with that of Arthur Symons, himself a
disciple of the French decadents; only one must add in
justice that no taint of moral degeneration has appeared
in the Irish writer — and that is much to concede to a
decadent. It would be easy to set forth this kinship by
parallel quotations; to show, for instance, how in both
writers the looseness of ideas betrays itself unmistakably
in a curious uncertainty of rhythm, wherein the accents
hover weakly and dissolve into a fluttering movement
utterly different from the marching order of the strong
poets. There is one trick of both (though it is much
more marked in Mr. Yeats) which may seem trivial, and yet
does in some way connect itself with the total impression of their art. This is an insistence on the hair in
describing women. Just why this habit should smack of
decadence, is not quite clear to me, but the feeling it
inspires is unmistakable. Out of curiosity I counted the
number of allusions to hair in the few poems that make up
Mr. Yeats's 'Wind among the Reeds', and found they mounted
up to twenty-three. It is 'the long dim hair of Bridget',
or 'the shadowy blossom of my hair', or 'passion-dimmed
eyes and long heavy hair', or 'a flutter of flower-like
hair', or 'dim heavy hair', or the command to 'close your
eyelids, loosen your hair'. There is a fragile beauty
in these expressions, no doubt, but withal something

troubling and unwholesome; one thinks of the less chaste
descriptions of Arthur Symons or the morbid women of
Aubrey Beardsley's pencil rather than of the strong
ruddy heroines of old Irish story. The trait is significant of much.

Yet I would not he held to deny the loveliness of many
of Mr.Yeats's poems; above all I have respect for the
pure patriotism that burns through his language like a
clear flame within a vase of thinly chiselled alabaster,
although I believe that the specific aims of the Gaelic
enthusiasts are tragically misdirected. It may even be
the half-avowed consciousness of this fatal mistake that
has so emphasised the note of defeat in their verse. At
times this patriotic fervour enables Mr. Yeats to catch
the old haunting magic that Matthew Arnold marked as the
chief characteristic of Celtic literature. So in one of
his earlier poems he pictures the supernatural creatures
that troubled the men who were digging into the hill of
the Sidhe folk, and his words might stand with the best of
such passages in the 'Cuchulain':

> At middle night great cats with silver claws,
> Bodies of shadow, and blind eyes like pearls
> Came up out of the hole, and red-eared hounds
> With long white bodies came out of the air
> Suddenly, and ran at them and harried them.

One does not soon forget those 'blind eyes like pearls'.
Elsewhere Mr. Yeats seems to be aware that the wanton
revery of his muse may cut him off from the fellowship
of the 'great legion of Ireland's martyr roll':

> Know that I would accounted be
> True brother of that Company,
> Who sang to sweeten Ireland's wrong,
> Ballad and story, rann and song. . . .

> Nor may I less be counted one
> With Davis, Mangan, Ferguson,
> Because to him who ponders well,
> My rhymes more than their rhyming tell
> Of the dim wisdoms old and deep,
> That God gives unto man in sleep.
> For the elemental beings go
> About my table to and fro.
> In flood and fire and clay and wind,
> They huddle from man's pondering mind;
> Yet he who treads in austere ways
> May surely meet their ancient gaze.

If this is the poetry of defeat, it still retains a
vision of pure beauty that is not without a message for
those whose ears ring with the din of loud materialistic
songs. Nay, I am not prepared to say that the poet of
failure has not his own place in the chorus that cheers and
soothes us when, at rare intervals perhaps, we seek the
consolation of verse. How few of us there are who do not
feel at times the wan lethargy of defeat steal upon us!
It is not easy amid the sordid business of life, even
amid the strong calls of generous action when these are
heard, to pay heed to the still small voice; and in our
moods of dejection there may perchance be some kinship
to spiritual things in this feeling of defeat, in this
surrender to the vague fleeting shadows that tremble on
the inner eye. The sadness of these poems of Ireland is
justified to us then, and we recall the stanzas of another
poet, 'in his misery dead', composed on the theme of that
strange phrase, 'To weep Irish':

The sadness of all beauty at the heart,
The appealing of all souls unto the skies,
The longing locked in each man's breast apart,
Weep in the melody of thine old cries.

Mother of tears! sweet Mother of sad sighs!
All mourners of the world weep Irish, weep
Ever with thee; while burdened time still runs,
Sorrows reach God through thee, and ask for sleep.

And though thine own unsleeping sorrow yet
Live to the end of burdened time, in pain;
Still sing the song of sorrow! and forget
The sorrow, in the solace, of the strain.

34. OLIVER ST JOHN GOGARTY ON YEATS AS DRAMATIST

1904-1906

These three comments, dated respectively 12 December 1904,
18 November 1905 and 24 November 1906, are taken from
letters to G.K.A. Bell, a friend of Gogarty's at Oxford
who later became Bishop of Chichester. They are included
in Oliver St John Gogarty, 'Many Lines to Thee' (1971),
edited by James F. Carens.

Oliver St John Gogarty (1878-1957), educated at
Trinity College Dublin, and the University of Oxford, was a
surgeon, poet and wit. He was a Senator of the Irish Free
State (1923-36). An excellent minor poet, his reminiscences 'As I was going down Sackville Street' (1937) led
to a famous libel action: a further volume of autobiography, 'It isn't this time of year at all', was published
in 1954. Gogarty, portrayed as Buck Mulligan in Joyce's
'Ulysses', was for a time a friend of Joyce, who for a
while lived in the Martello tower Gogarty rented in
Dublin. His close friendship with Yeats (whose tonsils
he removed with panache) dated from about 1910, and he
was probably responsible for Yeats's being made a Senator.
Gogarty's exploit of escaping from his executioners in
the Civil War by plunging into the Liffey (in December)
delighted Yeats, and particularly Gogarty's dedication of
two swans to the river in gratitude, commemorated in
Gogarty's volume 'An Offering of Swans' (1924), as well
as his Rabelaisian conversation. Yeats included several
of Gogarty's poems in 'The Oxford Book of Modern Verse'
(1936).

(a)

Yeats and George Moore are reconciled now. Yeats was at
Moore's the other Saturday & drank whiskies & sodas &
recited a passage from a play he is composing now,
'Dei[r]dre'. He has succeeded in it in giving a kind
of classical heroic value to a commonplace or folk work, eg.

But her *goodman* answered her.

It was perhaps most from his voice that I derived the
impression but the effect to me was charming because it
so suddenly though subconsciously makes you realize that
Naoise & Dei[r]dre were flesh and blood, human — almost
homely. Then when Angus & Adene enter,(1) the chorus
sings — Angus & Adene are talking together as lovers:

But [Is] Adene worth a song?
Now the hunt begins anew,
Praise the beautiful and strong,
Praise the redness of the yew,
Praise the blossoming apple stem,
But our silence had been wise
What is all this Speech [Praise] to them
Who [That] have one another's eyes?(2)

The effect of his reading this is not to be transmitted
to you. He forgot himself and his face seemed tremulous
as if an image of impalpable fire — & not red[,] black
& white coloured Yeats. His lips are dark cherry red &
his cheeks too, take colour & his eyes actually glow black
and then the voice gets all vibrating as he sways like a
Druid with his whole soul chanting. No wonder the mechanics in America were mesmerized! I know no more beautiful
face than Yeats' when lit with song. Moore of course
talked bawdy too. Yeats gave his opinion on a version of
a Limerick. The conversation was very interesting to me.
At Moore's everyone becomes inspired to talk without
affectation. Moore is the most sincerely affected man
I know. His mannerism has become real Moore. Yeats said
that all great poems were capable of being estimated &
compared first: by the essential mythus, secondly by the
power showed in working the myth out and sustaining it
with incidents. Eg. Homer, his myth is the wandering of
a man, but then all the adventures that befall him ere
he reaches home. Then Cervantes' myth — the idealist
in contact with reality and the innumerable adventures
& the marvellous invention they show. 'Invention' was
the word Keats used if I mistake not when discussing a
similar theme in connection with his writing 'Endymion'.
Yeats would rather have signed 'Don Quixote' than 'Hamlet'!
I hope you will be soon a friend of Yeats. Let our home
be full of song.

(b)

I think that Yeats will have many moments [un]occupied in
Oxford. You say he will be there only a day. Were he
influenced by me as he is by his ladies, he would spend
his time with you. My spirit is making the discovery
and experiencing somewhat of the disillusionment that yours
experienced when you gazed on Algy too long in Life.
Yeats in a word, has outlived his singing season and he
is now a bare ruined choir save that an attractive kind
of mannerism helps him yet. You will only think the plays
good when you have forgotten great drama and remembered
only contemporary revivals. I intend soon to denounce
this lilliputianism in Art: this making ordinary common
people protagonists, sending Apollo not even to Admetus
but to the swineherd's hamlet; investing the peasant with
divinity, reducing God to the ancestral Ape. Of old the
protagonists were better than ourselves and capable of
intense and grand suffering; and by contemplating these
we became ourselves ennobled — katharsis. Nowadays,

the passions fit for gods are grafted on to non-representative and ignoble peasants, incapable of feeling greatly, even if they were not incapable of inspiring their audience with sentiments noble awful and divine. And the peasant protagonist cannot be ennobled to the dignity of drama without making drama more undignified by not painting the peasant true. This is what Aristophanes probably kicked Euripedes for — Dressing his Kings in rags: appealing to sentiment. It was indecorous in a dramatist and indecent in Art. Awful Aeschylus, glorious Sophocles, how we are fallen! And that sanest Aristophanes foresaw it all. Shakespeare's natural intuition forbade him to dethrone his Kings — though Lear wandered crownless. Ibsen is indecent beyond the expression of disgust, though I grant him all genius. And then the little theatre disgracing us in England! Go, but when returning write to me endorsing this — you will then avoid discomforting disappointments.

(c)

I would you were here. Yeats and Co. are in full swing and supplying many pleasantries. 'Dei[r]dre' a dusty production, impossible as it stands, had Yeats not remembered Lady Macbeth & the last scene of 'Romeo & Juliet', was produced on Saturday for the first time. I did not like his Dei[r]dre. His attempted conception of her is nauseating: he has whorified a fine old lover with little lascivities — But I will send you the text. I hope you got your books; they were delayed by dalliance. . . . Life here is amusing and as barbarous as ever. I am now angry at Yeats' petulant impertinence: calling Spenser's sonnets 'intolerable'. So — ever yours affectionately

Oliver Gogarty

Notes

1 Professor Carens comments, 'As Deirdre, Naoise and Fergus enter the musicians sing this song about the fabulous lovers Aengus and Edain (to use Yeats's later spelling of the names)'.
2 Professor Carens remarks that Gogarty, writing from memory, comes very close to the actual phrasing of the original, though his punctuation differs from Yeats's early versions and later revisions.

35. PERFECTION IS OF MANY KINDS

1905

An unsigned review of 'Stories of Red Hanrahan' (1905),
'The Academy', 22 July 1905.

In Mr. Yeats' 'Secret Rose' there were several stories of
Hanrahan, the passionate and unlucky hedge schoolmaster.
There were 'The Book of the Great Dhoul and Hanrahan';
'The Twisting of the Rope'; 'Kathleen the daughter of
Hoolihan and Hanrahan'; 'The Curse', 'The Vision', and
'The Death' of Hanrahan. The stories were full of strangeness involved in simplicity, and of all the characteristic excellences of Mr. Yeats' earlier work, not without
some of that rhetoric and descriptiveness which he has
now triumphantly done with. The pleasant volume before
us contains all of these stories, save 'The Book of the
Great Dhoul', which is replaced by an introductory story
about Hanrahan and a game of cards and a vision of 'Echtge,
daughter of the Silver Hand'; and it is prefaced thus:
'A friend has helped me to remake these stories nearer to
the mind of the country places where Hanrahan and his
like wandered and are remembered.' Take, for example,
one of the best of the tales, containing the poem:

> The poet, Owen Hanrahan, under a bush of May
> Calls down a curse on his own head, because it withers
>   grey.

It used to be called 'The Curse of Hanrahan the Red'; now
it is 'Red Hanrahan's Curse'. 'One morning in spring,' it
used to begin; now it begins with 'One fine May morning'.
Even so Plato changed the opening of his dialogue, but
not in public. Our own feeling about the changes that
follow, changes of earlier work, is that they are un-
principled and founded upon a misconception of the nature
of perfection; so that one may say that one version is
not better than the other, but different, in mood, aim,
and result; the later version in this case being admirably chaste, but leading us to fear that the writer's
final view of perfection may be a blank. In the old
version, the girl Nora was lying with her face in long
grass; now she sits with her face in her hands under a
thorn; and now she reminds Hanrahan of Margaret 'Gillane'
not 'Gillen', 'Maeve' Connellan, not 'Maurya'. Almost
every sentence is changed, often simplified, but seldom

without making us feel that the new form is the work of
another man, who should not have been allowed to touch
the old. The book is chiefly valuable because it gathers
the stories of Red Hanrahan together, and because it
shows that perfection is of many kinds, and that there
is no reason why a man should not write the same story in
a hundred ways, all good, if he has leisure.

36. JOHN BUTLER YEATS ON THE DANGERS OF GERMAN THEORIES

1906

These passages from a letter dated 1906 are taken from
John Butler Yeats, 'Letters to his son W.B. Yeats and
others: 1869-1922' (1944), edited with a memoir by
Joseph Hone. Yeats's father wrote many letters to his
son; they are lively and stimulating. Professor William
Murphy of Union College, Schenectady, who is writing a
life of John Butler Yeats, is drawing upon his vast
collection of them to illuminate the originality and
freshness of the painter's approach to art, literature
and life itself.
        For note on John Butler Yeats see p. 61.

. . . . As regards the other matter in your letter. As
you have dropped affection from the circle of your
needs, have you also dropped love between man and woman?
Is this the theory of the overman, if so, your demi-
godship is after all but a doctrinaire demi-godship.
        Your words are idle — and you are far more human than
you think. You would be a philosopher and are really a
poet — the contrary of John Morley, who is really a
philosopher and wants to be a statesman. Morley is never
roused except when some pet synthesis is in jeopardy.
        The men whom Nietzsche's theory fits are only great men
of a sort, a sort of Yahoo great men. The struggle is
how to get rid of them, they belong to the clumsy and
brutal side of things. . . .
        I never show your letters to them at home. Women are
always apt to treat every utterance as if it is something
final — and I don't think anything you say at present or
for some time to come *if ever* is to be treated as final.
You are haunted by the Goethe idea, interpreted by Dowden,
that a man can be a complete man. It is a chimera — a

man can only be a specialist.
    Robert called here this morning. I hope he will give
a good report of things. I am awfully worried but in the
highest spirits — but I fear I am wasting your time
and that this is *trivial fond record* to a man who has cast
away his humanity. — Yours affectionately — J.B. YEATS

37. GEORGE A. BIRMINGHAM ON HIS INTRODUCTION TO THE
CELTIC NOTE IN LITERATURE

1907

Extract from George A. Birmingham, The Literary Movement
in Ireland, 'Fortnightly Review', December 1907
    George A. Birmingham was the pen-name of Canon J.O.
Hannay (1865-1950): a clergyman of the Church of Ireland,
who spent over 20 years in the west of Ireland, the locale
for many of his successful novels, some of which are now
being reprinted. These include 'Spanish Gold' (1908);
'Lalage's Lovers' (1911); and 'Millicent's Corner' (1935).
He was a chaplain in the British Embassy in Budapest, later
with the British Army in France. He held a living in Somer-
set and later lived in London. He published 'The Spirit and
Origin of Christian Monasticism' (1903) and 'The Wisdom of
the Desert' (1904) under his own name; both books influenced
Yeats.

. . . Mr. Standish O'Grady wrote on. His 'Early Bardic History of Ireland' was followed by his 'History of Ireland,
Critical and Philosophical', by 'Cuculain', 'The Flight of
the Eagle', 'Finn and his Companions', 'The Bog of Stars',
and other books. Mr. Standish O'Grady never won great popularity. His was a nobler reward. He is the father of the
Irish literary movement. From him the poets and dramatists
who are writing in Ireland now drew their first inspiration.
Nor do his services to Ireland stop here. By his publication
of 'The Library of the Nore' while he was editor of 'The
Kilkenny Moderator', he gave young writers their first
chance of finding a public. In his 'All Ireland Review',
now, alas! dead, he steadily maintained great ways of
thought, high and pure views of vexed questions, an heroic
attitude of soul, which have done much to elevate and keep
lofty in spirit our new literature. Yet for a long time
Mr. Standish O'Grady was alone, a voice in a midnight

wilderness full of ravening creatures.

But the dawn came, and if we have not yet got done
with the howlings of wolves, at least there is a hope that
when the daylight fully comes to us they will get them
away to their dens. In 1888 Miss Katharine Tynan published her first volume of verse. She and another young
poet, Miss Frances Wynne, who died before she had done
more than give promise of good work, owed much to the wise
encouragement of Father Matthew Russell, editor of 'The
Irish Monthly'. Here was work, not of great power or
striking originality, but distinctively Irish in tone.
The following year Mr. Yeats published his 'Wanderings of
Oisin'. I can recall now the effect produced on my mind
by the reading of this book. I had just left college
after winning an undeserved honour degree in modern
literature. I was more or less capable of appreciating
English poetry. I knew Palgrave's 'Golden Treasury'
almost off by heart. I was totally unprepared for what I
found in 'The Wanderings of Oisin'. The subjects of the
poems were new to me, the verse harmonies unfamiliar.
It was my first introduction to the Celtic note in
literature. Fortunately the book was given to me by a
man whose literary judgment I trusted. I persevered
with it, and bewilderment passed into admiration. I
note this effect of Mr. Yeats's poetry on my mind, not
because it matters in the least to any one how I felt or
thought, but because there are many even now to whom the
new Irish literature is repellent on account of its
strangeness; people who have been educated as I was to
understand the English literary tradition and who find it
extremely difficult to understand anything else. . . .

The Collected Works in Verse and Prose of William Butler Yeats (1908)

38. LYTTON STRACHEY ON YEATS AS EXTREME ROMANTIC

1908

An unsigned review of the first two volumes of 'The
Collected Works in Verse and Prose of William Butler
Yeats' (8 vols, 1908) [by Lytton Strachey] Mr Yeats's
Poetry, 'The Spectator', 17 October 1908.
   Giles Lytton Strachey (1880–1932). Educated at Liver-
pool University and Trinity College, Cambridge, his
'Eminent Victorians' (1918) marked the reaction of the
'Bloomsbury group', among whom he formed his close friendships, against the Victorian middle-class culture they
inherited. He continued his ironic attack on legendary
figures with 'Queen Victoria' (1921), though this biography has some sentimentality about it.
   'Books and Characters: French and English' (1922),
'Elizabeth and Essex' (1928), 'Portraits in Miniature
and Other Essays' (1931), and 'Characters and Commentaries'
(1933) show his wide interests. He more than compensated
for occasional inaccuracy by his liveliness of mind and
desire to probe the inner nature and motivation of his
subjects.

The publication of a living writer's collected works
implies a claim to a recognised and permanent place in
the literature of a nation. None but classics deserve
complete editions, and an author who appears in one during
his lifetime is, in effect, making pretensions to classical
honours. These are bold pretensions to make; and they
seem all the bolder when, as in the case of Mr. W.B.
Yeats's sumptuous volumes, they are made with pomp and

elaboration. The books are perfect examples of beautiful
printing and binding; they are to contain several finely
reproduced portraits of the author; and the text is
illustrated and amplified by a number of variant readings
and notes. The two volumes already issued are devoted
to Mr. Yeats's lyrical and narrative poems and to four of
his poetical plays. The six subsequent volumes will contain the rest of his plays, together with his essays and
tales in prose. Mr. Yeats is a prose writer of originality and talent, but it is, of course, upon his work in
verse that his claim to high distinction really rests, and
thus the two volumes now before us afford the means for a
judgment as to his true position in English literature.
Historically, Mr. Yeats's poetry belongs to the great
romantic tradition which came into being with the publication of the 'Lyrical Ballads', and, in particular, to that
part of the tradition which owes its inspiration to
Coleridge. The revolution in English poetry which followed the appearance of 'The Ancient Mariner' was the
result of a reaction against the narrow poetical outlook
of the eighteenth century. The great poets of that age
had been content to look for their subject-matter among
the facts of civilised society, beyond which they were
either unable or unwilling to let their imaginations
range. Coleridge's genius was the first to shatter this
convention; he turned his back upon the common-sense and
the artificial beauties of his predecessors, and plunged
boldly into the unbounded regions of imagination and
romance. His influence, carrying poetry further and further away from the actualities of life, may be traced
throughout the nineteenth century; Keats's masterpieces
belong to the world of imagination, and not of fact;
so do the early poems of Tennyson, and so does much of
the finest work of Mr. Swinburne. In Mr. Yeats's poetry
we find this tendency pushed to its furthest point. Here
the sober earth, the common doings and reasonable thoughts
of ordinary men, have vanished so completely as to seem,
as one looks back at them through the mist of Mr. Yeats's
verses, to have left 'not a rack behind'. Mr. Yeats
transports us into a strange dominion 'beyond Time and
Fate and Change', where everything is vague and wonderful
and dreamy, and endowed, in some transcendental manner,
with mysterious significance. He is, in fact, the example
par excellence of the extreme romantic. His poetry might
almost be defined as romance in process of decomposi-
tion. For this reason it is of peculiar interest to the
student of English verse, for, through its faults no less
than its merits, it provides the material for a criticism
of the whole romantic school. The simplest way of

realising the true characteristics of a style or a convention is to examine them, not in their best forms, but
in their most pronounced.

It is easy to imagine the kind of criticism which Mr.
Yeats would have received from eighteenth-century readers.
Dr. Johnson would have reserved for him his most annihila-
ting common-sense, while Voltaire would have covered him
with sparkling ridicule. Such criticisms would have been
by no means final, because they would have lacked the
quality which is as necessary in criticism as salt in
cooking, — the quality of sympathy; yet it can hardly be
doubted that Mr. Yeats might have learnt something from
Dr. Johnson, and even from Voltaire. They would have
accused him of being too unreasonable to be a good poet;
and would they have been altogether wrong? Is it not true
that, even in poetry, reason has its place? The opinion
is no doubt an unfashionable one, but we have only to turn
to Mr. Yeats's volumes to find an object-lesson of the bad
results which may follow when reason is left out of
account in the making of poetry. One of these volumes
is devoted to four essays in poetic drama, of which the
best known are 'Deirdre' and 'On Baile's Strand'. There
is much charm in these pieces, and much beauty; but they
show not a trace of that rare power of uniting poetry and
dramatic force without which 'poetic drama' is merely
another name for dialogue in verse. Curiously enough,
the solitary instance in these plays in which Mr. Yeats
gives proof of a dramatic sense is to be found in those
passages in 'On Baile's Strand' which are written in
prose. Here Mr. Yeats, adopting a manner somewhat similar
to that of M. Maeterlinck, succeeds in producing an unmistakably dramatic effect, — an effect which disappears as soon as he returns to blank verse. And his
verse is undramatic because it is too unreasonable to
follow the actual workings of human thoughts, and to take
shape from the actual pressure of human feelings. His
characters are the creatures of his poetry, with motives
which are not real motives, and experiences unfelt below
the moon. More than this, his verse itself suffers, and
becomes 'subdued to what it works in'. It is only in
his plays — and only in those parts of his plays which
are intended to be dramatic — that Mr. Yeats writes
positively badly. 'We will go away,' says Deirdre at the
climax of the drama,

> Into some country at the ends of the earth.
> We'll trouble you no more. You will be praised
> By everybody if you pardon us.

The last line is a fair example of the weakness and
emptiness into which throughout this volume Mr. Yeats's
technique constantly falls. His narrative poems are far
more successful, but they are not without faults of a
similar nature. In 'The Wanderings of Oisin' the incoherence is so great that the reader obtains no sense
of an artistic whole. The poem is not only completely
divorced from the common facts of life, but its structure
is essentially unreasonable, because it depends upon no
causal law, and thus the effect which it produces is
singularly fragmentary and vague. It is full of beauties,
but they are all unrelated, and slip out of one's grasp
like unstrung pearls. Mr. Yeats's narrative style
resembles to a remarkable degree that of William Cham-
berlayne, whose 'Pharonnida' fills the same sort of place
in the Elizabethan tradition as Mr. Yeats's work in the
Romantic. In both there is the same looseness, the same
flow, the same love of detail, the same negligence of
unity; both are instances of a great manner run to seed:

                        We rode between
     The seaweed-covered pillars, and the green
     And surging phosphorus alone gave light
     On our dark pathway, till a countless flight
     Of moonlit steps glimmered; and left and right
     Dark statues glimmered over the pale tide
     Upon dark thrones. Between the lids of one
     The imaged meteors had flashed and run
     And had disported in the stilly jet,
     And the fixed stars had dawned and shone and set,
     Since God made Time and Death and Sleep: the other
     Stretched his long arm to where, a misty smother,
     The stream churned, churned, and churned — his lips apart,
     As though he told his never-slumbering heart
     Of every foamdrop on its misty way:
     Tying the horse to his vast foot that lay
     Half in the unvesselled sea, we climbed the stair
     And climbed so long, I thought the last steps were
     Hung from the morning star.

How much there is to admire here in felicity of expression and boldness of imagination, and yet how faint is
the total effect which the lines produce! This is Mr.
Yeats's fundamental weakness, — an inability to make a
really profound and lasting impression upon the mind.
It is a weakness which is inherent in his poetical method,
and one which, given that method, only a writer of colossal
force could have avoided. It requires a Coleridge to
create, out of the loose and drifting fantasies of

dreamland, the unforgettable marvel of a 'Kubla Khan'.
    It is right to dwell upon Mr. Yeats's limitations,
partly because they are the limitations of a whole school,
and partly because they are bound up with merits of a
very high order. Nothing can be vainer than promiscuous
praise. It is by virtue of his lyrical writing — and,
if we are not mistaken, by virtue of his lyrical writing
alone — that Mr. Yeats deserves a niche in the temple
of Apollo. He possesses the true lyrical gift; he can
write with spontaneity, with melody, with haunting charm;
and it is difficult to think of any other writer of this
generation of whom it can be said with equal certainty
that he has given proof of inspiration. His lyrics are
weak where the rest of his work is weak, — in clarity
of thought and in construction; but these are precisely
the qualities with which lyrics can most easily dispense,
and at his best Mr. Yeats dispenses with them quite successfully. Who can stop to notice that the exquisite
'Innisfree' lacks certainty of design? We are content
when we have read this verse:

> And I shall have some peace there, for peace comes
>   dropping slow,
>   Dropping from the veils of the morning to where the
>   cricket sings;
>   There midnight's all a glimmer, and noon a purple glow,
>   And evening full of the linnet's wings.

That is truly beautiful, and those lovers of poetry who
have not already become acquainted with Mr. Yeats's
work will find scattered through these volumes passages
no less deserving of remembrance and of admiration. The
whole bulk of what is best in his achievement is certainly not large; but it is genuine poetry, and that is
enough. Even a few lines of poetry carry with them a
peculiar glory, for a poet differs from other writers not
in degree but in kind. One can no more be partly a poet
than — to compare great things to small — one can partly
catch a train. Poetry is like gold; it can be mixed with
baser materials, but it can never partake of their nature.
When the alloy has been sifted away, posterity will treasure up the pure and shining fragments of this precious
substance in the work of Mr. Yeats.

39. DOWDEN'S COMMENTS ON ALTERATIONS IN THE POEMS AND
ACHIEVEMENT IN THE PROSE

1909

A review of 'The Collected Works in Verse and Prose of
William Butler Yeats' (8 vols, 1908), The Writings of Mr.
W.B. Yeats, 'Fortnightly Review', 1 February 1909. This
was signed E.M.D., and attributed to Professor Edward
Dowden by K.G.W. Cross and R.T. Dunlop, 'A Bibliography
of Yeats Criticism' (1971).
For note on Edward Dowden see pp. 62-3.

The first volume of the Collected Edition contains the
lyrical and narrative poems, and to compare the earlier
forms of some of these with the later versions is
instructive. 'The Wanderings of Oisin' is one that has
been largely altered and thereby greatly improved; poor
lines have been struck out, weak lines strengthened,
the right word found at last, so that what was merely
verse is turned into poetry. 'The Meditation of the Old
Fisherman' is now among the most beautiful of the early
lyrics, but it was not so in the beginning. Then the
second of the verses ran:

> The lines are not heavy, nor heavy the long nets brown —
> Ah me! full many a creak gave the creel in the cart
> That carried the fish for sale in the far-away town,
> When I was a boy with never a crack in my heart.

This is how it stands revised in the Collected Edition:

> The herring are not in the tides as they were of old;
> My sorrow! for many a creak gave the creel in the cart
> That carried the take to Sligo town to be sold,
> *When I was a boy with never a crack in my heart.*

Now the Master's hand has touched it, and we hear, in
the third line, the rumbling of the heavy, mud-caked
wheels on the rutted country road, and this, I take it, is
what we were always meant to hear. Unfortunately, it
cannot be said that the alterations are invariably happy;
and some of the poems, to those of us who have long known
and loved them, seem to be but the shadow of their old
selves, as for example the musical 'Cradle Song', where
the first form is incomparably the better. But the best
poems are for the most part untouched, or else only

touched (as in 'When You are Old' and 'The Sorrow of
Love') to give an added grace.
   It was not until 1891, five years after the publication of 'Mosada', that Mr. Yeats made his first essay
in prose with a thin volume containing 'John Sherman' and
'Dhoya'. 'John Sherman' is remarkable as being Mr. Yeats'
only novel. Of late the word novel has fallen upon evil
days and suggests to the ordinary reader something merely
ephemeral, to be glanced through in an idle hour and as
quickly forgotten. Used in this sense, it would be singularly ill-applied to 'John Sherman', which, in spite of
sundry crudities, gives us some of the best of Mr. Yeats'
prose, while, as he himself confesses in the tenderly-
written preface to be found in the seventh volume, the
story is in part an autobiography: 'Having been persuaded
somewhat against my judgment to include these early
stories ('John Sherman' and Dhoya'), I have read them for
the first time these many years. They have come to interest me very deeply; for I am something of an astrologer, and can see in them a young man — was I twenty-
three? and we Irish ripen slowly — born when the Water-
Carrier was on the horizon, at pains to overcome Saturn in
Saturn's hour, just as I can see in much that follows his
struggle with the still all-too-unconquered Moon, and at
last, as I think, the summons of the prouder Sun. Sligo,
where I had lived as a child and spent some months or
weeks of every year till long after, is Ballah, and Pool
Dhoya is at the river mouth there, and he who gave me
all of Sherman that was not born at the rising of the
Water-Carrier has still the bronze upon his face, and is
at this moment, it may be, in his walled garden, wondering as he did twenty years ago, whether he will ever
mend the broken glass of the conservatory where I am
not too young to recollect the vine-trees and grapes
that did not ripen.'
   If the grapes did not ripen, the boy who wondered at
their greenness has more than fulfilled the promise of
his early work. Yet even to-day when all are agreed as
to the beauty of the poetry, there are widely different
opinions as to the worth of the prose. Though one critic
has declared it to be 'the most beautiful prose in the
world', others have described it as over-elaborated,
self-conscious, tortured, and, at its best, reminiscent
of Pater and the school that cultivated refinement of style
until it robbed itself of very life. There is a measure of
truth in the blame, but the praise is more likely to be the
enduring verdict. In his prose, Mr. Yeats is, as it were,
constantly reciting his *Credo*; giving reasons for the faith
that is in him and telling us of new things, or rather of

old things the world has forgotten so long, that they
seem to us new. Writers, or at all events critics and
journalists, live for the most part in cities, and the
life and thought of cities is ever taken up with eager
activities; so that what lies outside the common vision
of common men seems but as foolishness, and those who would
speak of high mysteries are dubbed dreamers and even the
honesty of their belief is called in question. Now, in
this preface to 'John Sherman', Mr. Yeats tells us, in the
ordered prose of his latest conviction, that he is 'something of an astrologer', and astrology is not to-day
reckoned a popular science. Long ago it fell into dis-
repute, being a happy hunting-ground for the charlatan and
other evilly-disposed rogues; yet there are some who
still claim that astrology is the only absolutely demonstrable science, and it certainly helps to explain much
that would be otherwise obscure in Mr. Yeats' later writings. Without this key it is possible to see only the
beauty of the prose and that is why it has sometimes been
called weak, vague, and obscure; with the key, we find
the thought lying concealed is clear as crystal, only it
is something strange and new.

'John Sherman' is the story of a young man told by a
young man, and there is in it no hint of the life-like
portraiture that has made 'Tom Jones' famous; yet, as
we read, we know this picture in half-tones is every whit
as true. It shows us a type never common, but happily
for the world never extinct, though the conditions of
life to-day make it rarer than it was half a century
ago. The people who are content with little, desire
little, and dread change, preferring the old furrows to the
new, must expect scant sympathy in an age of experiment and
progress; but they are not the less wise, and their
stories, bare of incident, often make better reading than
the adventures of the more successful. Just such a man is
John Sherman; content with the narrow life he lives with
his mother in the little country town, happy in his idle
dreams, loving (though he does not know it) one woman,
yet leaving her with but little regret to go into his rich
uncle's London office. In London he is unhappy as a sea-
bird in a cage, until he meets with a beautiful girl who
promises to marry him. Then slowly self-knowledge comes,
and he determines to set himself free and go back to the
old life in the little town and to the old love.

> The others had gone and Sherman was alone in the
> drawing-room by himself, looking through the window.
> Never had London seemed to him so like a reef whereon
> he was cast away. In the Square the bushes were

covered with dust; some sparrows were ruffling their
feathers on the sidewalk; people passed, continually
disturbing them. The sky was full of smoke. A terrible feeling of solitude oppressed him. A portion of
his life was ending. He thought that soon he would be
no longer a young man, and now, at the period when the
desire of novelty grows less, was coming the great
change of his life. He felt he was of those whose
granaries are in the past. And now this past would
never renew itself. He was going out into the distance
as though with strange sailors in a strange ship.

A remarkable piece of writing that for so young a man,
and as characteristic now as then of Mr. Yeats, for he,
too, is of those 'whose granaries are in the past'. Like
Sherman, he is out of touch with the busy ways of cities,
but their unloveliness is not so depressing to him as
the poverty of their purposes and aims. He is for ever
telling us that with the complicated machinery of our
existence and our gospel of work and hurry we have made
the world intolerable, and in his heart we know he agrees
with the old woman on the Irish cattle-boat who was
making her monthly journey with geese for the Liverpool
market and said to John Sherman, 'For what have we in this
life but a mouthful of air?' The ending of the book, with
its story of the homecoming of the awakened man, is more
beautiful, because it is more true, than the ending of
any other book I knew.

40. GEORGE MOORE ON YEATS AS TALKER, ASTROLOGER, ORATOR
AND COLLABORATOR

1911

These passages are from 'Hail and Farewell, Ave' (1911),
George Moore's magnificently mischievous account of his
experiences in Dublin from the turn of the century till
his departure for London.
    George Augustus Moore (1852-1933), landowner, novelist,
autobiographer, short-story writer, playwright and art
critic, went to Paris to become an artist, but found his
métier in writing 'A Modern Lover' (1883) in a realistic
manner learned from Zola; this was not successful, but
'A Mummer's Wife' (1885) established him as a serious
novelist, a reputation deepened by 'Esther Waters' (1894).

He returned to Dublin in the early 1900s to join in the
Irish renaissance. He write several plays and helped
Yeats and Lady Gregory in the early days of the Irish
Literary Theatre, but Yeats and he quarrelled over their
collaboration in 'Diarmuid and Grania', which was performed in 1901. His novel 'A Drama in Muslin' (1886) had
dealt with Ireland in the period of the Land League, and
now he wrote the Turgenev-like stories of Irish life, 'The
Untilled Field' (1903) and 'The Lake' (1905), his experiment with the melodic line. His trilogy 'Hail and Farewell' (1911-14) marked his departure from Dublin to London. His remarks on Lady Gregory and Yeats in this funny
and malicious account of Dublin received Yeats's counter-
blow in 'Dramatis Personae' (1935). Some of Moore's
Irish material appeared in 'A Storyteller's Holiday' (1918).
After 'The Brook Kerith' (1916) and 'Avowals' (1919) his
style settled into the smoothly flowing rich prose which
makes 'Heloise and Abelard' (1921) so pleasant to read.
A return to medieval Ireland in 'Ulick and Soracha' (1926)
was not so successful. 'A Communication to My Friends'
(1933) is a final account of 'how writing was forced on me'
and 'the persecution' he had undergone as a result for
forty years.

. . . English was becoming a lean language. We have lost,
Yeats, and I fear for ever, the second person singular of
the verbs; thee and thou are only used by peasants, and
the peasants use them incorrectly. In poetry, of course —
Yeats shook his head — thee and thou were as impossible
in verse as in prose, and the habit of English writers
to allow their characters to thee and to thou each other
had made the modern poetic drama ridiculous. Nor could
he sympathise with me when I spoke of the lost subjunc-
tive, and I understood him to be of the opinion that a
language might lose all its grammar and still remain a
vehicle for literature, the literary artist always
finding material for his art in the country.
    Like a landscape painter, I answered him. But we
are losing our verbs; we no longer ascend and descend,
we go up and we go down; birds still continue to alight,
whereas human beings get out and get in.
    Yeats answered that even in Shakespeare's time people
were beginning to talk of the decline of language. No
language, he said, was ever so grammatical as Latin, yet
the language died; perhaps from excess of grammar. It
is with idiom and not with grammar that the literary
artist should concern himself; and, stroking his thin
yellow hands slowly, he looked into the midnight fire,

regretting he had no gift to learn living speech from
those who knew it — the peasants. It was only from them
one could learn to write, their speech being living speech,
flowing out of the habits of their lives, struck out of
life itself, he said, and I listened to him telling of a
volume of folklore collected by him in Sligo; a welcome
change truly is such after reading 'The Times', and he
continued to drone out his little tales in his own incomparable fashion, muttering after each one of them,
like an oracle that has spent itself — a beautiful
story, a beautiful story! When he had muttered these
words his mind seemed to fade away, and I could not but
think that he was tired and would be happier tucked up in
bed. But when I rose out of my chair he begged me to
remain; I would if he would tell me another story. He
began one, but Symons came in in the middle of it, tired
after long symbolistic studies at the Empire, and so hungry
that he began to eat bread and butter, sitting opposite to
us and listening to what we were saying, without, however,
giving us much of his attention. He seemed to like
listening to Yeats talking about style, but I gathered
from his detachment that he felt his own style had been
formed years ago; a thing of beauty without doubt, but
accidentally bestowed upon him, so much was it at variance with his appearance and his conversation; whereas
Yeats and his style were the same thing; and his strange
old-world appearance and his chanting voice enabled me
to identify him with the stories he told me, and so completely that I could not do otherwise than believe that
Angus, Étaine, Diarmuid, Deirdre, and the rest, were
speaking through him. He is a lyre in their hands; they
whisper through him as the wind through the original
forest; but we are plantations, and came from England in
the seventeenth century. There is more race in him than
any one I have seen for a long while, I muttered, while
wending my way down the long stairs, across Fountain
Court, through Pump Court, by the Temple Church, under
the archway into King's Bench Walk. . . .

Rising from the low stool in the chimney-corner, he led
me to a long box, and among the manuscript I discovered
several packs of cards. As it could not be that Yeats
was a clandestine bridge-player, I inquired the use the
cards were put to, and learnt that they were specially
designed for the casting of horoscopes. He spoke of
his uncle, a celebrated occultist, whose predictions were
always fulfilled, and related some of his own successes.
All the same, he had been born under Aquarius, and the
calculations of the movements of the stars in that con-
stellation were so elaborate that he had abandoned the

task for the moment, and was now seeking the influences
of the Pleiades. He showed me some triangles drawn on
plain sheets of cardboard, into which I was to look while
thinking of some primary colour — red, or blue, or
green. His instructions were followed by me — why not? —
but nothing came of the experiment; and then he selected
a manuscript from the box, which he told me was the new
rules of the Order of the Golden Door, written by himself.
There was no need to tell me that, for I recognise always
his undulating cadences. These rules had become necessary;
an Order could not exist without rule, and heresy must be
kept within bounds, though for his part he was prepared
to grant every one such freedom of will as would not
endanger the existence of the Order. The reading of the
manuscript interested me, and I remember that one of its
finest passages related to the use of vestments, Yeats
maintaining with undeniable logic that the ancient priest
put on his priestly robe as a means whereby he might
raise himself out of the ordinary into an intenser life,
but the Catholic priest puts on an embroidered habit because it is customary. A subtle intelligence which delighted me in times gone by, and I like now to think of
the admiration with which I used to listen to Yeats talking
in the chimney-corner, myself regretting the many eloquent
phrases which floated beyond recall up the chimney, yet
unable to banish from my mind the twenty-five men and
women collected in the second pair back in West Kensington,
engaged in the casting of horoscopes and experimenting in
hypnotism.

As has been said before, analogies can be discovered in
all my boon companions. Could it be otherwise, since they
were all collected for my instruction and distraction?
Yeats will sit up smoking and talking of literature just
like Dujardin, Edward the same; and Yeats and Edward are
both addicted to magic: it matters little that each
cultivates a different magic, the essential is that they
like magic. And looking towards the armchairs in which
they had been sitting, I said: Yeats likes parlour
magic, Edward cathedral magic. A queer pair, united for
a moment in a common cause — the production of two plays:
'The Heather Field' and 'The Countess Cathleen'. 'The
Heather Field' I know, but 'The Countess Cathleen' I have
not read, and wondering what it might be like, I went
to the bookcase and took down the volume. . . .

My eyes went to Yeats, who sat, his head drooping on
his shirt-front, like a crane, uncertain whether he
should fold himself up for the night, and I wondered what
was the beautiful eloquence that was germinating in his
mind. He would speak to us about the Gods, of course,

and about Time and Fate and the Gods being at war; and
the moment seemed so long that I grew irritated with Gill
for not calling upon him at once for a speech. At
length this happened, and Yeats rose, and a beautiful
commanding figure he seemed at the end of the table, pale
and in profile, with long nervous hands and a voice
resonant and clear as a silver trumpet. He drew himself up and spoke against Trinity College, saying that it
had always taught the ideas of the stranger, and the songs
of the stranger, and the literature of the stranger, and
that was why Ireland had never listened and Trinity
College had been a sterile influence. The influences
that had moved Ireland deeply were the old influences
that had come down from generation to generation, handed
on by the story-tellers that collected in the evenings
round the fire, creating for learned and unlearned a
communion of heroes. But my memory fails me; I am dis-
figuring and blotting the beautiful thoughts that I heard
that night clothed in lovely language. He spoke of
Cherubim and Seraphim, and the hierarchies and the clouds
of angels that the Church had set against the ancient
culture, and then he told us that Gods had been brought
vainly from Rome and Greece and Judaea. In the imaginations of the people only the heroes had survived, and from
the places where they had walked their shadows fell often
across the doorways; and then there was something wonderfully beautiful about the blue ragged mountains and the
mystery that lay behind them, ragged mountains flowing
southward. But that speech has gone for ever. I have
searched the newspapers, but the journalist's report is
feebler even than my partial memory. It seemed to me
that while Yeats spoke I was lifted up and floated in
mid-air. . . . But I will no longer attempt the impossible;
suffice it to say that I remember Yeats sinking back like
an ancient oracle exhausted by prophesying. . . .

It is not until the language has been strained through
many minds that tragedy can be written in it. Balzac
wrote 'Les Contes Drôlatiques' in Old French because Old
French lends itself well to droll stories. Our play had
better be written in the language of the Bible. Avoiding
all turns of speech, said Yeats, which immediately recall
the Bible. You will not write Angus and his son Diarmuid
which is in heaven, I hope. We don't want to recall the
Lord's Prayer. And, for the same reason, you will not use
any archaic words. You will avoid words that recall any
particular epoch.

I'm not sure that I understand.

The words honour and ideal suggest the Middle Ages, and
should not be used. The word glory is charged with modern

idea — the glory of God and the glory that shall cover
Lord Kitchener when he returns from Africa. You will not
use it. The word soldier represents to us a man that
wears a red tunic; an equivalent must be found, swords-
man or fighting man. Hill is a better word than mountain;
I can't give you a reason, but that is my feeling, and
the word ocean was not known to the early Irish, only
the sea.

We shall have to begin by writing a dictionary of the
words that may not be used, and all the ideas that may not
be introduced. Last week you wrote begging me not to
waste time writing descriptions of Nature. Primitive man,
you said, did not look at trees for the beauty of the
branches and the agreeable shade they cast, but for the
fruits they bore and the wood they furnished for making
spear-shafts and canoes. A most ingenious theory, Yeats,
and it may be that you are right: but I think it is safer
to assume that primitive man thought and felt much as
we do. Life in its essentials changes very little, and
are we not writing about essentials, or trying to?

Yeats said that the ancient writer wrote about things,
and that the softness, the weakness, the effeminacy of
modern literature could be attributed to ideas. There
are no ideas in ancient literature, only things, and,
in support of this theory, reference was made to the
sagas, to the Iliad, to the Odyssey, and I listened to
him, forgetful of the subject which we had met to discuss. It is through the dialect, he continued, that one
escapes from abstract words, back to the sensation
inspired directly by the thing itself.

But, Yeats, a play cannot be written in dialect; nor
do I think it can be written by turning common phrases
which rise up in the mind into uncommon phrases.

That is what one is always doing.

If, for the sake of one's literature, one had the
courage to don a tramp's weed — you object to the word
don? And still more to weed? Well, if one had the
courage to put on a tramp's jacket and wander through the
country, sleeping in hovels, eating American bacon, and
lying five in a bed, one might be able to write the
dialect naturally; but I don't think that one can acquire
the dialect by going out to walk with Lady Gregory. She
goes into the cottage and listens to the story, takes
it down while you wait outside, sitting on a bit of wall,
Yeats, like an old jackdaw, and then filching her manuscript to put style upon it, just as you want to put style
on me.

Yeats laughed vaguely; his laugh is one of the most
melancholy things in the world, and it seemed to me that

I had come to Coole on a fruitless errand — that we
should never be able to write 'Diarmuid and Grania' in
collaboration.

41. KATHARINE TYNAN REMEMBERS THE YOUTHFUL WILLIE YEATS

1913

These passages are taken from Katharine Tynan, 'Twenty-
five Years: Reminiscences' (1913).
     For note on Katharine Tynan see p. 66.

. . . Willie Yeats was always about the studio. He had
not ceased at that time to be an art student, although
he was writing poetry. He used to be very quiet in a
corner doing some work of his own, and ever willing to
do anything he was asked to do for others. He was very
gentle, simple, and generous. He asked you to be profoundly interested in his poetry. On the other hand, he
was always profoundly interested in yours. He would
read his poetry to you for hours, if you would allow it;
on the other hand, he would listen for hours, absorbed
in yours, if you chose to absorb him. He was a wonderful
critic. At that time he was apt, I think, to be over-
generous to the work of those whom he liked. He asked
from poetry something of sincerity, of truth, of character and personality, and he would make the beauty for
himself.
     If you brought him a new poem he would chant it over
to himself with his head on one side. Nearly always one
was surprised by the generosity of his admiration.
     He would be at work quietly in his corner painting,
perhaps, or perhaps only cleaning his father's brushes or
palette. When the time came for the midday light lunch
he was always at hand to fill the kettle, to go out to
buy bread or milk or anything else that was wanted. Once
he was very quiet for a long time in his corner. At
last his father asked, 'What *are* you doing, Willie?' 'I'm
trying to get the paint off my coat with turpentine, but
it won't come off,' said the poet. 'I've been at it for
an hour, but it seems only to get worse.' 'Where did you
find the turpentine?' 'In this can.' 'Oh but that is
oil!'

Sometimes after lunch, in a quiet hour, Willie would read poetry for us. I heard Chapman's 'Homer' in that way. Once I nodded, and would have dropped asleep if I had not laughed. After that I had my early afternoon cup of tea to keep me wakeful.

Sometimes during the sitting a knock would come to the door. Mr. Yeats would go to it, and there would be a colloquy, ending in the visitor's being sent away. It was usually someone who was paying for his or her portrait and wanted a sitting, who was thus rejected.

Occasionally I stayed the night at the Yeatses' house on the outskirts of Dublin. I used to be awakened in the night by a steady, monotonous sound rising and falling. It was Willie chanting poetry to himself in the watches of the night.

He never had the remotest idea of taking care of himself. He would go all day without food unless someone remembered it for him, and in the same way would go on eating unless someone checked him. That first winter, a hard one, he would come to see me, five miles from Dublin, striding along over the snow-bound roads, a gaunt young figure, mouthing poetry, swinging his arms and gesticulating as he went. George Russell complained to me the other day that Willie Yeats had said somewhere of him, and printed it, that he used to walk about the streets of Dublin swinging his arms like a flail, unconscious of the alarm and bewilderment of the passers-by. It was Willie's own case. I remember how the big Dublin policemen used to eye him in those days, as though uncertain whether to 'run him in' or not. But, by and by, they used to say, 'Shure, 'tisn't mad he is nor yet drink taken. 'This the poethry that's disturbin' his head,' and leave him alone.

Once he had a very bad cough — he very often had a cough or a cold from his inability to take care of himself. I was sorry for him, and I bestowed upon him some cough lozenges which contained opium or chlorodyne or both, with instructions to suck one two or three times a day. He ate through the whole box at a sitting, and thereafter slept for some thirty hours. Fortunately he awoke none the worse, else I should have done a very ill service to the world.

There were moments when poetry ceased to charm others, but never him. He was always ready to squire me anywhere I would. I remember one very wet night, after we had been to a meeting of the Protestant Home Rule Association, when we waited in Westmoreland Street for a tram; I in my smart clothes, my high-heeled French shoes, standing in a pool of water; the wind driving the rain as it

does only in a sea-bound city; Willie holding the um-
brella at an acute and absent-minded angle which could
shelter nobody, pouring the while into my ears 'The
Sensitive Plant'. It was a moment to try any woman's
temper, and mine did not stand the trial well. . . .
     The later developments took the form of a spiritual-
istic séance in which I participated most unwillingly.
Willie Yeats was also of the party. The remaining ones
were undistinguished, if occult.
     In spite of my protestations my host gently but firmly
made me take part. We sat round a table in the darkness
touching each other's hands. I was quite determined to
be in opposition to the whole thing, to disbelieve in it,
and disapprove of it as a playing with things of life and
death. Presently the table stood up slowly: the host was
psychic. There were presences. The presences had com-
munications to make and struggled to make them. Willie
Yeats was banging his head on the table as though he had
a fit, muttering to himself. I had a cold repulsion to
the whole business. I took my hands from the table.
Presently the spirits were able to speak. There was someone in the room who was hindering them. By this time I
had got in a few invocations of my own. There was a
tremendous deal of rapping going on. The spirits were
obviously annoyed. They were asked for an indication as
to who it was that was holding them back. They indicated
me, and I was asked to withdraw, which I did cheerfully.
The last thing I saw as the door opened to let me pass
through was Willie Yeats banging his head on the table.
     He explained to me afterwards that the spirits were
evil. To keep them off he had been saying the nearest
approach to a prayer he could remember, which was the
opening lines of 'Paradise Lost': 'Of Man's first disobedience, and the fruit.'
     . . . Whenever I hear of vegetarianism I recall how
Willie Yeats and I dined at a vegetarian restaurant somewhere about Charing Cross, when I was in London in 1889.
There was a long and elaborate menu, but after the first
or second course I felt that never again, as long as I
lived, could I have any appetite, so Willie had the rest
of the meal, my portions as well as his own. Afterwards
we went to the Southwark Junior Irish Literary Society,
founded by Mrs. Rae and Miss Skeffington Thompson, where
Irish children were trained in the way they ought to go.
Mr. Frank Fahy, who is a very delightful Irish poet,
accompanied us back to Westminster Bridge Station. I
have a horrid recollection of the pangs of hunger I
suffered, positive starvation, on the homeward journey,
while Willie Yeats chanted poetry into my ear, being

quite unconscious of inflation or depression in his own
case, as he would have been indeed if he were a fasting
man, or if he was one of those entertainers who undertake
to consume an enormous amount of food within a very short
given time.
    And this carries me on to the time when we used to
visit at the O'Learys. There was a thieving maid, of whose
proclivities Miss O'Leary was unaware till her wine-bottles
began, most unaccountably, to yield up not wine, but water;
it was only by the repetition of this strange occurrence
that she came to the conclusion that someone must be empty-
ing and filling and resealing the bottles. Willie Yeats
knew more about her proceedings, as indeed did I. On one
occasion he hung his overcoat in the hall, with a couple of
golden sovereigns just paid to him for an article in its
pocket. When he resumed his overcoat the money was gone.
He was chronically hard up, yet he was not at all concerned about the loss of the money. What absorbed his
thoughts was speculation as to the state of mind of the
thief and what her motives were, and as to how a dipso-
maniac must feel deprived of drink, and so on.
    He had an uncanny way of standing aside and looking
on at the game of life as a spectator. He told me
about this time of how he had sat a night long with a
youth who had fallen into disgrace, and was in the depths,
not to be left alone for fear of what he might do. I
often thought of what a *macabre* situation it was — the
aloof, speculative poet, and the poor human failure, dis-
traught with his own misery.

42. LADY GREGORY'S ENTHUSIASM FOR YEATS'S VERSE PLAYS

1914

These passages are taken from Lady Gregory, 'Our Irish
Theatre: A Chapter of Autobiography' (1913).
    Lady Isabella Augusta Gregory (1859-1932) came from a
landowning family, the Persses of Galway. In 1880 she
married a neighbouring landowner, Sir William Gregory, a
former governor of Ceylon, who died in 1892. She first
met Yeats in 1896 when he visited Coole Park, her house
in Co. Galway. They became close friends and he spent
most of his summers at Coole up to his marriage in 1917.
She joined Yeats and Edward Martyn, who lived at Tulira
Castle, another neighbouring estate, in founding the Irish

Literary Theatre, out of which the Abbey Theatre developed.
She was a Director of the Abbey with Yeats and Synge and
did much to administer it, writing plays for it as well
as assessing the work of other playwrights. Her encouragement of Sean O'Casey was notable.

She gave Yeats a peaceful environment at Coole, lent
him money, and encouraged him to return to his earlier
interest in folklore and peasant speech. (She created her
own version of Anglo-Irish speech known as 'Kiltartan'.)
She collaborated — more than has yet been realised — with
him in playwriting, and he rightly praised her excellent
versions of Gaelic legend, 'Cuchulain of Muirthemne' (1902)
and 'Gods and Fighting Men' (1904). Her plays are lively
and very well made, the best known being 'Spreading the
News', 'The Rising of the Moon', 'The Workhouse Ward'
and 'The Gaol Gate'. All these are included in 'Seven
Short Plays' (1909). She wrote a biography of her nephew
Sir Hugh Lane (her earlier efforts culminated in 1959 in
the return from London of half his pictures on semi-
permanent loan to Dublin); and her 'Our Irish Theatre: a
Chapter of Autobiography' (1914), 'Coole' (1931; and, in
expanded version, 1971) and her 'Journals' (edited by
Lennox Robinson, 1946) give some idea of her unselfish
and firm character.

When we first planned our Theatre, there were very few
plays to choose from, but our faith had no bounds and as
the Irish proverb says, 'When the time comes, the child
comes.'

The plays that I have cared for most all through, and
for love of which I took up this work, are those verse
ones by Mr. Yeats, 'The Countess Cathleen' with which we
began, 'The Shadowy Waters', 'The King's Threshold', and
the rest. They have sometimes seemed to go out of sight
because the prose plays are easier to put on and to take
from place to place; yet they will always be, if I have
my way, a part of our year's work. I feel verse is more
than any prose can be, the apex of the flame, the point of
the diamond. The well-to-do people in our stalls sometimes say, 'We have had enough of verse plays, give us
comedy.' But the people in the sixpenny places do not
say they get too much of them, and the players themselves
work in them with delight. I wrote to Mr. Yeats when
'On Baile's Strand' was being rehearsed: 'Just back from
rehearsal, and cheered up on the whole. . . . As to
'Baile's Strand', it will be splendid. . . . The only
real blot at present is the song, and it is very bad.
The three women repeat it together. Their voices don't

go together. One gets nervous listening for the separate
ones. No one knows how you wish it done. Every one
thinks the words ought to be heard. I got Miss Allgood to
speak it alone, and that was beautiful, and we thought if
it didn't delay the action too long, she might speak it,
and at the end she and the others might sing or hum some
lines of it to a definite tune. If you can quite decide
what should be done, you can send direction, but if you
are doubtful, I almost think you must come over. You
mustn't risk spoiling the piece. It is quite beautiful.
W. Fay most enthusiastic, says you are a wonderful man,
and keeps repeating lines. He says, "There is nothing
like that being written in London."'

43. CORNELIUS WEYGANDT ON YEATS'S SYMBOLISM

1913

This passage is taken from Cornelius Weygandt, 'Irish
Plays and Playwrights' (1913).
    Cornelius Weygandt (1871-1957) also wrote 'The Red
Hills', 'Tuesdays at Ten' and 'Wissahickon Hills'. Two
of his books have been reprinted: 'Red Hills: A Record
of Good Days Outdoors and In, with Things Pennsylvania
Dutch' (1929) and 'Philadelphia Folks: Ways and Insti-
tutions in and about the Quaker City' (1938).

. . . There have been constant to it [his verse] since
'The Wanderings of Oisin' all the qualities that distinguish it to-day, — its eloquence, its symbols that
open up unending vistas through mysteries, its eeriness
as of the bewildering light of late sunset over gray-green
Irish bog and lake and mountain, its lonely figures as
great in their simplicity as those of Homer, its plain
statement of high passion that breaks free of all that is
occult and surprises with its clarity where so much is
dim with dream. First one and then another of these
qualities has most interested him. He has written in
explanation of patriotic verse, of folk-verse, of verse
based on the old court romances, of symbolism, of Rosicrucianism, of essences, of speaking to the psaltery, of
dramatic art; and all the time he has practised poetry,
the interest of the time resulting in now the greater
emphasis on one quality in the poetry, and now on another

quality. It would be superfluous to do more than point
out most of these qualities, but a word on his use of
symbols may help to a fuller understanding of his poetry.
I am very sure that I read wrong meanings from many of
these symbols, as one who has not the password must. They
require definite knowledge of magical tradition, and of
the poet's interpretation of Celtic tradition, for a full
understanding. As the years go by, I think their exact
meaning will escape more and more readers until they will
have no more significance than Spenser's allegories have
to us. Only to the student deeply read in Elizabethan
politics do these mean to-day what must have been patent
to the inner circle at Elizabeth's court. Those symbols
of Mr. Yeats that we may understand intuitively, as we
may 'The white owl in the belfry sits', other generations
also may understand, but hardly those that have meanings
known only to a coterie. But we may read Spenser with
enjoyment even if all the inner allegories are missed,
and so, too, many read Mr. Yeats to-day, neglectful of
the images of a formal symbolism.

I do not know that I get more enjoyment from the poetry
of the verses entitled 'The Valley of the Black Pig'
because Mr. Yeats's note tells us that it is the scene
of Ireland's *Götterdämmerung,* though it is an unquestionable gratification to the puzzle interest I have with my
kind, and I would at times be more comfortable were I
sure that the 'Master of the Still Stars and of the Flaming
Door' was he who keeps the gates of the Other World, the
real world we shall enter when death sets us free of that
dream men call life. Mr. Yeats is not so kind to the men
'in the highway' as the old Irish bards. When they wrote
enigmas they were apt to explain them fully, as does the
poet of 'The Wooing of Emer' when he tells what was meant
by the cryptic questions and answers exchanged between
that princess and Cuchulain. When the symbolism is of
the kind found in 'Death's Summons' of Thomas Nashe,
which of all poems Mr. Yeats quotes oftenest, all cultivated men may understand —

> Brightness falls from the air;
> Queens have died young and fair;
> Dust hath closed Helen's eye.

The difference between the symbol Helen and each one of
the several symbols Mr. Yeats employs in 'The Valley of
the Black Pig' is the difference between a symbol universally recognized throughout the world and a symbol
recognized by one people; but there is the further difference that one is intimately associated with the thing

symbolized, is the name of a woman the context tells us
is a queen and beautiful, and the other is only the scene
of a battle that symbolizes the ending of the world. It
is more natural to use a beautiful woman as a symbol of
all beauty than to use a black boar that shall root up all
the light and life of the world as a symbol of the ending
of the world. But neither of these is a symbol that would
be understood intuitively, as the rose used as a symbol
of beauty or the wind as a symbol of instability. Sometimes Mr. Yeats's symbols are very remote, but perhaps
they were remote in the old stories in which he found
them. The details in

> the phantom hound
> All pearly white, save one red ear,

and 'the hornless deer' which it chases, seem arbitrary.
The hound, it is true, is known of all men as the pursuer,
and the deer as the pursued; but does this knowledge
suggest immediately 'the desire of the man which is for
the woman, and the desire of the woman which is for the
desire of the man'? Mr. Yeats does not, as I take it,
expect all his symbols to be understood so definitely as
this hound and deer, which, of course, are not only
symbols, but figures from the tapestry of fairyland. It
is often enough, perhaps, that we understand emotionally,
as in 'Kubla Khan' or 'The Owl'. From some of his writing
it would appear he believed many symbols to be of very
definite meaning and to be understood by generation upon
generation. In the note to 'The Valley of the Black Pig'
he writes, 'Once a symbol has possessed the imagination
of large numbers of men, it becomes, as I believe, an
embodiment of disembodied powers, and repeats itself in
dreams and visions, age after age.'
    This is but another phase of Mr. Yeats's belief that
when a poem stirs us as by magic, it is a real magic has
been at work. The words have loosened the seals that the
flesh has fastened upon the universal memory which
is subconscious in all of us, until that memory possesses
us and we are one with all that has been since the beginning of time, and may in such moments live over all that
has been lived. He thinks that in such moments the poet's
magic brings before us the past and the unseen as the
past and the unseen were brought before our pagan ancestors by the magical rites of their priests. . . .

44.   EZRA POUND ON YEATS'S CHANGE OF MANNER

1914

A review of the Cuala Press edition of 'Responsibilities'
(1914), by Ezra Pound, 'Poetry' (Chicago), 11 May 1914.
This is also included in 'Literary Essays of Ezra Pound'
(1954; 1960) ed. T.S. Eliot.

Ezra Loomis Pound (1885-1973), American poet, critic,
translator and composer, was born at Hailey, Idaho and
educated at the University of Pennsylvania and Hamilton
College, Clinton.   fter brief visits to Europe he came to
London in 1908, and met Yeats, who described him as a
'queer creature' to Lady Gregory in October 1909, but
later as 'a solitary volcano' to Mrs Shakespear and her
daughter Dorothy (whom Pound married in 1914).   He was
friendly with John Butler Yeats in New York in 1910 and
1911, editing a selection of his letters in 1917.   By
1913 Yeats wrote to Lady Gregory to say he found Pound a
stimulating critic: 'To talk over a poem with him is
like getting you to put a sentence in dialect.   All
becomes clear and natural.'   In November of that year he
acted as Yeats's secretary for three months when they
shared a cottage in Sussex.   He and his wife spent the
winters of 1914-15 and 1915-16 there.   Yeats's wife,
Georgiana Hyde Lees, whom he married in 1917, was a friend
of Dorothy Pound, and the friendship continued over the
years.   In 1928 the Yeatses saw the Pounds at Rapallo,
Yeats using Wyndham Lewis's phrase 'a revolutionary
simpleton' about Pound, and explaining 'A Vision' in
'A Packet for Ezra Pound' (1929).   They met again in 1929
when Yeats took a flat at Rapallo.   It was at Rapallo in
1930 that he made his famous comment on Yeats's 'The
King of the Great Clock Tower': 'putrid'.
     Pound co-edited 'Blast' (1914-15), was London Editor
of the 'Little Review' (1917-19), and became Paris Editor
for 'The Dial' in 1920.   He spent much time and energy
helping other writers, notably Joyce, Eliot and Hemingway.
His own 'Cantos' appeared first in 1933 and culmiated in
the 'Pisan Cantos' (1949).   'The Translations of Ezra
Pound' appeared in 1933, his 'Literary Essays' in 1934.
The story of Pound's wartime broadcasting, his indictment
for treason and incarceration for over twelve years in a
lunatic asylum and release, and his final days in Italy have
been well described by Noel Stock, 'The Life of Ezra
Pound' (1970).

I live, so far as possible, among that more intelligently
active segment of the race which is concerned with today
and tomorrow;   and, in consequence of this, whenever I
mention Mr Yeats I am apt to be assailed with questions:
'Will Mr Yeats do anything more?', 'Is Yeats in the movement?', 'How *can* the chap go on writing this sort of
thing?'

And to these inquiries I can only say that Mr Yeats'
vitality is quite unimpaired, and that I dare say he'll do
a good deal; and that up to date no one has shown any
disposition to supersede him as the best poet in England,
or any likelihood of doing so for some time; and that after
all Mr Yeats has brought a new music upon the harp, and
that one man seldom leads two movements to triumph, and
that it is quite enough that he should have brought in
the sound of keening and the skirl of the Irish ballads,
and driven out the sentimental cadence with memories of
'The County of Mayo' and 'The Coolun'; and that the production of good poetry is a very slow matter, and that, as
touching the greatest of dead poets, many of them could
easily have left that *magnam partem,* which keeps them with
us, upon a single quire of foolscap or at most upon two;
and that there is no need for a poet to repair each
morning of his life to the Piazza dei Signori to turn a
new sort of somersault; and that Mr Yeats is so assuredly
an immortal that there is no need for him to recast his
style to suit our winds of doctrine; and that, all these
things being so, there is nevertheless a manifestly new
note in his later work that they might do worse than
attend to.

'Is Mr Yeats an Imagiste?' No, Mr Yeats is a symbolist, but he has written *des Images* as have many good
poets before him; so that is nothing against him, and
he has nothing against them (*les Imagistes*), at least so
far as I know — except what he calls 'their devil's
metres'.

He has written *des Images* in such poems as 'Braseal
and the Fisherman'; beginning, 'Though you hide in the
ebb and flow of the pale tide when the moon has set'; and
he has driven out the inversion and written with prose
directness in such lyrics as, 'I heard the old men say
everything alters'; and these things are not subject to
a changing of the fashions. What I mean by the new note —
you could hardly call it a change of style — was apparent
four years ago in his 'No Second Troy', beginning, 'Why
should I blame her,' and ending —

[With] Beauty like a tightened bow, a kind
That is not natural in any [misprint for 'an'] age like this,

Being high and solitary and most stern?
Why, what could she have done being what she is?
Was there another Troy for her to burn?

I am not sure that it becomes apparent in partial
quotation, but with the appearance of 'The Green Helmet
and Other Poems' one felt that the minor note — I
use the word strictly in the musical sense — had gone or
was going out of his poetry; that he was at such a cross
roads as we find in

Voi che intendendo il terzo ciel movete.(1)

And since that time one has felt his work becoming
gaunter, seeking greater hardness of outline. I do not
say that this is demonstrable by any particular passage.
'Romantic Ireland's Dead and Gone' is no better than Red
Hanrahan's song about Ireland, but it is harder. Mr Yeats
appears to have seen with the outer eye in 'To a Child
Dancing on the Shore' (the first poem, not the one printed
in this issue). The hardness can perhaps be more easily
noted in 'The Magi'.
Such poems as 'When Helen Lived' and 'The Realists'
serve at least to show that the tongue has not lost its
cunning. On the other hand, it is impossible to take any
interest in a poem like 'The Two Kings' — one might as
well read the 'Idylls' of another. 'The Grey Rock' is,
I admit, obscure, but it outweighs this by a curious
nobility, a nobility which is, to me at least, the very
core of Mr Yeats' production, the constant element of his
writing.
In support of my prediction, or of my theories, regarding
his change of manner, real or intended, we have at least
two pronouncements of the poet himself, the first in 'A
Coat', and the second, less formal, in the speech made
at the Blunt presentation. The verses, 'A Coat', should
satisfy those who have complained of Mr Yeats' four and
forty followers, that they would 'rather read their Yeats
in the original'. Mr Yeats had indicated the feeling
once before with

Tell me, do the wolf-dogs praise their fleas?

which is direct enough in all conscience, and free of the
'glamour'. I've not a word against the glamour as it
appears in Yeats' early poems, but we have had so many
other pseudo-glamours and glamourlets and mists and
fogs since the nineties that one is about ready for hard
light.

And this quality of hard light is precisely what one
finds in the beginning of his 'The Magi':

Now as at all times I can see in the mind's eye,
In their stiff, painted clothes, the pale unsatisfied ones
Appear and disappear in the blue depth of the sky
With all their ancient faces like rain-beaten stones,
And all their helms of silver hovering side by side.

Of course a passage like that, a passage of *imagisme*, may
occur in a poem not otherwise *imagiste*, in the same way
that a lyrical passage may occur in a narrative, or in
some poem not otherwise lyrical. There have always been
two sorts of poetry which are, for me at least, the most
'poetic'; they are firstly, the sort of poetry which
seems to be music just forcing itself into articulate
speech, and secondly, that sort of poetry which seems as
if sculpture or painting were just forced or forcing
itself into words. The gulf between evocation and description, in this latter case, is the unbridgeable difference between genius and talent. It is perhaps the
highest function of art that it should fill the mind with
a noble profusion of sounds and images, that it should
furnish the life of the mind with such accompaniment and
surrounding. At any rate Mr Yeats' work has done this in
the past and still continues to do so. The present
volume contains the new metrical version of 'The Hour
Glass', 'The Grey Rock', 'The Two Kings', and over thirty
new lyrics, some of which have appeared in these pages, or
appear in this issue. In the poems on the Irish gallery
we find this author certainly at *prise* with things as
they are and no longer romantically Celtic, so that a lot
of his admirers will be rather displeased with the book.
That is always a gain for a poet, for his admirers
nearly always want him to 'stay put', and they resent any
signs of stirring, of new curiosity or of intellectual
uneasiness. I have said that 'The Grey Rock' was obscure;
perhaps I should not have said so, but I think it demands
unusually close attention. It is as obscure, at least, as
'Sordello', but I can not close without registering my
admiration for it all the same.

Note

1 The quotation is the opening line of Dante's 'Con-
   vivium': 'You who fully understand [by having had
   the experience] move the third heaven [of Venus].'

45. GEORGE MOORE ON YEATS'S INFLUENCE ON OTHER WRITERS

1914

From a letter from Moore to Ernest Boyd, included in
Joseph Hone, 'The Life of George Moore (1936). Boyd
(1887-1946), the author of 'Ireland's Literary Renaissance' (1916), was one of the first critics to assess
the importance and trace the origins of the literary
revival. An Irishman, he served in the British consular
service until 1919. He spent the rest of his life in
New York.
     For note on George Moore see pp. 172-3.

If it had not been for Yeats, Synge would never have
written anything but board-school English. Yeats trained
him through dialect, he dunged the roots, and when this
was done, Synge grew and strengthened, and putting forth
new shoots he wearied of the dialect and began writing in
English. The Wicklow and Kerry sketches are full of
good things; but it was Yeats who taught him to write;
and it was Yeats who taught Lady Gregory. She had not
written anything at all until she met Yeats. . . . He
seems to me to be a very fine schoolmaster. I owe something to him myself and I take this opportunity of acknow-
ledging it. He seems to me to have devised a method of
testing, or to speak more plainly, he has devised literary
formulæ not unlike the pictorical formulæ that Walter
Sickert invented and that have enabled countless ladies
to paint gable ends barely distinguishable from the
'master's'. Walter Sickert teaches how 'values' may be
dispensed with — how vermilion worked into ultra-marine
will produce a symbolic sky that harmonises with the brown
roofs in which Indian red is used largely. Ultramarine
broken with vermilion is not a sky but it stands for a
sky. The drawing can also be dispensed with by means of
a photograph which is enlarged and squared out upon the
canvas. 'Quality' is necessary in oil painting, and it
cannot be dispensed with, but a sort of wholesale 'quality'
is arrived at by a series of little dabs; and these dabs
protect the artist from linoleum. The London County
Council pays for all this teaching and every year a tribe
of little female Sickerts go forth all over Europe bringing back endless gable ends. It seems to me that Yeats
can do very much the same in literature as Sickert does
in painting.

46. FORREST REID ON YEATS'S PROSE

1915

These comments are from Forrest Reid, 'W.B. Yeats: A Critical Study' (1915), the first book-length study of Yeats's work.

Forrest Reid (1876-1947), novelist and essayist, born in Belfast and educated at Cambridge, wrote 'W.B. Yeats: A Critical Study' (1915). His best known novel is 'Peter Waring' (1937); he wrote two volumes of autobiography, 'Apostate' (1926) and 'Private Road' (1940).

[The] spirit of mysticism broods over every word of those strange and sometimes disquieting stories that are gathered together under the title of 'The Secret Rose'. The book is of a much more serious and subjective nature than 'The Celtic Twilight'. Mr. Yeats no longer speaks for others, but for himself, and the atmosphere of folklore and fireside tale is replaced by a darker atmosphere, through which flame wild unearthly lights that lure the soul to its destruction.

The stories of 'The Secret Rose' have all the profound inwardness of the poems. The substance is, indeed, very similar — that endless war of the spiritual upon the material world; and the prose as prose, has the same melodious and vocal quality as the verse has as verse. It seems made for reading aloud. To pass from verse to prose is still to remain in the same world. The beat of the rhythm becomes hardly less musical, but only a little less accentuated, moving in broader waves of sound. The prose that he writes in his book, and in the 'Ideas of Good and Evil', is elaborate in the extreme, yet it is not precious. It has none of the purple patches of an inferior and slightly vulgar artist like Wilde. Its peculiar, haunting quality depends in great measure on a richness of metaphor, on an imaginative use of words as if they were living things, with a power and a life that can be commanded as Prospero ruled his spirits. Mr. Yeats's vocabulary is not large. Unlike another modern master of style, Mr. Henry James, he never uses either 'dictionary words' — such a word as 'interlocutor', for example — which exist only for the printed page, or words taken from the slang of the day; and the elaboration of his style has not yet begun to make it difficult. There are few very long, no involved, sentences. His style, unlike the later style of Meredith or James, does not make use of any

eccentricity of pattern or construction. It is without
lightness and buoyancy, the exquisite delicacy of touch
which distinguishes the prose of an Anatole France (whose
style is certainly the most perfect of all styles), but
it is admirably suited to his matter, his purpose. The
rhythm is monotonous and full, with, at its best, a dark
magnificence of colour, that is like the colour on the
wings of a moth; while the imagery he uses is largely the
same as that employed in the poems. In 'Rosa Alchemica'
the rich, sombre beat of the rhythm is more pronounced
than in any other of the stories, and this, too, is
appropriate, for our senses must be drugged almost to the
verge of trance before the occult world begins to glow and
flame against the blackness beyond.
I know of no writer since Jeremy Taylor who gets so
splendid and rich a harmony as Mr. Yeats gets in certain
passages of 'The Secret Rose':

> Some believed that he found his eternal abode among
> the demons, and some that he dwelt henceforth with
> the dark and dreadful goddesses, who sit all night
> among the pools in the forest watching the constel-
> lations rising and setting in those desolate mirrors.(1)

> He was of those ascetics of passion who keep their
> hearts pure for love or for hatred as other men for
> God, for Mary and for the saints, and who, when the
> hour of their visitation arrives, come to the Divine
> Essence by the bitter tumult, the Garden of Gethse-
> mane, and the desolate Rood ordained for immortal
> passions in mortal hearts.(2)

Let me set beside these passages a passage from Taylor's
'Holy Dying':

> For so the wild foragers of Lybia, being spent with
> heat, and dissolved by the too fond kisses of the sun,
> do melt with their common fires, and die with faintness,
> and descend with motions slow and unable to the little
> brooks that descend from heaven in the wilderness; and
> when they drink, they return into the vigour of a new
> life, and contract strange marriages; and the lioness
> is courted by a panther, and she listens to his love,
> and conceives a monster that all men call unnatural,
> and the daughter of an equivocal passion and of a sudden
> refreshment.(3)

But at this point, as, alas! so frequently happens, I
am drawn up sharply by the contrast presented by existing

texts; all that I have said of his style applying more
essentially to the older text, and to those stories, 'Rosa
Alchemica', 'The Tables of the Law', 'The Adoration of the
Magi', which have been left unchanged; and to those other
stories, 'The Binding of the Hair', 'The Rose of Shadow',
'The Book of the Great Dhoul', which are no longer published with 'The Secret Rose'; and to the essays in 'Ideas
of Good and Evil'; rather than to the rewritten tales.
The 'Red Hanrahan' stories, which were originally included in 'The Secret Rose', have indeed been so thoroughly
revised that they quite cease to belong to this, his
middle period, and need not be considered here. What,
however, probably very few of his readers on our side of
the Atlantic know, is that there exists a revised edition
of the stories of 'The Secret Rose' proper. It has been
published in America, but never in this country. The
versions printed in the 'Collected Works', and in the
English new editions of 'The Secret Rose', follow the
original text. In the American revised edition, 'Rosa
Alchemica' remains practically unchanged, but all the other
tales have been subjected to a greater or lesser amount
of revision, though the alterations affect the form alone.
I have found it more difficult to choose between the two
texts here than anywhere else in Mr. Yeats's work. The
rewriting of the stories has undoubtedly improved them in
some respects, while it has weakened them in others. The
simplifying of the proper names is a distinct, though it
may appear a slight, advantage; but, in the simplification
of the style, too frequently the rhythm has been sacrificed,
simplicity sometimes being obtained by the very drastic
method of cutting off the latter half of a sentence, or
by lifting a clause out of the middle of a sentence while
leaving the beginning and the end untouched. The prose —
how could it be otherwise? — no longer flows with quite
the old mellifluous sleepy melody. It is balder, more
broken, not only for the reason I have given, but because
many of those wonderful images which Mr. Yeats, like
Taylor, scattered with so lavish a hand up and down his
pages, have been removed. It is difficult to see why a
beautiful simile like this should be struck out from
the story of 'Costello the Proud':

> He rode . . . on over the Mountains of the Ox, and
> down towards the sea; his eyes almost continually
> resting upon the moon which glimmered in the dimness
> like a great white rose hung on the lattice of some
> boundless and phantasmal world.(4)

The sentence now ends with the word 'moon', and this
is a fair enough example of Mr. Yeats's method of revision, of the kind of loss the stories have suffered.
What they have gained, on the other hand, is a certain
rapidity of movement. They have shaken off much of their
solemnity, and those to whom in the first instance the
story was the main thing, will have little quarrel with
their present form. For myself, I cling obstinately to
the older text, while admitting that familiarity with it
may to some extent be responsible for this preference.
What is doubtless the important thing, the thing to rejoice
in, is that both texts are extremely beautiful.
    'The Secret Rose' is a collection of Irish tales,
some founded upon old legends, some invented by their
author, but all in the highest degree individual and personal. For in his telling of the older tales beautiful
meanings creep in, glimmering behind the words and actions
of his heroes like a flame shining through a curtain; and
there is little difference between these heroes and the
brotherhood of the Alchemical Rose, or Owen Aherne of
'The Tables of the Law', a little book which may be considered in conjunction with 'The Secret Rose'. They are
consumed, most of them, by a devouring spiritual fever,
and spend their lives in a restless search for a knowledge that has been forbidden to man, for impossible
experiences, or ineffable loves, that hurry them to the
abyss, to death, to evil, to the outer darkness of horror.
And none of them finds peace. Even he who renounces the
strange unholy rites of the temple of the Alchemical Rose,
and turns to fasting and to prayer, still hears the voices
of the lawless demons in his ears; and, while he clasps
the rosary to his breast, their fatal beauty floats
before his eyes, colouring his dreams, and filling his
days and nights with the terror of insecurity. Yet
in these perishing lives we seem to see Mr. Yeats's own
ideal reflected, though it may be in a dark mirror, and
are confronted by a sort of paradox. For the very doctrines he preaches, not here only but in nearly all his
work, seem in his stories to lead inevitably to disaster.
Or is it only to the breaking of the body? Can they, in
the end, cry with Cleopatra, 'I am fire and air; my
other elements I give to baser life'?(5) How far it is
all but a form of imaginative beauty, but a material for
art to work upon, I think it would be impossible for the
poet himself to tell us, though we may try to find a
solution of this question when we come to deal with his
philosophy.
    Not one of these stories is without beauty, whether it
be the sombre, lyrical beauty of 'Costello the Proud', or

the glittering, jewelled beauty of 'Rosa Alchemica', or
the softer, sunlit beauty of 'The Heart of the Spring'.
It is difficult to indicate the particular quality which
gives them at once their originality and their charm without somewhat lengthy quotation; but it seems to me to
arise from a metaphysical subtlety of thought, in conjunction with an intensely vivid pictorial presentation.
The actual scene is always evoked with a clearness as of
something conjured up before our physical vision. The
detail is never submerged in the general, but on the other
hand it is never there for its own sake, and is used with
the utmost economy, each stroke being put in for a
definite purpose, and by the hand of an artist who can
make sacrifices that we sometimes almost regret.

Notes

1 'The Secret Rose', p. 24.
2 Ibid., p. 111.
3 'Holy Dying', chap. v, sec. 8.
4 'The Secret Rose', p. 118.
5 'Antony and Cleopatra', V, ii, 288-9.

47. JOSEPH HONE ON YEATS'S VIEW OF BLAKE AND NIETZSCHE

1915

These comments are taken from J.M. Hone, 'The Poet in
Contemporary Ireland' (1915).
    Joseph Maunsel Hone (1882-1959), an Irishman, was
educated at the University of Cambridge, and became a
director of the publishing house of Maunsel & Company.
He was a biographer, whose 'The Life of George Moore'
(1936), 'The Life of Henry Tonks' (1939), and 'W.B. Yeats
1865-1939' (1942) are all excellent in their provision of
detailed information based on first-hand knowledge of
the subjects. Hone wrote on Swift, Berkeley and Thomas
Davis, as well as compiling a brief 'Dictionary of Irish
Writers'. His edition of J.B. Yeats, 'Letters to his son
W.B. Yeats and others 1869-1922' (1944) contains an
excellent memoir outlining the painter's life.

As a rule Mr. Yeats' prose cannot be read in fragments.
He will not treat a subject from the point of view of
general interest, and he makes no concession to casual
readers. To those who are impatient of personal idio-
syncracies Mr. Yeats' prose is a far severer test than
his poetry.

The essays on Blake, 'William Blake and the Imagination', and 'William Blake and his Illustrations' are
studies of an æsthetic faith that knew no bounds. Swinburne and other commentators had shrugged their shoulders
in despair at certain passages in Blake's 'prophetic'
writings. Mr. Yeats and Mr. Ellis in bringing out their
three-volume edition of the mystical poet made their attitude clear by the defiant quotation from Hamlet: 'Bring
me to the test, and I the matter will reword, which madness would gambol from.'

In the 'Ideas of Good and Evil' Mr. Yeats did not
attempt to rebuild the ruined house of Blake's mythology,
but confined himself to interpreting Blake's ruling
ideas, so nearly akin to his own. When Blake wrote of
vision and objected to allegory, he anticipated the
modern symbolists, and when he 'announced the religion
of art, of which no man dreamed in the world about him,
he understood what he was saying more perfectly than the
thousands of subtle spirits who have received the baptism.
When Blake cried out that everything that lives is holy,
and that nothing is unholy except things that do not
live — lethargies, cruelties, timidities, and that
denial of the imagination which is the root they
grow from in old times; when he asserted that passions
because most living are most holy . . . and man shall
enter into eternity borne upon their wings'; when he
opposed one 'philosophy' which is 'worldly', and established for the ordering of the body, and the 'fallen will',
a philosophy made by 'men of action', to another which is
'divine' and 'established for the peace of the imagination and the unfallen will', and, even when obeyed with
too literal a reverence can make men sin against no higher
principality than prudence'; when he 'called the followers
of the first philosophy pagans, no matter by what name
they knew themselves, because the pagans, as he understood the word pagan, believe more in the outward life,
in what he called war, princedom, and victory than in
the secret life of the spirit; and the followers of the
second philosophy Christians, because only those whose
sympathies have been enlarged and instructed by art and
poetry can obey the Christian command of unlimited for-
giveness'; — whom did he resemble if not the most
celebrated of modern philosophers, Frederick Nietzsche?

Mr. Yeats, was, I think, the first observer to find a
likeness between Blake, the Christian mystic, and a
thinker whose boast was that he had parted with the last
vestiges of transcendental belief.   'One is reminded'
(by Blake), he wrote, 'of Shelley . . . but still more of
Nietzsche,   whose thought flows always, though with an
even more violent current, in the bed Blake's thought has
worn'.   There is truth in the apparent paradox, and though
Mr. Yeats has not developed the theme, or referred elsewhere in his printed works even to the name of Nietzsche,
we have a hint here of certain changes about to come into
his own thought and work.   They were not revolutionary
changes, for though Mr. Yeats may cross rivers, he is one
of those who leave the bridges behind him intact, and the
chief of these bridges has been William Blake.

48.   THOMAS MacDONAGH ON YEATS'S GAELIC AND ANGLO-IRISH
USAGE

1916

This comment comes from Thomas MacDonagh, 'Literature in
Ireland, Studies Irish and Anglo-Irish' (1916).
   Thomas MacDonagh (1878-1916), poet, playwright and
critic, was a graduate of University College, Dublin,
where he became a lecturer;   he helped Padraic Pearse
to found St Enda's College, and was one of the signatories
of the Proclamation of the Irish Republic in 1916.   He was
shot after the 1916 Rising.   His play 'When the Dawn is
Come' was produced in 1908;   his 'Poetical Works' and
'Literature in Ireland, Studies Irish and Anglo-Irish'
were published in 1916.   Yeats alluded to him as Pearse's
'helper and friend', and described his thought as 'daring
and sweet' in 'Easter 1916'.

. . . Irish has been regarded as fair game for almost
any treatment.   A language with an elaborate grammatical
system, with delicate phonetic changes to indicate changes
of sense, is treated as if it had no system and as if it
could suffer nothing from barbarous mispronunciation.   If
the ignorance or carelessness of the writers who use it
so mattered only to the Irish language, the Irish language
could well afford to let it pass: it would affect it no
more than does the fact that now, half a century after the
time of O'Donovan and O'Curry, the Royal Irish Academy has

for its president a man so grossly ignorant of the language
that he is incapable of pronouncing the names of the books
in its library. But to the new generation of Irish readers
who know the two languages, many otherwise fine books are
spoiled or at least made a little foolish and ridiculous
by the grotesque disguises under which Irish words appear
in them. And this ignorance of the authors is like that
of the old sham philologists. A modern writer who made
an image from the derivation *lucus a non lucendo,*(1) who
referred to a wood as 'that which the Roman named from
darkness', would be doomed to unintelligible obscurity or
to absurdity. What then of Mr. W.B. Yeats who confesses
that when he wrote the greater number of his poems, he
had hardly considered seriously the question of the pronunciation of Irish words, who copied at times somebody's
perhaps fanciful spelling, and at times the ancient spelling as he found it in some literal translation, pronouncing the words always as they were spelt? That is,
pronouncing the words as if they were English. Mr. Yeats,
however, is quite honest in the matter. He would not, he
says, have defended his system at any time. If ever he
learns the old pronunciation of the proper names he has
used he will revise the poems. He is content to affirm
that he has not treated his Irish names as badly as the
mediæval writers of the stories of King Arthur treated
their Welsh names. But Mr. Yeats is not living in the
Middle Ages. Whether we regret it or not, we cannot
ignore the knowledge of those to whom we communicate our
works. In the lines:

> The host is riding from Knocknarea
> And over the grave of Clooth-na-Bare

nothing is gained, surely, by that extraordinary per-
version of the Irish name of the Old Woman of Beare,
Cailleach na Béara. The word *clooth* is not Irish; it
has no meaning. Even for others than Irish scholars the
right word would have served as well. And — if it be not
too Philistine a question — would not:

> And over the grave of the Hag of Beare,

have been better in this poem in English? In his revision
of 'The Wind Among the Reeds', Mr. Yeats has changed
Irish words into English, 'colleens' into 'women'. Lately
he has set his face against all this use of Irish words
and Irish stories; but he cannot undo his work. Let me
admit, before passing from him, that his constant use of
the form used before him by Ferguson, has fixed a new

word in the English language. *Danaan* is impossible in
Irish, which has *Dannan* (in *Tuatha De Dannan*) accented
on the first syllable. Mr. Yeats has, as he claims, the
excuse that the words he uses are of the old language.

Two examples from different stages of Anglo-Irish
literature will illustrate this tendency of our poetry.
The reading of the first we know from its whimsical tune:

> The town of Passage
> Is both wide and spacious
> And situated upon the sea,
> 'Tis neat and decent
> And quite contagious
> To go to Cork on a bright summer's day.

The last line of this verse is always sung in such a
way as to be almost spoken with rapid and even enunciation of all the syllables. The effect may be got by
reading the line with little or no stress on the words,
'go', 'Cork', 'bright', 'day'. In the song this effect
adds to the drollery of the words and the tune.

Very different is the well-known 'Lake Isle of Inishfree'
of W.B. Yeats.

[Quotes the poem, see 'Collected Poems', p. 44.]

In the line

> And I shall have some peace there, for peace comes
>   dropping slow,

it would be as wrong to mark, as heavily stressed, the
syllables 'I', 'some', 'there', as to scan it:

> And I | shall have | some peace | there . . .

as some English metrists might read it.

Take the line frankly as if it were a line of prose,
only with that beauty of vibration in the voice that
goes with the fine grave words of poetry. (It is impossible to mark the reading by punctuation or the like.)
Read it so, and you will understand the true quality of
this mode in Anglo-Irish poetry. It is wrong to scan this
verse, to cut off the syllables according to the measure
of a rhythm that rises and falls sharply and regularly.
Even with some marks to indicate that though unstressed,
a syllable is slow and long:

> And I shall have some p$\overline{\text{ea}}$ce there

the scansion is wrong. There is a recurrence in this
verse, but it is not the recurrence of the foot. I have
been able to take half a line to illustrate my meaning.
The first three lines of each stanza have a cesura in the
middle. I believe that that is the only division to make
in them, and that as a rule open to exception. In
general the second part of the line has a more obvious
recurrence of stress than the first, as:

      . . . of clay and wattles made.

Of course, as in all musical verse, there are contrasts,
exceptional first half lines that run with a regular
scannible rhythm, and exceptional second half lines like:

      . . . with low sounds on the shore.

This general movement, changing from a slow beat to an
easy rise and fall, happens constantly. I sometimes
think it expresses, whether in accentual verse or quantitative, the mingled emotion of unrest and pleasure that
comes with the break up of winter, with the south wind,
with the thought of the shortness of life and the need to
make haste to explore its good and simple joys — the
desire to leave the unlovely, mingled with a vivid conception of the land of heart's desire. It is the rhythm
of that fourth ode of Horace's first book. In the long
lines the four solemn bars, dactyls or spondees, are
followed by three light trochaic feet; and the short
lines, after the unrest of one syllable taken alone,
continue the movement:

      Solvitur acris hiemps grata vice veris et Favoni,
         trahuntque siccas machinæ carinas;
      ac neque iam stabulis gaudet pecus aut arator igni,
         nec prata canis albicant pruinis.(2)

The system is:

$$- \underline{\underset{\smile\smile}{}} \,\Big|\, - \underline{\underset{\smile\smile}{}} \,\Big|\, - \underline{\underset{\smile\smile}{}} \,\Big|\, - \underset{\smile\smile}{} \,\Big|\, - \underset{\smile}{} \,\Big|\, - \,\smile \,\Big|\, - \,\smile$$

$$\underline{\underset{\smile}{}} \,\Big|\, - \,\smile \,\Big|\, - \underline{\underset{\smile}{}} \,\Big|\, - \,\smile \,\Big|\, \underset{\underline{\smile}}{\smile} \,\Big|$$

It would be possible to treat the second line taken above
as iambic, but, considering the dactyls and trochees in the
first, it must be read as trochaic.
      It may be objected that owing to the utter difference
between accentual and quantitative verse, it is wrong to
apply these remarks to the two. I have elsewhere drawn
attention to the difference, for instance, between the

dactyl (quantitative) and the triple falling accentual measure of 'merrily'. This difference does not affect the similarity between the contrast of first half line and the second half line in both 'Inishfree' and this ode of Horace's. For the rest, a rhythm may be produced not only in music, in noise, in words and in other things heard, but in things seen and things felt. And not merely the words of verse express the emotion. In true poetry, as the meaning of the words comes second to their rhythm, and the rhythm expresses an emotion, it will be found that the words mean the expression of this emotion as well as the rhythm.

To read correctly Anglo-Irish poetry one must follow either Irish music or Anglo-Irish prose speech. My earliest conscious observation, and notation, so to call it, of this speech was in Cork city about ten years ago. In the house at which I stayed there were two children. One was continually looking for the other and calling all over the house. 'Is Maudie in the garden?' Jimmy would chant in a most wonderfully sweet voice, lingering on every syllable. Later I was delighted to note, when living in a little mountain lodge above Rathfarnham in County Dublin, that a blackbird which came to wake me every morning in the spring sang just the notes of Jimmy's chant — a blackbird with a Cork accent. One need not think that Jimmy was guilty of that sin of childhood never committed by the Anglo-Saxon Saint Guthlac, who 'did not imitate the various cries of birds'. Jimmy was not peculiar in his accent.

In such instances song and speech are not far apart; and Mr. Yeats, for all his want of musical ear, owes, I believe, this peculiar musical quality of his early verse to that Irish chant which at once saves Irish speech from too definite a stress and from an utterance too monotonous and harsh.

At the same time one must not deduce from all this that Gaelic verse is a footless thing of sinuous windings. Nothing could be more clearly marked than most Gaelic measures. And these too have had their effect on Anglo-Irish verse. To do Mr. Yeats justice, since I have quoted from him to show the serpent, I shall now quote, to show the eagle, the Musicians' song from 'Deirdre':

> FIRST MUSICIAN.

> 'Why is it,' Queen Edain said,
>   'If I do but climb the stair
> To the tower overhead,
>   When the winds are calling there,

Or the gannets calling out,
  In waste places of the sky,
There's so much to think about,
  That I cry, that I cry?'

        SECOND MUSICIAN.

But her goodman answered her:
  'Love would be a thing of naught
Had not all his limbs a stir
  Born out of immoderate thought;
Were he anything by half,
  Were his measure running dry.
Lovers, if they may not laugh,
  Have to cry, have to cry.'

        THREE MUSICIANS *(together)*.

But is Edain worth a song
  Now the hunt begins anew?
Praise the beautiful and strong;
  Praise the redness of the yew;
Praise the blossoming apple-stem.
  But our silence had been wise.
What is all our praise to them,
  That have one another's eyes?

The poem is really syllabic, seven syllables to the line,
like one species of Debhidhe poems in Irish — without, of
course, the arrangements of assonance. I do not know if
Mr. Yeats is aware of this syllabic measure; but again
and again in his poems and in the poems of many contemporary Irishmen I find this tendency. Indeed I should say
that the effects of our more deliberate Irish speech on
our verse are these two: first, a prose intonation, not
monotonous, being saved by the natural rise and fall of
the voice, a remnant of the ancient pitch — a quality, as
it were, of chanted speech — and second, a tendency to
give, in certain poems, generally of short riming lines,
almost equal stress value to all the syllables, a tendency to make the line the metrical unit. From the first
of these effects comes a more reasoning, not to say conversational tone, which disallows inversions, quaint
words and turns of speech. Not conforming in our way of
verse to the regular English stress rhythm we have not the
same necessity as the English poets to depart from the
natural word order. We have not to manufacture a rhythm
in that unnatural way. . . .

Note

1 A grove from its not giving light.
2 'Sharp winter is breaking up at the pleasing change to
  spring and the Zephyr, and the tackles are hauling
  dry hulls to the sea. No longer now does the flock
  delight in the fold nor the ploughman in his fireside,
  nor are the meadows white with hoar frost' (Horace,
  'Odes', I, iv).

49.   DARRELL FIGGIS ON A.E., YEATS AND THE LITERARY CON-
VENTION OF THE CELTIC TWILIGHT

1916

These comments are from Darrell Figgis, 'AE: A Study
of a Man & Nation' (1916).
    Darrell Figgis (1882-1925) was born in Dublin, spent
his childhood in India, and then worked in London. He
joined the Irish Volunteers, and joined Erskine Childers
and others in the Howth gun-running incident. He drew
up the constitution of the Irish Free State, and represented County Dublin in the Dàil. He committed suicide in
1925. He wrote under the pseudonym 'Michael Ireland'. His
work included a play 'Queen Tara', poetry and fiction.

. . . For some years W.B. Yeats had lived in London,
engaging in literary journalism. Already he had established himself as a poet of very rare beauty; and his
choice of subject, a certain atmosphere laden with mist
that wrapped the beauty (for which he himself 'coined
the funny nickname' 'The Celtic Twilight'), and the fact
that he travelled to and fro between Ireland and England,
caused the right ascription of his poetry to this country,
though it was framed in the English tongue. He and A.E.
were close friends. He knew the circle that met in Ely
Place. He even once for a short while joined the 'household' that lived in Ely Place, sharing the life of
spiritual experiment. Admiring A.E., as he was in turn
admired by A.E., and conceivably not being averse to
another text in his own special subject in London
journalism (for to succeed in London journalism, then as
now, was to make a special corner, with a certain allow-
ance for versatility), it came about therefore, with the

publication of 'Homeward, Songs by the Way', that he and
A.E. were hailed as the leaders of a queer thing known as
the Irish Literary Revival.   It was queer in this, that
neither of them knew Irish;   but they came at a time when
Englishmen had the inward conviction, hardly to be pub-
licly admitted, that their language had exhausted its
chances of beautiful usage, and was only of avail thence-
forward for journalism.   There was, to be sure, some
justification for this suspicion, for poets and prose-men
had become afraid of beauty;   they regarded fine writing
askance (and do yet);   they defied new forms that should
give greater suppleness, and had long and bitterly fought
the greatest living master of their language;   and it was
therefore not altogether a strange thing that the best
of its music at the time was won by those who used the
tongue as foreigners, these two Irishmen in verse and
Joseph Çonrad, a Pole, in prose.   Even the very great
poem that succeeded to them from the pen of an Englishman, 'The Dynasts', was cast into a verse that simulated
prose;   and was a feat of imagination rather in the greatness of its conception than in the making of its verses,
being fearful of the metaphor in which the elder poets
delighted, and tucking its legerdemain into stage-
directions.
     What was called the 'Irish Literary Revival' was
truly an English Literary Revival conducted by Irishmen.
In this W.B. Yeats had a conscious part;   but A.E. was
rather caught into it from his own separate world, that
was only literary in the sense that to convey spiritual
experiences from soul to soul was to put them into writing,
and that to convey them justly was to write them finely,
with a commensurate music and imagination.   W.B. Yeats'
apostleship was designed and deliberate, and the immediate
results were excellent though the work became spoiled in
time;   but A.E. was rather an unsuspecting apostle, a
little bewildered in the white light of publicity that
had so suddenly fallen about him in his emergence from the
household in Ely Place.   The difference may be seen in
their work.   In Yeats' poetry there is the same deliberate
disavowal of splendour that marked the work of his peers
in London;   and it arose from the same literary fear of
the past — a fear that if splendour were permitted it
would slip into the grooves cut by the prowess of the
elder poets.   Francis Thompson might have reassured them;
but the critics took good care that he should not by at
once likening him, in much dreary nonsense, to Crashaw, and
deriving him from the Restoration poets, till one wonders
if they had bothered to read Thompson's fiery page of
metaphors or had turned down Crashaw's taut music from its

slumber on the shelves.   However, for the most part the
critics were the poets and the poets were the critics,
and in this literary genealogy-hunting they showed their
own fear of the past.   In this fear Yeats shared;   but,
coming to it from the County Sligo and the city of Dublin,
and with the soul of a poet born not made, he made beautiful poetry where Ernest Dowson (save for one solitary cry
of passion) played with trivialities, where Lionel
Johnson wrought scholarly verse, and Robert Bridges
relied for the most part on bald statement.   He made a
convention as they did.   'The Celtic Twilight' was a
literary convention, conceived in London and conceivably
revolting from London;   for the old Gaelic poets were
not afraid of splendour, of metaphor, of big musics;
indeed, they rioted in them;   they splashed in them as a
swimmer glad of the sea, laughing back to the bright
laughter of the wave.   Yet conventions are a little thing,
for he made poetry;   and 'The Countess Cathleen', wrought
in those days, justifies nothing, and asks to justify
nothing, but itself, for Beauty needs no creed for its
making or its defence.

50.   A.E.   (GEORGE RUSSELL) ON YEATS'S MASK

1916

A letter of [?] 6 April 1916 to George Moore, included in
'Letters from AE' (1961), ed. Alan Denson.
     For note on George Russell see p. 130.

Your account of Yeats is very amusing, quite in the 'Ave
Vale' mood, but I don't think you have dealt seriously
with the psychology of Yeats.   He began about the time of
'The Wind among the Reeds' to do two things consciously,
one to create a 'style' in literature, the second to
create or rather to re-create W.B. Yeats in a style which
would harmonise with the literary style.   People call this
posing.   It is really putting on a mask, like his actors,
Greek or Japanese, a mask over life.   The actor must talk
to the emotion on the mask, which is a fixed emotion.
W.B.Y. began twenty years ago vigorously defending Wilde
against the charge of being a poseur.   He said it was
merely living artistically.

51.   ANONYMOUS COMMENT ON THE NATURE OF YEATS'S MIND

1918

An unsigned review of Yeats's 'Per Amica Silentia Lunae'
(1918), Reality by Moonlight, 'Times Literary Supplement',
7 February 1918.

In reading Mr. Yeats, whether it be his verse or his prose,
we have often felt, even at the height of enjoyment, an
unusual curiosity about the nature of his mind, as if it
were a strange fowl — a silver pheasant, perhaps —
among the familiar winged creatures of our own literature.
In this little book he tells us something about that mind
and whets our curiosity more than ever. His theme is
the fact that in their art, men often seem to be the
opposite of what they are in their conduct, the opposite,
perhaps, even of what they seem to themselves. He says
of himself:

> When I shut my door and I light the candle, I invite
> a Marmorean Muse, an art, where no thought or emotion
> has come to mind because another man has thought or
> felt something different, for now there must be no
> reaction, action only, and the world must move my
> heart but to the heart's discovery of self, and I begin
> to dream of eyelids that do not quiver before the
> bayonet; all my thoughts have ease and joy. I am
> all virtue and confidence.

And he speaks of a friend 'whose only fault is her habit
of harsh judgment with those who have not her sympathy,
and she has written comedies where the wickedest people
seem but bold children.' 'To me it seems that her ideal
of beauty is the compensating dream of a nature wearied
out by overmuch judgment.' He gives also the case of
Synge and of Dante; and he might give, above all, the
case of Correggio, who was timid, anxious, melancholy
and penurious, 'always at work for the family which depended upon him', yet who painted the Antiope, the Io,
and the Paradise of careless joy in the Dome at Parma.
His art was the compensating dream of a nature wearied
by overmuch self-denial. And that very word self-denial
lets us into the secret. In life we are always denying
ourselves; but in art, if it is art at all, there can
be no denial of self. Mr. Yeats thinks that the artist
finds another self, 'an anti-self or antithetical self,

who comes but to those who are no longer deceived, whose
passion is reality'. He says, truly, that the senti-
mentalists are practical men who believe in money, in
position, in a marriage bell, and whose understanding of
happiness is to be so busy, whether at work or at play,
that all is forgotten but the momentary aim. To them
happiness is merely pleasure. But true happiness is
always belief; and, when a man is filled with pleasure,
he has no room for belief — and so for happiness. The
practical man fears belief above all things lest it
should be unpleasant. But the dreamer, as he is called,
knows that without it pleasure is unconscious, discon-
nected, merely something that happens to him. Happiness
is conscious pleasure; and it becomes conscious only
when it becomes belief. The practical man sees pleasure
as a matter of circumstance; and his effort is to con-
trive the circumstances that will give him pleasure. He
is active in contriving them, but at the mercy of the
circumstances themselves. The dreamer knows that happiness comes of his own experience of circumstances, whatever they may be. He is concerned, therefore, with the
manner in which he experiences them, with the manner in
which he attains to belief through them.

But often in actual life he fails to experience them as
he would. His mind is all reaction, not action. Things
happen to him, people happen to him; and he is affected,
against his will and casually, by the opinions of others,
whether he accepts them or revolts against them with
violence. In either case it is not pure action of the
mind, but reaction; and what he desires is the simple
action of his own mind; 'the world must move his heart
but to the heart's discovery of self'. So, to Correggio,
himself was not the timidity, the penuriousness, the
anxiety of his actions; all of these were but a misex-
perience of tyrannous circumstance. The real self was
that which made of the universe the Paradise in the Dome,
or which sought passionate adventures in the forest;
and to this real self he attained in his art.

Mr. Yeats calls it the anti-self, as if it were something that had to be assumed, as if it were an imitation
of a really foreign character. 'Active virtue,' he
says, 'as distinguished from the passive acceptance of a
code, is theatrical, consciously dramatic, the wearing of
a mask.' But is it not rather the making of experience in
life itself, as the artist makes it in his art? Is it
not the finding of the real self in action, the refusal
of mere reaction? For what is art but the making of
experience? In that making the artist escapes from that
common self of his, which is at the mercy of things as

they happen to him, which he denies to be his real self,
to a self that makes things happen as he will. The
actual world happened to Correggio so that it made of
him not himself, but a common type, the anxious, saving,
father of a family, a domestic animal, in fact. And
what we all hate in ourselves or in others is the type,
the generic. That is what bores us because it is unreal;
because we can classify it, and one cannot classify
the real. You can classify bad pictures or poems, but
not good. Each one of those is itself; and so each
real human being is himself, and when we can classify human
beings, it is because they are not real to us, are not expressing themselves. So a man hates himself when he
seems a type to himself, a domestic or any other kind of
animal, a subject of natural history. And the artist, in
his art, escapes from this animal that he seems to himself
in his actual experience and makes an experience in which
he is no longer a type but himself. That true self
making its own experience is what Mr. Yeats calls the
anti-self. It is not a mask, but the throwing off of the
mask, the type, as all masks are, which actual experience
has imposed on him. Passive virtue, as Mr. Yeats says,
is the acceptance of a code, of the typical mask of the
virtuous man; active virtue is the throwing off of this
mask, as the artist throws it off in his art; it is the
self experiencing actual things as it would, and being
utterly itself in the process.

This real self, to which the artist attains in his
art, often seems an anti-self just because it is a rebellion against his defects of actual experience. It is the
compensating dream of a nature wearied out by falsity to
itself. But it is not merely a dream; it is an escape,
not from reality, but to it. For reality in us all is to
be found not in what we have been, but in what we are
trying to be; and this reality is revealed in art, a
reality not merely of the individual artist, but of all
mankind. The philosopher tells us what we are; the
moralist tells us what we ought to be; but the artist
tells us the real secret about ourselves, what we wish
to be. He removes the mask and shows us life, not as it
misexpresses itself under the tyranny of actual experience,
but as it would be in actual experience if it could. And
he tells us also this secret, if only we would listen to
it; that the victory for man consists not in making his
circumstances, but in making his experience of them. At
the end of his book Mr. Yeats says:

I think the common condition of our life — I know that
this is so with me — is irritation with public or

private persons or events. There is no great matter
in forgetfulness of servants, or the delays of trades-
men, but how forgive the ill-breeding of Carlyle or
the rhetoric of Swinburne, or that woman who murmurs
over the dinner table the opinion of her daily paper?

It is always the typical, the generic, that we hate in
people. That ill-breeding, that rhetoric, we can classify;
it belongs not to the individual Carlyle or Swinburne,
but to ill-bred or rhetorical types. And that woman is
not a woman, but a gramophone, a monstrous mechanical
potence of life. To escape from this condition of hatred
is to be aware of the self in others which is individual.
And so we try to escape to the self in ourselves. But
we cannot do that except through being aware of the self
in others. The type all round us, the gramophone, makes
us seem types and gramophones to ourselves. It robs us of
belief, and so of happiness; and that is why we hate it.
    But Mr. Yeats has other explanations of these facts;
and it is these that provoke us to curiosity about the
nature of his mind. At a certain point he passes away
into a moonlight world of his own where we cannot follow
him; a world of magic in which everything is not itself,
but means something else, as the moon gets its light not
from itself, but from the sun. For him things are symbols;
and one has need of magic to discover what they mean; and
this view of reality is not a pose with him or a game; it
is a habit of his mind. To him the universe, as we know
it, is all moonlit, and we never see the sun except by
means of some incantation. Now we know that we cannot
see reality as it is. We have, through ages, been used
to see it only as it is of use to us. It is not only that
we see a bit of it, but that we see that bit, as it were,
in an unreal relation to ourselves; we see it, uncon-
sciously, with the object of making use of it; and
reality itself does not exist so that we may make use of
it. But Mr. Yeats goes further, and for him it is not
reality at all that we see, but something that is but a
show of reality, something, not merely that we deceive ourselves about, but which deceives us.
    Into that 'Celtic twilight' we cannot follow him;
but we are the more curious about his habit of passing
into it because of his wisdom and subtlety before he has
passed into it. Where we can follow him, he is a guide
to be trusted; and then suddenly he leaves us in a cloud.
Suddenly he talks a language we do not understand; we
do not know whether it is a language at all or gibberish.
Is that but one instance of the eternal difficulty between
the Irishman and the Englishman? Always they seem to

understand each other up to a point; and then suddenly
there is an end of understanding. We do not know what
they mean or why they act; they seem to have a different
notion of the nature of reality. We believe that the
thing itself will show itself to us if we try hard enough;
for we believe that the thing itself is there. But they
seem to believe that it is not there at all, that all
reality wears masks, that in all things there is an anti-
self. And so we are bewildered by their curious coldness
behind all their surface passion, the coldness of moonlight and make-believe. And yet, with it all, Mr. Yeats
is a poet, as moonlight is beautiful. The beauty that
we see is the only thing common between his mind and ours.
There may not be sense to us, but there is music; and
in that there is a common language, though we cannot translate it into words. The Irishman speaks to us still only
in his art, but when shall we understand his actions?

The Wild Swans at Coole (1917; 1919)

52. MARIANNE MOORE ON YEATS'S TALKING HEART

1918

A review of 'The Wild Swans at Coole', by Marianne Moore,
'Poetry' (Chicago), October 1918.
   Marianne Moore (1887-1972) American poet, verse
translator and critic, is well represented in 'Poems'
(1921); 'Selected Poems' (1935); 'Collected Poems' (1951)
and 'Complete Poems' (1967). Her translation of Jean de La
Fontaine's 'Fables' was published in 1954.

For a poet with such a personality as Yeats, it seems
almost indecorous to bare it before us, in the midst of
our social, political and literary lives. Yeats makes
poetry out of the fact that he is a proud, sensitive,
cultivated Irishman. He hardly has to make poetry —
except the rhymes, which don't matter; he just lets his
heart talk, as in the poems about the dying lady.
   In a despondent mood, the poet, like some of the admirers of his earlier manner, longs for the leopards of
the moon, and complains of the harsh and timid sun. Whatever the lights are of 'Ego Dominus Tuus', 'Presences',
'Men Improve With Years', 'The Collarbone of a Hare',
'The Fisherman', 'The Hawk', they shine. The invading
hawk too, if not indecorous, is unfair, as unfair as some
similarly naive passages in the Bible are:

> What tumbling cloud did you cleave,
> Yellow-eyed hawk of the mind,
> Last evening? that I who had sat
> Dumbfounded before a knave,

Should give to my friend
A pretence of wit.

The weighing and measuring, the critical care evidently
spent on this thin volume, save the reviewer most of his
labor. If the longer poems seem to him, in spite of their
shrewdness and spells of passion, somewhat old-fashioned,
he is willing to bend to the opinion of the author of the
others. One can not but pay reverence to a poet who,
after having written poetry for many years, can still be
read with the same critical alertness that one would give
to the best of the younger poets. And if there is a
drooping line here and there, the author is too proud,
too able, and too conscientious to arouse misgivings
that he will ever bank on his reputation.
Here is Yeats in a very gentle mood:

[Quotes 'Presences', 'Collected Poems', p. 174.]

In 'Ego Dominus Tuus', the beautiful poetic dialogue
which appeared first in 'Poetry' and is reprinted here
and in his latest prose volume, the poet would have us
believe that great poems are the result of the poet's
'opposite' image — an expression of what the poet is not.
I think this opposite, and not his little every-day
thoughts and actions, *is* the poet; Dowson's drunkenness,
and Dante's lecherous life, are somewhat beside the mark,
as their effects on the poet's soul are mainly those of
health and sickness. They are ethical and civil sins,
but hardly poetic *sins*. Their scars on the poet are not
of .the same character as Turner's miserliness, or as
malice, envy, etc. But even these, when present, are
hardly more than masks of the poet's soul — perhaps hardly more than masks of any soul; it is in his poems that
the real soul can be seen. Nor is indulgence due, as
Yeats thinks, to the poet's desire to escape from himself; but rather, in so far as it is more than mere
exhaustion, due to his desire to find himself. It is the
disappointment with pleasure, and life's egging on.
'At the Hawk's Well', beautiful as it is as poetry and
as a poetic play, does not to me seem to be a Noh play
in the full sense of the term. The Noh play is based on
something nearer to the lives of the Japanese people than
a legend. A modern Noh play, to have a similar appeal,
would have to be based on something nearer the lives of
the Irish people. A play based on Davitt or Parnell
might come nearer the Japanese; or, perhaps best, a play
based on something in modern life treated mystically. But
it has the great merit of being the first attempt at a Noh
play in English.

53.   EASY, LAZY, MASTERLY FIDDLING TO AN OLD TUNE

1919

An unsigned review of 'The Wild Swans at Coole' (1919),
Tunes Old and New, 'Times Literary Supplement', 20
March 1919.

Mr. Yeats is like a fiddler taking down his old dust-
covered violin and lazily playing an old tune on it;   or
it seems an old tune at first that he is taking liberties
with.   How often one has heard it;   and yet, suddenly, it
is as new as the sunrise — or the moonlight.   Go on,
go on, we cry.   No one can play like that;   and then he
ceases carelessly, and puts the fiddle away, and talks of
other things.   All through this book he has the effect
of remembering old tunes and playing them over again and
making them new.   There are some players who possess you
with the sense of their mastery by the way they look over
the fiddle before they sound a note;   and he has this
power with the first words of a song.   But he likes best
to begin with the variation upon an old tune, the tune
being implicit in the variation and fading away out of it
into a last line, that seems to stop lazily as if it were
just capriciously tired of itself.   So in 'The Wild Swans
at Coole' we are tantalized;   he seems to love the mere
sound of his fiddle that only he can draw from it and then
to grow weary as if all tunes were played and stale.
       He himself is aware of this mood and even makes poetry
out of it:

       I am worn out with dreams;
       A weather-worn, marble triton
       Among the streams;
       And all day long I look
       Upon this lady's beauty
       As though I had found in book
       A pictured beauty,
       Pleased to have filled the eyes
       Or the discerning ears,
       Delighted to be but wise,
       For men improve with the years;
       And yet and yet
       Is this my dream, or the truth?
       O would that we had met
       When I had my burning youth;
       But I grow old among dreams,

> A weather-worn, marble triton
> Among the streams.

There he seems to be living on memories and to resent some
malignancy in the nature of things which has made of him
a work of art incompatible with artless reality.   It is
this sense of a malignance in things which makes Irish
writers themselves so often seem malicious.   It is in
Synge, and even in Mr. Shaw;   they whisper malice about
men because to them there is malice in reality.   In the
second verse of another poem Mr. Yeats says:

> I would find by the edge of that water
> The collar-bone of a hare
> Worn thin by the lapping of water,
> And pierce it through with a gimlet and stare
> At the old bitter world where they marry in churches,
> And laugh over the untroubled water
> At all who marry in churches,
> Through the white thin bone of a hare.

Irish writers do seem to look at reality through the
white thin bone of a hare, through some magic and isolating
medium of their own, which makes reality to them far off,
absurd, meaningless.   And the world of meaning which they
desire, for them is not.   Hence their malice.   They would
put us out of conceit with the reality that is at least
real to us, because they are out of conceit with it; and
Mr. Yeats wanders lost, unable to find that universe
which is yet real to him because he so much desires it.
   Through all his poetry there is this beauty, a little
malign, of desire that has not only failed to find its
object but despairs of finding it.   That is why he picks
up his fiddle so lazily and plays us such short, sweet
tantalizing tunes on it.   Stray things suggest to him
that state of being he can never find, like the wild
swans at Coole themselves:

> The trees are in their autumn beauty,
> The woodland paths are dry,
> Under the October twilight the water
> Mirrors a still sky;
> Upon the brimming water among the stones
> Are nine and fifty swans.

And the poem ends:

> But now they drift on the still water
> Mysterious, beautiful;

> Among what rushes will they build,
> By what lake's edge or pool
> Delight men's eyes when I awake some day
> To find they have flown away?

Because they are so beautiful they are to him visitants
and have the transitoriness of his own delight in them.
In his music he seems to inhabit a world that will tremble
away at a touch like reflections in still water. Even in
the beautiful poem in memory of Major Gregory, full of
concrete things and characters, he says:

> Always we'd have the new friend meet the old
> And we are hurt if either friend seem cold,
> And there is salt to lengthen out the smart
> In the affections of our heart,
> And quarrels are blown up upon that head;
> But not a friend that I would bring
> This night can set us quarrelling,
> For all that come into my mind are dead.

Friends too, and even friendships, are like the
wild swans at Coole. But how good the poem is; both
racy and passionate, like the poetry of Donne, and like
that, without imitation, in its very turns of speech.
While we analyse the poet's mind and seem to judge it, we
are fidgeting away from the real matter, the beauty of
his poetry. That justifies his mind and all its moods;
and in 'The Wild Swans at Coole' there are many beautiful
poems, some more homely than Mr. Yeats is wont to write.
Every one can enjoy the 'Two Songs of a Fool', or 'The
Cat and the Moon', which is a miracle of things exactly
said that seemed unsayable; and there is a truth most
delicately captured in 'An Irish airmen foresees his
death':

> I know that I shall meet my fate
> Somewhere among the clouds above;
> Those that I fight I do not hate,
> Those that I guard I do not love;
> My country is Kiltartan Cross
> My countrymen Kiltartan's poor,
> No likely end could bring them loss
> Or leave them happier than before.

There he fiddles to an old tune, but what a new surprise
of meaning he gets out of his easy, lazy, masterly
fiddling. And we can only listen and be grateful.

54. J. MIDDLETON MURRY REGARDS 'THE WILD SWANS AT COOLE'
AS YEATS'S SWAN SONG

1919

A review of 'The Wild Swans at Coole' (1919) by J. Middleton Murry, Mr Yeats's Swan Song, 'The Athenaeum', 4 April
1919. The text is taken from his 'Aspects of Literature'
(rev. ed., 1934).

John Middleton Murry (1889-1957), critic, biographer,
novelist and editor, educated at Brasenose College,
Oxford, subsequently worked for the 'Westminster Gazette',
the 'Nation' and the 'Times Literary Supplement'. He
married Katherine Mansfield in 1913. He edited 'The
Athenaeum', of which he was the last editor, and founded
'The Adelphi' in 1923. His best known critical study is
'Keats and Shakespeare' (1925); he wrote books on William
Blake and D.H. Lawrence, who was a friend of his, as well
as a 'Life of Jesus' (1926). (He was himself a humourless
Christian Marxist.) His life of Katherine Mansfield was
published in 1933.

In the preface to 'The Wild Swans at Coole', Mr. W.B.
Yeats speaks of 'the phantasmagoria through which alone I
can express my convictions about the world'. The challenge could hardly be more direct. At the threshold we
are confronted with a legend upon the door-post which
gives us the essential plan of all that we shall find in
the house if we enter in. There are, it is true, a few
things capable of common use, verses written in the seeming-
strong vernacular of literary Dublin, as it were a hospi-
table bench placed outside the door. They are indeed in-
side the house, but by accident or for temporary shelter.
They do not, as the phrase goes, belong to the scheme,
for they are direct transcriptions of the common reality,
whether found in the sensible world or the emotion of the
mind. They are, from Mr. Yeats's angle of vision (as
indeed from our own), essentially *vers d'occasion*.(1)
    The poet's high and passionate argument must be sought
elsewhere, and precisely in his expression of his convictions about the world. And here, on the poet's word
and the evidence of our search, we shall find phantasmagoria, ghostly symbols of a truth which cannot be otherwise conveyed, at least by Mr. Yeats. To this, in itself,
we make no demur. The poet, if he is a true poet, is
driven to approach the highest reality he can apprehend.
He cannot transcribe it simply because he does not possess

the necessary apparatus of knowledge, and because if he
did possess it his passion would flag. It is not often
that Spinoza can disengage himself to write as he does at
the beginning of the third book of Ethics, nor could
Lucretius often kindle so great a fire in his soul as
that which made his material incandescent in *Æneadum
genetrix*.(2) Therefore the poet turns to myth as a
foundation upon which he can explicate his imagination.
He may take his myth from legend or familiar history, or
he may create one for himself anew; but the function it
fulfils is always the same. It supplies the elements
with which he can build the structure of his parable,
upon which he can make it elaborate enough to convey the
multitudinous reactions of his soul to the world.

But between myths and phantasmagoria there is a great
gulf. The structural possibilities of the myth depend
upon its intelligibility. The child knows upon what
drama, played in what world, the curtain will rise when
he hears the trumpet-note: 'Of man's first disobedience
. . .' And, even when the poet turns from legend and
history to create his own myth, he must make one whose
validity is visible, if he is not to be condemned to
the sterility of a coterie. The lawless and fantastic
shapes of his own imagination need, even for their own
perfect embodiment, the discipline of the common perception. The phantoms of the individual brain, left to
their own waywardness, lose all solidity and become like
primary forms of life, instead of the penultimate forms
they should be. For the poet himself must move securely
among his visions; they must be not less certain and
steadfast than men are. To anchor them he needs intelligent myth. Nothing less than a supremely great genius
can save him if he ventures into the vast without a landmark visible to other eyes than his own. Blake had a
supremely great genius and was saved in part. The mascu-
line vigour of his passion gave stability to the figures
of his imagination. They are heroes because they are
made to speak like heroes. Even in Blake's most recondite
work there is always the moment when the clouds are parted
and we recognise the austere and awful countenances of
gods. The phantasmagoria of the dreamer have been mastered by the sheer creative will of the poet. Like Jacob,
he wrestled until the going down of the sun with his angel
and would not let him go.

The effort which such momentary victories demand is
almost superhuman; yet to possess the power to exert it
is the sole condition upon which a poet may plunge into
the world of phantasms. Mr. Yeats has too little of the
power to be able to vindicate himself completely from the

charge of idle dreaming. He knows the problem; perhaps he has also known the struggle. But the very terms
in which he suggests it to us subtly convey a sense of
impotence:

> Hands, do what you're bid;
> Bring the balloon of the mind
> That bellies and drags in the wind
> Into its narrow shed.

The languor and ineffectuality conveyed by the image
tell us clearly how the poet has failed in his larger
task; its exactness, its precise expression of an ineffectuality made conscious and condoned, bears equal
witness to the poet's artistic probity. He remains an
artist by determination, even though he returns down-
cast and defeated from the great quest of poetry. We
were inclined at first, seeing those four lines enthroned
in majestic isolation on a page, to find in them evidence of an untoward conceit. Subsequently they have
seemed to reveal a splendid honesty. Although it has
little mysterious and haunting beauty, 'The Wild Swans
at Coole' is indeed a swan song. It is eloquent of
final defeat; the following of a lonely path has ended in
the poet's sinking exhausted in a wilderness of grey. Not
even the regret is passionate; it is pitiful.

[Quotes 'Men Improve with the Years', 'Collected Poems',
p. 152; see text on pp. 213-14.]

It is pitiful because, even now in spite of all his
honesty, the poet mistakes the cause of his sorrow. He
is worn cut not with dreams, but with the vain effort to
master them and submit them to his own creative energy.
He has not subdued them nor built a new world from them;
he has merely followed them like will-o'-the-wisps away
from the world he knew. Now, possessing neither world,
he sits by the edge of a barren road that vanishes into
a no-man's land, where is no future and whence there is
no way back to the past.

> My country is Kiltartan Cross,
> My countrymen Kiltartan's poor;
> No likely end could bring them loss
> Or leave them happier than before.

It may be that Mr. Yeats has succumbed to the malady of
a nation. We do not know whether such things are possible;
we must consider him only as a poet whose creative vigour

has failed him when he had to make the highest demands
upon it. His sojourn in the world of the imagination,
far from enriching his vision, has made it infinitely
tenuous. Of this impoverishment, as of all else that has
overtaken him, he is agonisedly aware.

[Quotes second stanza of 'The Collar-Bone of a Hare',
'Collected Poems', p. 153; see text on p. 214.]

Nothing there remains of the old bitter world, which
for all its bitterness is a full world also; but nothing
remains of the sweet world of imagination. Mr. Yeats has
made the tragic mistake of thinking that to contemplate
it was sufficient. Had he been a great poet he would have
made it his own by forcing it into the fetters of speech.
By re-creating it, he would have made it permanent; he
would have built landmarks to guide him always back to
where the effort of his last discovery had ended. But
now there remains nothing but a handful of the symbols
with which he was content:

A Sphinx with woman breast and lion paw,
A Buddha, hand at rest,
Hand lifted up that blest;
And right between these two a girl at play.

There are no more than the dry bones in the valley of
Ezekiel, and, alas! there is no prophetic fervour to make
them live.
Whether Mr. Yeats, by some grim fatality, mistook his
phantasmagoria for the product of the creative imagination, or whether (as we prefer to believe) he made an
effort to discipline them to his poetic purpose and
failed, we cannot certainly say. Of this, however, we
are certain, that somehow, somewhere, there has been
disaster. He is empty, now. He has the apparatus of
enchantment, but no potency in his soul. He is forced to
fall back upon the artistic honesty which has never forsaken him. That it is an insufficient reserve let this
passage show:

For those that love the world serve it in action,
Grow rich, popular, and full of influence,
And should they paint or write still it is action:
The struggle of the fly in marmalade.
The rhetorician would deceive his neighbours,
The sentimentalist himself; while art
Is but a vision of reality. . . .

Mr. Yeats is neither rhetorician nor sentimentalist.   He
is by structure and impulse an artist indeed.   But
structure and impulse are not enough.   Passionate apprehension must be added to them.   Because this is lacking
in Mr. Yeats those lines, concerned though they are with
things he holds most dear, are prose and not poetry.

Notes

1 Occasional verses.
2 Mother of the children of Aeneas (the opening of
  Lucretius, 'De Rerum Natura').

55.   ROBERT LYND ON YEATS CREATING THE TASTE BY WHICH HE IS ENJOYED

1919

A comment on Mr. W.B. Yeats in Robert Lynd, 'Old and New
Masters' (1919).
     Robert Wilson Lynd (1879-1949), essayist and critic,
was born in Belfast.   For many years he was literary
editor of the 'News Chronicle':   he contributed to the
'New Statesman' under the pseudonym Y.Y.   A strong Irish
nationalist, he wrote 'Home Life in Ireland' (1909) and
'Ireland a Nation' (1919).   His essays are reminiscent
of Lamb in their personal and witty style.   'The Art of
Letters' (1920), 'The Blue Lion' (1923), 'Dr Johnson and
Company' (1927) and 'In Defence of Pink' (1939) are
good examples of his work.

It is distinctly surprising to find Mr. Yeats compared
to Milton and Jeremy Taylor, and Mr. Forrest Reid, who
makes the comparison, does not ask us to apply it at all
points.   There is a remoteness about Milton's genius,
however, an austere and rarefied beauty, to which Mr.
Reid discovers certain likenesses in the work of Mr. Yeats.
Mr. Yeats is certainly a little remote.   He is so remote
that some people regard his work with mixed feelings, as
a rather uncanny thing.   The reason may partly be that Mr.
Yeats is not a singer in the ordinary tradition of poets.
His poems are incantations rather than songs.   They seem
to call for an order of priests and priestesses to chant

them. There are one or two of his early poems, like
'Down by the Sally Garden', that might conceivably be
sung at a fair or even at a ballad-concert. But, as Mr.
Yeats has grown older, he has become more and more
determinedly the magician in his robes. Even in his prose
he does not lay aside his robes; it is written in the
tones of the sanctuary: it is prose for worshippers.
To such an extent is this so that many who do not realize
that Mr. Yeats is a great artist cannot read much of his
prose without convincing themselves that he is a great
humbug. It is easy to understand how readers accustomed
to the rationalism of the end of the century refused to
take seriously a poet who wrote 'spooky' explanations of
his poems, such as Mr. Yeats wrote in his notes to 'The
Wind Among the Reeds', the most entirely good of his books.
Consider, for example, the note which he wrote on that
charming if somewhat perplexing poem, 'The Jester'. 'I
dreamed,' writes Mr. Yeats:

> I dreamed this story exactly as I have written it, and
> dreamed another long dream after it, trying to make
> out its meaning, and whether I was to write it in
> prose or verse. The first dream was more a vision
> than a dream, for it was beautiful and coherent, and
> gave me a sense of illumination and exaltation that
> one gets from visions, while the second dream was
> confused and meaningless. The poem has always meant
> a great deal to me, though, as is the way with sym-
> bolic poems, it has not always meant quite the same
> thing. Blake would have said, 'The authors are in
> eternity'; and I am quite sure they can only be
> questioned in dreams.

Why, even those of us who count Mr. Yeats one of the
immortals while he is still alive, are inclined to shy at
a claim at once so solemn and so irrational as this. It
reads almost like a confession of witchcraft.
     Luckily, Mr. Yeats's commerce with dreams and fairies
and other spirits has not all been of this evidential
and disputable kind. His confessions do not convince us
of his magical experiences, but his poems do. Here we
have the true narrative of fairyland, the initiation into
other-worldly beauty. Here we have the magician crying
out against

> All things uncomely and broken, all things worn out
>   and old,

and attempting to invoke a new — or an old — and
more beautiful world into being.

> The wrong of unshapely things is a wrong too great to
>   be told,

he cries, and over against the unshapely earth he sets
up the 'happy townland' of which he sings in one of his
later and most lovely poems. It would not be easy to
write a prose paraphrase of 'The Happy Townland', but
who is there who can permanently resist the spell of
this poem, especially of the first verse and its refrain
[quotes them]? . . .

Mr. Yeats, in his desire for this other world of colour
and music, is no scorner of the everyday earth. His early
poems especially, as Mr. Reid points out, give evidence
of a wondering observation of Nature almost Wordsworthian.
In 'The Stolen Child', which tells of a human child that
is enticed away by the fairies, the magic of the earth
the child is leaving is the means by which Mr. Yeats
suggests to us the magic of the world into which it is
going, as in the last verse of the poem:

> Away with us he's going,
> The solemn eyed:
> He'll hear no more the lowing
> Of the calves on the warm hillside;
> Or the kettle on the hob
> Sing peace into his breast,
> Or see the brown mice bob
> Round and round the oatmeal-chest.
>
> *For he comes, the human child,*
> *To the waters and the wild*
> *With a faery, hand in hand,*
> *From a world more full of weeping than he can*
>   *understand.*

There is no painting here, no adjective-work. But no
painting or adjectives could better suggest all that the
world and the loss of the world mean to an imaginative
child than this brief collection of simple things. To
read 'The Stolen Child' is to realize both that Mr. Yeats
brought a new and delicate music into literature and that
his genius had its birth in a sense of the beauty of
common things. Even when in his early poems the adjectives seem to be chosen with the too delicate care of an
artist, as when he notes how

> in autumnal solitudes
> Arise the leopard-coloured trees,

his observation of the world about him is but proved
the more conclusively. The trees in autumn *are* leopard-
coloured, though a poet cannot say so without becoming
dangerously ornamental.

What I have written so far, however, might convey the
impression that in Mr. Yeats's poetry we have a child's
rather than a man's vision at work. One might even
gather that he was a passionless singer with his head in
the moon. This is exactly the misunderstanding which has
led many people to think of him as a minor poet.

The truth is Mr. Yeats is too original and, as it
were, secret a poet to capture all at once the imagination
that has already fixed the outlines of its kingdom amid
the masterpieces of literature. His is a genius outside
the landmarks. There is no prototype in Shelley or Keats,
any more than there is in Shakespeare, for such a poem as
that which was at first called 'Breasal the Fisherman',
but is now called simply 'The Fisherman':

> Although you hide in the ebb and flow
> Of the pale tide when the moon has set,
> The people of coming days will know
> About the casting out of my net,
> And how you have leaped times out of mind
> Over the little silver cords,
> And think that you were hard and unkind,
> And blame you with many bitter words.

There, in music as simple as a fable of Æsop, Mr. Yeats
has figured the pride of genius and the passion of
defeated love in words that are beautiful in themselves,
but trebly beautiful in their significances.

Beautifully new, again, is the poem beginning, 'I
wander by the edge', which expresses the desolation of
love as it is expressed in few modern poems:

> I wander by the edge
> Of this desolate lake
> Where wind cries in the sedge:
> *Until the axle break*
> *That keeps the stars in their round*
> *And hands hurl in the deep*
> *The banners of East and West*
> *And the girdle of light is unbound,*
> *Your breast will not lie by the breast*
> *Of your beloved in sleep.*

Rhythms like these did not exist in the English
language until Mr. Yeats invented them, and their very
novelty concealed for a time the passion that is immortal in them. It is by now a threadbare saying of
Wordsworth that every great artist has himself to
create the taste by which he is enjoyed, but it is worth
quoting once more because it is especially relevant to
a discussion of the genius of Mr. Yeats. What previous
artist, for example, had created the taste which would be
prepared to respond imaginatively to such a revelation of
a lover's triumph in the nonpareil beauty of his mistress
as we have in the poem that ends:

I cried in my dream, *'O women bid the young men lay*
Their heads on your knees, and drown their eyes with your hair,
Or remembering hers they will find no other face fair
Till all the valleys of the world have been withered away.

One may doubt at times whether Mr. Yeats does not too
consciously show himself an artist of the æsthetic school
in some of his epithets, such as 'cloud-pale' and 'dream-
dimmed'. His too frequent repetition of similar epithets
makes woman stand out of his poems at times like a decoration, as in the pictures of Rossetti and Burne-Jones,
rather than in the vehement beauty of life. It is as if
the passion in his verse were again and again entangled
in the devices of art. If we take his love-poems as a
whole, however, the passion in them is at once vehement
and beautiful.
   The world has not yet sufficiently realized how deep
is the passion that has given shape to Mr. Yeats's
verse. 'The Wind Among the Reeds' is a book of love-
poetry quite unlike all other books of love-poetry. It
utters the same moods of triumph in the beloved's beauty,
of despair, of desire, of boastfulness of the poet's immortality, that we find in the love-poetry of other ages.
But here are new images, almost a new language. Sometimes
we have an image which fills the mind like the image in
some little Chinese lyric, as in the poem 'He Reproves
the Curlew':

   O, curlew, cry no more in the air,
   Or only to the waters of the West;
   Because your crying brings to my mind
   Passion-dimmed eyes and long heavy hair
   That was shaken out over my breast;
   There is enough evil in the crying of the wind.

This passion of loss, this sense of the beloved as
of something secret and far and scarcely to be attained,
like the Holy Grail, is the dominant theme of the poems,
even in 'The Song of Wandering Aengus', that poem of almost
playful beauty, which tells of the 'little silver trout'
that became

> a glimmering girl
> With apple blossom in her hair,
> Who called me by my name and ran
> And faded through the brightening air.

What a sense of long pursuit, of a life's quest, we
get in the exquisite last verse — a verse which must be
among the best-known of Mr. Yeats's writing after 'The
Lake Isle of Innisfree' and 'Had I the Heaven's Embroidered Cloths':

> Though I am old with wandering
> Through hollow lands and hilly lands,
> I will find out where she has gone,
> And kiss her lips and take her hands;
> And walk among long dappled grass,
> And pluck till time and times are done
> The silver apples of the moon,
> The golden apples of the sun.

This is the magic of fairyland again. It seems a
little distant from human passions. It is a wonderful
example, however, of Mr. Yeats's genius for transforming
passion into elfin dreams. The emotion is at once deeper
and nearer human experience in the later poem called 'The
Folly of Being Comforted'. I have known readers who professed to find this poem obscure. To me it seems a
miracle of phrasing and portraiture. I know no better
example of the nobleness of Mr. Yeats's verse and his
incomparable music.

The Cutting of an Agate (1919)

56. FINE PROSE FOR A LITTLE CLAN

1919

An unsigned review of 'The Cutting of an Agate' (1919)
[by Walter de la Mare], A Lapidary, 'Times Literary
Supplement', 1 May 1919. The contents of this edition
of 'The Cutting of an Agate' differ from the earlier New
York Macmillan edition of 1912, 'Thoughts on Lady Gregory's
translations', being replaced in the later edition by 'Certain Noble Plays of Japan'.

Walter de la Mare (1873-1956) became a clerk with the
Standard Oil Company at the age of eighteen. Eighteen
years later he received a Civil List pension and spent
the rest of his life writing. He published fifty volumes
of poetry, short stories, novels and essays. His 'Collected Poems' were published in 1942; his 'Collected Rhymes
and Verses' in 1944; and his 'Collected Stories for
Children' in 1947. He published his early work under
the pseudonym of Walter Ramal. He was made a Companion
of Honour at seventy-five, and given the Order of Merit in
his eightieth year. His work blended dream and reality,
gaiety and the grotesque, and a delight in natural beauty.

With one exception the papers collected in this volume
were written before 1912. The time which we have lived
through since then is not measurable in years. A nightmare has intervened, and we have to piece together a
thread violently broken. In 1914 we could have quietly
woven these essays into our literary life. Now we follow
Mr. Yeats's intricate and rarified prose hesitantly, doubtful to what extent the atmosphere of dream which hangs

between our mind and his is the dissipating of that nightmare or an emanation for which he alone is responsible.
Here is our 'agate', shaped by a skilled hand, and of an
elaborate design. The thoughts expressed are unquestionably
'important', the principles closely applicable to 'life
itself'; but never were we less certain what precisely
we mean by life, and where exactly, to put it crudely,
'we are'.

    This is one passing perplexity. But Mr. Yeats was
never in approach an easy writer. He is an ineffable,
rather than an affable expounder. Englishmen he has ever
seemed to regard as dunces who must be 'larned', to be
insensitive and incorrigible barbarians. He talks, in
tone if not in substance, well over our heads, not as a
stranger within the gates (an observer easily indulged
or explained away), but as might a rabbi visiting the
children of a step-brother who has removed into, and
prospered in, Philistia — 'finished and finite clods,
untroubled by a spark'. That little matters if so be we
'welcome each rebuff', each sting that bids — not go,
but stand or kneel. England assuredly would be none the
poorer, spiritually, if heed were paid to his counsels,
even to his anathemas; though it is doubtful if Ireland
would be any the friendlier, or Mr. Yeats the less remote.

    That the stars are in his sky it needs no other instru-
ment than our sand-blind eyes to discover. That he seems
deliberately to attempt to hide his face amid them is
regrettable, for our own sake. When Mr. Yeats says of
Synge, 'He could not have loved had he not hated, nor
honoured had he not scorned,' the accents are so much his
own that we do not apply to Synge an aphorism extremely
dubious, unless we preclude from the odious and contemptible
all men, all nature, and all the gods. The faithful, however ardent in evangelization they may be, do not readily
welcome raw recruits into their ranks. To Mr. Yeats the
English, or, for that matter, the Irish, heretic is a mortal foe; not merely a child — of wrath, naughty and
wilful, it may be, but still a child — that will presently storm itself to sleep and be only its own virtue
in repose. Yet he realizes that though humanity may, like
an ass, break into a gallop under the whip, its heart is
not to be won by violence, nor its love and obedience by
the ecstatic abstraction of a carrot dangling unattain-
ably between its long ears.

    'Only that which does not teach, which does not cry
out, which does not persuade, which does not condescend,
which does not explain is irresistible.' This is a net of
narrow mesh, though it excludes the 'strong silent man',
a blind, deaf, tongueless beggar, a briar rose, and the

soul of goodness.   But Mr. Yeats does not follow his own
counsel.   What man does?   He teaches — and castigates
the scholar for vaunting himself that he can learn.   He
cries out, always in deliberate and dignified, often in
beautiful and moving, at times in a kind of echoing and
phantasmal English — a St. John who prefers to remain in
the wilderness since his own imagination is its verdant and
serene, if occasionally sand-vexed, oasis.   He seldom fully
explains, preferring to leave his symbols symbolical and
his runes esoteric.   And so long as he condescends he may
convince, but he will never persuade.   His book is full of
wise things, of thoughts and conclusions not pieced together, not deduced, not distilled out of mere knowledge,
but which have sprung, as if by the magic of nature, out
of experience, out of solitary reverie, out of enthusiasm and self-sacrifice.   He has given himself to his art,
and has.been rewarded.   But from a rare truth, the child
of intuition and life, he is apt to draw a dubious in-
ference, and perhaps in making his self-surrender he rather
too consciously appraised the gift.

He expresses his love of simplicity, yet in these
flowers from his secret garden there is always a tinge of
the exotic.   By an over-close cultivation he seems to
have 'made' them beautiful.   It is a delight to surprise
an author's happiness in some unforeseen felicity or beauty
that he has chanced on on his way.   But we seldom seem to
overhear Mr. Yeats exclaiming not merely 'Why did I say
this?' but 'Did *I* say this?'   Not that *naïveté* is a charm
that it is not dangerous to indulge too much.   But what
may be called his keywords sound at times like empty
shells, only remotely murmuring of the ocean of life —
his 'naked', 'passionate', 'exquisite', 'dangerous',
even his 'art', his 'artist', his perilous 'natural', his
still more perilous 'life'.   His loyalest epithets wear
the look of the conscript.   His 'Serpent' devours its tail
with a certain langour;   his 'Phœnix' plays the incendiary
with rather too manifest a faith in its ashes.   He has
ensnared his Beauty, and is a little weary in her possession.
He describes symptoms, yet fails to perceive that he is in
danger of the malady: — 'All art is sensuous, but when a
man puts only his contemplative nature and his more vague
desires into his art, the sensuous images through which
it speaks become broken, fleeting, and uncertain, or are
chosen for their distance from general experience, and all
grows unsubstantial and fantastic.'   The poet, too, who
attempts to distil the waters of his inspiration, to
enumerate the 'points' of his Pegasus, is bent on the most
treacherous of achievements.   He may criticize and appre-
ciate the work of other men justly and generously.

He may talk of technique to his heart's content.   But
to enter in and scrutinize his self's self, to 'fix' his
secret impulses, to master, and so circumscribe, his
own philosophy, may lead not merely to self-satisfaction
but to self-security — a giddy equilibrium.
   It is a lovely place where dwells Mr. Yeats's imagination, but now and then we find ourselves gracelessly
wishing he were not so skilled a cartographer.   His poems,
though we are liberty — a liberty he takes himself — to
choose between their kinds, rarely play him false as a
poet, never as an artist.   His prose, though it does
not exactly cheat him, insists on rather high stakes;   and
the cards are all 'on the table'.   Lovely, again, is his
Ireland, however wildly vexed with storms and the dim
Hyades, its Trinculos and Calibans.   Yet Prospero somehow
succeeds in screening his Miranda from the enamoured
glances of the hated stranger.   Many a reader of these
essays — at heart as sympathetic and remorseful as an
Englishman may humbly and tactfully confess himself to be —
will be tempted to give up Ireland in a sense which even
the most extreme of Sinn Feiners must self-respectingly
deplore.
   When Mr. Yeats forgets Jerusalem, forgets that he is
the only 'adventurer' of his admirable and remote 'discoveries', is no longer concerned with such confessions
as 'Without knowing it, I had come to care for nothing
but impersonal beauty,' or 'One part of me looked on,
mischievous and mocking,' and with such rather solemn
little warnings to trespassers as 'When Lionel Johnson
and Katharine Tynan (as she was then) and I myself began
to reform Irish poetry,' he becomes thrice as free, happy,
engrossing, and invigorating.   He praises nobly and with
the clearest discrimination.   Without sacrificing one iota
of his rare and natural distinction and reserve, he makes
Synge live in these praises.   When he refers to a fellow-
creature whom he loves or is quietly amused at, that fellow-
creature is ours.   He can so depict himself spinning Gaelic
fairy-tales to two delightful nuns that not even Max would
need to sharpen a line.   His three pages telling how, with
'certain followers of St. Martin' in Paris, he took the
Indian hemp, are a sheer joy — vaguely suggesting, queerly
enough, a masterpiece as remote from it as Defoe's 'Journal
of the Plague Year':

   The poet was wholly above himself, and presently he
   pointed to one of the street lamps, now brightening
   in the fading twilight, and cried at the top of his
   voice, 'Why do you look at me with your great eye?' . . .
   After a while a Martinist ran towards me with a piece of

paper, on which he had drawn a circle with a dot in it,
and pointing at it with his finger he cried out, 'God,
God!' Some immeasurable mystery had been revealed,
and his eyes shone; and at some time or other a lean
and shabby man, with rather a distinguished face, showed
me his horoscope and pointed with an ecstasy of melancholy at its evil aspects.

It was a light o'love who finally in the grey of dawn
dragged back these dreamers to stepmother Earth. Far
easier it is, of course, to be amused than to be edified.
But Mr. Yeats's edification, his aphorisms, chiselled,
recondite, and profound, on art and conduct, poetry,
religion, life, will convert only the converted. He
engraves his fine prose for a little clan. 'The peering
and peeping persons who are but hawkers of stolen goods',
the 'scientists', the readers of newspapers, whom he so
bitterly detests, if they open his book, will quickly shut
it up again and return to their husks and gewgaws. 'There
is something of an old wives' tale in fine literature.
The makers of it are like an old peasant telling stories.'
It is for such stories finely told that our minds and our
hearts long. We have been preached at for four years.
Not even a change of text can much comfort us, not even
a poet in the pulpit, not even if that poet be Mr.
Yeats — since from the open window of our old church
our eyes pine for the long historied woods and meadows, the green hills and valleys of his native paradise.

57. T.S. ELIOT ON YEATS'S UNKNOWN AND UNKNOWABLE WORLD

1919

A review by T.S. Eliot of 'The Cutting of an Agate' (1919),
A Foreign Mind, 'The Athenaeum', 4 July 1919.
   Thomas Stearns Eliot (1888-1965) poet, critic, dramatist, editor, and publisher, was born in St Louis, Mis-
souri, and educated at Harvard University; he attended
the Sorbonne, Marburg University and Oxford University.
His first volume of poetry 'Prufrock and Other Observations' (1917), published with Ezra Pound's help, was
followed by a volume of criticism, 'The Sacred Wood' (1920)
and 'The Waste Land' (1922), which brought him fame. Eliot
became a director of Faber and Gwyn (later Faber and Faber),
a British subject, and an Anglican.

Eliot's criticism of Yeats began with this review of 'The Cutting of an Agate'; in 'After Strange Gods' (1934) he praised Yeats's austerity, his arrival, against the greatest odds, at greatness. In 1935 (in 'The Criterion', which he edited with distinction from 1922 to 1939) he repeated the idea of Yeats's dropping unnecessary trappings, in this case 'the more superfluous stage properties of Ireland'. He regarded his influence on English poetry as 'great and beneficial'. The lecture Eliot gave at the Abbey Theatre in Dublin in 1940 did not disguise the fact that he found aspects of Yeats's thought and feeling unsympathetic, but assessed him for his importance in the history of his own time, his part in the consciousness of an age, while also praising his ability 'to remain always a contemporary'.

Mr Yeats, more than any of the subjects that have engaged his attention, is what engages our attention in this book. When we read it we are confirmed in the conviction — confirmed in a baffling and disturbing conviction — that its author, as much in his prose as in his verse, is not 'of this world' — *this* world, of course, being our visible planet with whatever our theology or myth may conceive as below or above it. And Mr Yeats's cosmos is not a French world, certainly. The difference between his world and ours is so complete as to seem almost a physiological variety, different nerves and senses. It is, therefore, allowable to imagine that the difference is not only personal, but national. If it were merely personal, it might be located, attached to ourselves as some eccentricity of our nature; but Mr Yeats is not an eccentric. He eludes that kind of relationship to the comprehensible. Everywhere the difference is slight, but thorough. For when we say 'not of this world', we do not point to another. Ghosts, mediums, leprechauns, sprites, are only a few of the elements in Mr Yeats's population, and in this volume they hardly appear at all. Mr Yeats cannot be localized as a *rond de cuir* of séances. When an Englishman explores the mysteries of the Cabala, one knows one's opinion of him, but Mr Yeats on any subject is a cause of bewilderment and distress. The sprites are not unacceptable, but Mr Yeats's daily world, the world which admits these monsters without astonishment, which views them more familiarly than Commercial Road views a Lascar — this is the unknown and unknowable. Mr Yeats's mind is a mind in some way independent of experience; and anything that occurs in that mind is of equal importance. It is a mind in which perception of fact, and feeling and

thinking are all a little different from ours. In Mr
Yeats's verse, in particular, the qualities can by no
means be defined as mere attenuations and faintnesses.
When it is compared with the work of any English bard of
apparently equivalent thinness, the result is that the
English work in question *is* thin; you can point to something which it ought to be and is not; but of Mr Yeats
you cannot say finally that he lacks feeling. He does
not pretend to more feeling than he has, perhaps he has a
great deal; it is not feeling that standards can measure as passionate or insipid.

58. C.L. WRENN ON YEATS'S THEORY AND PRACTICE

1920

Extract from an article by C.L. Wrenn, W.B. Yeats: A
Literary Study, 'Durham University Journal', 1920.
    Charles Leslie Wrenn (1895-1969) was a lecturer at
Durham University; Principal and Professor, Pachai
Yappa's College, Madras; Head of Department in the Uni-
versity of Dacca; Lecturer in the University of Leeds;
Lecturer then Professor in the University of London;
before becoming Professor at the University of Oxford.
He held many visiting Professorships. His publications
included 'Beowulf', a revision of Clark Hall's transla-
tion (1940), and 'The English Language' (1949).

His is the subjective view of art, as it is the subjective
view of nature; he will explain to us his emotions, his
imaginings, his visions; but he will not write a critique
ofthe work of another, such as Coleridge made for the
poetry of Wordsworth. 'I think my style is myself,' he
wrote in an essay in his 'Ideas of Good and Evil' in
1901;(1)· 'I might have found more of Ireland if I had
written in Irish, but I have found a little, and I have
found all myself.' And again in another essay in the
same collection he says with obvious satisfaction, 'This
age of criticism is about to pass, and an age of imagination, of emotion, of moods, of revelation, (is) about
to come in its place.' For he accepts to the full Blake's
doctrine that the Imagination is the eternal enemy and
rightly the ultimate conqueror of the Reason. Nevertheless, since he has written plays and critical essays, and

since these have indubitably a real value, though not the
value suggested by these titles, we should examine them
as such. But let us consider first and mainly his work as
a lyric poet, as the singer of his dreams.
Mysticism, the most comprehensive yet the most indefinite creed of the world, has certain definite attributes.
We all know what these are, though most of us would be
hard put to it to formulate them logically and clearly.
But we think we grasp what Shelley meant by

             that sustaining love,
   Which, through the web of being blindly wove
   By man and beast and earth and air and sea,
   Burns bright or dim as each are mirrors of
   The fire for which all thirst.

We think we understand the view of life Blake meant to
inculcate when he denied divinity to the moral law, as
the product of the devil of Reason, and gave it to the
human passions and to the Imagination. Mysticism connotes
too what may be described as some form of universal monism.
But as these illustrations show, our ideas on the subject
however clear to ourselves, tend always to be vague in
expression. Especially is this vagueness characteristic
of those mystics who have also been poetic artists: for
they have expressed themselves in products of the creative
imagination, with the added aid of allegory or symbolism.
Consider, for instance, two of the most outstanding and
significant English mystics in poetry, the originator of
the 'Vision of William concerning Piers Plowman' and
William Blake.
   Yeats is a mystic in the sense that his mental attitude towards the world partakes of those vague qualities
which we usually associate with the term mysticism —
concentrated introspection, pervasive subjectivity, intense
and visionary consciousness of definite spiritual presences from a world beyond, and monistic philosophising.
And vagueness is everywhere in his poetry. But we must
differentiate him from other poets of this mystic class
in two ways at least: first, in his essentially individual
qualities, and secondly, in his literary relations and antecedents.
   Yeats often dreams of the regeneration of mankind in a
new heaven and a new earth: but his is not the 'passion
for reforming the world' which Thomas Love Peacock smiled
at in Shelley: he is not the perfervid mystic. He has
'Immortal longings'; but they are rather for some 'Land
of heart's desire' — where fairy children dance in the

wind, and Lethe and the Lotus plant are ever near, and
Love and the Imagination are free and full — than for any
place of ascetic reformation or direct and conscious regeneration. So absorbed indeed is he in his dreaming
exemplifications of the doctrine of Art before all things,
that for him, even patriotism is 'an impure desire'.

And this brings us to another somewhat individualistic
quality which separates him from other mystics. He is of
Anglo-Irish origin — born of the land-owning middle
classes of Ireland descended from the English colonists.
But his antecedents on the maternal side were all pure
Irish-Celtic: and he himself assures us that a man of
genius inherits most from his mother. Moreover, his
childhood was passed in a country district of Sligo, where
the Celtic tradition had been but little touched by
exotic influences; and in later life he often went to
gather his favourite folklore sitting beside turf-fires
in Connaught. We are therefore rightly led to regard
Yeats' temperament as being to a great extent Celtic; and
it is certain that his mysticism is of the kind which
Matthew Arnold, in his essay on Celtic Literature, has
called Celtic. It is a mysticism founded on a basis of
pure emotion and an exquisite sensibility, expressing
itself in the melancholy of reverie or in happy dreams
which to more prosaic races seem insubstantial. 'The
Celt,' says Arnold, is 'so eager for emotion that he has
not patience for science': and again he describes him
as 'always ready to react against the despotism of fact'.
This is why Yeats is not generally a good critic: this
is why his volume of mainly topical poems, 'Responsibilities and other Poems', of 1917(2) is often petulant
and crudely violent in treating of contemporary happenings instead of the old Irish legends and folk-tales
which he has made so happily his own. Yeats has written
no more characteristic lines than these: and we vaguely
feel them to be Celtic in tone:

> And God stands winding his lonely horn,
> And time and the world are ever in flight:
> And love is less kind than the grey twilight,
> And hope is less dear than the dew of the morn.

It was Yeats' deliberate aim to form both the theory
and the practice of his art as the conscious disciple of
Blake: but, owing, it would seem, to his Celtic nature,
he cannot preach us into a better world with anything
like his Master's inspired and impassioned homilies, but
must needs persuade and allure us to some intangible
spiritual salvation in some ever-happy faery-world, by

the 'natural magic' of beautifully narrated dreams, and
'cloud-pale' musical symbols. Still, all his work, both
prose and verse, is filled with the memory and
the influence of Blake, and we do not need the beautiful
edition of their loved Master by Yeats and Edwin Ellis
to remind us that without Blake there could have been no
Yeats as we know him. The two essays devoted to Blake in
'Ideas of Good and Evil' are the clearest and most convincing interpretation of his complicated doctrine and
system of symbolism that England has yet seen: and Yeats
too has often striven to express himself in an elaborate
system of symbols, often indeed taking them directly from
his Master. For example, we recognise at once Blake's
doctrine of the eternal holiness of passion in these lines
from 'The Wind among the Reeds' in a poem entitled 'The
Blessed':

> O blessedness comes in the night and the day,
> And whither the wise heart knows:
> And one has seen in the redness of wine
> The incorruptible Rose.

Here the wine symbolises passion, and the Rose — as the
writer is at pains to explain in a note which is quite
superflouous to those who know Blake — is a symbol of
the highest spiritual ideal. We are again reminded of
Blake in the song in 'The Rose' addressed 'To Ireland in
the coming times':

> My rimes more than their riming tell
> Of the dim wisdoms old and deep
> That God gives unto men in sleep.
> For the elemental beings go
> About my table to and fro.

We remember that a fairy sat on Blake's table, and dictated
to him prophetic mysteries! But always when we think of
Blake's earlier and more obviously poetical lyrics — those
which bring us nearest to Yeats (for it is only in the very
recently published 'Per Amica Silentia Lunae' that Yeats
reaches the serene obscurity of the 'Prophetic Books') —
we feel that the poetic visions of his disciple

> Come from a more dream-heavy land,
> A more dream-heavy hour than this.

We see plainly that universal monism of outlook, which
is a generic character of mysticism, in the *Anima Mundi*
which Yeats describes in his latest volume referred to

above — of which he regards all our memories, dreams,
visions and imaginings as the emanations, and which he
believes can be evoked by symbols in the exercise of the
magic of the mediæval magicians. But here we notice at
once that the association of this universal Mind with the
ideas of men like Paracelsus and Cornelius Agrippa —
whom he reverently cites as authorities — is a thing peculiar among our poets to Yeats himself. And similarly,
his philosophy — applying this term loosely in the vulgar
manner to his views merely for the sake of convenience,
and with apology by Bertrand Russell — owes not a little
to Neo-Platonic varieties of mysticism like those of the
so-called 'Cambridge Platonists' of the seventeenth
century whom he has evidently been studying.

Like all artists of genius, Yeats is easily indivi-
dualised from the fashions of his age and from its prevailing temper: and he has so given his heart to his Art
that extra-literary things, such as politics or religious
controversy, seldom damage the purity of the artistic
significance of his work. Though keenly devoted to the
aspirations of that tendency to literary and journalistic
productivity in Ireland which its participators love to
call the 'Celtic Renaissance', or the 'Neo-Celtic Renaissance', and always sympathetic towards the nationalistic
activities of Young Ireland, he has yet clung with fair
consistency to his ambitions for a great Irish salvation
through art and the innate potential excellences of the
Celtic race. Even his friends could not make him serve
patriotic causes with his art in their merely political
bearings; and, not knowing the Irish language (on his own
confession he cannot even pronounce correctly the Celtic
names of the mythological characters of his poems), he has
never shown active enthusiasm for Sinn Fein or even the
Gaelic League. However, no man — not the greatest — can
be entirely independent of his age: and we have not to
look far for signs that Yeats shares, and always has
shared, in some measure, the tendencies — even the follies
in literature — of his co-ævals. More than once too his
difficulties in managing the new Irish theatre or the
obtuseness and prejudice of the public have drawn from him
a querulous, and therefore inartistic set of verses.

Though Yeats stands almost alone in our time in the great
literary qualities of the Celtic character, we occasionally
are reminded in his poems that he was born in 1865, and
that Lionel Johnson and Ernest Dowson were the friends of
his youth. He shared something of the life, and sometimes
felt the Acrasian charm of that pessimism in philosophy and
that almost cynical pursuit of Beauty for itself alone or of
Art for Art's sake only, which signalised the Æsthetic

'Decadents' of the '90's, of whom Yeats and Arthur Symons
are somewhat belated and lonely survivors. Aleel, the
wandering poet in 'The Countess Cathleen', clearly belongs
to that last luxuriant decade of the nineteenth century,
and he sells his soul to the Demon-merchants in words which
Yeats must often have heard from the lips of literary companions:

> Here, take my soul; for I am tired of it:
> I do not ask a price.

Seldom indeed does Yeats refer in his poetry to contemporary persons or events by name: but in the volume of
'Responsibilities and Other Poems' of 1917 already
alluded to, he directly addresses in 'The Grey Rock' those
glorious decadent Æsthetes of the '90's with whom he too
had 'flung roses riotously' in London:

> You had to face your ends when young—
> 'Twas wine or women or some curse—
> But never made a poorer song
> That you might have a heavier purse,
> Nor gave loud service to a cause
> That you might have a troop of friends.
> You kept the Muses' sterner laws,
> And unrepenting faced your ends:
> And therefore earned the right—and yet
> Dowson and Johnson most I praise—
> To troop with those the world's forgot,
> And copy their proud steady gaze.

And now that Yeats has well passed his fiftieth year, his
latest utterances on Art still seem to echo thoughts of
the literary coteries of the '90's. In his book published early in this present year he writes:

> I think that we who are poets and artists, not being
> permitted to shoot beyond the tangible, must go from
> desire to weariness and so to desire again, and live
> but for the moment when vision comes to our weariness
> like terrible lightning, in the humility of the
> brutes.

Something should here be said of Yeats' relations with
the symbolist movement in art: but this subject is very
technical and the few observations that seem really
necessary will be more conveniently made when we come to
comment on his critical writings. After all, it is simply
as a lyric poet that he is important to us.

>   For the crown of our life as it closes
>   Is darkness, the fruit thereof dust.

These words of Swinburne come home to the mind with an
added poignancy if we think how many poets who have lived
on past middle life into a tranquil and easy senescence
have lived also to versify long after the springs of pure
poetic inspiration had run dry. Wordsworth made an admirable Poet Laureate when he had long ceased to be a poet,
and Bridges has become a skilled technician delivering
formal lectures to the aspirants of Labour on 'The
necessity of Poetry'. Milton indeed is a great exception;
but with us he is almost unique in the power of his old
age: but even he could not recapture in later life the
spontaneity of expressed emotion which he had inherited
from the Elizabethan singers. Happy were Keats and Shelley
and Byron in their early graves in that they never lived
to versify passionless platitudes or to become the accepted
teachers of the orthodox. And this distinction which has
so often to be made between the earlier and the later work
of the poets must be applied perhaps a little to Yeats too.
For there are signs in his recent writings that the man
begins to influence too greatly the artist, that he has
been in the world so long that he finds it more and more
difficult to keep his work unspotted, and that like our
Poet Laureate he too tends to turn his art into a lesson-
book. His 'Responsibilities and Other Poems' published
last year is full of contemporary references and grumblings
and of rather carelessly expressed instructions: and in
his last volume he writes:

>   I think the common condition of our life is hatred — I
>   know that this is so with me — irritation with public
>   or private events or persons.

The reading public has accepted Yeats; and perhaps he,
like Tennyson, has written most of his best poetry before
being overtaken by the dangers of public recognition. It
is at least certain that among his most enthusiastic lovers
it is the lyrics of his earlier life that are most known
and read. When a man's theories of his art begin to crys-
tallise and he feels that he has a place of power in the
republic of letters and therefore begins to systematise
his thoughts, then it seems almost inevitable that his
writing should become less universal in its appeal: and
men have usually agreed since Aristotle's time that the
best poetry will always be the most universal in its appeal.
Man is an animal only potentially rational, and most of his
actions are not prompted by reasoning: he wants to hear

of the tranquilly recollected emotions of a poet set to
music, the songs and the dreams which have comforted and
expressed his youth, rather than what the poet would advise
him to do, or what is his theory of symbols or rhythms.
Hence it is that for ten readers of 'The Wind among the
Reeds', or 'The Rose', or 'In the Seven Woods', you will
find but three of 'Responsibilities and Other Poems', and
but one of 'Per Amica Silentia Lunae'. . . .
. . . Admirers of Yeats will certainly not wish for any
detailed criticism of 'Responsibilities and Other Poems';
they will rather pass it by on the other side with bewildered regret. For, beyond question, this is the volume
on which the poet is least to be congratulated. Its
poetry is in depressing contrast to the bulk of its pages,
and it is a disagreeable reminder that human littlenesses
must beset even the poet consecrated to his art.
It is, with some noble exceptions, a collection of topical verse, in which two main strata are visible throughout — either querulous commentary on contemporaneous
events in the world of art and letters which annoyed the
author, or pointed moralizing of those aphorisms which
constitute so much of the wisdom of all ages.
'I think that we who are poets and artists . . . must
go from desire to weariness, and so to desire again,' wrote
Yeats last year; but these verses would seem to suggest
a diagnosis of the writer's case rather as the weariness
which comes of impotent desire. For here we have the work
of a man tired with human ephemeral affairs, tired with
the hopeless fight for ideals. So that it is but natural,
therefore, that the thoughts of this volume — and almost
generally the language — are lacking in poetic feeling
and artistic restraint. There is too a touch of bitterness
which occasionally betrays the poet into actual ugliness
in expression. 'The Three Beggars' and the 'Three Hermits'
are very forcibly written little moralities, but no one
would call them poetry: they are too full of the dust and
heat of daily life. In 'The Hour before Dawn' we find
'minute' rhymed with 'within in'; and in the same piece
we read:

> I should not be too down in the mouth
> For anything you did or said,
> If but this wind were in the South.

This is surely the 'poetic diction' and the prosaic
fallacy which Wordsworth had committed a century earlier!
But nothing will show in epitome the characteristic
features of 'Responsibilities and Other Poems' more clearly
than the verses entitled 'A Coat', in which the artist

obviously loses his temper with cheap and successful
imitations of his work:

> I made my song a coat
> Covered with embroideries
> Out of old mythologies
> From heel to throat;
> But the fools caught it,
> Wore it in the world's eyes
> As though they'd wrought it.
> Song, let them take it:
> For there's more enterprise
> In walking naked.(3)

Anatole France somewhere remarks, 'The wise smile, pity,
and wait!' In September 1913 Yeats wrote:

> Romantic Ireland's dead and gone;
> It's with O'Leary in the grave.

And it was at this time that most of 'Responsibilities and
Other Poems' were written; but one may risk the extra-
vagant-sounding conjecture that the Easter rising in
Dublin of 1916, which so vividly brought home to people
in this country the force and spirit of the Irish national
Revival, dates also a recovery — if only partial — in
the strength of the creative genius of Yeats: for the
volume of poems which he published little more than twelve
months ago (unhappily in a limited edition) gives us once
more something of the dream-power and the languid beauty
of his earlier work, though it can hardly be said to contain much that is definitely novel. Be this as it may,
Yeats himself has categorically withdrawn his statement
that Romantic Ireland is dead, and the success of his
recent literary energy is foreshadowed in the note which
he appended in July 1916 to the verses of September 1913:
'"Romantic Ireland's dead and gone" sounds old-fashioned
now. It seemed true in 1913, but I did not foresee 1916.
The late Dublin rebellion, whatever one can say of its
wisdom, will long be remembered for its heroism. "They
weighed so lightly what they gave"; and gave too, in
some cases, without hope of success. . . . '

Notes

1 1903. (Ed.)
2 The date of the second impression of the 1916 edition.
  The first edition was that of the Cuala Press (1914).(Ed.)

3 Elsewhere in the same volume he remarks more wittily that it would be politic to praise his imitators: 'But was there ever dog that praised his fleas!'

59. DIFFERENT ATTITUDES OF WRITERS BORN IN BELFAST AND CORK TO THE TALK OF A DUBLINER

1920 and 1939

The first extract is from St John Ervine, Some Impressions of my Elders: William Butler Yeats, 'North American Review', February 1920 and March 1920. This was reprinted in 'Some Impressions of my Elders' (1923). To offset the northern Puritanism of the first extract(a), a second (b) has been included from Frank O'Connor, Two Friends: Yeats and A.E., 'The Yale Review', September 1939, even though this falls outside the period of this volume. Ervine was at one time and briefly manager of the Abbey Theatre, and O'Connor was later a director of the Theatre. St John Ervine was thirty-seven, Yeats fifty-five when this piece was written.

Ervine, born in Belfast, was a man of letters, best known for his dramatic work, which includes the realistic plays 'Mixed Marriage' (1911); 'Jane Clegg' (1913); and 'John Ferguson' (1915). Many of his later plays tended to domestic comedy. The comedy of 'Boyd's Shop' (1936) was followed by a satire on nationalisation, 'Private Enterprise' (1947). Ervine wrote several novels and biographies, the latter including lives of Sir Edward Carson, General Booth, Oscar Wilde and Bernard Shaw.

Frank O'Connor (Michael O'Donovan, 1903-66) novelist, critic, translator, and, particularly, short-story writer, was influenced by Daniel Corkery in his youth. His knowledge of the Gaelic language and literary tradition emerged in his translations of Gaelic poetry, notably, of Brian Merriman's 'The Midnight Court' and of early Irish poetry in 'Kings, Lords and Commons' (1959). He was a friend of Yeats, on whose poetry he lectured impressively in later years. He was a director of the Abbey Theatre (1936-9), and he wrote movingly in his autobiography 'My Father's Son' (1968) of the effect of Yeats's death on him. This book gives a good account of Yeats's influence and of the in-fighting on the Board of the Abbey Theatre.

(a)

He is a tall man, with dark hanging hair that is now
turning grey, and he has a queer way of focussing when
he looks at you. I do not know what is the defect of
sight from which he suffers, but it makes his way of
regarding you somewhat disturbing. He has a poetic
appearance, entirely physical, and owing nothing to any
eccentricity of dress; for, apart from his neck-tie,
there is nothing odd about his clothes. It is not easy
to talk to him in a familiar fashion, and I imagine that
he has difficulty in talking easily on common topics. I
soon discovered that he is not comfortable with individuals: he needs an audience to which he can discourse
in a pontifical manner. If he is compelled to remain in
the company of one person for any length of time, he begins
to pretend that the individual is a crowd listening to him.
His talk is seldom about common-place things: it is either
in a high and brilliant style or else it is full of reminiscences of dead friends. I do not believe that any one
in this world has ever spoken familiarly to him or that
any one has ever slapped him on the back and said 'Hello,
old chap!' His relatives and near friends call him
'Willie', but it has always seemed to me that they do so
with an effort, that they feel that they ought to call him
'Mr Yeats!' I doubt very much whether he takes any intimate interest in any human being. It may be, of course,
that he took less interest in me than he took in any one
else, for I am not a very interesting person; but I
always felt that when I left his presence it was immaterial
to him whether he ever saw me again or not. I felt that,
on my hundredth meeting with him, I should be no nearer
intimacy with him than I was on my first meeting. My
vanity has since been soothed by the knowledge that he has
given a similar impression regarding themselves to other
people who know him better than I do. I have seen him
come suddenly into the presence of a man whom he had
known for many years, and greet him awkwardly as if he
did not know what to say. He never offers his hand to a
friend: he will often stand looking at one without
speaking, and then bow and pass on, with perhaps a fumbled
'Good evening!' but never with a 'How are you?' or 'I'm
glad to see you!'
   It is, I suppose, the result of some natural clumsiness
of manner. He has trained himself to an elegance of
demeanour, an elaborate courteousness, which is very
pleasing to a stranger, but he has spent so much time
in achieving this elegance that he has forgotten or never
learned how to greet a friend. . . .

. . . It may be that Mr. Yeats's aloofness from men is
due to the fact that he thinks too much and feels too
little. . . .
    I think of him as a very lonely, isolated, aloof man.
He is, so far as I am aware, the only English-speaking
poet who did not write a poem about the War, a fact which
is at once significant of the restraint he imposes upon
himself and of his isolation from the common life of his
time. I have never met any one who seems so unaware of
contemporary affairs as Mr. Yeats, and this unawareness
is due, not to affectation, but to sheer lack of interest.
He probably would not have known of the War at all had
not the Germans dropped a bomb near his lodgings off the
Euston Road. When Macaulay's New Zealander comes to
examine the ruins of London, he will probably see Mr.
Yeats, disembodied and unaware that he is disembodied or
that London is in ruins, sitting on a slab with a planchette.
He is younger than Mr. Shaw by ten years, but might be ten
years older. His verse and his speech and his manner are
all elderly. . . .

(b)

. . . At first, one was only aware — pleasantly aware —
of a touch of dandyism in the lofty, ecclesiastical stare,
the ritual motion of the hands, the unction of the voice,
and an occasional elaborate mispronunciation like 'weld'
for 'world' or 'medder' for 'murder'. And perhaps if one
had analyzed those careful sentences of his, one would have
found at times the rhythms of oratory rather than the
rhythms of good speech — certain cadences linger in my
ear.
    There was something about him that suggested the bird:
the strange inhuman cock of the head; the bird's sloping
eyes, which at times seemed to be at the side rather than
the front of his face; his long nose, which he tweaked;
his laugh, which was abrupt and remote — a caw, Moore
called it. Sometimes he laughed without moving his lips,
his eyebrows raised, only his eyes smiling, and the laugh
dwindled into a sad thoughtfulness as though dying upon
the air. Sometimes he laughed excitedly, jerking and
moving about, shaking himself within his clothes, stam-
mering slightly; but it was always the eyes that smiled.
When he was very happy and forgot himself, animation flowed
over him in waves, as I have seen it flow over his sister.
He sat forward, arms on his knees, washing his hands over
and over, the pose broken sometimes by a loud harsh throaty
laugh like a croak and the throwing back of the bird's

head, while he sat bolt upright holding on to the lapels
of his coat; sometimes by a tweaking of the nose, most
characteristically perhaps by a sudden raising of the
indix finger for attention. But he was always alert,
dramatic, and amazingly brilliant. When he told a funny
story, he had a trick of looking suddenly at the ceiling,
rolling his eyes with little snorts of laughter, and
spreading out his beautiful hands as if he were juggling
invisible balls. He was a really lovely man to watch.
Every pose was right. . . .

60. JOHN BUTLER YEATS ON POETRY AND THE GAME OF LIFE

1921

From a letter written on 30 June 1921, when Yeats's father
was in his last year of life — he was born in March 1839,
and died in February 1922. The text is from John Butler
Yeats, 'Letters to his son W.B. Yeats and others, 1869-
1922' (1944), edited with a memoir by Joseph Hone.
    For a note on John Butler Yeats see p. 61.

. . . When is your poetry at its best? I challenge all
the critics if it is not when its wild spirit of your
imagination is wedded to concrete fact. Had you stayed
with me and not left me for Lady Gregory, and her friends
and associations, you would have loved and adored concrete
life for which as I know you have a real affection. What
would have resulted? Realistic and poetical plays —
poetry in closest and most intimate union with the positive realities and complexities of life. And that is the
world that waits, so far in vain, its poet. I have always
hoped and do still hope that your wife may do for you what
I would have done. Not idea but the game of life should
have been your preoccupation, as it was Shakespeare's and
the old English writers', notably the kinglike Fielding.
The moment you touch however lightly on concrete fact,
how alert you are! and how attentive we your readers
become! Whistler was a fine artist, but as a portrait
painter a failure. His Carlyle is ridiculous, a mere
conventional coat of a prophet, the picture merely a good
decorative arrangement. Every artist, poet and painter,
should have many visions — first the poem itself or the
picture — and with Whistler this included the frame — and

then as part and parcel of that the vision of the man or
woman or landscape. Da Vinci had his immortal vision of
that great lady with the smile. But Whistler was too
arrogant or rather too insolent — and insolence I do not
love, it makes me think of the nobleman's footman. So he
had not the patience to become the student and lover of
life itself. Carlyle the man was to him nothing except
an occasion for an artistic picture. In Shakespeare's
time that kind of insolence was not known among the poets.
France had not ennobled and decorated them, they were
little better than noblemen's servants or servants to the
public — so that there was nothing to prevent their making
a close study of life itself — and they had not despised
their fellow creatures as did the Puritan and does the
modern English gentleman. For this kind of study you
have by nature every natural qualification — your conversation shows it. Never are you happier and never more
felicitous in words than when in your conversation you
describe life and comment on it. But when you write
poetry you as it were put on your dress coat and shut
yourself in and forget what is vulgar to a man in a dress
coat.

   Probably you will have a long life, in which will be
many revolutions and epochs. It is my belief that some
day you will write a play of real life in which poetry
will be the inspiration as propaganda is of G.B. Shaw's
plays.

   Am I talking wildly? Am I senile? I don't think so,
for I would have said the same any time these 20 or 30 years.
The best thing in life is the game of life, and some day a
poet will find this out. I hope you will be that poet. It
is easier to write poetry that is far away from life, but it
is *infinitely more exciting* to write the poetry of life —
and it is what the whole world is crying out for as pants
the hart for the water brook. . . .

61. PADRAIC COLUM ON YEATS'S CAPACITY FOR RENEWING HIS
POETIC LIFE

1921

Extract from a review by Padraic Colum of 'Selected
Poems' (New York, 1921), Mr Yeats' Selected Poems, 'Dial',
October 1921.

Padraic Colum (1881-1973), born in Longford, was one of
the early Abbey playwrights, much of whose life was spent
in the United States. His plays, 'Broken Soil' (1903),
'The Land' (1905) and 'Thomas Muskerry' (1910) are well
known. His 'Collected Poems' appeared in 1932, 'The
Poet's Circuits' in 1960. He also wrote travel books,
criticism, books for children and biography; he was a
fine conversationalist and reader of poetry.

As one goes through this collection of beautiful poems
and impressive plays one is struck, first of all, by the
poet's capacity for renewing his poetic life. There are
poets who have strung a poetic period out through a whole
life-time. Not this poet. After writing poems and a play
that are full of the feeling of Irish country life, and
after writing a long poem that had in it the elemental
things of Celtic romance, he produced the deliberately
esoteric poems of 'The Wind Among the Reeds'. The liquid-
escence of the Symbolist movement showed him that there
could be no advance in that direction. He sought for 'a
more manful energy' in the direct statements of dramatic
poetry. The new effort brought him a great renewal; out
of it came 'The King's Threshold', 'On Baile's Strand',
'Deirdre', 'The Green Helmet'. Then his interest in the
theatre he created lapsed: he made no new plays, but he
brought back to the lyric the direct and living utterance
of the drama — 'words with a spit on them' as they used
to say in Dublin when discussing his insistence upon
'living speech'. The directness of speech that he learnt
in the theatre and through the range of interests that the
theatre opened for him, makes his later lyrics stirring
in a way that few lyrics since the XVII century are
stirring.
     Mr Yeats, then, is not only a first-rate poet, but he
is an abundant poet. And no poet writing in English in
our time has given out so many fruitful influences.
Thomas Hardy is a first-rate poet also. But Thomas Hardy
has few sons in Apollo. Mr Yeats has fathered most of
the Irish poets of to-day. And by his insistence upon the
importance of local life, local speech, and local tradition, he created in English-speaking countries the movement to which is due John Masefield in England, and Edgar
Lee Masters and Vachel Lindsay in America.
     He is a court poet in a country that had no court, and
in a world in which courts are vanishing. His sense of
the office and his detachment from the office have both
been a gain to him. His sense of the office has kept him
out of both the Market Place and the Ivory Tower; his

detachment from it permitted him to use his abundant
secular energy in a way that meant the widening of his
interests. But for all that he remains a poet of the
court, responding to forms and courtesies, to rank, and
to all authentic traditions.

Above all, his sense of the office has given style
to his poetry. Swinburne had substituted sound for style,
and the next poet would have to return to plainer verse.
William Morris made his verse plain and freed it from
inversions. The youthful Yeats learnt to do with verse all
that Morris could do with it, and he made it more intrin-
sically poetic.

And he was to do something else to this straight verse —
something that was to give it a distinction that Morris
had never attained. Did Mr Yeats come to this new distinction through his knowledge of the rare achievements
of Anglo-Irish poetry — achievements that brought into
English verse the unemphatic rhythms of the Irish folk
song? To the straightness that William Morris had brought
into verse he added a stillness:

> Had I the heavens' embroidered cloths,
> Enwrought with golden and silver light,
> The blue and the dim and the dark cloths
> Of night and light and the half light,
> I would spread the cloths under your feet.

Here was verse as near as could be in English to the verse
that the French symbolists dreamed of — a verse that would
be, not a hymn to beauty, nor a description of beauty, but
an evocation of beauty.

From what region do these poems come? From a region
beyond the world, certainly, but not from any irresponsible Fairyland. These are the poems of an ascetic —
of a man who has taken to himself 'a secret discipline'.

His vision of the world made perfect is in the race
course where 'delight makes all of the one mind'. Those
who shared in that delight had to have one discipline —
the discipline of horsemanship. Mr Yeats is an ascetic
for the sake of ecstasy — of an ecstasy that awakens
body and spirit. All the things that bring ecstasy in
Mr Yeats' poetry come through labour — 'Beauty that we
have wrought from bitterest hours'. The men he celebrates
are:

> Bred to a harder thing
> Than triumph.

Labour and discipline have not always an end in
ecstasy, and in some moods the poet is ready to cry out
against them —

> I would be—for no knowledge is worth a straw—
> Ignorant and wanton as the dawn.

He has that queer mood, too, in which he makes the hero of
'On Baile's Strand' 'live like a bird's flight from tree
to tree'. But the very texture of his verse shows how
much labour and discipline are a part of his being. The
child dancing in the wind brings to him, not images of
freedom, but thoughts of a discipline to be imposed and
a work to be accomplished.

He has called 'The Land of Heart's Desire' the most
feminine of his plays in deprecating its popularity. And
yet 'The Land of Heart's Desire' is a play that has a
firm texture; in it character is really projected, the
people in it live and move, and the verses that they speak
have relation to their character. It is one of the few
plays that have a real poetry — the poetry of the hearth-
side and of the hill-top are matched in it.

This little play will have a place in literary history.
It is remarkable that a young man, writing out of the
tradition of an Irish countryside should have succeeded in
doing what Tennyson and Browning and Swinburne failed in
doing — in writing dramatic verse that an audience could
not only listen to, but be stirred by. With 'The Land of
Heart's Desire' dramatic verse comes back to the English-
speaking stage for the first time after its flickering out
in Jacobean days.

Mr Yeats places 'The Land of Heart's Desire' before
'The Countess Cathleen'. But he dates 'The Land of Heart's
Desire' 1894, and 'The Countess Cathleen' 1893. In his
notes, however, he speaks of the production of 'The Land
of Heart's Desire' as in 1891. I have always regarded 'The
Land of Heart's Desire' as being prior to 'The Countess
Cathleen' and for that reason I have spoken of it and not
of 'The Countess Cathleen' as being the innovating play.
'The Countess Cathleen' is in conception a great play. The
idea — that of a great soul sacrificing itself for the
sake of lesser souls, and in sacrificing itself attaining
to fulfilment — is one of the great dramatic ideas of
literature — it is an idea comparable to the idea in
Antigone. But this great idea is not given adequate
illustration. It is spoiled by what seems mere fantasy.
And the fantasy that dissipates all the clearness and the
fineness of the idea is all gathered around the poet Aleel.
Aleel, the antagonist to Countess Cathleen's other-worldli-

ness, should represent some part of common life; he
should be firmly made and have a firm enunciation. But
we are made to know Aleel only as a mutterer.

Both these plays were written before Mr Yeats got his
hand upon a theatre; both, however, were re-written in
1911 when the poet was in the extremely fortunate situation
of having a malleable theatre to his hand and a growing
dramatic movement behind him. The other two plays included
in the 'Selected Poems', 'On Baile's Strand' and 'Deirdre',
were written in the course of the dramatic movement that
he headed, and one has to speak of them as his mature
plays.

Both have passages of verse that, to speak of work sinc
Jacobean days, are unequalled except in 'The Cenci'; this
verse is informed, moreover, as the verse of 'The Cenci'
is not informed, with the spirit of the theatre.

The verse is triumphant. But the plays representing
his mature dramatic work that Mr Yeats has selected are
both, even more seriously than 'The Countess Cathleen',
marred by fantasies. Cuchulain, in 'On Baile's Strand'
goes out to fight the young man who had won his liking
just because somebody talks of 'a witch of the air' and
suggests that the young soldier had bewitched him. And
'Deirdre', for all its fine verse and for all its excellent invention, has an over-emphasized fantastic element —
Libyan dragon-stones and outlandish soldiers. It seems
to me that the real dramatic poetry of this play is in
the two pages that follow on Deirdre's movement to kill
herself on Naisi's body.

After the plays come the great lyrics written between
1904 and 1919. Truly men improve with years, and one has
to say of 'A Woman Homer Sung', 'The Cold Heaven', 'The
Wild Swans at Coole', that they are even more remarkable
than 'The Folly of Being Comforted'. They are thrilling
in their austerity, in their renunciation of what is merely
emotional. And these particular poems are only the outstanding ones in a group of extraordinary poems — poems
in which speech seems to flow into verse simply through
its own energy.

Every poem in this latter group gives one the impres-
sion of something dimensional — a poem that one might
handle like a blade — 'That the Night Come', 'Friends',
'Against Unworthy Praise', 'These are the Clouds', 'At
Galway Races', 'The Mountain Tomb', 'To a Friend whose
Work has come to Nothing', 'When Helen Lived', 'The
Player Queen', 'The Mask', 'An Irish Airman faces Death',
'Men Improve with Years'. These poems must make for us all
a rare, an austere standard of perfection.

Towards the end there comes another change in this
poetry. In 'The Collar Bone of a Hare', 'Under the Round
Tower', 'The Cat and the Moon', he gets the waywardness
of the folk-rhymer. With these poems the circle is made
complete, the singer of the countryside goes back to the
countryside, to its roads and its ditches; the court-poet
goes from where the wax candles are lighted, and comes to
sit by the kitchen fire-side.

Plays in Prose and Verse: written for an Irish Theatre, and generally with the help of a friend (1922) and *Later Poems* (1922)

62. YEATS'S TRUST IN DREAMS AND THE STEADY GROWTH OF HIS POETRY

1922

An unsigned review of 'Plays in Prose and Verse: written for an Irish Theatre, and generally with the help of a friend' (1922) and 'Later Poems' (1922), Mr Yeats's Dreams, 'Times Literary Supplement', 28 December 1922.

The word 'dream', more particularly when it occurs in the work of a young poet, is usually considered a sort of counter; and it occurred very frequently in the early work of Mr. Yeats — in those poems which he wrote up to his twenty-seventh year and which are included in a collection previous to this. But the division between the two collections is arbitrary. This volume contains 'The Wind among the Reeds' and 'In the Seven Woods', books of verse quite plainly belonging to the first half of Mr. Yeats's development as a poet. Here the word is still prominent:

> But I, being poor, have only my dreams:
> I have spread my dreams under your feet;
> Tread softly because you tread on my dreams.
>
> For that pale breast and lingering hand
> Come from a more dream-heavy land,
> A more dream-heavy hour than this.
>
> I bring you with reverent hands
> The books of my numberless dreams.

251

No critic could be forgiven for not having seen in these
earlier volumes that Mr. Yeats was an original and substantial poet; but any critic might be forgiven for having
thought that there was something a little too facile and
conventional in his use of certain poetic counters, among
which this was the chief. But the second half of his
poetic development, which begins about half-way through
this new collection, after an interval of eight years from
'In the Seven Woods', instructs us that he uses the word
'dream' with a definite and fundamental meaning, not
merely to produce a large, vague and easy effect.
   Mr. Yeats is so much the most considerable poet brought
forth by his own period that we often forget that any
period at all is to be held responsible for him. Yet he
is clearly a poet of the Nineties. Now the Nineties
produced John Davidson, Francis Thompson, and Mr. A.E.
Housman. But it is not of these that we think when we
use the word with a capital, nor does Mr. Yeats refer
to them when he recalls his contemporaries:

>Poets with whom I learned my trade,
>Companions of the Cheshire Cheese,
>. . . You kept the muses' sterner laws,
>And unrepenting faced your ends,
>And therefore earned the right—and yet
>Dowson and Johnson most I praise—
>To troop with those the world's forgot,
>And copy their proud, steady gaze.

The Nineties were, indeed, less a period than a way of
thinking which flourished during a particular period. This
way of thinking, organized, manageable, applicable, because
it was derived entire from foreign sources, coloured the
poetry of nearly a decade; but, with one exception, the
important poets of that decade were unaffected by it. The
exception was Mr. Yeats, the only Symbolist poet seriously
to be considered in English literature.
   Such he was, such he still is, and literally, strictly,
not only in the vague and associative way in which the term
is most often applied to both French and English writers.
He composes almost always, and deliberately, in symbols.
But his individual peculiarity, a thing in him native and
unalterable, is that he derives most of his symbols from
dreams. When he speaks of dreams, it is not to colour his
verse: he does mean precisely that activity of the imagination which goes on during sleep. In a note to some of
his latest pieces he says of Michael Robartes and Owen
Aherne: 'They take their place in a phantasmagoria in
which I endeavour to explain my philosophy of life and

death, and till that philosophy has found some detailed
exposition in prose certain passages in the poems named
above may seem obscure.' Of 'The Cap and Bells' he
writes:

> I dreamed this story exactly as I have written it, and
> dreamed another long dream after it, trying to make
> out its meaning, and whether I was to write it in
> prose or verse. The first dream was more a vision
> than a dream, for it was beautiful and coherent, and
> gave me the sense of illumination and excitation that
> one gets from visions, while the second dream was
> confused and meaningless. The poem has always meant
> a great deal to me, though, as is the way with sym-
> bolic poems, it has not always meant quite the same
> thing. Blake would have said, 'the authors are in
> eternity', and I am quite sure they can only be ques-
> tioned in dreams.

Forgael, in 'Shadowy Waters', says:

>   All would be well
> Could we but give us wholly to the dreams,
> And get into their world that to the sense
> Is shadow, and not linger wretchedly
> Among substantial things; for it is dreams
> That lift us to the flowing, changing world
> That the heart longs for.

Thomas Hearne, in 'The Unicorn from the Stars' (and even
if the words are Lady Gregory's, the meaning is plainly
Mr. Yeats's), sets up the opinion of the world in order
that it may be knocked down:

> But work must go on and coachbuilding must go on, and
> they will not go on in the time there is too much
> attention given to dreams. A dream is a sort of a
> shadow, no profit in it to anyone at all. A coach,
> now, is a real thing and a thing that will last for
> generations and be made use of to the last, and maybe
> turn to be a hen roost at its latter end.

These passages, which might be multiplied a score of times,
sufficiently illustrate the poet's preoccupation. He
puts a real trust in the world of dreams. He looks there
for symbols, imagery, he even composes there; and sometimes it seems that that world is to him more real, more
substantially satisfying, than the ordinary world of the
waking senses and mind.

A realization of this gives a preciser significance
to his early vocabulary, as exemplified in the lines here
first quoted. Nevertheless, that early vocabulary does
remain a little vague and slack; and even in 'The Wind
among the Reeds' the verse occasionally seems to ramble
on more loosely than it need, as in such a passage as this:

> Far off, most secret and inviolate Rose,
> Enfold me in my hour of hours; where those
> Who sought thee in the Holy Sepulchre,
> Or in the wine vat, dwell beyond the stir
> And tumult of defeated dreams; and deep
> Among pale eyelids, heavy with the sleep
> Men have named beauty.

But in this later work Mr. Yeats's poetry, without losing
or changing any inner quality, becomes tauter and firmer
in style, more rarefied, less languid, luscious and
luxurious. He himself writes:

[Quotes 'A Coat', 'Collected Poems', p. 142; text on
p. 240.]

The explanation given here is, no doubt, as wrong as can
be. A poet does not, whatever women may do with their
hats, discard a style that is his natural expression
merely because it has been freely imitated. But Mr. Yeats's
natural expression has kept pace with the development of his
mind; and as this has grown more mature, so that has grown
firmer and terser, less in need of lavish decoration.
Mr. Yeats has a philosophy. He tells us so, and he
adds that it stands in need of exposition in prose. What
it is we may not adventure here to discover. Even when his
prose and his verse play into one another's hands the up-
shot is not superfluously clear. 'The Player Queen', he
says, comes from 'an attempt to write a poetical play where
every character became an example of the finding or not
finding of what I have called the Antithetical Self'. But
most readers of 'Per Amica Silentia Lunæ', in which this
idea is expounded, have remained in the dark as to precisely what it means; and the play will give them hardly
any new light. Mr. Yeats's 'philosophy', it may be suspected, outside a few simple rules of conduct and feeling,
is commonly more an emotional than either an intellectual
or an intuitional affair. He appears to regard himself
as a mystic; but his rejection of concrete and tangible
reality takes him only half-way in that direction.
But even if there were no heart of philosophy in what
he has written, if his symbols and imagery were to be taken

only for their beauty as they stand, if he were only a
describer of dreams, as a poet may be only a describer of
landscape or persons or events, nevertheless he is a
considerable poet and his poetry is a substantial work.
The development of his style has permitted the widening
of his range and has allowed him to use subjects which he
could not have attempted before. In his beginnings there
was something dim, remote and trance-like about all he
did. But now that with his stripped austere style he
gives to his dreams the firm outline of real things, he
can also on occasion write about real things themselves.
Hence come the verses on the 'Playboy', or Sir Hugh Lane's
pictures, and on the Easter Week Insurrection. Hence come
also, it must be owned, somewhat pitiful followings of
Milton or Wordsworth and such crawling lines as

> I think it better that in times like these
> A poet keep his mouth shut, for in truth
> We have no gift to set a statesman right.

But the good outweighs the bad; and, though Mr. Yeats's
occasional verses are not a large part of his work, yet
any extension of range is good. He is now able also to
exercise a certain human and graceful playfulness which
would have been impossible to the mournful writer of 'The
Wind among the Reeds'. 'His Phœnix' is a toy, it is
decidedly without the poignancy of earlier things, but it
is a charming toy:

> There'll be that crowd, that barbarous crowd,
>   through all the centuries,
> And who can say but some young belle may walk
>   and talk men wild
> Who is my beauty's equal, though that my heart denies,
> But not the exact likeness, the simplicity of a child,
> And that proud look as though she had gazed into the
>   burning sun,
> And all the shapely body no tittle gone astray.
> I mourn for that most lovely thing; and yet God's
>   will be done,
> I knew a phœnix in my youth, so let them have
>   their day.

If we consider the whole spread of Mr. Yeats's lyrical
work, we find in it a steady growth which, after all, not
many of our lyrical poets have surpassed — not many
of them, indeed, having had the opportunity to do so. The
earlier poems are specially endeared to us by familiarity
and hence, often, by their faults; the later are sometimes

strange, difficult and disconcerting. But when we have
had a little time we shall see the whole as an harmonious
and self-consistent development. Let us add to this that
Mr. Yeats is a dramatist of some weight. He, almost
alone among English-speaking poets, has contrived to write
plays in verse which are nearly free of the paralysing
influence of the Elizabethans. Favoured, indeed, by
environment and upbringing, he has written blank-verse
dialogue in a style of his own and has proved, though
the proof is as yet without consequences, that the thing
is at least possible. Moreover, in that 'heroic farce'
'The Green Helmet', he has made a new departure, and has
shown that it is not even necessary to run the risks of
blank verse.

63. PADRAIC COLUM ON THE PLAYS AND LATER POEMS

1925

A review of 'Plays in Prose and Verse' and 'Later Poems',
by Padraic Colum, Mr Yeats's Plays and Later Poems, 'The
Yale Review', January 1925.
    For a note on Padraic Colum, see p. 246.

In the notes at the end of 'Plays in Prose and Verse' Mr.
Yeats has something suggestive to say of the two plays
that open the volume: 'The dialect of "Cathleen ni
Houlihan" is, I think, true in temper, but has no richness,
no abundance'; and, 'I hardly know how much of the play
["The Pot of Broth"] is my work, for Lady Gregory helped
me as she has helped me in every play of mine where there
is dialect. . . . In those first years of the Theatre we
all helped one another with plots, ideas, and dialogue,
but certainly I was the most indebted as I had no mastery
of speech that purported to be of real life.' He goes on
to say of 'The Pot of Broth', 'The dialect has not, I
think, the right temper, being gay, mercurial, and suggestive of rapid speech.' It should be added to these
judgments that the gay, mercurial dialogue suggestive of
rapid speech is quite appropriate to the farce that comes
out of a folk-tale, and that any richness or abundance
of dialogue in 'Cathleen ni Houlihan' would take from the
austerity of a play that has in it a grand and simple
invention. The point I make by quoting these sentences

as criticism is that on account of their being in a
dialect that carries a hint of even a remote collaboration,
these firstling plays stand in a different relation to
Yeats's mind than the others that go to make up the collection.

The last play in the volume, 'The Player Queen', is
really the typical Yeats play, in spite of the fact that
it is the only play he has written the scene of which is
not laid in Ireland and the fable of which is not based
on Irish tradition. It is a play of fantasy. 'You will
give me straw to lie on,' says the old beggar to Septimus
the poet. 'Asphodels!' he replies. 'Yet indeed the
asphodel is a flower much overrated by classical authors.
Still, if a man has a preference, I say for the asphodel.'
So it goes on, every speech, every scene a fantasy. And
the fantasy that is pure and unadulterated in 'The Player
Queen' goes through all the other plays, sometimes
wronging a dramatic idea, sometimes attaining to a high
and memorable expression.

There is fantasy in 'The Hour Glass', a fantasy that
is out of place, when the Fool puts the butterfly that
symbolizes the soul of the Wise Man into a box; there
is fantasy in 'The King's Threshold', a high fantasy and
a lower fantasy — a high fantasy in the spectacle of the
poet starving on the kind's stairway, and speaking to the
procession of courtiers, students, soldiers, and beggars,
and a lower fantasy when Yeats would have us believe that
poetry itself is endangered because a poet has been sent
away from a king's table; there is fantasy again in
'Baile's Strand' when the hero insists upon fighting the
young man whom a minute before he had admired merely
because someone calls out 'witchcraft!' 'Deirdre' has
fantasy, too — a fantasy that works against the high
poetry that is in it, and that makes hero and heroine
speculate upon their places in people's memory when their
doom has come upon them. The fantasy is heroic and magnificent in 'The Green Helmet', a play in rhymed verse that
is successful, that is stirring, and that has in it
authentic national character. To how many Irish leaders
from Parnell to Michael Collins might the last lines be
addressed:

I have not come for your hurt, I'm the Rector of this land,
And with my spitting cat-heads, my frenzied moon-bred band,
Age after age I sift it, and choose for its champion-ship
The man who hits my fancy.
                          And I choose the laughing lip
That shall not turn from laughing whatever rise or fall,
The heart that grows no bitterer although betrayed by all;

The hand that loves to scatter;   the life like a gambler's
   throw;
And these things I make prosper, till a day comes that I
   know,
When heart and mind shall darken that the weak may end
   the strong,
And the long-remembering harpers have matter for a song.

The 'Rector of this land', the 'spitting cat-heads',
belong to fantasy, but, in this case, to a high, moving,
and prophetic fantasy. I repeat the word, for fantasy,
I believe, is the element that Yeats has brought into the
theatre.

But to insist upon his bias towards fantasy is to
give a false impression if one does not insist, too,
that Yeats is the first since Jacobean days — leaving
out one man's one play, Shelley's 'Cenci' — to bring
poetry into the theatre, poetry that can be spoken and
that can move an audience. 'The King's Threshold' may
be fantasy, and have an existence that can be challenged,
but what splendid verse is in it! The poet who has
brought such verse into the theatre has brought another
element besides his fantasy.

Yeats turned from the verse of 'The Wind Among the
Reeds', the verse that was so much influenced by the
French symbolists, to the theatre, so that he might bring
a 'more manful energy' into his work. The theatre helped
him to discover and bring into his lyrical work a new
rhythm, a new vocabulary. In the verse that follows 'The
Wind Among the Reeds' he no longer uses words that seem
to belong to an initiate; he uses words that might be
used by anyone in a fine excitement. Had he not gone
into the theatre, he never could have made poems like
'Ireland, September 1913', 'To a Friend whose Work has
come to Nothing', 'The Cold Heaven', 'The Wild Swans at
Coole', 'To a Wealthy Man who had promised a Subscription
to the Dublin Municipal Gallery if it were proved that the
People wanted Pictures', nor could he have produced a
song like this:

[Quotes 'The Mask', 'Collected Poems', p. 106.]

The last section of 'Later Poems', the section that has
the title 'Michael Robartes and the Dancer', shows, I
think, where the danger to Yeats as a poet lies. He has
been described as a mystic; he is not; he is an intellectual poet, and as an intellectual he constructs his
philosophical system; in the poems in the last section
he permits his philosophy to enter, and he makes them

obscure by making them depend upon some private reflection.

The poem that gives title to a section in these 'Later
Poems', 'The Wild Swans at Coole', is one of Yeats's most
beautiful poems. Once I remember walking with the poet
in Galway — it was in Coole, the place he has celebrated
in this poem — and he spoke of the great clouds and the
grayness of the landscape that sometime he would work
into his poems. In 'The Wild Swans at Coole', he has
the West of Ireland atmosphere, the grayness, the cold
light. And what a cycle he has completed with this poem!
Once no word that might be used by a journalist would be
permitted in his canon; now he can put the adjective
'brilliant' before 'creatures' and make a beautiful
line, 'I have looked upon those brilliant creatures and
now my heart is sore.'. . .

64.   NO PLACE IN THE MODERN THEATRE FOR YEATS

1924

An unsigned review of 'Plays and Controversies' (1923),
Mr Yeats's Theatre, 'Times Literary Supplement', 10
January 1924.

In this volume, in which Mr. Yeats has collected his
earliest and his latest dramatic pieces, he includes
also a series of essays on the theatre, mostly written
between 1901 and 1906 and reprinted from the little
journal called 'Samhain', which was founded to defend the
'Irish Dramatic Movement'. At the end of these comes an
open letter to Lady Gregory, written in 1919, a summing-up
which expresses satisfaction and a little regret and
some aspirations for the future.

This collection makes a valuable document for any
student of the Irish Literary Revival. Some years hence,
when recent Irish history has fallen into some kind of
perspective, when perhaps, as Mr. Yeats hopes may happen,
the Government of the Free State has founded a National
Theatre, this book will be indispensable to anyone who
wants to know how Ireland was served by her poets and
dramatists. It shows, too, in a very interesting manner
the effect of newly awakened and easily exacerbated
national feeling on the poetic activity which accom-

panies it, and tries to help it but is not always helped
by it. Years before 'The Playboy of the Western World'
was howled down by a too devout and patriotic mob (armed
with tin trumpets) Mr. Yeats found himself again and
again obliged to argue rather pathetically with those who
would judge new plays by wrong standards:

> A little play, 'The Rising of the Moon' . . . has, for
> instance, roused the suspicions of a very resolute
> leader of the people, who has a keen eye for rats
> behind the arras. A Fenian ballad-singer partly
> converts a policeman, and is it not unwise under any
> circumstances to show a policeman in so favourable a
> light? It is well known that many of the younger
> policemen were Fenians: but it is necessary that the
> Dublin crowds should be kept of so high a heart that
> they will fight the police at any moment. Are not
> morals greater than literature? Others have objected
> to Mr. Synge's 'Shadow of the Glen' because Irish
> women, being more chaste than those of England and
> Scotland, are a valuable part of our national argument.
> Mr. Synge should not, it is said by some, have chosen
> an exception for the subject of his play, for who knows
> but the English may misunderstand him? Some even deny
> that such a thing could happen at all, while others
> that know the country better, or remember the statis-
> tics, say that it could but should never have been
> staged.

These details are interesting, and so are many other
details of the various stages in the progress of the Irish
Dramatic Movement. But for many readers they will to some
extent spoil what is perhaps Mr. Yeats's best essay
in criticism, and what is certainly one of the best books
on the theatre published for several years. It is true,
as Mr. Yeats says, that even an atmosphere of ignorance
and intolerance is better for the stage than an atmosphere of indifference. Even the shop-girls who complained of 'The Countess Cathleen' that 'to describe an
Irishwoman as selling her soul to the devil was to slander
the country' played their part in forcing him to consider
and to express very clearly to what end great plays are
written.
    These pages are all written in the rather dreamy and
drawling prose with which Mr. Yeats has long made us
familiar. It is a distinctive style and, in its way,
a charming, even a beautiful, style; but it has its
defects as a vehicle for criticism. (He says, in 1905, 'I
shall, I think, have to cast away the hope of ever having

a prose style that amounts to anything'; and one sus-
pects that he may previously have nursed this hope with
a little too much concentration.) But every now and
again, as he wrestles with the preconceptions of those
whom he is endeavouring to persuade, he brings out such
passages of admirably lucid statement as this:

> What attracts me to the drama is that it is, in the
> most obvious way, what all the arts are upon a last
> analysis. A farce and a tragedy are alike in this,
> that they are a moment of intense life. An action is
> taken out of all other actions; it is reduced to its
> simplest form, or at any rate to as simple a form as
> it can be brought to without our losing the sense of
> its place in the world. The characters that are in-
> volved in it are freed from everything that is not a
> part of that action; and whether it is, as in the less
> important kinds of drama, a mere bodily activity, a
> hair-breadth escape or the like, or as it is in the
> more important kinds, an activity of the souls of
> the characters, it is an energy, an eddy of life
> purified from everything but itself. The dramatist
> must picture life in action, with an unpreoccupied
> mind, as the musician pictures her in sound and the
> sculptor in form.

In 1919 Mr. Yeats, writing to Lady Gregory, confesses
something like failure: 'You and I and Synge, not understanding the clock, set out to bring again the Theatre
of Shakespeare, or rather perhaps of Sophocles.' But
the Irish Theatre moved stadily away from heroic and poetic
plays in the direction of peasant comedy. It produced 'The
Countess Cathleen', but that was not the true direction
of its growth. Mr. Yeats, so far from following it, moved
away as fast from it as it from him, till he found himself
wanting to create 'an unpopular theatre and an audience
like a secret society where admission is by favour and
never to many'. This is perhaps the natural destiny of
his genius; and he seems at least to have secured, in
his 'Four Plays for Dancers', that it shall have no other.

> When you and Synge [he says] find such an uneasy foot-
> ing, what shall I do there who have never observed
> anything or listened with an attentive ear, but value
> all I have seen or heard because of the emotions they
> call up or because of something they remind me of that
> exists, as I believe, beyond the world?

Such a man has no place in the modern theatre, nor is he
fitted to remould the modern theatre to his own use. And
this, which is betrayed in 'The Countess Cathleen' and
'The Land of Heart's Desire', is almost paraded in 'At
the Hawk's Well' and 'Calvary'. He retires to his own
'Unpopular Theatre', and writes for it these mysterious
and beautiful little pieces. Some day an influence from
them will enter the modern, the popular, theatre and be
powerful there; but they themselves never will.

65. THE LONELY AND DISTINGUISHED RITUAL OF YEATS'S PROSE

1924

An unsigned review of 'Essays' (1924) [by Hugh L'Anson
Fausset], Mr Yeats's Prose, 'Times Literary Supplement',
22 May 1924.
    Hugh L'Anson Fausset (b. 1895) reviewed regularly for
the 'Times Literary Supplement', the 'Guardian' and other
periodicals. His essays appeared in 'Poets and Pundits'
(1947), and 'Towards Fidelity' (1952) was a volume of his
personal philosophy of life. He also wrote two novels,
'Between the Tides' (1942) and 'The Last Days' (1945).

Mr. Yeats has collected in this volume the material of
three earlier books, 'Ideas of Good and Evil', 'The
Cutting of an Agate', and 'Per Amica Silentia Lunae'. It
contains therefore, with the considerable exception of
'The Trembling of the Veil', still protected by a limited
edition, all the best of his prose written over a period
of twenty years. What must strike the reader at once is
the supple sameness of its quality from first to last.
There is no such change both of tone and rhythm as to be
found here as can be traced in his poetry from the early
lyrics through 'The Wind Among the Reeds' to 'The Wild
Swans at Coole'. The years have deepened somewhat his
sophistication, intensified his passivity, purified or
over-involved, as we like to regard it, his purpose. But
essentially he conceals the same difficult and esoteric
quest behind the same dreamy indolence of manner in the
essay on the nature of 'Popular Poetry', with which this
book begins, and in the Oriental musings on the self and
the anti-self with which it concludes. To turn from the
agitations of an age over which Blake's 'Spectre', the

critical reason, presides with unexampled authority, in
which truth is so universally sought by psychological
rather than spiritual avenues, and to immerse oneself
in a pool at once so limpid and mysterious, simple and
secretive, as this, is to experience at first a delicious
sense of relief, a loosening of the fetters of the mind,
a solution of the discord of the world and of warring
faculties. But imperceptibly the charm weakens, and the
critical faculty reasserts itself. We remember Pater
and the nineties, which wrote his epitaph in decorative
word-patterns. We remember Butler's curt admonition:

> I never knew a writer yet who took the smallest pains
> with his style and was at the same time readable. . . .
> A man may, and ought to, take a great deal of pains to
> write clearly, tersely, and euphemistically . . .
> he will be at great pains to see that he does not
> repeat himself, to arrange his matter in the way that
> shall best enable the reader to master it, to cut out
> superfluous words and, even more, to eschew irrelevant
> matter; but in each case he will be thinking not of
> his own style but of his reader's convenience.

Butler, it may be admitted, embraced the practical
in his dislike of the precious; but has Mr. Yeats reversed
the process? That is the essential question in any consideration of his prose. Butler's 'just common, simple
straightforwardness' is, of course, an entirely inadequate criterion of literary style, which must be effective
not only as a communicative but also as an expressive
act. It must be sensitive to all the delicate distinc-
tions of its author's personality, and, in so far as he
is subtle and sincere, has apprehended truth and organized
his experience, his style will achieve permanence and
reflect beauty. No disharmony will then exist between form
and substance, grace and utility. In this sense Butler's
own style has a beauty in exact accordance with his personality, and Mr. Yeats has supplied us with sufficient
evidence to prove that, unlike Newman or Stevenson, against
whom Butler preached, he never sought to acquire a style
as a preliminary measure or as a thing of value in itself.
If he has fallen anywhere into preciosity, it is because
the vision of which his style has been the persistent
embodiment has failed him. An experience over-systematized
has ceased momentarily to have organic life; it has degenerated into a formula with the inevitable lapse into
self-consciousness and mannerisms. We think these occasions are rare, because Mr. Yeats's lifelong aim has been
to escape from the self-consciousness generated by contact

with the world of appearance and to invoke from the subconscious a world of purer reality, so to deepen self-
consciousness in fact that it dies in the infinite. It
is an aim which may easily encourage too blind a confidence in irrelevant images or the multiplication of
symbols which have no more than a private significance,
but Mr. Yeats has pursued it with such ardour and simplicity of heart as to set him quite apart from contemporaries who sought to conceal emptiness behind an artificial manner. In his 'Per Amica Silentia Lunae' he
tells through what self-discipline he had to pass before
he was able to suspend will and intellect and tap the
'subconscious' as he wished.

> I had no natural gift for this clear quiet, as I
> soon discovered, for my mind is abnormally restless;
> and I was seldom delighted by that sudden luminous
> definition of form which makes one understand almost
> in spite of oneself that one is not merely imagining.

And of the reality achieved he writes:

> When all sequence comes to an end, time comes to an
> end, and the soul puts on the rhythmic or spiritual
> body or luminous body and contemplates all the events
> of its memory and every possible impulse in an eternal
> possession of itself in one single moment; that con-
> dition is alone animate, all the rest is phantasy.

Elsewhere he writes: 'Only in rapid and subtle thought,
or in faint accents heard in the quiet of the mind, can
the thought of the spirit come to us but little changed.'
And such passages only state explicitly what is implicit
in all his writing, a desire to avoid all the surface
fluctuations of thought and feeling, the rhetoric which
is born of 'our quarrel with the world', or the mists with
which bodily passions dim the clear mirror of the soul.
   This ideal of passive contemplation, of self-forget-
fulness in self-absorption, which Mr. Yeats shares with
the fakir, is not without its dangers to the artist, in
whom perception and conception, receptivity and creative-
ness, should be complementary functions. In consciously
setting out to purge his imagination of all physical alloy
Mr. Yeats has inevitably narrowed its range while deepening
its content. It is possible too to carry the virtue of 'a
wise passiveness' too far, to mistake in the languid quiet
of the mind the faint accents of fancy for the real symbols
of imagination, to confuse simplicity and sophistication,
and to cloud the vision as surely by the fumes of emotional

idleness as by those of a too hasty and combative activity.
There are passages in these essays in which such a confusion seems to us to exist, in which Mr. Yeats's necro-
mancy strikes us as purely fantastic and arbitrary, and
his style as limp, for all its gesture of pride and
courtesy. We feel then that through over-cultivation the
subconscious has ceased to feed his imagination, that an
ideal activity has degenerated into a doctrine, and we
yearn for that 'rapid and subtle thought' for the deci-
sive speech of overmastering and unconscious intuition,
upon which Mr. Yeats has turned his back. But as an
interpreter of pure aesthetic values, of mystical or
metaphysical art, or of the Celtic element in literature he has made a contribution to his time in prose
which we believe to be as sure of permanence as much
of his poetry. Like Shelley, he has sought 'more in
life than any understood', but he has schooled himself
to live down desire's impatience and to shut himself
away from the discords and irrelevancies of life in a
cloister of reverie. In so doing he has favoured the
saint, it may be, at the expense of the artist. The
momentary mutations of nature, the rush of wind and cloud,
the haste and hunger of men, have their place in aesthetic
experience, and they have ceased to intrude upon the
peace, studied and a little autumnal, where he conducts
his lonely and distinguished ritual as he liked to imagine
Shelley conducting his:

> I think too that as he knelt before an altar, where
> a thin flame burnt in a lamp made of green agate, a
> single vision would have come to him again and again,
> a vision of a boat drifting down a broad river be-
> tween high hills where there were caves and towers,
> and following the light of one star; and that voices
> would have told him how there is for every man some
> one scene, some one adventure, some one picture that
> is the image of his secret life, for wisdom first
> speaks in images, and that this one image, if he would
> but brood over it his life long, would lead his soul,
> disentangled from unmeaning circumstance and the ebb
> and flow of the world, into that far household, where
> the undying gods await all whose souls have become
> simple as flame, whose bodies have become quiet as
> an agate life.

66.   FROM THE SIMPLE TO THE COMPLEX

1925

An unsigned review of 'Early Poems and Stories' (1925),
[by Hugh L'Anson Fausset], 'Mr Yeats in Transition',
'Times Literary Supplement', 8 October 1925.
     For note on H. L'Anson Fausset see p. 262.

This fifth volume of Mr. Yeats's collected works contains
the first fruits of his genius in poetry and prose.   It
begins with 'The Wanderings of Usheen' and the early
lyrics first published in 1889, and ends with the two
mystical narratives entitled 'The Tables of the Law' and
'The Adoration of the Magi', which appeared eight years
later.   Between these two dates his sensibility had
advanced from the simple to the complex.   He has described
himself how Nature filled his head with thoughts of making
a whole literature and plucked him from the art shcools
at Dublin and drove him into a library to read translations from the Irish, and at last down into Connaught
to sit by turf fires, enshrining the legendary lore he
gleaned there in 'The Celtic Twilight'.   By thus steeping
himself in traditions of an imaginative people he deepened
the roots of that lyrical impulse which had already expressed itself with such a delicate, instinctive simplicity
in poems like 'The Stolen Child', 'To an Isle in the Water',
and 'Down by the Salley Gardens'.   The songs and stories
handed down among the cottages carried his memory back to
ancient verses and forgotten mythologies.

> Folk art [as he wrote] is, indeed, the oldest of the
> aristocracies of thought, and because it refuses what
> is passing and trivial, the merely clever and pretty,
> as certainly as the vulgar and insincere, and because
> it has gathered into itself the simplest and most un-
> forgettable thoughts of the generations, it is the soil
> where all great art is rooted.

Apart then from its intrinsic value, 'The Celtic Twilight'
represents a significant point in Mr. Yeats's development. The cottages of Connaught preserved him from suc-
cumbing to the atmosphere of preciosity which enveloped
him when he left them for the London and Paris of the
'nineties.   The influence of these literary circles upon
him was, of course, considerable.   He played with the
theosophy of Mme Blavatsky as he played with the artificial

and elaborate English consciously cultivated by devotees
of Walter Pater, but both his mysticism and his style were
too well-grounded in a rural tradition to be lastingly
corrupted by urban refinements. The poet who found the
streets of London hateful was not merely a sick dreamer,
who sought, like some of his contemporaries, to sop
realism with narcotics, but one whom the herons at Rosses
Point and Mayo women and Leinster fishermen had set seeking a reality that underlay the real and might be re-
invoked and reinterpreted in the present by those who had
struck down to its deep natural roots in the past. It
was because Mr. Yeats's mysticism continued to derive
from naturalism even when it became erudite by the study
of esoteric literatures that it never ceased to have
literary value or to reflect individual experience. The
same essential innocence has conditioned his experience
while he has advanced from the simplicity of instinct,
to which his early writing owes its popularity, to that of
refined sophistication, which marks his maturity. The
present volume illustrates certain stages in the transition. The illumination of the seer is a development of
the credulity of the child and the simpleton, and the
stories of ghosts, fairies, and devils which Mr. Yeats
took down from the lips of peasants in 'The Celtic
Twilight' inclined him for long towards a too credulous
acceptance of the fantastic for its own sake. At the
same time they enriched his sense of the mystery of life
and of the overlapping of time and eternity.

> To the wise peasant the green hills and woods round
> him are full of never-fading mystery. When the aged
> countrywoman stands at her door in the evening and, in
> her own words, 'looks at the mountains and thinks
> of the goodness of God', God is all the nearer be-
> cause the pagan powers are not far.

It was the same instinct which led Mr. Yeats to attempt by
various experiments that 'transmutation of the weary heart
into a weariless spirit' which he later described in
'Rosa Alchemica'. The experience, as he records it, is
at times tainted by an indolent, æsthetic connoisseurship,
characteristic of a period which opposed 'dreams' to
'Grey Truth', and pursued a reality which had little
organic relation with fact. But behind the 'elaborate
spiritual beauty' which he invoked as alone able to 'up-
lift souls weighted with so many dreams' there lurked
continually 'a pagan's delight in various beauty', and it
is this which enabled him to outgrow the self-consciousness that at that time threatened his attempt to graft

thought on to instinctive sensibility and to purge his
imagination of the merely arbitrary and picturesque.
   In the later prose included in this volume, however,
the process is by no means complete. It is too often
both fantastic and sophisticated, and, while the fantasy
of the peasant is delightful because its naivety is inevitable, the cultivated dreaming of 'Rosa Alchemica' is
'full of lassitude, and of wavering purpose'. The same
process may be traced through Mr. Yeats's poetry as
through his prose. Although there is nothing in his second
book of poems, now entitled 'The Rose', so mystically
pondered as in its successor, 'The Wind Among the Reeds',
it contains more

>   Of things discovered in the deep,
>   Where only body's laid asleep.

than in its predecessor 'Crossways'. He had begun to imagine beauty as 'suffering with man and not as something
pursued and seen from afar', and his verse therefore inevitably became more subtle and complicated. In the
present edition he has altered several of these poems in
an attempt to express better what he thought and felt as
a young man. The alterations entail the sacrifice of
several lines felicitous in themselves and endeared by
association, and in the case of two poems, 'The Song of
the Old Pensioner' and 'The Sorrow of Love', are so considerable as to transform them completely. Generally,
however, Mr. Yeats has effected a finer crystallization
of emotion, and he has wisely confined himself to those
poems of which he has not outgrown the experience.

A Vision (1925)

67. A.E. (GEORGE RUSSELL) ON THE COHERENCE OF 'A VISION',
THIS EXTRAORDINARY BOOK

1926

A review of 'A Vision' (1925; 600 copies were issued to
subscribers in January 1926), by George Russell, 'The
Irish Statesman'. 13 February 1926.
For note on George Russell see p. 130.

A sage out of the ancient world possibly might write with .
more understanding of 'A Vision' than any of Mr. Yeats'
contemporaries. It is an interpretation of life and history, but the interpreter has a compass in his hand, and
he measures and divides the cycles as if he had at heart
more than any other saying that profundity of Plato,
'God Geometrises'. It might be compared with Henry Adams'
mathematical interpretation of history in the astonishing essay on 'Phase', but it is infinitely more complicated, infinitely more difficult to understand. Subtle
as the thought was in 'Phase' it was an exercise in simplicity compared with 'A Vision'. Here I fall away from
a mind I have followed, I think with understanding, since
I was a boy, and as he becomes remote in his thought I
wonder whether he has forgotten his own early wisdom,
the fear lest he should learn 'to speak a tongue men do
not know'. I allow myself to drift apart because I feel
to follow in the wake of Mr. Yeats' mind is to surrender
oneself to the idea of Fate and to part from the idea of
Free Will. I know how much our life is fated once life
animates the original cell, the fountain from which the
body is jetted; how much bodily conditions affect or even

determine our thought, but I still believe in Free Will
and that, to use the language of the astrologers, it is
always possible for a man to rise above his stars. Now
Mr. Yeats would have me believe that a great wheel turns
ceaselessly, and that I and all others drop into inevitable
groove after groove. It matters not my virtue to-day, my
talent which I burnish, the wheel will move me to another
groove where I am predestined to look on life as that new
spiritual circumstance determines, and my will is only
free to accept or rebel, but not to alter what is fated.

The 'Vision' is so concentrated, the thought which in
other writers would be expanded into volumes, is here continually reduced to bare essences, to tables of the faculties and their interactions, that I may have missed some
implication, and there may be some way out, and it may be
that in his system we are more masters of our fate than
my study of the book has led me to suppose. The weighty
core of the book is relieved by a preliminary fantasy.
Owen Aherne and Michael Robartes, old creatures of the
poet's imagination, meet, and Robartes tells Aherne of his
wanderings, and how in Cracow he discovered a mediæval
tractate, 'Speculum Angelorum et Hominorum', written by
one Giraldus, and how later in Arabia, among the Judwalis,
he found men learned to the same philosophy. He instructs
Aherne in this, then quarrels with him, and Aherne brings
his notes to Yeats, who writes from them his 'Vision'.
All this fantasy and the philosophical poems set in the
book create about its hard geometrical core an air of
cold beauty like a wintry sunrise playing on a pyramid of
stony rock, and once the difficult geometry of 'Anima
Mundi' is expounded there is a long and brilliant meditation upon history, its changes and cycles related to the
movements of divine powers. As I looked at the diagrams
and tables, so difficult to relate to life, I encouraged
myself to explore by remembering what Neander wrote in
his 'Church History' when he was confronted by the task of
elucidating the bewildering mythology of the Gnostics.
We must remember, he said, that the mind of man is made
in the image of God, and therefore even in its wildest
speculations it follows an image of truth. That is, there
is something in the very anatomy of the soul which pro-
hibits its adventure into that which is utterly baseless
and unrelated to life. It may discolour what is true,
but by its very nature it cannot escape from a truth.
Just as we find shapely or unshapely people, but they all
conform to a human model, so the soul in its remotest
imaginations conforms in some transcendental way to its
microcosmic relation to the macrocosm.

We live our lives in an erratic rhythm, waking and
sleeping alone sure in their return, for in our lives
one day never repeats exactly the rhythm of another.
But let us imagine an Oversoul to humanity whose
majestic motions have the inevitability of the rising
and setting of constellations. Let us assume, as we well
might, that that majesty in its in-breathing and out-
breathing casts a light upon our own being as the sun in
its phases of dawn, noon and sunset makes changing the
colours of all it illuminates. Well, Mr. Yeats takes the
Great Year of the Ancients, a cycle of 'Anima Mundi'
symbolised by the passage of the sun through the Zodiacal
constellations, a period of about 26,000 years of our
time, but in his system it is considered but as one year
of that mightier being whose months and days, all with
their own radiant vitality, influence our own evolution.
One of its days may be the spiritual light of many of our
generations. It moves from subjective to objective.
There are cycles within cycles, action and recoil, contrasted and opposing powers, all of a bewildering complexity, and caught within this great wheel the lesser
wheel of our life revolves, having phases as many as the
days of a lunar month, all re-echoing the lordlier cycle
and its phases. When he illustrates these phases of
human life, thirty in all, by portraits of men and women,
dead and living, typical of the phase, I suspect the
author to be animated not only by a desire to elucidate
the system, but by an impish humour. I ask myself was it
insight or impishness which made him link Bernard Shaw,
H.G. Wells and George Moore as typical men of the twenty-
first phase, or what old lady did he discover in Mr.
Galsworthy to make him unite that novelist with Queen
Victoria? I am a little uncomfortable with some of my
fellow-prisoners in phase twenty-five. I welcome George
Herbert, but am startled to find myself along with Calvin,
Luther and Cardinal Newman, as no doubt the last three
would be incredulous of their own affinities to associate
pilgrim souls. I am inclined to think all the good
qualities of Carlyle were pruned by Mr. Yeats' geometrical scissors to make him fit into his phase. But these
character tellings, illustrative of the phases, will be
to many the most interesting part of the book. For all
its bewildering complexity the metaphysical structure he
rears is coherent, and it fits into its parts with the
precision of Chinese puzzle-boxes into each other. It
coheres together, its parts are related logically to each
other, but does it relate so well to life? Do we, when
we read about the cycles and their attributions, say to
ourselves, yes, so men have gone changed from mood to

mood. We can say from our reading of history that there
is action and reaction, that the philosophers of one age
are antithetical to those who preceded them, that the
political ideas of our age must face in the next a recoil
of contrary, equal and opposing forces: nay, that the
very moment one power starts out for dominion over the
spirit, it calls into activity an opposing power, 'one
lives the other's death, one dies the other's life'.
But as they are immortals they never truly die, and the
life of the antithetical powers is like that combat of
hero and demon the poet imagined so many years ago in
his 'Wanderings of Usheen'. Yes, we see this interaction,
recoil and succession of mood in history, but are they
the interaction, recoil and succession of moods Mr. Yeats
sees? We have a tendency to make much of all that has
affinity with our mood or our argument, and not to see
or to underrate the importance of all that is not akin.
I, with a different mentality from Mr. Yeats, see figures
as important which are without significance to him. If I
summed up the character of an age I might read black where
he reads white. Doubtless, every age has a distinctive
character, or predominant mood, and I am not learened
enough in history to oppose confidently my own reading
against his. I have written round and round this extraordinary book, unable in a brief space to give the slightest idea of its packed pages, its division of the faculties
of man, the Will, the Creative Genius, the Mask and the
Body of Fate and their lunar gyrations, or of its division
of the transcendental man, the diamoniac nature and its
cycles and their relations to our being, or of the doctrines of the after life. Almost any of its crammed pages
would need a volume to elucidate its meanings. It is not
a book which will affect many in our time. It is possible
it may be discussed feverishly by commentators a century
hence, as Blake's prophetic books so ignored, so unintelligible a hundred years ago, are discussed by many editors
in our time, and he is found to be the profoundest voice
of his own age. It is possible 'A Vision' may come to
be regarded as the greatest of Mr. Yeats' works. It is
conceivable also that it may be regarded as his greatest
erring from the way of his natural genius, and the lover
of his poetry may lament that the most intense concentration of his intellect was given to this book rather
than to drama or lyric. Personally, I am glad it was
written. I do not doubt that though the seeds of his
thought do not instantly take root and fructify in my
mind that they will have their own growth, and later I may
find myself comprehending much that is now unintelligible.
So far as the mere writing is concerned, the part dealing

with the Great Wheel and History is as fine as any prose
he has ever written, and the verses set here and there
have a fine, clear, cold and wintry beauty. The poetic
intellect has devoured the poetic emotion, but through
the transformation, beauty, the spirit animating both,
maintains its unperturbed life.

                                                    A.E.

68. FRANK PEARCE STURM ON THE GREAT WHEEL

1929

Extract from a letter written on 26 August 1929 by
F.P. Sturm, included in 'His Life, Letters and Collected
Work' (1969), edited by Richard Taylor.
   Frank Pearce Sturm (1879-1942) poet, mystic and translator, was born in Manchester and educated at the University of Aberdeen. He had been in touch with Yeats
(whose poetry he admired and by which his own was influenced) by 1903. In 1904 he married and went to France
to translate Baudelaire: he and his wife returned —
perforce — to their medical studies, and he bought a
practice at Leigh in Lancashire. After the war he and
his wife became interested in Anthroposophy; he
published 'Umbrae Silentes' (1918), a subjective dis-
quisition on the immortality of the soul. His occult
belief was similar to that of Yeats, and there are some
marked similarities between Sturm's poetry (which Yeats
encouraged him to publish) and Yeats's. The two men met
and corresponded. Their correspondence (together with the
editor's valuable commentary on their friendship and the
parallels between their work) is included in 'Frank
Pearce Sturm, His Life, Letters and Collected Work'
(edited by Richard Taylor, 1969). Sturm, a likeable man,
had an ironic sense of humour and one letter records his
view of Yeats clearly. 'Yeats,' he wrote on 25 August
1936, 'appeals to those few of us who are so cultured that
we dare not write the word shit.'

My dear Yeats:
This place [the Royal Hotel, Southport] only remotely
resembles the Tavern of the Screaming Seraph at Byzantium.

Old men come here also, & argue together, but they talk money not philosophy.

I have been reading your new introduction to the Great Wheel, which I suppose is to be a remoulded 'Vision'. Do get some friend who knows Latin to read the proofs this time. I know that I am a pedant, but pedants read you. We cough in the ink till the worlds end, as you cruelly said, but the least of us would save you from the errors which spoil The Vision as it is now.

Personally I think your philosophy smells of the fagot. Some dead & damned Chaldean *mathematikoi* have got hold of your wife & are trying to revive a dead system.

All these gyres & cones & wheels are parts of a machine that was thrown on the scrap heap when Ptolemy died. It won't go. There is no petrol for such.

The ghosts of the *mathematikoi* are weeping over their broken toy universe: the *Primum Mobile* no longer moves, the seven planetary spheres of crystal are dull as a steamy cookshop window — so they are trying to speak through your wife & are using much that she has read in the past.

However, all that you write is letters. No doubt many an Inquisitor has signed as he condemned some author to the flames. You would not have escaped. . . .

My new book, when I write it is to be in seven parts, & is to be called 'Seven Fagots for the Burning of the Great Heretic Yeats' — or 'The Wheel Dismantled' — printed for the author by Michael Paleologus and is to be purchased at the Sign of the Screaming Seraph in Byzantium.

> Yours
> F.P. Sturm

69. RICHARD CHURCH ON YEATS'S CONCEPT OF LIFE AS A TRAGEDY

1927

A review of 'Autobiographies' (1926) by Richard Church, W.B. Yeats and the Creative Mask, 'Calendar of Modern Letters', January 1927.

Richard Church (1893–1973) poet, novelist, autobiographer and essayist, worked as a civil servant and publisher's adviser. His volume of 'Collected Poems' (1948) was followed by two volumes of autobiography, 'Over the Bridge' (1955) and 'The Golden Sovereign' (1957). The auto-

biographies show his interest in poetry engagingly; his
own poems were in the tradition of Wordsworth and had a
Georgian flavour.

Browsing recently over Mr. Yeats's 'Autobiographies' —
a valuable book for the person given to speculation on
the origin and machinery of literary activity — I came
upon the following passage:

> Years afterwards when I had finished 'The Wanderings
> of Oisin', dissatisfied with its yellow and its dull
> green, with all that overcharged colour inherited
> from the romantic movement, I deliberately re-shaped
> my style, deliberately sought out an impression as of
> cold light and tumbling clouds. I cast off traditional
> metaphors and *loosened my rhythm,* and, recognizing
> that all the criticism of life known to me was alien
> and English, became as emotional as possible but with
> an emotion which I described to myself as cold.

Mr. Yeats has certainly achieved that crystallization
of emotion for which he strove. By creating for himself
a myth opposite and complementary to that of Pygmalion
he has learned how to imprison life in art. The process
is that which Wordsworth more humanely described as
'remembering emotion in tranquillity'. Sooner or later,
every artist must come to that process as his consciousness develops, as he rises above instincts, impulses,
and the mechanical suggestion of environment, towards a
subtle and blandly-suspicious condition of mind which
alone is capable of valuable creative power. Only then
can he be sure that he is speaking with his own voice;
that he is reaching down to the permanent relationship
existing between him and his fate. The discovery of that
permanent and real self, shorn of all conventions, sub-
missions, courtesies, and other disguises, is the aim of
every being who possesses human dignity. Some find it
soon and without effort, as for instance, Chatterton and
Mozart. Others run on, in agonies of suspense and trial,
from experience to experience, crisis to crisis, mentor
to mentor, always about to reach self-realization, but
only fully achieving it towards the end of life. The
majority of us never succeed. We live and die obscured,
masked by crowd-traditions and ideas, and so emerge at
birth from oblivion to pass into the same oblivion at
death, our sojourn here un-utilized.
How are we to know when we are truly ourselves? Mr.
Yeats has a criterion:

As life goes on we discover that certain thoughts
sustain us in defeat, or give us victory, whether over
ourselves or others, and it is these thoughts, tested
by passion, that we call convictions. Among subjective men (in all those, that is, who must spin a web
out of their own bowels) the victory is an intellectual daily recreation of all that exterior fate
snatched away, and so that fate's antithesis; while
what I have called 'The Mask' is an emotional antithesis to all that comes out of their internal nature.
We begin to live when we have conceived life as a tragedy.

Here he sketches more deliberately the process of self-
discovery. His 'Mask' can surely be no more than that
line of conduct and thought which is most difficult for
our individual nature. I look out on the world and see
where I succeed, where I conquer environment, where I
make my personality most felt. In those directions I am
complete and have fulfilled that part of my destiny. But,
apart from that very limited field of conquest, I see
myself baffled, overcome by helplessness before a too-
complex problem of existence. A little circumstance,
repeating itself as though at the prompting of some too-
knowing and malicious demon, throws me down — fearful
and chagrined. Certain planes of life, certain fields of
activity or speculation, I *know* to be impossible to me.
Perhaps my flair is for intuitive solutions of the problems
of life. I may be able to glance at a face and leap to a
correct estimate of the character behind it. I may be
able to cleave through intellectual knots with sudden
swords of vision. Let me beware of all these facilities.
Let me treat them as self which is already fully grown and
finished. If I believe in re-incarnation, let me say that
these native powers of mine are an inheritance from former
existences, and are nothing to my credit. What I achieve
with them, I do not achieve of myself. It is done for me.
How then shall I prove that I have a daemon of creation,
a will to impose upon fate? I must turn my mind to those
thoughts and mental processes of which I am afraid. I
must plunge into actions from which I shrink in dread or
shyness. I must assume a Mask to hide my grimaces of
fear from the world, and I must set up before my eyes an
Image of perfection in these matters in which I am so
imperfect. By a gradual changing of my features to fit
that Mask; by a quiet but persistent dissolution of
myself into that Image, I shall bring to my inherited
strengths and faculties newer ones, more immediately suited
to the particular accidence of my environment.

This may sound very old-fashioned, very reminiscent of
Emerson's dogma of self-reliance; of the rigid and wearing discipline of Sparta, and its mechanical and unintel-
ligent imitation, the English Public-School code. But,
nevertheless, it seems to be the only way of developing
one's personality so that one can stand four-square
against the world. One may argue that there is a danger
of self-destruction in such a practice; that the strain
will dull the nerves, kill spontaneity, and banish from
one's life the quality of joy without which there can be
no triumph over circumstance. But I think the reply to
that argument is that a certain repression gives us
greater potential energy, just as a gas by compression has
more dynamic force. Morbid conditions have their value,
for they are significant of change and development. Who
is more active-minded than the so-called pessimist? So
we find Mr. Yeats insisting that 'we begin to live when
we have conceived life as a tragedy'.

Without that conception, we are not sufficiently wary;
we are not, as I hinted above, *suspicious* enough of the
world around us, which, by the strength of its multi-
fariousness, is always tending to dissipate our energies,
to break down that coherence of idea and conduct, that
continuity of purpose, by which a personality is made.

The conception of life as a tragedy is really the
acknowledgment of one's own vulnerability to the onslaughts
of the external world. How can one, from that basis, be
satisfied to exploit the faculties with which one is already well equipped, and to ignore the weaknesses in one's
armour? It is a policy of self-deception and cowardice,
and is bound to lead to disaster. Our strengths are as
strong as our weaknesses. Until we realize that, we can
have no unity of being, that blessed state in which our
inherent faculties attempt perfect freedom and expression. We come thus to a paradox: that to develop originality, we must suppress originality, and give our attention to those parts of our being in which we are commonplace. Who is more dreadful than the artist who works his
talent to death? He becomes a repeating machine in his
work; and in himself he degenerates into an irritable
vanity that just fails to cover the sore of humiliation
and failure. I cannot agree with Mr. Yeats when he says:

I now know that there are men who cannot possess 'Unity
of Being', who must not seek it or express it — and who,
so far from seeking an anti-self, a Mask that delineates
a being in all things the opposite to their natural
state, can but seek the suppression of the anti-self,
till the natural state alone remains. These are those

who must seek no image of desire, but await that which
lies beyond their mind — unities not of the mind, but
unities of nature, unities of God — the man of science,
the moralist, the humanitarian, the politician, St.
Simon Stylites upon his pillar, St. Anthony in his
cavern, all whose preoccupation is to seem nothing;
to follow their hearts till they are void and without
form, to summon a creator by revealing chaos, to become the lamp for another's wick and oil; and, indeed,
it may be that it has been for their guidance in a very
special sense that the 'perfectly proportioned human
body' suffered crucifixion.

The man who seeks no image of desire, but awaits that
which lies beyond his mind — well, I believe he will
continue to wait. That process of 'seeming nothing', of
'hollowing one's heart' — is an effort of agony, the
sumpreme act of energy. The integral parts of our being
are so curiously integrated, and articulated each to the
other, that, by the effort to stir up our weaker members,
we set the whole hive working. John Keats's efforts and
failures with the surgeon's knife had their value, as he
discovered.
    I think Mr. Yeats analyses this paradox of the human
mechanism when he asks:

Does not all art come when a nature, that never ceases
to judge itself, exhausts personal emotion in action
or desire so completely that something impersonal,
something that has nothing to do with action or desire, suddenly starts into its place, something which
is as unforeseen, as completely organized, even as
unique, as the images that pass before the mind between sleeping and waking?

    I cannot see how Mr. Yeats reconciles this with his
theory that there are men who achieve by shaping themselves like cups, into which the wine of inspiration is to
be poured by some gracious external Hand. The only way
by which this mortal, this blood-supported self can plunge
through the obscurations of the physical world is by way
of the intellect. We have to be logical, coherent, and
scientific, before we can emerge into that plane of inspiration where the being becomes illogical and *more*
coherent. Such a condition is one of crisis, which, as
Mr. Yeats says, 'joins our hidden self for certain
moments to the trivial daily mind'. I wish he would not
occasionally deny himself by preaching that these divine
crises can be induced by passivity in conduct and idea.

He is too practical-minded, and too deeply experienced
in the artist's life of self-immolation, to believe in
this theory. I can only imagine that, when he supports
it, he is playfully posing; indulging in one of those
fits of impish irresponsibility which are the only leisure
for men who spend their lives faithfully trying to fulfil
their own genius.

70. LADY GREGORY ON YEATS'S REMARKS

1927

Two entries from 'Lady Gregory's Journals 1916-1930'
(edited by Lennox Robinson, 1946) dated respectively
17 June 1927 and 20 June 1927.
    For note on Lady Gregory see p. 181.

(a)

Yeats read me his poem, the Woman section fine but rather
difficult to understand in one reading. I said his
poetry is like the Bible, the beginning, Wanderings of
Usheen and Countess Cathleen — as easy as the Book of
Moses; then the more reasoning ones, and now the Book of
Revelation that has to be interpreted. He says he sometimes gets a thought and ascribes it to another — he
had been quoting from Gentile, 'the world is so incredible
that we go about touching it with our hands to convince
ourselves that it exists'. But now he has been looking for
it in Gentile's book and can't find it.

(b)

Yeats met old Putnam in London and said, 'Mr. Putnam,
you were my first publisher, and you told me I did not
know how to spell. And I still do not know how to spell.'
And then they got on very well. He says, 'Mrs. Phillimore
belongs to the generation of reasoners. When I said I
could not read Bertrand Russell and said I might as well
make love to a woman with a bald head, she said "But why
could you not make love to a woman with a bald head?"' and
was prepared to reason it. He says, 'They sent me an
invitation signed by thirty to the Trinity College dinner,

so, though I had refused, I did go. I spoke chiefly on
the Lane pictures. About our tradition I said, "Berkeley
was the first to say the world is a vision; Burke was the
first to say a nation is a tree. And those two sayings
are a foundation of modern thought."
    'At some house where I lunched they were speculating
as to what Lindbergh thought when he was coming over the
Atlantic. A millionaire woman said he probably thought of
a line from some American poem, "on a sea of rapture". I
said, "No, whatever a man in that position thinks of, it
is not rhetoric. I am an imaginative poet and I know."'
He thought he had offended some writer who was there, but
next day his hostess, bringing him a super-chocolate box,
told him this man had said, 'I have only in my life heard
two good talkers, Shaw and Yeats.'

71. I.A. RICHARDS ON YEATS'S USE OF TRANCE, HIS DISLIKE
OF SCIENCE AND CONTEMPT FOR THE GENERALITY

1927

From I.A. Richards, Some Contemporary Poets, 'Science
and Poetry' (1927).
    Ivor Armstrong Richards (b. 1893) was educated at
Magdalene College, Cambridge, where he became a Fellow.
He visited China (1929-30) and was Director of the Harvard
Commission on English Language (1939-44), a post which
arose out of his interest in Basic English which he
developed with C.K. Ogden and James Wood. He has been a
poet, but is perhaps better known for his critical work
which includes 'Principles of Literary Criticism' (1925)
and 'Practical Criticism' (1929).

Mr. Yeats' work from the beginning was a repudiation of
the most active contemporary interests. But at first
the poet of 'The Wanderings of Usheen', 'The Stolen
Child' and 'Innisfree' turned away from contemporary
civilization in favour of a world which he knew perfectly,
the world of folklore as it is accepted, neither with
belief nor disbelief, by the peasant. Folklore and the
Irish landscape, its winds, woods, waters, islets and
seagulls, and for a while an unusually simple and direct
kind of love poetry in which he became something more
than a minor poet, these were his refuge. Later, after

a drawn battle with the drama, he made a more violent repudiation, not merely of current civilization but of life itself, in favour of a supernatural world. But the world of the 'eternal moods', of supernal essences and immortal beings is not, like the Irish peasant stories and the Irish landscape, part of his natural and familiar experience. Now he turnes to a world of symbolic phantasmagoria about which he is desperately uncertain. He is uncertain because he has adopted as a technique of inspiration the use of trance, of dissociated phases of consciousness, and the revelations given in these dissociated states are insufficiently connected with normal experience. This, in part, explains the weakness of Mr Yeats' transcendental poetry. A deliberate reversal of the natural relations of thought and feeling is the rest of the explanation. Mr Yeats takes certain feelings — feelings of conviction attaching to certain visions — as evidence for the thoughts which he supposes his visions to symbolize. To Mr Yeats the value of 'The Phases of the Moon' lies not in any attitudes which it arouses or embodies but in the doctrine which for an initiate it promulgates.

The resort to trance, and the effort to discover a new world-picture to replace that given by science, are the two most significant points for our purpose in Mr Yeats' work. A third might be the singularly bitter contempt for the generality of mankind which occasionally appears.

The Tower (1928)

72. HIGHLY PERSONAL POETRY DEALING IN A COMMON STOCK

1928

An unsigned review of 'The Tower' (1928) [by Austin Clarke],
Mr. Yeats's New Poems, 'Times Literary Supplement', 1 March
1928.
   Austin Clarke (1896-1974) was educated at University
College, Dublin, where he succeeded Thomas MacDonagh as
a lecturer in English when MacDonagh was executed in 1916.
He lived as a literary journalist in England from the
1920s to 1938, when he returned to Ireland. His autobiographical writings include 'Twice Round the Black
Church' (1962), and 'A Penny in the Clouds' (1968). He
wrote several volumes of poetry including the 'Cattle-
drive in Connaught' (1925); 'Flight to Africa' (1963);
'Mnemosyne Lay in Dust' (1966) and 'A Sermon on Swift'
(1969). His 'Collected Poems' appeared in 1936, his
'Later Poems' in 1961. Clarke was deeply interested
in verse-speaking and his verse-speaking group often
performed on the Irish radio and staged verse plays in
Dublin.

When the later poetry of Mr. Yeats had shown a complete
abnegation of imaginative festivity, a deliberate poverty
at table and gate, the dismissed reader was inclined to
believe that the poet had mistaken mocking rags and an
empty state for true austerity. Impatient with an
earlier and lovelier mood that had never been easily won,
Mr. Yeats had seemed to choose to resentfully, as images
against life, 'all things uncomely and broken, all things
worn out and old'. Disturbing as that phase of disillusion

had been, one believed that it would pass into contentment.   Although there is no philosophic peace in this new book of poems, the acerbity has changed, as often as not, into intellectual anxiety and indignation: one becomes aware of a deeper sorrow at the roots of being that one cannot read of without being strangely moved.   More constantly than in preceding books, perhaps, there is a quality in these poems which seems at variance with their personal disquiet, a freedom of the poetic elements, an imaginative and prosodic beauty that brings one the pure and impersonal joy of art.

This highly personal poetry, which is self-analytic and preoccupied with the workings of the mind, has come to pause over a learned or literary image, a memory of person or time, a Quattrocento loveliness or a Greek commonplace.   It may appear more approachable, despite its aloofness of opinion, than the work of Mr. Yeats's middle age, for it is concerned with problems of the natural mind, age or destiny: it deals in a common stock.   Those who found themselves as frightened foreigners in that Celtic twilight, where symbols moved independently as mythological beings and had taken upon themselves another existence may be still puzzled, if their wits are poor, but they have a lessening reason for being mystified.   One scarcely has to recall 'Il Penseroso' to find a tower, with its solid and bleak masonry, a fitting place and image for meditation.   Mr. Yeats, in his title poem, calls up gracious or fantastically touched memories of the past and weighs them against the realities of his present.   Here, indeed, is a poetry that has come painfully to face the plain fact, if not to out-stare it, avoiding those agreeable hypotheses which are so often mistaken either as the substance of poetic thought or the beginning of wisdom.   The intensity of the poem carries with it melancholy or derogatory images, as when the poet writes of his years, finding no consolation in numbers:

> Decrepit age that has been tied to me
>   As to a dog's tail,

or again, in another poem, he speaks of the resentful intellect, 'fastened to a dying animal'.   The sharp division in these poems of physical from mental fact calls to mind, in passing, those popular medieval dialogues between body and soul in Latin, but with a difference, since here an individual doubt is substituted for the commonplaces or mysteries of creed.   Here the quickness of the intellect is set against those stern facts of age, against 'slow decay of blood', 'testy delirium', and

that worse evil of the affections, the death of friends,
'or death of every brilliant eye, That made a catch in
the breath'. In that mood of grief a confession of faith
becomes a protest of individualism and has little in
common with, for instance, the gracious idealism of
Berkley:

> I mock Plotinus' thought
> And cry in Plato's teeth,
> Death and life were not
> Till man made up the whole,
> Made lock, stock and barrel
> Out of his bitter soul.

And as he tells us —

> I have prepared my peace
> With learned Italian things.

The recurring mood compels one to realize a loneliness of
mind fallen back upon itself. One realizes, too, how
completely the poet is exiled, in faith though not in art,
from his earlier work which had drawn so much upon impersonal belief and upon traditional imagination.

Upon these poems, despite their isolation, their manifestation of pride as refuge, other realities obtrude as
suddenly as the armed young men who arrived at Thoor
Ballylee to blow up the bridge, as Mr. Yeats tells us in
a note, 'saying at last, "Goodnight, thank you," as
though we had given them the bridge.' In the policies of
the time and the conflict of issues Mr. Yeats has taken
his own stand; remembering a great house or two of his
youth or hearsay of a magnanimous gesture, and praising an
Anglo-Irish aristocracy that produced wit and oratory
(which Mr. Yeats really hates) but spent all its imagination upon extravagant behaviour, leaving only its pride:

> The pride of people that were
> Bound neither to Cause nor to State,
> Neither to slaves that were spat on,
> Not to the tyrants that spat,
> The people of Burke and of Grattan,
> That gave, though free to refuse —
> Pride, like that of the morn,
> When the headlong light is loose,
> Or that of the fabulous horn,
> Or that of the sudden shower
> When all streams are dry.

Personal discontents and the commotion of Irish public
times mingle, indeed, in these verses, satirical or
lyrical; but happily the imagination, despite its own
inhibitions, remains as free and symbolic. There is,
indeed, a constant awareness in the lines of this secret
industry of art:

> Never had I more
> Excited, passionate, fantastical
> Imagination, nor an ear and eye
> That more expected the impossible —
> No, not in boyhood, when with rod and fly,
> Or the humbler worm, I climbed Ben Bulben's back
> And had the livelong summer day to spend.

Poets, as much as politicians or publicists, may be permitted to observe the emotions which move through the
multitude as greater moods. That Mr. Yeats should still
find picturesque or heraldic expression for moods of
public hate, enthusiasm or violence, is a particular gain.
So in the seventh of his Meditations he sees from the
tower top, in the moon, when 'A mist that is like blown
snow is sweeping over all,' sees for a moment, clearly
before they have been dispersed by the phantoms of hatred,
those other images of 'the heart's fullness'.

> Their legs, long, delicate and slender, aquamarine
>   their eyes,
> Magical unicorns bear ladies on their backs.
> The ladies close their musing eyes. No prophecies
> Remembered out of Babylonian almanacs,
> Have closed the ladies' eyes, their minds are but a pool
> Where even longing drowns under its own excess;
> Nothing but stillness can remain when hearts are full
> Of their own sweetness, bodies of their loveliness.

One may remark again upon the prosodic beauty of the
poems, since criticism has lost its ear. The alexandrine
has been a curiously neglected metre in English; how
fascinating that may be, when its possibilities
of equipoise and of delicate substitution have been used,
may be seen in some of these poems. But the curious will
discover vibrancy of word and subtle cadence for themselves. In a note Mr. Yeats pays tribute to a beautiful
poem by Mr. T. Sturge Moore, and one may remark in conclusion on the delightful cover design of this book by
the artist poet.

73. JOHN GOULD FLETCHER SEES YEATS AS A GREAT MODERN POET

1928

From a review of 'The Tower' (1928) by John Gould Fletcher,
'The Criterion', September 1928.
    John Gould Fletcher (b. 1886), born at Little Rock,
Arkansas, educated at Harvard, lived fifteen years in
England before returning to the family home in Little
Rock in 1933. He joined the Imagists in 1914 after the
publication of five of his books of poems in 1913. He
changed his style in 1917. His 'XXIV Elegies' (1935)
took him twenty years to write. He translated Elie Faure
and J.J. Rousseau and wrote a prophetic essay contrasting
Russia and America as well as commenting on similarities
between them.

. . . Here ['The Tower'] we have not a collection of
anthology specimens, good or bad, but what is essentially
a *Weltanschauung* worked out at high tension in poetic form.
To Mr Yeats, the world of myth and legend and the world of
objective fact are extraordinarily close to each other.
He sees the whole of outward phenomena and the whole of
subjective fantasy as being in some sense like the creation of man:

> Death and life were not
> Till man made up the whole,
> Made lock, stock and barrel
> Out of his bitter soul,
> Aye, sun and moon and star, all;
> And further add to that
> That being dead, we rise,
> Dream, and so create
> Translunar Paradise.

This attitude enables him to see Troy burning in a hay-
stack set on fire, and old legends coming to life in the
tumult and fury of Ireland torn by civil war. Yet in
thus moving closer to the epic (and the best parts of
his book are brief, concentrated epics) he has not over-
looked his own beginnings which were lyric evocations of
'old mythologies', akin to Keats and Shelley. Thus the
sensitive critic can find in him alike echoes of the old
romantic yearning and subrational love for the undisci-
plined world of imagination, alongside of Greek epic
fatalism of contemplation directed to the outer world of

fact. He corresponds, or will correspond, when the true
literary history of our epoch is written, to what we
moderns mean by a great poet.

74. THEODORE SPENCER ON THE AUTHORITY OF YEATS'S SYMBOLISM

1928

From a review of 'The Tower' (1928) by Theodore Spencer,
'New Republic', 10 October 1928.
    Theodore Spencer (1902-49), American critic and poet,
was educated at Princeton, Cambridge and Harvard, where
he taught from 1927 to 1939. He was then appointed to a
lectureship in English at Cambridge — the first American
to be elected to such a post — but because of the breaking out of the wear he stayed at Harvard and became
Boyleston Professor of Rhetoric and Oratory in that University in 1946. 'Poems: 1940-1947' (1948) contained
much of his work published in earlier volumes. He wrote
two books of criticism, 'Death and Elizabethan Tragedy'
(1936) and 'Shakespeare and the Nature of Man' (1943).

No one has been more aware of the contemporary problem
than Mr Yeats; the question of an external order, and the
individual's relation to it, has been his constant preoccupation. In his earliest poems he sought 'some symbolic language reaching far back into the past and associated with familiar names and conspicuous hills that I
might not be alone amid the obscure impressions of the
senses'; and in the poems of his second period he strove
to express 'those simple emotions which resemble the more,
the more powerful they are, everybody's emotion. . . .
I was soon to write many poems where an always personal
emotion was woven into a general pattern of myth and
symbol'.
    But a reference to Irish legend or the mere expression
of emotion, no matter how universal it may be, was, to
Mr Yeats, not enough. Description and analysis must be
followed by synthesis, and for the past ten or fifteen
years, the construction of such a synthesis, in a form
outside of poetry, has been Mr Yeats' chief concern. He
has worked out an elaborate scheme, which explains, on the
authority of medieval magic, spiritism, and personal
revelation, the relationship between the elements of the

individual life, between different lives, and between the
individual and his age. An account of this system was
privately printed in 1925 under the title, 'A Vision'.
    This is not the place to discuss the validity of Mr
Yeats' philosophy; what we are concerned with is its
effect on his poetry. And for a time it seemed unfortunate. Such poems as 'The Phases of the Moon', and 'Ego
Dominus Tuus', written some eight years ago, though they
are by no means without fine lines, are jerky and uneven;
they are too didactic to be musical; they do not represent the proper marriage between thought and emotion.
    One awaited, therefore, Mr Yeats' next volume of verse
with considerable interest, and one was prepared to attack
it with several questions. Would the philosophy be sufficiently absorbed not to override the emotion? Would the
escapist element, now that a philosophic symbolism had
been substituted for a nationalistic one, still be too
predominant? Would the personal feeling be so related
to the external order that they would be fused into a
single whole?
    And now that 'The Tower' has appeared, one may answer
all these questions to Mr Yeats' advantage. It is true
that there are some reservations, and those will appear
in a moment, but, on the whole, the poems in this book
are among the finest Mr Yeats has written. They are, in
a sense, less dependent on 'A Vision' than their immediate predecessors; they are not, that is, expository.
The philosophy is used as a mine for symbols, instead of
itself being the subject-matter of the poems; this is, of
course, the way in which poetry should always make use
of philosophy. And it is symbolism employed in this
fashion which gives to Mr Yeats' poems a quality peculiar
to them alone. They have, in the first place, an air
of authority obtained by their reference to a system outside themselves, and, in the second place, they have a richness of tone which makes them echo and reëcho in the mind.
    But the use of a symbolism drawn from personal philo-
sophy implies a considerable danger. The symbols may be
too private, they may fail to communicate the emotion they
represent. And if this is the case, then the construction
of the philosophy will have, for poetry, little immediate
significance, and the poet will have to wait, like Blake,
a century or so before he is understood. Such, however,
it is safe to remark, will not be the fate of Mr Yeats.
His symbols are, as a rule, sufficiently related to the
common cultured memory so that they awaken a response in
the intelligent reader. Where the danger comes is in the
assignation to certain symbols of a greater emotional
value than they would have for anyone unacquainted with

Mr Yeats' own system. The subject of the poem called
'Sailing to Byzantium', for instance, is the determination
of the poet, now he has become old, to leave sensuous
things, and turn to the things of the spirit.

> And therefore I have sailed the seas and come
> To the holy city of Byzantium.

This is perfectly satisfactory, for one is willing to
accept the use of Byzantium as a symbol for age and wisdom,
especially when it is qualified by what follows:

> O sages standing in God's holy fire
> As in the gold mosaic of a wall,
> Come from the holy fire, perne in a gyre
> And be the singing masters of my soul.
> Consume my heart away: sick with desire
> And fastened to a dying animal
> It knows not what it is; and gather me
> Into the artifice of eternity.

This is admirable writing, and the only snag is the reference to Mr Yeats' system in the words, 'perne in a gyre'.
But when, as the climax of the poem, the poet tells us that once
'out of nature', he will only take his bodily form from

> Such a form as Grecian goldsmiths make
> Of hammered gold and gold enamelling
> To keep a drowsy emperor awake,

one feels, without a knowledge of Mr Yeats' sense of
values, that this is a trivial ambition, unworthy of the
strong feeling that has preceded it, and it is only when
one turns to page 191 of 'A Vision' and finds that the
craftsmanship of sixth-century Byzantium has for Mr
Yeats a special significance, that one can feel the poem
as it was meant to be felt.

Privacies like this are the chief fault of this book.
They are largely responsible for a sensation of trailing
off, of inconclusiveness, that the reader is not infre-
quently aware of. Just as, in Mr Yeats' prose, one feels
that thought and emotion are not clearly enough distinguished, so here one sometimes gets an impression of
mistiness, of a mind clad too obviously in flesh, that
prevents successful communication.

But such blemishes are outweighed by the positive
achievement which this book represents. There is no one
living to whom poetry is more important than to Mr Yeats,
there is hardly anyone more important to poetry. He has

made of poetry a method of life, and he has kept his art
steadily alive by adapting it to the changing circumstances of his thought. This book is different from its
predecessors, not only because it is concerned with different emotions, and because its style is in many ways
different from Mr Yeats' previous style, but also because
it gets closer to reality; it is more centripetal.
Even if the symbolism is on occasion remote, the emotions,
particularly those connected with old age, are more
convincing than they ever have been, and many of these
poems — 'The Tower', 'Nineteen Nineteen', 'Among School
Children' — will remain a permanent part of English
poetry.

75. THE SIMPLICITY AND GRAVITY OF YEATS'S VERSION OF
'OEDIPUS TYRANNUS'

1928

An unsigned review of 'Sophocles' King Oedipus: A
Version for the Modern Stage' (1928) [by a reviewer
named Smyth], 'Times Literary Supplement', 22 November
1928.

Mr. Yeats's version of the ' Œdipus Tyrannus' has already
received a practical proof of its worth in the enthusiasm with which it was received by a popular audience
in Dublin. So at least we learn from a newspaper extract printed on the cover, which seems to show that it
achieved a remarkable success at the Abbey Theatre.
Having thus completely fulfilled the end for which it was
made, it is immune from a mere reader's criticism, which
can only note some of the points that may have contributed to its triumph. It presents the dialogue considerably abridged in prose; and though this has necessitated the shearing away of heightened and ornamental turns
of speech permissible to a writer in verse, the simplification has its advantage in allowing the steady march
of the drama toward its catastrophe to be more clearly
followed. Moreover, the prose is always stately and
measured prose, uniform in tone, and depending for its
excitement on the gathering weight of the dreadful facts
that it invests. As it proceeds gravely on its way we
receive a greater sense of tragedy pure and unmitigated

than if the writer had tried to diversify it by adhering
more closely to the elaborated diction of Sophocles. 'The
one thing that I kept in mind,' he says, 'was that a word
unfitted for living speech, out of its natural order, or
unnecessary to our modern technique, would check emotion
and tire attention.' On all these points the taste of
Mr. Yeats is to be trusted. As regards the chorus,
which is in verse also much abridged, though it does not
complete with the impassioned beauty of the Greek, even
for a reader it attains its professed object, 'to
preserve the mood while it rests the mind by change of
attention'.

76. CHARLES WILLIAMS ON YEATS'S ENLARGING THE BOUNDARIES
OF POETRY AND MYTHOLOGY

1930

An extract from W.B. Yeats in Charles Williams, 'Poetry
at Present' (1930).
    Charles Williams (1886-1945), critic, novelist, essayist
and playwright, worked for the Oxford University Press,
during which time he had much to do with W.B. Yeats when
the 'Oxford Book of Modern Verse' was in the making. His
novels contained some of the mystical and supernatural
elements which he considered more seriously in his theological writings. His best work is to be found in
'Shadows of Ecstasy' (1933), 'Descent into Hell' (1937),
'The Image of the City' (1958), and 'Collected Plays'
(1963).

'Dreams' is a word that occurs often enough in Mr. Yeats's
work, but it seems that we should do him wrong if we
took it to mean only the confused nonsense of our own
sleep. It may include that, but it is more than that;
it is more than the refuge of the minor poet and weak
artist who so often claim for their negligible fantasies
the attention of the world which has, if nothing better,
at least something as good to concern itself with. It is
more even than the beautiful vaguenesses which Mr. Yeats
himself has sometimes made for us out of his own lesser
imaginations. It is prophecy, it is vision, it is sight
of and belief in a mode of existence much more real and
intense than that of every day. It is the hunger for

that mode of being which, in the earlier poems with
lament, in the later with a certain bitterness, causes
Mr. Yeats to think of the world of 'bankers, school-
masters, and clergymen'. The poetry itself is proof
enough of his sincerity; no such beauty, no such vivid
insolence, ever sprang from a mind that was not set with
all its strength of desire upon some other than a mortal
end. But what was once, so beautiful was the verse, in
the earlier poems a sorrow to linger in, an exquisite
sadness in the heart of love, has become in the later a
read suffering. 'Time and Fate and Change' were spoken
of dramatically, or else woven into the tapestries of
the chamber of love; but in later days they themselves
help to make the verse.

> A pity beyond all telling
> Is hid in the heart of love —

but the poignancy of it was, even so, a sweet enjoyment.
Sorrow will not consent even so tenderly to be lulled
with words, and Mr. Yeats would be a lesser poet than he
is if grief and disaster did not also speak in his verse.
There are no more beautiful poems in English than some of
his laments for 'dear dead women' —

> A crowd
> Will gather and not know it walks the very street
> Whereon a thing once walked that seemed a burning cloud;

and that exquisite one which has for refrain

> I knew a phoenix in my youth, so let them have their day.

Over the political poems, too, a change has come.
'Romantic Ireland's dead and gone', but the poem that says
so is itself a contradiction. The anger which an aristocratic and poetic mind feels for the corruption and greed
and malice of his fellows, and for the blatant stupidities
of the crowd, his scorn and his despair, are at least
equalled by the poems on the heroes of the Easter Rebellion
— 'a terrible beauty is born' — in one of which he
deliberately includes among that great company one who had
done his own dear friends 'most bitter wrong':

> He too has been changed in his turn,
> Transformed utterly,
> A terrible beauty is born.

In another poem, 'The People', where he laments —
almost fretfully — that all he has tried to do for the
town has been wasted, and that he might have been living
all that time, in ease and according to his desire, in
Italy, he puts also into the mouth of 'his phoenix' the
grave reply that, though 'the drunkards, pilferers of
public funds', have done her grievous harm,

> 'Yet never have I, now nor any time,
> Complained of the people.'
>   All I could reply
> Was: 'You, that have not lived in thought but deed,
> Can have the purity of a natural force,
> But I, whose virtues are the definitions
> Of the analytic mind, can neither close
> The eye of the mind, nor keep my tongue from speech.'
> And yet, because my heart leaped at her words,
> I was abashed, and now they come to mind
> After nine years, I sink my head abashed.

This mind, that was set, like Donne's, on other modes
of being, has engaged itself also with the world, and out
of that conflict has made (as it was its business to do)
most moving verse. 'Out of the strong came forth sweetness'. The marvellous song of these earlier years, the
inappeasable desire which was sometimes a lament, and
sometimes a tenderness, and sometimes an incantation,
and sometimes a questing call after faerie, and sometimes
a cry so near the borders of humanity that only the songs
of Ariel went beyond it — all these things have changed
and yet still exist.
    The change is clear, not only in the tone of the mind,
but in the sound of the verse. If there was a danger to
the earlier poems it was that the slight languor which
seemed sometimes to accompany those dreams should be
changed into a slight weariness with them, through the
over-repetition of certain words and phrases — 'pearl-
pale', 'dim hair', 'white feet', and so on. In its weaker
moments (since all poetry must have its weaker moments)
the verse sank a little towards a blurred emotionalism.
Compare, for example, the too rhetorical note of

> My master will break up the sun and moon,
> And quench the stars in the ancestral night
> And overturn the thrones of God and the angels,

with the much better rhetoric of

> We must be tender with all budding things.
> Our Maker let no thought of Calvary
> Trouble the morning stars in their first song.

If anything troubled us when we heard Mr. Yeats's first
song it was an anxiety whether this music, ghostly in all
senses of the word, could go on. It has reassured us by
taking a new movement, under which the older is still felt,
sometimes in opposition, sometimes in alliance. Line
such as

> We that are old, old and gay,
> O so old,
> Thousands of years, thousands of years,
> If all were told,

have tended to speak more like those other lines on Dante,
'the chief imagination of Christendom',

> He found the unpersuadable justice, he found
> The most exalted lady loved by a man.

There is still something of a sigh in that last line, but
it is the inevitable sigh of humanity.

There is another thing, besides awakening our minds to
dreams, more or less imaged in actuality, which Mr. Yeats
has done. He has given to English verse, and made native
to it, a new mythology. Until he wrote, our literature had
had, on the whole, three mythologies to draw on — the
Greek and the Norse and the Christian; now it has also
the Celtic. Names and shapes unapprehended till now are
now its possession; its boundaries are so far enlarged.
This certainly is an accident of time and place and
genius, but it is an accident for which we can hardly
be too grateful. It is less of an accident that he has
renewed in us the sense of great interior possibilities
by his use of the traditions of magic and faerie, and made
his own verse tremble with their imagined presence. It is
by the most happy accident of his personal genius that he
has given to us so large a number of poems of beauty and
power, so many memorable lines, that we may say to him, in
his own phrase,

> our bodies have begun to dream,
> And you have grown to be a burning sod
> In the imagination and intellect.

End Piece

The ecstasy of adoration dies;
   speaking with four strong poets other than you,
   I have felt the frenzy half itself renew,
worshipping, trembling, a fool where they were wise:
but O the crowded theatre, and the cries
   shaking the dark air, if so loud a cue
   might bid you speak! the tumult still runs through
my memory and my dreams, and still my eyes
behold you solitary, when the show
   was done, sweet music making an end thereof,
   shutting the sorrow and pageant of Cathleen:
was it a marvel I adored you so,
   being twenty, a poetaster, never in love,
   and you the only poet I had seen?

77. WILLIAM EMPSON ON AMBIGUITY IN YEATS

1930

An extract from William Empson, 'Seven Types of Ambiguity'
(1930).
   William Empson (b. 1906) was educated at the University
of Cambridge, where he was influenced by I.A. Richards.
He taught in China and Japan, worked with the BBC in the
war, then taught in Peking before becoming Professor at
the University of Sheffield (1953-72). Empson's 'Seven
Types of Ambiguity' (1930) was followed by 'Some Versions
of Pastoral' (1935); 'The Coming Storm' (1940); 'The
Structure of Complex Words' (1951); and 'Paradise Lost:
Milton's God' (1961). His 'Collected Poems' were published in 1955. His work has had marked effects upon
contemporary poetry and criticism.

One of the finest poems of W.B. Yeats is an example of an
ambiguity of the sixth type, under the sub-heading 'irrelevant statements'.

   Who will go drive with Fergus now,
   And pierce the deep wood's woven shade,
   And dance upon the level shore?
   Young man, lift up your russet brow,
   And lift your tender eyelids, maid,
   And brood on hopes and fears no more.

> And no more turn aside and brood
> Upon Love's bitter mystery;
> For Fergus rules the brazen cars,
> And rules the shadows of the wood,
> And the white breast of the dim sea
> And all dishevelled wandering stars.
> *(Who Goes with Fergus?)*

There is another poem in the volume explaining about
Fergus ['Fergus and the Druid']. He appears as a king,
who has left the judgement-hall, and the pleasures of
the court, and the chariot races by the seashore, who has
grown weary of active life, and has sought out a Druid
to be given the bag of dreams. The Druid warns him that

> No woman loves me, no man seeks my help,
> Because I be not of the things I dream.

Fergus, insisting, is given the dreams and awakes to what
they imply, the intellectual or contemplative life, so that

> now I am grown nothing, being all,
> And the whole world weighs down upon my heart,

and so that he cries out

> Ah! Druid, Druid, how great webs of sorrow
> Lay hidden in the small slate-coloured bag!

One may notice the way a foreign idiom is implied by the
two uses of *how*: 'how great were the webs' and 'how the
webs of sorrow lay hidden'.

The first poem, of course, assumes this story, but *now*
may mean before or after the transformation. If after,
the first line means: 'Now that the awful example of
Fergus is in front of you, surely you will not be so
unwise as to brood?'; to *drive* with him would be to
wander through the woods like a ghost, as he does; the
dancing would be that of the fairy child who danced upon
the mountains like a flame and stole away the children.
Or 'Now who will be so loyal as to follow him?' or 'Can
you be so cruel as to abandon him now?'; or with a different feeling: 'Now that Fergus knows everything, who
will come and join in his meditations; who will share his
melancholy and his knowledge; which of you will pierce
the mystery of the forest and rejoice in sympathy with
the whole of nature?' If before, so that the force of
now is: 'There is still time to drive with Fergus, as
he is still a king in the world', or 'There is still time

to give a warning as the fatal thing has not yet happened';
then the first line gives: 'Who will come out with the
great figures of the court, and join in their sensible
out-of-door pleasures?'

   If before, the second verse means: 'You need not
brood, because Fergus is guardian of common-sense; he
is a strong man to drive war-chariots, as you should be;
he owns all the territory on which magic takes place; he
will keep it under decent control; there is no need for
you to worry about it.' If after: 'Do not brood; be
warned by Fergus, who though still king, still technically in command of war-chariots, is true ruler only of
the dim appurtenances of magic dreams,' or, since there is
no mistaking the triumph of the line about *cars* into whatever melancholy the verse trails away, 'Remember that
though Fergus is a great poet or philosopher or what not,
though he drives some mythological chariot of the Muses,'
of whose details I am afraid I am ignorant, 'yet even he,
because these victories involved brooding, is reduced to
the dim and ghostly condition of the last three lines.'

   I said that an example of the sixth type must say
nothing, and this poem says: 'Do not brood.' But the
words have little of the quality of an order; they convey rather: 'How strange and sad that you should still
be brooding!'; and one may interpret variously the transition from advice to personal statement, from such of an
imperative as was intended to the mere pain of loss, in
the repetition of *no more*. 'I, in that I am Fergus, can
no more turn aside from brooding,' is a sort of false
grammar by juxtaposition,which may be felt in the line,
and there is a suggestion that they must now lose their
dreams, as they have already lost the real world, without
getting anything in exchange for either. 'All has grown
bitter, and who can join in either activity of Fergus
any longer?' One might finally distinguish the erotic
brooding of the young persons from the philosophical
brooding of Fergus, which as hoping for nothing is at once
grander and more empty; no doubt this distinction is only
intended faintly, since it is part of the wisdom of the
language of the poet that it treats these two as of the
same kind. But, in so far as it is intended, it allows
of an opposite meaning for 'Do not brood' — 'Do not
brood in this comparatively trivial fashion but go and
drive with Fergus, who will teach you to brood about
everything, who will teach you to wander, untouchable, and
all-embracing, in an isolation like that of the stars.'

   The wavering and suggestive indefiniteness of nineteenth-
century poetry is often merely weak. When, as here, it has
a great deal of energy and sticks in your head, it is

usually because the opposites left open are tied round a
single strong idea;   thus here, on the one hand, the
condition of brooding is at once to be sought out and
to be avoided;   on the other, the poet, 'nothing, being
all', contemporaneously living all lives, may fitly be
holding before him both the lives of Fergus, and drawing
the same moral from either of them.

78.   A POET ON YEATS'S EARLIER POEMS

1930

This poem, Yeats's Earlier Poems, by Monk Gibbon was
published in 'The Irish Statesman', 29 March 1930.
    Monk Gibbon (b. 1896), born in Dublin, was educated at
Keble College, Oxford, and has been a school teacher in
Switzerland, England and Ireland.   'This Unsubstantial
Pageant', his collected poems, was published in 1951.
His autobiographical novels are 'Mount Ida' (1948) and
'The Climate of Love' (1961).   He has written a book on
Yeats entitled 'The Masterpiece and the Man: Yeats as
I knew him' (1959).

YEATS' EARLIER POEMS

On sands untrodden,
Barefoot from the tide,
With smoke from sodden
Bogs blown to sweetness on the causeway wide
To islands low,
Green islands low surmised still more than seen;
Fleet as the spray,
As lonely as the scene,
And mild-eyed as the moon that rises now;
Too sure to slip,
They run exultant, then stop suddenly,
Sobered by this grave stranger,
Scenting danger,
Some scorn of lip,
Some slight impatience of the moving hand
Tracing strange figures on the soon-swept strand,
Till he
Stops absently,
Sees tresses salt with brine.
'Whose are these children? They indeed are mine.'

79. A COMMENT ON OVER-MUCH SHORTHAND IN THE SYMBOLISM
OF 'THE WINDING STAIR'

1930

An unsigned review of 'The Winding Stair' (1930), 'Times
Literary Supplement', 6 November 1930.

The two sets of poems in this slight volume are bound
together, rather loosely, each by a common idea. But
what these ideas are it is not easy to say, or for Mr.
Yeats to explain. For here Mr. Yeats is deliberately
using an elaborate symbolism. The winding stair is that
of a tower 'where I have written most of my poems of
recent years. My poems attribute to it most of the meanings attributed in the past to the tower — whether watch
tower or pharos, and to its winding stair those attributed to gyre or whorl.' Perhaps it is our ignorance of
occult symbolism that is at fault if the meaning of the
tower does not at once leap to the mind. But 'what those
meanings are,' Mr. Yeats continues, 'let the poems say.'

> Alexandria's was a beacon tower, and Babylon's
> An image of the moving heavens, a logbook of the
>   sun's journey and the moon's,
> And Shelley had his towers, thought's crowned
>   powers he called them once.
>
> I declare this tower is my symbol; I declare
> This winding, gyring, spyring treadmill of a stair
>   is my ancestral stair;
> That Goldsmith and the Dean, Berkeley and Burke
>   have travelled there.

The ascent of these Irish writers is not a matter of deep
obscurity. But the tower and the stair seem to have a
symbolism at once vaguer and more universal.

> I summon to the windy ancient stair;
> Set all your mind upon the steep ascent,
> Upon the broken crumbling battlement,
> Upon the breathless starlit air;
> Fix every wandering thought upon
> That quarter where all thought is done,
> The pole star and the silence of the pole.

One cannot say that this sort of symbolism, which naturally
becomes more obscure as the poem proceeds, does not awake

certain responses. One recognizes the divisions which
mystics like to make, as of thought from feeling, sense
from soul, and so forth. Actually the verse quoted comes
from a dialogue between self and soul. But one cannot
understand the meaning of Mr. Yeats's lines in the same
way as, for example, a poem by Donne. Donne may require
a great deal of reading and rereading before one can understand his notions, but one knows from the start that Mr.
Yeats's knots can never be untied in the same way.
     Perhaps this may seem an irrelevant criticism of poetry.
We are accustomed to find great beauty in poetry which is,
as an argument or as a statement of fact, nonsense or
untrue; and therefore it would seem absurd to complain of
a poem simply because it does not seem to make sense.
Equally poetry is almost always very difficult, so that
we should not complain of the trouble to which Mr. Yeats
puts his readers. Nor should our attitude to poetry be
much affected by our attitude to mysticism. But the
obscurity and difficulty of Mr. Yeats's poems seems to be
of a distinct and unusual kind. For Mr. Yeats is sometimes difficult in the way that most poets are, and we
at once recognize the difference. He tells us, for
example, that he symbolizes a woman's love as the struggle
of darkness to keep the sun from rising from its earthly
bed, an idea which can have little or no meaning to most
people. But Mr. Yeats thus converts the idea into poetry:

> Scarce did he my body touch,
> Scarce sank he from the west,
> Or found a subterranean rest
> On the maternal midnight of my breast
> Before I had marked him on his northern way,
> And seemed to stand although in bed I lay.

Here there is no great difficulty, and we can accept the
idea without trouble while poetry flowers from it. Any
idea whatever seems to serve for poetry, and it is fortunate that it should be so. But the idea has to be in
some measure self-consistent; mere symbols which act as
the shorthand of an idea but without our knowledge of the
key have no connexion with each other, do not seem perfectly suited for poetry. For that inevitability of
phrasing which is the chief part of poetry requires a
precise idea, and one that has fully emerged from shapeless thought. Once a connexion between such symbols is
clearly established, however illogical and absurd such a
connexion may be, the entire poem may assume its own
internal order. But too often Mr. Yeats does not really
expose any connexion between the symbols which he employs,

or between the symbol and the thing symbolized, so that
one feels as if a cog had slipped and the images succeed
without connexion. The close contraction of ideas which
seems necessary for poetry is interrupted by the diffu-
sion of loose symbols which might appear in any order.
But nevertheless it is not seldom that in the midst of
this confusion of symbols a clear image or idea emerges,
and we come upon such beautiful lines as these:

> But the dark changed to red, and torches shone,
> And deafening music shook the leaves; a troop
> Shouldered a litter with a wounded man,
> Or smote upon the string and to the sound
> Sang of the beast that gave the fatal wound.

Then one may recognize what a very remarkable poet Mr.
Yeats is.

80. EDMUND WILSON ON YEATS'S SENSE OF REALITY

1931

This extract is taken from Edmund Wilson, 'Axel's
Castle: A Study in the Imaginative Literature of 1870-
1930' (1931).
    Edmund Wilson (1895-1972) was born in New Jersey and
educated at Princeton University. He was associate
editor of the 'New Republic', 1926-31, and book critic of
the 'New Yorker'. 'Axel's Castle' (1931) discussed the
symbolist movement. His other works include 'The Wound
and the Bow' (1941), 'The Scrolls of the Dead Sea' (1955),
and 'The American Earthquake' (1958). As well as plays
and verse he also wrote the autobiographical 'Memoirs of
Hecate County' (1946).

As we read all this [the comments on 'A Vision' in 'A
Packet for Ezra Pound'], we say to ourselves that Yeats,
growing older, has grown more credulous. But we come, at
the end, to the following passage: 'Some will ask if I
believe all that this book ['A Vision'] contains, and I
will not know how to answer. Does the word belief,
used as they will use it, belong to our age, can I think
of the world as there and I here judging it?' And he
intimates that, after all, his system may be only a set

of symbols like another — a set of symbols, we recognize, like the Irish myths with which he began.
    Into the personal situation suggested by Yeats's
account of his revelations, it is inappropriate and unnecessary to go: the psychological situation seems
plain.   When Yeats, at the crucial period of his life,
attempted to leave fairyland behind, when he became
aware of the unsatisfying character of the life of iri-
descent revery, when he completely recreated his style
so as to make it solid, homely and exact where it had
formerly been shimmering or florid — the need for dwelling with part of his mind — or with his mind for part
of the time — in a world of pure imagination, where the
necessities of the real world do not hold, had, none
the less, not been conjured away by the new artistic and
intellectual habits he was cultivating.   Where the early
Yeats had studied Irish folk-lore, collected and sorted
Irish fairy tales, invented fairy tales for himself, the
later Yeats worked out from the mediumistic communica-
tions of his wife the twenty-eight phases of the human
personality and the transformations of the soul after
death.   Yeats's sense of reality to-day is inferior to
that of no man alive — indeed, his greatness is partly
due precisely to the vividness of that sense.   In his
poetry, in his criticism and in his memoirs, it is the
world we all live in with which we are confronted — the
world we know, with all its frustrations, its defeats,
its antagonisms and its errors — the mind that sees is
not naïve, as the heart that feels is not insensitive.
They meet reality with comprehension and with passion —
but they have phases, we are astonished to discover,
when they do not seem to meet it at all.   Yet the scientific criticism of supernatural phenomena is actually as
much a part of the reality of Yeats's world as it is of
that of most of the rest of us.   And when Yeats writes
of his supernatural experiences, this criticism, though
it may be kept in the background, is nevertheless always
present — his realistic sense is too strong, his intellectual integrity too high, to leave it out of the picture.
Though he is much addicted to these fantastic imaginings,
though he no doubt needs their support to enable him to
sustain his rôle of great poet — yet when he comes to
write about his spirits and their messages, he cannot help
letting us in on the imposture.   He believes, but — he
does not believe: the impossibility of believing is the
impossibility which he accepts most reluctantly, but still
it is there with the other impossibilities of this world
which is too full of weeping for a child to understand.
    It is interesting to compare 'A Vision' with that

other compendious treatise on human nature and destiny
by that other great writer from Dublin: Bernard Shaw's
'Guide to Socialism and Capitalism'.   Here we can see
unmistakably the differences between the kind of literature which was fashionable before the War and the kind
which has been fashionable since.   Shaw and Yeats, both
coming as young men to London from eighteenth-century
Dublin, followed diametrically opposite courses.   Shaw
shouldered the whole unwieldy load of contemporary socio-
logy, politics, economics, biology, medicine and journalism, while Yeats, convinced that the world of science
and politics was somehow fatal to the poet's vision, as
resolutely turned away.   Shaw accepted the scientific
technique and set himself to master the problems of an
industrial democratic society, while Yeats rejected the
methods of Naturalism and applied himself to the intro-
spective plumbing of the mysteries of the individual
mind.   While Yeats was editing Blake, Shaw was grappling
with Marx;   and Yeats was appalled by Shaw's hardness and
efficiency.   'I hated it,' he says of 'Arms and the Man';
'it seemed to me inorganic, logical straightness and not
the crooked road of life and I stood aghast before its
energy.'   And he tells us that Shaw appeared to him in a
dream in the form of a sewing machine,'that clicked and
shone, but the incredible thing was that the machine
smiled, smiled perpetually.'
    In his Great Wheel of the twenty-eight phases, Yeats
has situated Shaw at a phase considerably removed from
his own, and where the individual is headed straight for
the deformity of seeking, not the soul, but the world.   And
their respective literary testaments — the 'Vision' and
the 'Guide' — published almost at the same time, mark the
extreme points of their divergence: Shaw bases all human
hope and happiness on an equal distribution of income,
which he believes will finally make impossible even the
pessimism of a Swift or a Voltaire;   while Yeats, like
Shaw a Protestant for whom the Catholic's mysticism was
impossible, has in 'A Vision' made the life of humanity
contingent on the movements of the stars.   'The day is
far off,' he concludes, 'when the two halves of man can
divine each its own unity in the other as in a mirror,
Sun in Moon, Moon in Sun, and so escape out of the Wheel.'
    Yet, in the meantime, the poet Yeats has passed into
a sort of third phase, in which he is closer to the common
world than at any previous period.   He is no longer quite
so haughty, so imperturbably astride his high horse, as
during his middle Dantesque period.   With the Dantesque
mask, he has lost something of intensity and something
of sharpness of outline.   in 'The Tower' (1928), certain

words such as 'bitter', 'wild', and 'fierce', which he
was able, a few years ago, to use with such thrilling
effect, have no longer quite the same force. He writes
more loosely, and seems to write more easily. He has
become more plain-spoken, more humorous — his mind
seems to run more frankly on his ordinary human satis-
factions and chagrins: he is sometimes harsh, sometimes
sensual, sometimes careless, sometimes coarse.

Though he now inhabits, like Michael Robartes, a lonely
tower on the outermost Irish coast, he has spent six years
in the Irish senate, presiding at official receptions in
a silk hat, inspecting the plumbing of the government
schools and conscientiously sitting through the movies
which it is one of his official duties to censor. He
is much occupied with politics and society, with general
reflections on human life — but with the wisdom of the
experience of a lifetime, he is passionate even in age.
And he writes poems which charge now with the emotion of
a great lyric poet that profound and subtle criticism of
life of which I have spoken in connection with his prose.

We may take, as an example of Yeats's later vein,
the fine poem in 'The Tower' called 'Among School
Children'. The poet, now 'a sixty year old smiling
public man', has paid an official visit to a girls'
school kept by nuns; and as he gazes at the children
there, he remembers how the woman he had loved had told
him once of some 'harsh reproof or trivial event' of her
girlhood which had changed 'some childish day to tragedy'.
And for a moment the thought that she may once have
looked like one of the children before him has revived the
excitement of his old love. He remembers the woman in
all her young beauty — and thinks of himself with his
present sixty years — 'a comfortable kind of old scare-
crow'. What use is philosophy now? — is not all beauty
bound up with the body and doomed to decay with it? —
is not even the divine beauty itself which is worshipped
there by the nuns inseparable from the images of it they
adore?

> Labour is blossoming or dancing where
> The body is not bruised to pleasure soul,
> Nor beauty born out of its own despair,
> Nor blear-eyed wisdom out of midnight oil.
> O chestnut tree, great rooted blossomer,
> Are you the leaf, the blossom or the bole?
> O body swayed to music, O brightening glance,
> How can we know the dancer from the dance?

Here the actual scene in the convent, the personal
emotions it awakens and the general speculations which
these emotions suggest, have been interwoven and made to
play upon each other at the same time that they are kept
separate and distinct. A complex subject has been treated
in the most concentrated form, and yet without confusion.
Perceptions, fancies, feelings and thoughts have all their
place in the poet's record. It is a moment of human
life, masterfully seized and made permanent, in all its
nobility and lameness, its mystery and actuality, its
direct personal contact and abstraction.

81. F.R. LEAVIS ON AN UNFORTUNATE HABIT OF MIND IN YEATS

1932

This comment is taken from F.R. Leavis, 'New Bearings in
English Poetry' (1932).
    Frank Raymond Leavis (b. 1895) literary critic, was
educated at Emmanuel College, Cambridge, and taught at
Downing College, Cambridge, becoming a visiting Professor at York University in 1965. He married Queenie
Dorothy Roth in 1929. He was one of the founders of
'Scrutiny' (1932-53), and through this journal and his
teaching and lecturing has been an influential and vigorous intellectual force, regarding, in the Arnoldian
tradition, English literature as a vehicle for the traditional and moral education of the young, and stressing
his preoccupation with great or serious writers. His
works include 'Mass Civilization and Minority Culture'
(1930); 'D.H. Lawrence' (1930); 'New Bearings in English
Poetry' (1932); 'Revaluation: Tradition and Development
in English Poetry' (1936); 'The Great Tradition' (1948);
and 'The Common Pursuit' (1952).

The long poem which gave its name to the collection of
1889 (his first) might be described as Mr. Yeats's
'Alastor' and 'Endymion'. Its importance is what is
indicated by this note: '. . . from the moment when I
began the 'Wanderings of Usheen'. . . my subject matter
became Irish.' Mr. Yeats starts in the English tradition,
but he is from the outset an Irish poet. The impulse
behind the poem is the familiar one. A poet's day-dream
could not easily be more cloudy and tenuous than the wist-

ful Elysium of his Irish theme, with its 'dim, pale
waters' and its realms

> Where Aengus dreams from sun to sun
> A Druid dream of the end of days;

and yet there is a paradoxical energy about the poem
that distinguishes it from any of Morris's day-dreams:
its pallor and weariness are not the exquisite aesthetic
etiolation familiar to the

> Poets with whom I learned my trade,
> Companions of the Cheshire Cheese.

For Mr. Yeats's Irishness is more than a matter of
using Irish themes and an Irish atmosphere. It means
that his dream-world is something more than private,
personal and literary; that it has, as it were, an
external validation. It gives him the kind of advantage that he has in mind here:

> I filled my mind with the popular beliefs of Ireland...
> I sought some symbolic language reaching far into the
> past and associated with familiar names and conspi-
> cuous hills that I might not be alone amod the obscure
> impressions of the senses, . . . or mourned the richness
> or reality lost to Shelley's 'Prometheus Unbound'
> because he had not discovered in England or in Ire-
> land his Caucasus.

The advantage is put even more significantly here:

> I did not believe with my intellect that you could be
> carried away body and soul, but I believed with my
> emotions and the belief of the country people made
> that easy.

In the world created with this kind of sanction he
could preserve the 'higher reality' that his imagination
and emotions craved, and without which life seemed worth-
less. His second collection of poems, 'The Rose' (1893),
frankly brings the cult of 'Eternal beauty wandering on
her way', with its Red Rose of 'an unimagined revelation',
into the world of Irish lore. But there is still a
certain esoteric languor about this phase:

> Beauty grown sad with its eternity
> Made you of us, and of the dim grey sea;

and we are again reminded that we are in the 'nineties.
('With a rhythm that still echoed Morris I played to the
Red Rose.') Here, too, belongs the unfortunate
'Innisfree', unfortunate, because it is Mr.
Yeats's most anthologized poem and recalls to us his own note:
'I tried after the publication of "The Wanderings of Oisin"
to write of nothing but emotion, and in the simplest
language, and now I have had to go through it all, cutting
out or altering passages that are sentimental from lack
of thought.'
    But with 'The Wind Among the Reeds' (1899) the dream-
reality takes on a new life, and the poet inhabits it
surely. And although the imagery of the Celtic Twilight
is heavily worked — 'pale', 'dim', 'shadowy', desolate',
'cloud-pale', dream-heavy', — there is no languor or
preciosity here. Indeed, 'passion-dimmed' and 'pale
fire' are equally important in the vocabulary. For a
new force has entered Mr. Yeats's poetry — love. It
is mainly despairing love, and the poetry is extremely
poignant. But for us the essential thing to note is how
Mr. Yeats turns both exaltation and despair to the height-
ening of his dream-world, his substitute for the drab
quotidian actuality of Huxley, Ibsen and Bastien-Lepage.

    When my arms wrap you round I press
    My heart upon the loveliness
    That long has faded from the world.

It is a perfectly sincere application of the platonic
habit, but a very odd one:

    For that pale breast and lingering hand
    Come from a more dream-heavy land,
    A more dream-heavy hour than this;
    And when you sigh from kiss to kiss
    I hear white Beauty sighing, too,
    For hours when all must fade like dew,
    But flame on flame, and deep on deep,
    Throne over throne where in half sleep,
    Their swords upon their iron knees,
    Brood her high lonely mysteries.

— Transcendental Beauty, the mystical reality, belongs
to a more dream-heavy hour even than that of the poetry,
which is thus the dream of a dream. The syntax of the
passage, curiously elusive as it is, suggests the equivocal status of Yeats's 'reality'. It is more than a
literary fiction; love and the Irish background ('I
believed with my emotions and the belief of the country

people made that easy') enabled him to make it so. The
resulting poetry has a fresh unliterary spontaneity comparable to that of Shelley's, but a spontaneity that has
behind it a Victorian literary sophistication instead of
Wordsworth and the French Revolution, and so is the more
remarkable an achievement. Yet everywhere there is a
recognition, implicit in the shifting, cloudy unseizable-
ness of the imagery, that this 'reality' must be illusory,
and that even if it could be reached it would leave human
longing unslaked. And this recognition is subtly turned
into a strength: it validates, as it were, the idealizing
fanaticism of the poetry and counterpoises the obsession
with the transcendental, just as the exaltations and
despairs of love are counterpoised by the sense that

>   time and the world are ever in flight;
> And love is less kind than the grey twilight,
> And hope is less dear than the dew of the morn.

The poetry of 'The Wind Among the Reeds', then, is a
very remarkable achievement: it is, though a poetry of
withdrawal, both more subtle and more vital than any
pure product of Victorian romanticism. We might, as
bearing on the strength it was to Mr. Yeats to be Irish,
note further that with the Irish element in the poetry
was associated a public and practical aim. Early and long
service in the cause of a national renaissance, and,
above all, of a national theatre might be expected to
turn even a poet of the Victorian dream-world into something else; and Mr. Yeats devoted to the Irish cause rare
qualities of character and intelligence. Yet his resolute attempt upon the drama serves mainly to bring out the
prepotence of the tradition he started in. His plays
repudiate the actual world as essentially as his incantatory lyrics and his esoteric prose repudiate it. 'As
for living, our servants will do that for us' — the
epigraph might cover all three. A drama thus devoted to
a 'higher reality' of this kind could hardly exhibit the
dramatic virtues.
    How insidious was the atmosphere that poets of his
time breathed comes out in his critical writings. 'Tragic
art,' he will tell us in a discussion of poetic drama,
'passionate art, the drowner of dykes moves us by setting
us to reverie, by alluring us almost to the intensity of
trance.' And so obviously acute is the critical intelligence at work that we try to find much virtue in that
'intensity'. Yet 'reverie' and 'trance' are dangerous
words, and in the critic who announces that 'All art is
dream' we fear the worst. 'Drama,' he will tell us again,

'is a means of expression . . . and the dramatist is as
free to choose where he has a mind to, as the poet of
'Endymion', or as the painter of Mary Magdalene at the
door of Simon the Pharisee. So far from the discussion of
our interests and the immediate circumstances of our life
being the most moving to the imagination, it is what is
old and far-off that stirs us the most deeply.' Reading
this, we may applaud the challenge to Shaw and Ibsen, but
we more than suspect the kind of dream he has in mind.
Indeed, we know, for the bent is inveterate. 'Every
writer,' he says, 'even every small writer, who has
belonged to the great tradition, has had his dream of an
impossibly noble life, and the greater he is, the more does
it seem to plunge him into some beautiful or bitter
reverie.' This comes from an essay on Synge, and of Synge's
rhythm he says: 'It is essential, for it perfectly fits
the drifting emotion, the dreaminess, the vague yet mea-
sureless desire, for which he would create a dramatic form.
It blurs definition, clear edges, everything that comes
from the will, it turns imagination from all that is of the
present, like a gold background in a religious picture,
and it strengthens in every emotion whatever comes to it
from far off, from brooding memory and dangerous hope.'
    Mr. Yeats the dramatist, that is, remains the poet who
had 'learned to think in the midst of the last phase of
Pre-Raphaelitism.' He differs from the Victorian romantics in the intensity with which he seeks his 'higher
reality'. This difference we have attributed to his being
Irish; but it will not do to let this explanation detract
from his rare distinction of mind and spirit. 'I had an
invincible conviction . . . that the gates would open as
they opened for Blake . . .' — this is not the anaemic
reverie of Victorian romanticism: to nurse a luxury of
defeat was not in Mr. Yeats's character; he was too strong
and alive. He fought, paradoxical as it may seem, for
victory, and it was not through any lack of intelligence
or contempt for it that he found such a Quixotry possible.
'The dream-world of Morris,' he writes, 'was as much the
antithesis of daily life as with other men of genius,
but he was never conscious of the antithesis and so knew
nothing of intellectual suffering.' Mr. Yeats knew much
of intellectual suffering, for the antithesis was terribly present to him: he had a magnificent mind, and less
than the ordinary man's capacity for self-deception. 'It
is so many years before one can believe enough in what
one feels even to know what the feeling is,' he notes,
exemplifying that rare critical self-awareness of which the
signs abound in his 'Autobiographies' and 'Essays'. 'I
ceased to read modern books that were not books of

imagination,' he reports; but he read these last, one might almost say, in a scientific spirit. Indeed, his dealings with spiritualism, magic, theosophy, dream and trance were essentially an attempt to create an alternative science. The science of Huxley and Tyndall he had rejected in the name of imagination and emotion, but he had an intelligence that would not be denied. He exhibits for us the inner struggle of the nineteenth-century mind in an heroic form — heroic, and, because of the inevitable frustration and waste, tragic. 'From the moment when these speculations grow vivid,' he tells us, 'I had created for myself an intellectual solitude.'

We may relate to this lonely struggle a remarkable change that manifests itself in Mr. Yeats's poetry when we compare 'The Wind Among the Reeds' (1889) with 'The Green Helmet' (1912). It is hard to believe that the characteristic verse of the later volume comes from the same hand as that of the earlier. The new verse has no incantation, no dreamy, hypnotic rhythm; it belongs to the actual, waking world, and is in the idiom and movement of modern speech. It is spare, hard and sinewy and in tone sardonic, expressing the bitterness and disillusion of a man who has struggled and been frustrated:

> The fascination of what's difficult
> Has dried the sap out of my veins, and rent
> Spontaneous joy and natural content
> Out of my heart.

It is true that the struggles he specifies here belong to the practical world, to 'this blind, bitter land':

> My curse on plays
> That have to be set up in fifty ways,
> On the day's war with every knave and dolt,
> Theatre business, management of men.

But this is not the whole tale; and if it is time that has brought this maturity, there are reasons why this maturity should be so sour.

> Though leaves are many, the root is one;
> Through all the lying days of my youth
> I swayed my leaves and flowers in the sun;
> Now I may wither into the truth

runs a quatrain headed 'The Coming of Wisdom with Time'. Actuality has conquered:

> The holy centaurs of the hill are vanished;
> I have nothing but the embittered sun;
> Banished heroic mother moon and vanished,
> And now that I have come to fifty years
> I must endure the timid sun.

It is like an awakening out of drugs, a disintoxication;
the daylight seems thin and cruel. He recognizes the
real world, but it is too late; his strength has been
wasted, and habit forbids readjustment.

> But I grow old among dreams,
> A weather-worn, marble triton
> Among the streams.

The poem this last comes from has for title 'Men Improve
with the Years', which suggests well enough Mr. Yeats's
peculiar bitterness, a bitterness mingled with scorn for
humanity.(1)
　　Nevertheless, the poetry of this later phase is a
remarkable positive achievement: Mr. Yeats was strong
enough to force a triumph out of defeat. He speaks of
a beauty

> 　　　　　　　won
> From bitterest hours,

and it is this he serves instead of the cloudy glamour of
the 'Celtic Twilight'; a

> 　　beauty like a tightened bow, a kind
> That is not natural in an age like this.

The verse, in its rhythm and diction, recognizes the actual
world, but holds against it an ideal of aristocratic
fineness. It is idiomatic, and has the run of free
speech, being at the same time proud, bare and subtle. To
pass from the earlier verse to this is something like passing from Campion to Donne. The parallel, indeed, is not
so random as it might seem. At any rate, Donne's name
in connection with a poet capable of passionate intellectual interests, who from such a start achieved such a
manner, leads us to reflect that if the poetic tradition
of the nineteenth century had been less completely unlike
the Metaphysical tradition Mr. Yeats might have spent less
of his power outside poetry. The speculation is perhaps
idle, but it calls attention to the way in which his
verse developed into something that has the equivalent of
certain seventeenth-century qualities. His use of the

idiom and rhythm of speech is not all:

> Plato thought nature but a spume that plays
> Upon a ghostly paradigm of things;
> Solider Aristotle played the taws
> Upon the bottom of a king of kings;
> World-famous golden-thighed Pythagoras
> Fingered upon a fiddle stick or strings
> What a star sang and careless Muses heard:
> Old clothes upon old sticks to scare a bird.

— This (and the context more than bears out the promise
of flexibility and variety of tone) is surely rather like
seventeenth-century 'wit', more like it than anything we
expect to find in modern verse outside the work of certain post-war poets — poets who exhibit no completed
escape from the Victorian poetical. The volume it comes
from, indeed appeared after the war. But 'The Tower'
(1928) merely develops the manner of 'The Green Helmet'
(1912), 'Responsibilities' (1914), and 'The Wild Swans at
Coole' (1919).

In 'The Tower' Mr. Yeats achieves a kind of ripeness in
disillusion. The scorn so pervasive before is gone: his
tragic horror at the plight of Ireland (as, for instance,
in 'Meditations in Time of Civil War') is something different and more generous. There is indeed bitterness,
but it is not the sterile kind. His raging against

> Decrepit age that has been tied to me
> As to a dog's tail

goes with a sense of ardent vitality:

> Never had I more
> Excited, passionate, fantastical
> Imagination, nor an ear and eye
> That more expected the impossible;

and the excitement is as apparent as the bitterness in
this poetry of the last phase. Each gives value to the
other. He is capable of excitement, for instance, about
the 'abstract things' that he describes as a *pis aller*.
He turns with a pang from the varied 'sensual music' of
the world, but he is drawn positively towards the 'monu-
ments of unaging intellect':

> An aged man is but a paltry thing,
> A tattered coat upon a stick, unless
> Soul clap its hands and sing, and louder sing
> For every tatter in its mortal dress.

This (though there is always an ironical overtone) is the
voice of one who knows intellectual passion. He does not
deceive himself about what he has lost, but the regret
itself becomes in the poetry something positive. His
implications, in short, are very complex; he has
achieved a difficult and delicate sincerity, and extraordinary subtle poise.

What, then, it might be asked after this account of
Mr. Yeats's achievement, is there to complain of? Does
it really show that the tradition in the nineteenth
century might with advantage have been other than it was?
If he had to struggle with uncongenial circumstances, has
not every great artist had to do so; and did he not, by
admission, make triumphs of them? Mr. Yeats himself
gives the answer in the bitter sense of waste he expresses characteristically, in the latest work as elsewhere.
His poetry is little more than a marginal comment on the
main activities of his life. No one can read his 'Autobiographies' and his 'Essays' without being struck by
the magnificent qualities of intelligence and character
he exhibits. His insight shows itself in his analysis
of his own case, an analysis that suggests at the same
time the complete achievement he was fated to miss: 'In
literature,' he wrote in 1906,(2) 'partly from the lack of
that spoken word which knits us to the normal man, we have
lost in personality, in our delight in the whole man —
blood, imagination, intellect, running together — but
have found a new delight in essences, in states of mind,
in pure imagination, in all that comes to us most easily
in elaborate music.' And we find him remarking in 'Autobiographies' 'how small a fragment of our own nature can
be brought to perfect expression, nor that even but with
great toil, in a much divided civilisation.' Again, by
quoting his own verse, he explicitly relates the general
reflection to his own case: 'Nor did I understand as yet
how little that Unity [of Being], however wisely sought,
is possible without a Unity of Culture in class or people
that is no longer possible at all.

> The fascination of what's difficult
> Has dried the sap out of my veins, and rent
> Spontaneous joy and natural content
> Out of my heart.'

At this point it might be commented that Mr. Yeats
turns out an unfortunate witness to have called. What
he testifies against is not the poetic tradition, but
the general state of civilization and culture; a state
which, he contends, makes waste inevitable for the sensi-

tive. But he implies nothing against holding that if the
poetic tradition had been different, as it might very well
have been, he might have brought more of himself to expression. Writing of the early Synge he says significantly: '. . . the only language that interested him was
that conventional language of modern poetry which has
begun to make us all weary. I was very weary of it, for
I had finished 'The Secret Rose', and felt how it had
separated my imagination from life, sending my Red Hanrahan, who should have trodden the same roads with myself,
into some undiscoverable country.' It is true that he
successfully dropped this 'conventional language of modern
poetry'; but early habits of mind and sensibility are
not so easily dropped. The incidental confession he makes
in a later poem —

> I have no speech but symbol, the pagan speech I made
> Amid the dreams of youth —

has such significance. For 'symbol' in his technical
sense — symbol drawn from his cult of magic and the
Hermetic sciences — is commonly felt to be an unsatisfactory element in his later verse, and to come from an
unfortunate habit of mind. And his magic and occultism,
of course, are the persistent and intense expression of the
bent that expressed itself first of all in the 'conventional language of modern poetry':

> The abstract joy,
> The half read wisdom of daemonic images,
> Suffice the aging man as once the growing boy.

Disillusion and waste were indeed inevitable; but not
in the form in which Mr Yeats suffered them. They might
have been more significant. For Victorian romanticism was
not the only possible answer to those modern conditions
that Mr. Yeats deplores. If it were, poetry would cease
to matter. Adult minds could no longer take it seriously.
Losing all touch with the finer consciousness of the age
it would be, not only irresponsible, but anaemic, as, indeed, Victorian poetry so commonly is. Mr. Yeats's career,
then, magnificent as the triumph was that he compelled
out of defeat, is a warning. It illustrates the special
disability of the poet in the last century, and impressively bears out my argument about the poetic tradition.
And it cannot be repeated. No Englishman in any case could
have profited by the sources of strength open to Mr. Yeats
as an Irishman, and no such source is open to any one now.
No serious poet could propose to begin again where Mr.
Yeats began.

Notes

1 Cf. We had fed the heart on fantasies,
      The heart's grown brutal from the fare,
      More substance in our enmities
      Than in our love.
                        'The Tower', p. 27.
2 Cf. 'Donne could be as metaphysical as he pleased . . .
      because he could be as physical as he pleased.' —
      'Autobiographies'.

82.   YVOR WINTERS ON INTELLECTUAL CONFUSION IN YEATS AND
THE ENTIRE GENERATION SUBSEQUENT TO HIM

1933

Excerpts from Yvor Winters, T. Sturge Moore, 'Hound and
Horn', April-June 1933.

Yvor Winters (1900-68) was born in Chicago and retired
after forty years' teaching in 1966. He won several
awards for his poetry, including the Bollingen Award.
'Primitivism and Decadence: A Study of American Experimental Poetry' (1937) was the first of the books in which
he defended the views of the moral value of poetry. His
'Collected Poems' were published in 1955 and revised in
1960; his experimental verse was reissued as 'The Early
Poems of Yvor Winters, 1920-28' (1966). He wrote 'The
Poetry of W.B. Yeats' (1960); 'Forms of Discovery'
(1965) also contained his adverse view of Yeats's poetry.

Mr Yeats began as a rather bad poet of a kind exactly
suited to the popular taste of his decade, and through
some miracle of destiny retained his following when he
became serious. . . . Mr Yeats, as a dramatist of his own
personality, writes with an histrionic tone seldom
entirely justified by his ideas and perceptions but which
beguiles many readers. . . .

The fundamental post-Romantic defect is the abandonment of logic, either in favour of an undisguised form of
what Mr Kenneth Burke calls 'qualitative progression'
(that is, progression governed wholly by mood), as in the
'Cantos', or as in 'Anna Livia Plurabelle', or in favour
of a pseudo-logic, such as one finds discreetly distri-
buted (amid much real logic) throughout Mr Eliot's

'Gerontion', in most of Crane, and frequently at crucial
moments in poems by Mr Yeats. The abandonment of logic
is a defect for two reasons: it eliminates a half of
human experience, and so limits the poet's range and
often falsifies his feeling; and it is an uneconomical
use of words, half only of the power of the words being
brought into play. These types of non-logical writing
represent the ultimate boundary of the uncritical emotionalism of the Romantics: they represent the stylistic
definition of that emotionalism, its ultimate formal
equivalent, to which the Romantics seldom attained, an
emotionalism which is frequently merely sensationalism,
and which is largely unmotivated (that is, unformulable).
    The defect which gives rise to Romantic irony, the
intellectual confusion which causes a greater or less
measure of meaningless feeling, Mr Yeats shares with the
entire generation subsequent to him. His irreducible
obscurities, his moments of inexplicable excitement,
have appeared to be kinds of profundity. . . .

Collected Poems (1933)

83. THE FORERUNNER: DESMOND MacCARTHY ON THE CONTINUITY
OF YEATS'S WORK

1934

A review of 'Collected Poems' (1933) by Desmond MacCarthy,
'The Sunday Times', 4 February 1934.
  Sir Desmond MacCarthy (1877-1952) was educated at
Eton and Trinity College, Cambridge, where he was a
friend of G.E. Moore, Bertrand Russell, Lytton Strachey,
Leonard Woolf and others. He became a distinguished
literary and dramatic critic. He edited 'Life and Letters'
and contributed regularly to the 'New Statesman', of
which he was literary editor in the twenties, and later to
'The Sunday Times'. His publications included 'Remnants'
(1918); 'Experience' (1935); 'Leslie Stephen' (1937);
'Drama' (1940); 'Shaw' (1951); 'Memories' (1935);
'Humanities' (1953); and 'Theatre' (1954).

Since the publication in one volume of W.B. Yeats's
collected poems many beside myself have also been living
intermittently in his company. It is to such readers I
address the following brief comments. They will have
discovered that there is depth as well as delight in the
work of this conscious and cautious artist, who has
lived so passionately in the imagination, and permitted
his poetry to assimilate only experience worthy of his
Muse. As the years passed (he is now an elderly poet) the
nature of those things assimilated has not unnaturally
changed, and this the perusal of his poems in the order in
which they were written brings to the notice of the reader.
I know from hearing others talk that it is not uncommon to

divide on that account his work into two halves: that
of the Yeats of the Celtic Twilight Period, and of the
later Yeats whom alone among the elder poets the younger
salute as a master. When I last wrote on Mr Yeats —
it was some years ago — I, too, stressed this change in
the venue of his poetry; this departure from the wistful
tenderness of such poems as 'I will arise and go now and
go to Innisfree' or from the romantic richness of others;
and I quoted then as a boundary mark the poem called 'The
Coat'.

[Quotes 'A Coat', 'Collected Poems', p. 142; see text,
p. 240.]

But on re-reading his poems in succession what has
impressed me as well was the continuity of his work. There
are not two poets, Yeats I and Yeats II; one whose poetry
the most modern poet can afford to ignore, the other one
whom they recognise as a master. From the first he wrote
out of the basis of his nature, which cannot change. The
poems of the Celtic period are not to be regarded as
poems of a youthful novitiate, but as an integral part of
his genius. No one but a fanatical theorist would omit
from a 'Selection', however rigorous, of Yeats's verse
poems from 'Crossways' (1889), 'The Wanderings of Oisin'
(1889), 'The Rose' (1893), 'The Wind Among the Reeds'
(1899), 'In the Seven Woods' (1904)(1).

YEATS AS A SYMBOLIST

        I heard the old, old men say,
        'Everything alters
        And one by one we drop away.'
        They had hands like claws, and their knees
        Were twisted like the old thorn-trees
        By the waters.
        I heard the old, old men say,
        'All that's beautiful drifts away
        Like the waters.'

I do not know the precise date at which that poem was
written, but it was long before the modern movement. In
Yeats's earlier poems there is many a passage marked by
the compression and sudden finality in suggestion which
were later to become (so pedantically) the sole aim in
verse of 'vorticists' and 'imagists'. (One such line
occurs to me: 'Our courage breaks like an old tree in a
black wind.') But such passages were never presented as
poems complete in themselves. The spoken word, the homely,

the perhaps harsh image, the detail fetched from life,
occur in his earlier work, and their presence, too, was
quite as Irish a treat as the dreaminess and the vaguely
magnificent musical imagery, labelled by English critics
as 'Celtic'. What was really more significant than the
mythology of his earlier poems, or their Celtic colour,
was the poet's method. That poetic method was the method
of the French Symbolists, to whom his friend Arthur Symons
had introduced him. There is no poetry more essentially
like Mallarmé's than certain passages and certain poems
in Yeats's earlier work. The symbols themselves are
different; but the poetic method is that of the French
Symbolist whose meaning runs to music. There is the same
indifference to the objective reality of symbols. Where
(so it appeared to me on re-reading his work) the poet *had*
changed was in that respect. He was still a symbolist;
but his symbols as time went on were chosen more and more
for their closer relation to experience, and later he
relied less on rhythmic pattern, more upon phrases. It
was not so when he wrote:

> O sweet everlasting Voices be still;
> Go to the guards of the heavenly fold
> And bid them wander obeying your will,
> Flame under flame, till Time be no more;
> Have you not heard that our hearts are old,
> That you call in birds, in wind on the hill,
> In shaken boughs, in tide on the shore?
> O sweet everlasting Voices, be still.

Or the still more famous 'Into the Twilight':

> Out-worn heart, in a time out-worn,
> Come clear of the nets of wrong and right;
> Laugh, heart, again in the grey twilight,
> Sing, heart, again in the dew of the morn. . . .
>
> And God stands winding His lonely horn,
> And time and the world are ever in flight;
> And love is less kind than the grey twilight,
> And hope is less dear than the dew of the morn,

which is a pure and lovely example of incantatory poetry.

AS A LOVE-POET
In the later poems the content is more philosophic and
perceptive. They are less dependent on incantation. The
reader must do more than listen and feel: he can win more
from the poem by thinking. The transition has been

through the poet's love-poetry, and that other theme which
has been with him an equal preoccupation; the relation of
the poet to experience. Mr Yeats will be recognised by
posterity as a great love-poet, and as a philosophic
poet of the poetic life. The balance he holds between
ideality and its roots in love-poetry is subtle and wise.
Whichever aspect he has at different times regarded, his
treatment has been marked by an incomparable dignity.
He has expressed the ideal content of passion and, with
the reserve which is necessary, the significance of the
body.

Compare the famous 'Tread softly, for you tread upon
my dreams' or 'The Lover tells of the Rose in his Heart'
with love-poems written at other times.

> All things uncomely and broken, all things worn out and
>   old,
> The cry of a child by the roadway, the creak of a
>   lumbering cart,
> The heavy steps of the ploughman, splashing the wintry
>   mould,
> Are wronging your image that blossoms a rose in the
>   deeps of my heart.
>
> The wrong of unshapely things is a wrong too great
>   to be told;
> I hunger to build them anew and sit on a green knoll
>   apart,
> With the earth and the sky and the water, re-made,
>   like a casket of gold
> For my dreams of your image that blossoms a rose in
>   the deeps of my heart.

Compare these poems with 'Parting'. It will suggest his
range as a love-poet:

> HE: Dear, I must be gone
>   While night shuts the eyes
>   Of the household spies;
>   That song announces dawn.
>
> SHE:No, night's bird and love's
>   Bids all true lovers rest,
>   While his loud song reproves
>   The murderous stealth of day.
>
> HE: Daylight already flies
>   From mountain crest to crest.

SHE: That light is from the moon.

HE: That bird . . .

SHE: Let him sing on,
    I offer to love's play
    My dark declivities.

Or with 'Memory', so lovely in its brief simplicity:

    One had a lovely face,
    And two or three had charm,
    But charm and face were in vain
    Because the mountain grass
    Cannot but keep the form
    Where the mountain hare has lain.

Or with 'The Deep-sworn Vow', which records a moment in
the memory of passion:

    Others because you did not keep
    That deep-sworn vow have been friends of mine;
    Yet always when I look death in the face,
    When I clamber to the heights of sleep,
    Or when I grow excited with wine,
    Suddenly I meet your face.

Does it not also appear true that the transition in his
poetry to closer contact with experience has been through
his love-poems? In the later work, too, there are gay,
light, acrid poems, though he never wastes cynicism on
the ideal.

POETRY AND LIFE
I am not in a position to illustrate here his treatment
of that other theme which runs so clearly through his
poems: the relation of the poet to the world — science,
industry, politics. The history of the poet's thought,
his successive absorption in folk-tales, in mythology, in
alchemistic speculation, in psychic phenomena, and latterly
in philosophy, seem to me to have been instinctive attempts
to keep actualities at a proper distance for his purpose;
to find the distance from which experience might be most
perfectly transmuted into poetry. Truth to the poet is
always a subordinate interest to this personal discovery.
From the first he was occupied with the solitude of the
poetic mind, and his closest relation to the nineties
lay perhaps in his sharing their conception of the artist
as a being apart, shut in the world of his reveries, the

only fit subjects for art.   In Yeats's prose we find deep
discourse upon the predicament of a poet in the modern
world.   There is the theory of the Mask or Anti-self
which the poet must impose upon his natural self.   Perhaps the verse dialogue 'Ego Dominus Tuus' shows best
how far he has travelled from an eighteen-ninety conception of the poet's vocation.   It suggests how, while
using his personal experience more and more as matter
for poetry, he has managed to maintain a splendid dignity
of utterance and combined it with wildest fantasy and
pungent vividness.

Note

1 This date is taken from 'Collected Poems' (1933);
  the separate volume was published in 1903.

84.   SIR HERBERT READ'S OBJECTIONS TO YEATS'S LATER VERSE

1934

A review of 'Collected Poems' (1933), by Sir Herbert
Read, The Later Yeats, 'The Criterion', April 1934.
This was included in 'A Coat of Many Colours: Occasional
Essays' (1945).
    Sir Herbert Read (1893-1968), poet, critic and pub-
lisher, was educated at the University of Leeds.   After
winning the DSO and MC in the First World War he became
a civil servant, then a Professor at the University of
Edinburgh, and subsequently a publisher.   He edited the
'Burlington Magazine' (1933-9) and consistently supported
avant garde work in art and literature.   His writings
include 'Reason and Romanticism' (1926), 'The Meaning
of Art' (1931);   his autobiographical 'The Innocent
Eye' (1933) and 'Annals of Innocence and Experience' (1940);
and his 'Collected Poems' (1946, 1966).

There is no doubt that Yeats was influenced, and influenced
for the good, by the technique of some of his juniors,
notably Ezra Pound.
    The change can best be examined in an early poem which
Yeats actually rewrote in his later manner.   'The Sorrow
of Love' was originally published in 1893;   as late as the

1912 edition of the 'Poems' and perhaps later, it read
as follows:

> The quarrel of the sparrows in the eaves,
> The full round moon and the star-laden sky,
> And the loud song of the ever-singing leaves,
> Had hid away earth's old and weary cry.
>
> And then you came with those red mournful lips,
> And with you came the whole of the world's tears
> And all the trouble of her labouring ships,
> And all the trouble of her myriad years.
>
> And now the sparrows warring in the eaves,
> The curd-pale moon, the white stars in the sky,
> And the loud chaunting of the unquiet leaves,
> Are shaken with earth's old and weary cry.

In the 1933 edition of the 'Collected Poems' this poem has
been rewritten and reads as follows:

> The brawling of a sparrow in the eaves,
> The brilliant moon and all the milky sky,
> And all that famous harmony of leaves,
> Had blotted out man's image and his cry.
>
> A girl arose that had red mournful lips
> And seemed the greatness of the world in tears,
> Doomed like Odysseus and the labouring ships
> And proud as Priam murdered with his peers;
>
> Arose, and on the instant clamorous eaves,
> A climbing moon upon an empty sky,
> And all that lamentation of the leaves,
> Could but compose man's image and his cry.

The change, it will be seen, is very drastic, but is
it altogether a change for the good? It is, let us
observe, in the first place, a change of diction and
not of structure; and that is true of all the changes
that occurred in Yeats's verse. 'All the revisions I
have made,' Yeats once said to me, 'have been in the
direction of making my poems less poetic.' His aim,
therefore, has been very much the same as Wordsworth's —
to get rid of 'the inane and gaudy phraseology' of an
outworn poetic tradition. The suggestion I wish to put
forward is that diction and structure are so closely
related in the generation of a poem, that you cannot
fundamentally change the one without changing the other.

But before elaborating that suggestion, let us look at
the actual changes which Yeats made in the poem quoted.
   Line 1. 'Brawling' is substituted for 'quarrel'.
In itself I do not think the word is any improvement, but
the change is necessitated by a change in line 2;
'quarrel' would not go well with 'brilliant', whereas
'brawling' provides a good alliterative and assonantal
match. 'Sparrows' becomes singular — a gain in precision.
   Line 2. 'Full round' was perhaps felt to be a commonplace epithet, but is 'brilliant' any better? It is
rather vaguer. But this change is perhaps in its turn
dictated by the change from 'star-laden' to 'milky'.
'Star-laden' is a very early-yeatsian, Celtic twilight
epithet of just the kind the poet presumably wanted to
get rid of; and since a brilliant moon will cancel out
the stars, 'milky' becomes a more expressive (incidentally
a metaphorical) epithet.
   Line 3. 'Ever-singing' was probably felt to be a cliché,
and 'loud' is not very exact for the sound of leaves. But
'famous harmony' seems to me to be a vaguer and weaker
substitute; it is a dead phrase, without any inherent
poetic tone. In fact, it is prose.
   Line 4. A completely new image is substituted.
'Earth's old and weary cry' was probably felt to be a
false and indefinite metaphor. 'Blotted' is a gain in
sound value, and links alliteratively with 'brawling'
and 'brilliant'; it has an onomatopœic value, and provides a much-needed acceleration of the rhythm.
   Line 5. A definite image of 'a girl' is substituted
for the vague 'you'; 'arose' gives alliteration with 'red'.
   Line 6. 'The whole of the world's tears' was perhaps
felt to be rather a ridiculous image; the new image is
more precise, but still difficult to visualize.
   Lines 7 and 8. A completely new image is substituted.
The repetition of 'And all the trouble of her' was
probably felt to be banal, and 'myriad years' to be a
cliché. The introduction of well-known classical allusions is a gain in precision and in the emotional surplus
attaching to legendary names.
   Line 9. The refrain motive of the sparrows in the
eaves is dropped — it is a romantic device, and two such
devices in one quatrain were felt to be a little too much.
The introduction of a time element, 'on the instant', adds
dramatic force to the poem. 'Clamorous' is a good
sonorous word, if a little too emphatic for the noise
made by a single sparrow; but it provides alliteration
with 'climbing', 'lamentation', 'leaves', 'could',
'compose' and 'cry'.

Line 10. The fresh and effective 'curd-pale' had to
be dropped, since the moon had become brilliant in the
first verse; for the same reason the white stars had to
be excluded. 'Climbing', though it sounds well enough,
is rather commonplace, and 'empty' is banal.
  Line 11. 'Loud' must be dropped to agree with the
first verse; 'chaunting' is an artificial metaphor. The
new line has a forceful alliterative movement. But I
doubt if a 'modern' poet would use a word like 'lamentation' in connection with 'leaves'; it is almost a *cliché*.
  Line 12. The changes are largely dictated by the new
form of line 4, and by the desire for alliteration. But
'compose' involves a process difficult to visualize, and
the line as a whole does not bring the poem to such a
definite and inevitable conclusion as in the first version.
  These are analytical notes, and perhaps on a reckoning
the plus and minus of it all cancels out. It is necessary,
in the end, to compare the synthetic feeling of the two
versions, and here one can only state a personal reaction.
My own is definitely in favour of the earlier version.
In spite of the romantic diction against which Yeats
rightly reacted, I feel that it produces a unity of effect
which, romantic as it is, is superior in force to the more
definite, more classical diction of the later version.
For the truth is, that the poem in essence and inception
is irradicably romantic, and had better retain its
romantic diction and imagery. As it is, the new version
has a patchy effect. The old suit may have been shabby,
but it was of a good cut and an even tone; the patches of
new classical cloth are too obvious and too disjointed.
  This image, with a little stretching, will serve for
my objection to Yeats's later verse (but naturally it is
only an objection on the highest plane of technical
criticism — the kind of criticism that poets exchange
between themselves, and which is not meant for laymen).
Though he makes his poems out of the latest suitings, all
of good classical (or, which comes to the same thing)
modernist cloth, the cut is still romantic.

> I dreamed as in my bed I lay,
> All night's fathomless wisdom come,
> That I had shorn my locks away
> And laid them on Love's lettered tomb:
> But something bore them out of sight
> In a great tumult of the air,
> And after nailed upon the night
> Berenice's burning hair.

The gesture here, in spite of its precision, is still

romantic and such poems stand out, luxuriant in the pruned
orchard of the later verse. The pruning has produced
a larger fruit, a clearer thought; but the effect is
rather bleak, the prose of scientific culture rather
than the poetry of natural growth. A complete change of
spirit requires a change of form; of structure as well as
of diction. And though one or two poems, such as
'Byzantium', seem to promise the necessary development,
Yeats remained to the end faithful to the spirit of another
age.

The Winding Stair
and Other Poems (1933)

85. YEATS'S MOVEMENT FROM CELTIC TO ANGLO-IRISH

1933

An unsigned review of 'The Winding Stair and Other Poems'
(1933) by George Buchanan , Mr Yeats's New Poems, 'Times
Literary Supplement', 5 October 1933.

George Henry Perrott Buchanan (b. 1904) was educated
at Queen's University, Belfast. He worked on the editorial staff of 'The Times', and the 'News Chronicle'.
He served in Coastal Command during the Second World
War and has written plays, 'A Trip to the Castle', 'Trésper
Revolution' and 'War Song'. His other books include
'Passage through the Present' (1932); 'A London Story'
(1935); 'Entanglement' (1938); 'Rose Forbes' (1950);
and 'Green Seacoast' (1959). His latest volume of poetry
is 'Minute-Book of a City' (1972).

Mr. Yeats is old — sixty-eight by the reference books —
and five years have passed since 'The Tower'. Expec-
tation of this new work, now before us, has been as eager
as though it had been by a young man reaching his prime.
Is the level that astonished us in 'The Tower' maintained?
It may be immediately observed that his passionate and
musical discourse is well continued — a discourse still
occupied with the sad fact of age. It is an austere subject, running the length of these pages, broken with
occasional bursts of anger or disgust or moments of
tenderness in which he feels endowed with almost the power
to bless.

In 1928 Mr. Yeats appeared to be purging his fears and
horror in sounding verse; generally now his mind appears

more ordered, more resigned to the so-much-spoken-of
event. Its proximity he feels, like a figure of the
Renaissance, to be a vivifier:

> No longer in Lethean foliage caught
> Begin the preparation for your death
> And from the fortieth winter by that thought
> Test every work of intellect or faith,
> And everything that your own hands have wrought,
> And call those works extravagance of breath
> That are not suited for such men as come
> Proud, open-eyed and laughing to the tomb.

Reminiscence, with appropriate comment, must naturally
form part of a book such as this. To see what elements
are drawn out and exposed is, therefore, of critical
importance. We are often shown the elder thinking not in
terms of what state he has arrived at but of the state
from which age has removed him: the skeleton (as it is
symbolized) talking about the vanished flesh. This humour
prevails in a series called 'A Woman Young and Old', which
was written before the publication of 'The Tower', but
'left out for some reason I cannot recall'. One of these
poems, dealing with a woman 'too old for a man's love',
should be referred to, since it possesses surprising
echoes of the early 'Wanderings of Oisin':

> But the dark changed to red, and torches shone,
> And deafening music shook the leaves; a troop
> Shouldered a litter with a wounded man,
> Or smote upon the string and to the sound
> Sang of the beast that gave the fatal wound.

In a group, 'Words for Music Perhaps', Crazy Jane, type
of a woman self-forgetful and abandoned in love, figures —
a noteworthy change from the cold proud woman celebrated
in so much of his earlier poetry.

Of other activity he refers to little, in looking back,
except the poetic activity: the mind contemplates its
own processes. Here again he is often regarding himself,
far-off, the young writer of fastidious courtship —
somewhat regretfully also, it may be. Modern poetry is
'the rattle of pebbles on the shore under the receding
wave'; but of himself and his early contemporaries, he says

> We were the last romantics — chose for theme
> Traditional sanctity and loveliness,

and adds later:

> But all is changed, that high horse riderless,
> Though mounted in that saddle Homer rode.

Homer is his touchstone. With Homer he defends his
paganism, which here is pronounced in a continual praise
of strong or beautiful bodies, and the ardours of physical
pleasure, from which illusions come:

> He fancied that I gave a soul
> Did but our bodies touch.

In recent books Solomon and Sheba were frequently sung
about; here we have Crazy Jane and Jack the Journeyman,
the coxcomb who is so much stronger in these matters than
the 'solid man'. Crazy Jane says: 'But should that other
come, I spit.' Mr. Yeats disdains, at this late hour,
the comforts of religion. He dismisses Von Hügel
('thought with blessings on your head'), explaining his
action thus:

> Homer is my example and his unchristened heart.

Another invocation of Homer is in an argument between the
Soul and the Heart, when the Heart, for ultimate sanction,
fries: 'What theme had Homer but original sin?' His
sympathy leans to the Heart, for the Soul, Mr. Yeats
fears, may be just a mysterious darkness. It is the pagan
position; but with it is the pagan courage and combative-
ness in face of human imperfection. Seeing his life, Mr.
Yeats can say:

> I am content to live it all again

even though it is not a pretty but a Swiftian picture he
takes of that life:

> I am content to live it all again
> And yet again, if it be life to pitch
> Into the frog-spawn of a blind man's ditch,
> A blind man battering blind men;
> Or into that most fecund ditch of all,
> The folly that man does
> Or must suffer, if he woos
> A proud woman not kindred of his soul.

What has endured in him is the unabated desire for life.
He has not finished with life before life has finished:
hence his great interest as a poet. In reading him one
does not feel sorry for brave spirits suffering the

inevitable assaults of time;   one rather rejoices on
account of them, seeing they are exemplars of the required
fortitude.
  The complaint will recur that these poems are obscure.
That is true, but they do not present a wall of incom-
prehension. Mr. Yeats is a veritable poet in this, that
the interplay of his thought and the words that express
it have reached the status of a dance, valuable to watch
in itself. A dancer, in his movements, does not *do* anything or *go* anywhere: this kind of poetic dance is
destroyed if it aims at the descriptive purposes of
prose. Recently M. Valéry well expressed these points:

> Si le sens et le son (ou si le fond et la forme) se
> peuvent aisément dissocier, le poème se *décompose*.
> Conséquence capitale: les 'idées' qui figurent dans
> une œuvre poétique n'y jouent pas le même rôle, ne
> sont pas du tout des *valeurs de même espèce,* que les
> 'idées' de la prose.(1)

M. Valéry recalls, also, an acute remark of Voltaire's:
'La poésie n'est faite que de beaux détails.' On similar
affirmations a defence might be built up of much of this
poetry. Mr. Yeats is a slow contriver; one may imagine
how these lines have been repeated and repeated until they
are worn smooth and made essential. The pictorial
quality of the imagery is usually small, and abstractions
are frequent, but these possess a curious concreteness
of their own. This may be noticed in 'Byzantium', the
magnificent centre-piece of the book, which opens with
these lines:

> The unpurged images of day recede;
> The Emperor's drunken soldiery are abed;
> Night resonance recedes, night-walkers' song
> After great cathedral gong;
> A starlit or a moonlit dome disdains
> All that man is,
> All mere complexities,
> The fury and the mire of human veins.

Such verses are written during no specified period. In
the present urban civilization like a forest about most of
us, Mr. Yeats does not serve us as a guide in matters of
sensibility. In one sense his is a lonely achievement —
an indoor activity with windows only upon the reaches of
some Irish stream. Allusions here to outer contemporary
events are fewer than ever; two poems, the introduction
tells us, were inspired by the death of Kevin O'Higgins,

'the finest intellect in Irish public life'. Yet it is
an achievement that fuses every plane of his own experience, which, if not wide or varied, is intense.
Mr. Yeats is not greatly receptive; he consciously
assumed a specialized role and, as he has told us, adopted
a mask. While effective in registering his personality
upon the outside world, this defended him much from the
free flow of natural experience. Keats at times felt a
loss of identity before the world: he became a recording
instrument. It is doubtful if Mr. Yeats has ever felt
that loss of identity.

He is a man who, with lovely romantic tales, pleased
many in his early youth, but who entirely shed that first
success, passing through years of critical disagreement,
and has earned the right in age to be applauded a second
time by the discerning. Has any other poet in the line of
the past known such an event, to have revived a fading
fame with a fresh one, quite dissimilar? His early poetry
ran like a quiver of ecstasy through young Irish poets,
all of whom fell beneath his influence; but now, since he
has resumed the Anglo-Irish tradition in place of the
Celtic cosmogony, it is noticeable how, even in his so-
called decline, he has stirred the marrow of the younger
English writers.

Note

1 If the meaning and the sound (or the essence and the form)
  can easily be dissolved, the poem becomes distorted.
  The main consequence of this is that 'ideas' in a poem
  do not play the same part, have in no way the same
  meaning as 'ideas' in prose.

86. HUGH GORDON PORTEUS ON THE REFINED AND DISCIPLINED
VISION OF 'THE WINDING STAIR'

1934

From a review of 'The Winding Stair and Other Poems' (1933),
by Hugh Gordon Porteus, 'The Criterion', January 1934.

An esteemed contemporary is not less difficult to write of
than a neglected contemporary. Here is a book which is
so much more than the sum of the verses in it; which is
important not less as revealing the poet than as poetry.
Yeats, alas, 'late Yeats', is fashionable. Already it is
impossible to discuss the new verse without mentioning,
reverently, his name. Even the 'Morning Post' has called
him, 'no question, the greatest of living poets'. Certainly
Yeats is the most outstanding, the most consistent, the most
romantic figure in poetry to-day. In fact, he is an interesting personality; and so we have eyed his poetry with
suspicion. Yet Yeats really is a magician. And he has
definite contributions to make not only to our literature
but to our craft of verse. Our admiration is real; it
is not merely respect for his silver hairs, for a still
unexpended energy, for an old man's skill, such as we had
for Bridges.

Of course, Yeats is romantic. He is, perhaps, more
romantic (because less precise) than Eliot or Pound, and
only less romantic than the surréalistes. It is indeed
his romanticism — a certain mistiness which obscures,
to the impatient, his finer virtues — that has got him
liked by the many, and disliked by a few. 'O it is not
because of the pictures that I said I liked Mr. Lane's
Gallery. I liked it because it has such a beautiful atmosphere, because of the muffed glass.' So said a certain
lady one day to Yeats. He himself has always liked to
envelope his work in a beautiful atmosphere. Only,
lately, the glass has cleared. If I may suggest a parallel
from another art — was there not a painter once who was
so seduced by 'the beautiful atmosphere' that only
rarely, and mainly in his later years,did he choose to
make pictures as 'solid and durable' as Cézanne's. I mean
Corot. Yeats, too, has plumbed the depths of romanticism;
but although he still employs a romantic idiom (it is
part of his programme, and he knows what he is doing) he
brings to it now a vision astonishingly refined and
disciplined. 'I put "The Tower" and "The Winding Stair"
into evidence to show that my poetry has gained in self-
possession and power,' he says in 'A Packet for Ezra
Pound'; but also: 'I owe this change to an incredible
experience.' When this incredible experience turns out
to be — as it does — an affair of automatic script
and supernatural smells, we realize that Yeats is still
the Romantic. For it goes to show the patience, humi-
lity, simplicity, curiosity and enthusiasm for the
strange which together make up, perhaps, the Romantic
attitude. Nevertheless Yeats is one of the rare sages
who can regard the stars with the eyes of a plain

shepherd, who can drag the moon through a pool and speak
his soul to us in the common words and not embarrass us.
This he can do because he knows so well the natural gait
of life ('the poet should know all men,' he once declared,
'should combine the greatest possible knowledge of the
speech and circumstances of the world') — and because
he 'knows death to the bone'; and their madnesses,
terror, darkness, and

> Brightness that I pull back
> From the Zodiac.

His 'magic' is not *all* nonsense, and anyone who dismisses
it as a weakness is missing something valuable in his
verse — that is to say, in poetry to-day. Even the
sceptical Mr. Herbert Read once spoke in these pages of
'the possibility of relating the types actualized by
the poetic imagination to their origin in the root-images
in the community'. (The notion of a 'race-memory' is
said to be discredited 'authoritatively' but who are the
authorities? Surely the visionaries rather than the
psychologists.) The artist has in any case to translate
his vision of the world into images and symbols before
he can communicate it; and although it is by their
quality that we decide his genius, it is by their uni-
versality that his work succeeds and endures. Emotion
produces a symbol, says Yeats, a symbol produces emotion;
and: 'certainly evocation with symbol has taught me that
much that we think limited to certain obvious effects
influences our whole being'. Images are only the scaf-
folding for the real thought, the essential gesture of
the human spirit, that hangs like a wraith about the
bone. Yeats uses invariably the elemental images — all
those primary elements and attributes which we can find
catalogued in the Fourth Book of Shang, and which go
directly into the Chinese 'radical'. (And I have found
in some of the Chinese radicals gestures of just such
universal force — for are they not race-images that
have withstood the usage of milleniums?) For Yeats, the
symbol is neither a sentimental counter nor a mental tag;
it has been emotionally and intellectually felt, and it
has a weight of experience behind it:

> I toiled long years and at length
> Came to so deep a thought
> I can summon back
> All their wholesome strength.

And again:

> I declare this tower my symbol;   I declare
> This winding, gyring, spiring treadmill
> Of a stair is my ancestral stair.

But the poet, he has told us, 'will play in all masks' —
so:

> In mockery I have set
> A powerful emblem up,
> And sing it rhyme upon rhyme
> In mockery of a time
> Half dead at the top.

In his latest book there are verses (e.g. 'Mohini
Chatterjee' and 'Coole and Ballylee') which would bring
fame overnight to any unknown poet.   And if as a whole
the book lacks the fine sweep of passion that distinguished 'The Tower', there is in the writing everywhere an added precision, some sharp memorable phrase,
as: 'Salt blood blocks his eyes.'   And we know of no
recent verse so poignant and sincere.

87.   PRISCILLA THOULESS ON THE EFFECT OF THE 'NO PLAYS'
AND ON MOOD IN THE 'FOUR PLAYS FOR DANCERS' (1921)

1934

This comment is taken from Priscilla Thouless, 'Modern
Poetic Drama' (1934).
    Priscilla Thouless obtained an MA in English Language
and Literature at the University of Manchester.   She
held a Research Fellowship in Italy and was an assistant
lecturer at the University of Manchester (1922-5).   In
1924 she married Dr R.H. Thouless, author of 'Straight
and Crooked Thinking' (1930;   revised edition 1953).

Yeats at all times found the close association between
realism and the theatre an irksome bondage.   Whatever
may be the author's view of drama, the actual physical
conditions of the stage and the relationship of the actors
to the audience does tend in Europe to make the tradition
of the theatre realistic.   Even so early as 1900 Yeats
was rebelling against this and prophesying that: 'The
theatre of art, when it comes to exist, must therefore

discover grave and decorative gestures . . . and grave
and decorative scenery, that will be forgotten the moment
an actor has said, "It is dawn"' ('Ideas of Good and
Evil'). He is aiming here at movements of the actor's body
and a decoration of the stage which will be symbolic
of emotion and not a realistic representation. The
experiments that Yeats made with Dolmetsch and Florence
Farr, in devising a method of reciting verse to notes,
have as their object the distancing of the actor, the
elimination of his own personality in so far as it is
possible, in order that the words and the verse itself
may retain their objective purity. Both 'Deirdre' and
'The Shadowy Waters' are dramas of the mind and of the
emotions; they are detached from ordinary life, and by
symbolism they express Yeats's inner world. But they
did not seem to Yeats to be written in the ideal form
of drama, and it is this form that he finds in the Nō
plays of Japan. . . .
    The subjects treated by the Nō dramatists are legendary
and from literary sources, and in many of the plays a
ghost appears in his own person or he takes possession
of one of his own characters, so that we are looking
back into the lives of the people and viewing their
emotions far down the stretch of human life. This does
not mean that they are unreal to us, but that they are
distanced and seen in perspective to life as a whole. . . .
    Yeats knew the Nō plays only through translation, but
he studied them with the help of a Japanese dancer, and
his genius was peculiarly fitted to understand a form of
art, characteristically Eastern; something subtle and
yet sensuous, something which could get past the envelope
of life to the inner harmony felt in time of trance,
this is what Yeats wanted, and what he found in the Nō
dramas. As he says in his 'Cutting of an Agate' (1919):
'The arts which interest me, while seeming to separate
from the world and us, a group of figures, images,
symbols, enable us to pass for a few minutes into a
deep of the mind, that had otherwise been too subtle
for habitation.' And for Yeats one of the essential
secrets of his art was the use of dancing in poetic
drama. He speaks of his Japanese drama as being able
'to recede from us into some more powerful life'. Yeats
realized that the aim of the poetic dramatist is to
remove the pressure of self from his audience so that it
may reach this more powerful life, and this aim is
most perfectly brought about by the union of dance and
music and verse.
    'Four Plays for Dancers' (1921) was the book of plays
which Yeats wrote with the new form of dramatic art in

his mind. The volume consists of 'The Dreaming of the
Bones' and 'The Only Jealousy of Emer' (1919), 'At the
Hawk's Well' (1917), and 'Cavalry'. Only one of these
plays, 'At The Hawk's Well', had been performed at the
time of publication, but Yeats intended the method of
production to be the same in all four plays. 'At the
Hawk's Well' was performed for the first time in 1916 in
an ordinary room without a platform, and the stage was a
bare space in front of a wall against which was placed a
patterned screen. Three musicians played certain instruments — drum, gong and zither, and also marked the beginning and end of the play by the ceremony of the folding of
the cloth. This ceremony is as follows: during their
song the first musician, standing still in the central
point of the front stage holds a black cloth, while the
two other musicians walk toward the back of the stage,
holding the two ends of the cloth so that it forms a
triangle with the first musician as the apex. While
the cloth is being held in this manner actors can arrive
on the stage or leave it, and simple stage properties
can be placed there: in addition its unfolding and folding is a sign that the play begins or ends. Masks were
worn in 'At the Hawk's Well' by the speaking characters —
the Old and the Young Man; the musician and the dancer,
the Guardian of the Well, had their faces painted to
resemble masks. The masks and the costumes were designed
by Dulac, who also composed the music for the songs and
dancing; Yeats, in his preface to 'Four Plays', suggests
that typical masks might be made by artists and used for
several plays. The central situation of this play, as
in all the plays, was the dance; in 'At the Hawk's Well'
the dancer was the Japanese Ito, and it was the wish of
Yeats that the dancing in all his plays should be formal,
resembling that of marionettes, and not human and personal.

    The subject matter of all the four plays of the volume
is symbolic and is connected with an account of some of
the mystical doctrines of the Arabs found in the papers of
Robartes, which Yeats was editing at the time of the
writing of these plays. The theories deal with the different grades of spiritual life found amongst men, and of
the grades of incarnation which take place throughout
life. Men are divided into subjective and objective
types, or as they are more commonly called introverted
and extraverted types, that is to say people whose centre
of interest is in the mind within, and those whose interest
is in people and objects outside the mind. Birds and
animals follow the same type, the solitary birds such as
the heron, the hawk, the swan being subjective, the
herd animal such as the dog being objective . . .

The 'Four Plays [for Dancers]' brings us once more to
the question of what symbolism means to Yeats. In certain poems of Blake the symbol and the thing symbolized
grow together and flower into perfect form, but Blake
was a visionary in a sense that Yeats was not, for to
Blake the world within his mind was real and concrete in
a way that the world outside could never hope to be. The
prophetic books of Blake are obscure because the world we
see lost all reality to him, and became completely obscured
by the flaming light of the world within him. The mind of
Yeats is of a different order; he does not see visually
a world within him, of which the world of objects is
only a distorted far-away image. His mind is subtle
intellectually; it delights in its own exercise and in
the perpetual seeking into the far corners of erudite
doctrines of the mind and its being. Many of his poems
therefore are written not to shadow forth the real world
within him, as are Blake's, but as poetical manifestations
of an intellectual idea.

The 'Four Plays' illustrate this side of Yeats's
nature, his absorbing interest in the intricacies of
esoteric doctrines, in the ranks of souls and spheres of
living of which Theosophists write so much. Yeats became
greatly interested in Theosophy as a young man, and throughout his life he is fascinated by the idea of peeling off
skin after skin from the nut of meaning. In 'Calvary', as
we have seen, Yeats illustrates symbolically the Arabian
mystical doctrines found in Robartes's papers. We are
told in the notes to the play that the herons and solitary
birds symbolize subjective temperaments, and with this
knowledge the musicians' song before and after the Calvary
scene fits into the scheme of the play; but this information seems to come to us from without the play, and
therefore to be æsthetically injurious. Though the
speeches of Lazarus are arresting and beautiful, the
play does not form a complete whole; there are intellectual ideas in the play and there is emotion, but these
things are not fused. The symbolism of the intellect,
fascinating as it is to the mind of Yeats, hinders rather
than helps the creation of an æsthetic world, complete
in itself and free from our world. But symbolism to Yeats
means different things at different times, and there is a
sense in which it is a living power within his mind. The
vital imaginative symbolism in Yeats is that in which his
heroic figures of ancient legend stand as symbols of the
deep imaginative life of mankind. To a child, the giant,
the unconquerable hero, the captured maiden, the sorcerer
are real inhabitants of an intensely real world, only
partially detached from his own waking one. The adult is

separated from this world, but these figures exist in
his dream life, symbolizing desires and struggles in the
depths of his mind, just as these figures symbolized the
desires and struggles of the race life in the past. To
Yeats these heroic figures, these legendary lovers, these
lost spirits open the world of reality, the world he is
always trying to escape to, from the life we know, the
world in which deep unconscious being flows. It is this
world he is seeking when he speaks of 'the vast passions,
the vagueness of past times, all the chimeras that haunt
the edge of trance'.

With the true symbolic subject which we find in the
'Four Plays' the image which draws up the wealth of the
mind such as 'the hot Istain stone, and the cold stone of
Fanes' of 'Deirdre' is gone. Instead we have the kind of
writing which cuts the mind free from the mind's store.
The image in 'Deirdre',

> O my eagle,
> Why do you beat vain wings upon the rock
> When hollow night's above?

is of this kind, as is the image in 'The Dreaming of the
Bones',

> And the tomb-nested owl
> At the foot's level beats with a vague wing.

In both these images the language is pared down, so that
the mind is cleansed of all confusing haphazard wealth
and only essential form is left behind. But, whereas in
'Deirdre' naked image appears side by side with the adorned
one, in 'Four Plays' Yeats makes no use of images calling
up a wealth of association. In these plays Yeats is
dwelling not on character nor on action, but on mood, the
mood of suspense, of suffering, of beauty expressed in
terms of legend. Above all in the greatest of these plays
he is giving to nature the expression of these emotions,
and it is by means of his peculiar imagery that Yeats
achieves this expression.

88.   EDITH SITWELL ON THE GREATNESS OF YEATS'S LYRICS

1934

These critical comments are taken from Edith Sitwell,
'Aspects of Modern Poetry' (1934).

   Dame Edith Sitwell (1887-1964), poet, prose writer
and anthologist, had an isolated childhood at Renishaw
Hall in Derbyshire until her governess Helen Rootham
interested her in French symbolism and music. Her anthology 'Wheels' (1916) and her poem 'Façade' (1922), set
to music by Sir William Walton, were *avant-garde* in intent,
and her subsequent poetry was a mixture of the fantastic
and an elegiac romantic strain. 'The Sleeping Beauty'
(1924) describes her early life. In 'Gold Coast Customs'
(1929) she changed to an awareness of the horror underlying
modern life, and her 'Street Songs' (1942), 'Green Song'
(1944) and 'Song of the Cold' (1945) reveal the depth of
her religious feeling. Her critical study 'Alexander
Pope' (1930) was one of the books which revived interest
in the Augustan poet.

How deep is the wisdom of this poem, and how intense and
strange its identity:

[Quotes 'The Three Hermits', 'Collected Poems', p. 127.]

   The strange beauty of this poem does not lie alone in
the knowledge that it is sung on the shore of eternity —

   (By a cold and desolate sea) . . .

   The beggar (who 'rummaged rags and hair, Caught and
cracked his flea') has turned over, sorted and summed
up all the remnants of mortality and has found life — in
one form. The praying beggar fears the approaching sleep;
but beside them is the strange saint-like ecstasy of one
who

   Giddy with his hundredth year,
   Sand unnoticed like a bird —

and who, like a bird, trusts in the love of God.

   Here already, the old men are faced with a more bitter,
a bleaker wind than that which sounds among the thorn-
trees. And in all these strangely beautiful, proud
poems, in which all life is compressed into the image of

a begger or of a tree, in which a black stone can hold all
the secrets of the heart, a cold wind blows from the shores
of eternity. The beings of whom Mr. Yeats writes, though
they bear names we know, and though we might call to
them with our mortal voices, exist in eternity and not in
time; their age is not the age of dust alone:

[Quotes 'The Friends of his Youth', VII, 'A Man Young
and Old'.]

Here, indeed, this great poet whose life as an artist
began under the influence of writers like Pater and
Villiers de l'Isle Adam, has removed himself from any
trace of those influences. His rhythmic line is bare
almost to austerity, but has all the nobility that such
a bareness of outline can give. The mood of these poems,
their particular lyrical impetus has changed from that
of the lovely earlier verses: that impetus is perhaps,
sharper, and darker, but in the later as in the early
poems, the lovely sound and sense are fused into one as
in no other lyrical poetry of our time. There is some
kinship (though scarcely a physical resemblance) between
certain of Mr. Yeats' earlier poems and certain of
Shelley's lyrics — 'A widow bird sat mourning on her
bough', for instance; but Mr. Yeats' individuality was
never shadowed by the presence of any other poet. Such
kinship as there was, lay in the peculiar impetus of the
rhythmic line in both poets. But the melodic schemes were
different. Writing of Shelley's lyrics in 'The Pleasures
of Poetry', Volume II, I said: 'The actual variations
of texture in the lyrics resemble, not so much the
differences between silk and marble and stone, as the
differences between the perfume of lily, dark rose,
tuberose, violet and narcissus. These melodic effects
are the result, in part, of his vowel-schemes, built up
often on a foundation of two vowels only, or on a foundation in which each vowel is used both poignantly and
dulled. But the beauty of the poems is often as intangible as the scent of the flowers, and is not to be
explained.'
Mr. Yeats' melodic schemes do not give us the feeling
of the different perfumes of flowers. The vowel-schemes —
so intensely fused with the rhythmic plan, or impetus,
that they are indivisible, and appear to have been born
into their form — not created by an outside handiwork —
seem to have all the different variations of wind and of
air, and it is a dew-laden, fresh wind or air, not one
laden with perfume.

The strange wisdom that is radiant round such a
poem as 'Mohini Chatterjee' for instance, takes another
form in the poem 'Crazy Jane on God', in which the fusion
of wisdom with the intensity of passion is such that we
feel the poem is a fire rather than a form of words
blown together.

That lover of a night
Came when he would,
Went in the dawning light
Whether I would or no;
Men come, men go;
All things remain in God.

Banners choke the sky;
Men-at-arms tread;
Armoured horses neigh
Where the great battle was
In the narrow pass:
All things remain in God.

Before their eyes a house
That from childhood stood
Uninhabited, ruinous,
Suddenly lit up
From door to top:
All things remain in God.

I had wild Jack for a lover,
Though like a road
That men pass over
My body makes no moan
But sings on:
All things remain in God.

In this poem the impression of those torn rags of
womanhood:

                a house
That from childhood stood
Uninhabited, ruinous,
Suddenly lit up

is conveyed by the tuneless half-rhymes that appear from
time to time: 'would-God' (a plunge into immeasurable
depths, this) in the first verse; 'sky-neigh', 'tread-
God', 'was-pass' in the second verse; 'house-ruinous'
(the extra syllable in the second word gives a feeling of
huddled misery), 'stood-God', 'up-top' in the third;

'lover-over', 'road-God', 'moan-on' in the fourth. It is
a memorable fact that the only pure rhymes are in the
first verse (where there is still the 'would-God' half
rhyme on which I have commented already) and this has
much psychological significance. In the second verse,
there is a mixture of rising, falling, and stretching
half-rhymes or dissonances; in the third all are falling;
in the last verse, the half-rhymes alternately fall and
stretch wildly onward into infinity. This is one of the
deeply significant technical interests of this great
poem.

'Words for Music' indeed, from which the foregoing and
the following poem are taken, are, to my feeling, undoubtedly the greatest lyrics of the last hundred years,
because of their intense fusion of spirit and matter,
because of their overwhelming fire and their strange
world-old wisdom, sung in the voice of one who is impatient with 'the loveless dust'.

89. GEOFFREY BULLOUGH ON THE COLD PASSION OF YEATS

1934

This critical account of Yeats's achievement is taken from
Geoffrey Bullogh, 'The Trend of Modern Poetry' (1934).

Geoffrey Bullough (b. 1901), professor and critic,
was educated at the University of Manchester and in Italy.
He has taught in the Universities of Manchester, Sheffield
and London. His publications include 'The Trend of Modern
Poetry' (1934, 1949); 'Narrative and Dramatic Sources
of Shakespeare' (1957-75), and 'Mirror of Minds' (1962).

In 'The Wanderings of Oisin' (1889), with its bright
tapestries of legendary figures, its regret for the
glories of a simpler civilisation, Mr Yeats strove to do
for Irish what Morris had done for Scandinavian myth, and
the lavish foreground of the pre-Raphaelites appears in
his decorative pictures of imaginary lands. He spun out
the brief fragments of the Ossianic cycle into dyeshot
gossamer with Tennysonian heroics and Swinburnian rhetoric.
With a dexterous use of couplet forms he evoked a poetry
of revolt and escape which became in 'The Rose' (1893) a
deliberate campaign to 'sing the ancient ways' of
Cuchulain, Fergus, and old Eire. His narrative and

dramatic poems were the chief embodiment of this aspiration to a lost heritage of beauty. Sometimes reminiscent of Swinburne in imagery and rhythm, sometimes
achieving a more personal note, he developed a wistful
suggestiveness. The poems by which he is best known,
'Innisfree', 'The Rose of the World', 'The Song of
Wandering Aengus', are marked by this romantic nostalgia.

> I am very religious, and deprived by Huxley and Tyndall,
> whom I detested, of the simple-minded religion of my
> childhood, I had made a new religion, almost an in-
> fallible church of poetic tradition, of a fardel of
> stories, and of personages, and of emotions, insepa-
> rable from their first expression, passed on from
> generation to generation by poets and painters with
> some help from philosophers and theologians ('The
> Trembling of the Veil').

But this was not the whole story; for these traditions
and stories derived their validity from an ambiguous
Celtic tradition, partly religious, partly magical. And
the indefiniteness of this background, its participation
in several levels of culture, appealed to the young poet,
though the spiritual power which he vaguely perceived was
not Beauty, nor the Christian God, nor a Lord of Magic,
but a blend of all three. His love of magic, his studies
in telepathy and spirit-lore, were rather an æsthetic toying with imaginative counters than a search for an absolute
essence. This distinguishes his poetry from that of A.E.
who was no magician, but a true mystic and wove myth and
legend into theosophic symbolism:

> Nearer to Thee, not by delusion led,
> Though there no house fires burn nor bright eyes gaze:
> We rise, but by the symbol charioted,
> Through loved things rising up to Love's own ways:
> By these the soul unto the vast has wings
> And sets the seal celestial on all mortal things.

Because of the coherence of his religious thought, A.E.
with a limited talent gives an impression more homo-
geneous and natural than the early Mr Yeats. The importance of the latter's work lay not so much in its content
as in the method of expression. Believing in the existence of a universal 'great mind' and a 'great memory'
which could be 'evoked by symbols', he came to regard
both imagery and rhythm as incantatory of universal emotions. Shelley's poetry became palatable to him only
when he realised the symbolism inherent in the recurrent

images of leaves, boats, stars, caves, the moon. In his
own verse the rose, white birds, foam, the wind, became
means of conjuring moods rather than sensations.
  'Blake,' he declared (in 1897), 'was a symbolist who
had to invent his own symbols. . . . He was a man crying
out for a mythology, and trying to make one because he
could not find one to his hand; had he been a scholar of
our time he would . . . [perhaps] . . . have gone to Ireland.' Mr Yeats's meaning was not so clear or so profound
as Blake's, and one questions whether the Celtic mythology as he took it over preserved its old vitality and
did not become too readily a vehicle of mere fantasy.
  He came, too, under the influence of French *Symbolistes*,
especially admiring Verlaine, Villiers De l'Isle Adam,
and Maeterlinck. In the 'Autumn of the Body' he described
(1898) how he found 'in the arts of every country those
faint lights and faint colours and faint outlines and
faint energies' to which he had himself turned. Rebelling against Parnassian exteriority and English impres-
sionism he hoped that with 'the casting out of descriptions of nature for the sake of nature, of the moral law
for the sake of the moral law, casting out of all anec-
dotes and of that brooding over scientific opinion that so
often extinguished the central flame in Tennyson and of
that vehemence that would make us do or not do certain
things . . . we would cast out of serious poetry those
energetic rhythms as of a man running . . . and we would
seek out those wavering meditative, organic rhythms, which
are the embodiment of the imagination.'
  He copied the Symbolist aim to evoke a complex of
emotion not by direct statement but by a multitude of
indirect strokes. In 'The Wind among the Reeds', (1899),
the affinity is marked. Here a great increase in the proportion of mythological to natural imagery is noticeable.
The symbolism of 'God stands winding his lonely horn', of
'your image that blossoms as a rose in the deeps of my
heart', is obvious, but a more recondite symbolism derived
from magical studies involved 'The Poet Pleads with the
Elemental Powers', while such lines as the following
demanded a commentary:

    Do you not hear me calling, white deer with no horns?
    I have been changed to a hound with one red ear; . . .
    I would that the Boar without bristles had come from
      the West
    And had rooted the sun and moon and stars out of the sky
    And lay in the darkness, grunting, and turning to his
      rest.

Such a learned symbolism, backed up frequently by references to the world-ranging anthropology of Sir James
Frazer, Mr Yeats was the first to present in English
poetry. We shall see its reappearance, with a deeper
significance in T.S. Eliot. Here it is almost purely
decorative, and (despite his theoretical distinction in
'Symbolism in Painting' (1898) between allegory and symbol) allegorical, that is, superimposed by the intellect
upon emotion.

At this time, form was all; his pursuit of beauty
was deliberate and somewhat 'decadent'; very salutary
no doubt in the heyday of Kipling, but tending to an
accumulation of epithets and an excess of word-music.
Yet the Celtic background gave an essential freshness
even within the limits of this artificiality, and in poems
like 'The Song of Wandering Aengus' or 'He wishes his
Beloved were Dead' energy and controlled fancy were
evident.

Certain poems of 'In the Seven Woods' (1904),(1) (e.g.
'Never Give all the Heart', 'The Arrow', 'The Old Men')
revealed a change in the direction of Mr Yeats's development, made clearer by what he wrote in 1906 ('Discoveries')
about Verlaine's assertion 'that the poet should hide
nothing of himself.'

'Without knowing it,' says Mr Yeats, 'I had come to
care for nothing but impersonal beauty. I had set out on
life with the thought of putting my very self into poetry,
and had understood this as a representation of my own
visions and an attempt to cut away the non-essential, but
as I imagined the visions outside myself my imagination
became full of decorative landscape and of still life. . . .
The more I tried to make my art deliberately beautiful the
more did I follow the opposite of myself. Presently I
found that I entered into myself and pictured myself and
not some essence when I was not seeking beauty at all,
but merely to lighten the mind of some burden of love or
bitterness thrown upon it by the events of life.' Now,
to attain 'style, mastery, that dignity and that lofty
and severe quality Verlaine spoke of', he saw that 'we
should ascend out of common interests, the thoughts of
the newspapers, of the market place, of men of science,
but only so far as we can carry the normal, passionate,
reasoning self, the personality as a whole.' He still
held that 'all art is dream', but it was now a representation of the waking dream of life, not merely of racial
memories. Banished were the indistinct meandering emotions, the sophisticated heroism. He turned to face his
growing bitterness in an Ireland no longer filled with
fairies. His struggles with the national theatre made
him reflect:

> The fascination of what's difficult
> Has dried the sap out of my veins, and rent
> Spontaneous joy and natural content
> Out of my heart.

But only this could save his poetry from mannerism and
produce the mature work in which 'passion and precision
have been one'. If at times he met disillusion harshly,
at others he achieved the nobility of 'To a Shade', and
'To a Friend whose work has come to Nothing'. He had to
discover that 'Romantic Ireland's dead and gone' before
he could achieve a simplicity and correctness whose nearest
parallel is in Ben Jonson.

In 'A Coat' he tells how his petty imitators stole his
song:

> Covered with embroideries
> Out of old mythologies,

and dismisses them with the reflection:

>   there's more enterprise
> In walking naked.

So 'The Green Helmet' (1910) and 'Responsibilities' (1914)
contain not only disgust at a life where 'all things at
one common level lie', but an epigrammatic force, an
economy of utternace which can be tested by comparing
'A Woman Homer Sung' with the cloudy, pretentious 'The
Rose of the World'.

Mr Yeats's increase in stature is revealed in these
volumes by the manner in which he reworked old themes, as
in 'When Helen Lived', 'Fallen Majesty', and the poignant
'Friends'.

His later volumes, too, 'The Wild Swans at Coole'
(1919), 'Michael Robartes' (1921), 'The Tower' (1928), and
'The Winding Stair' (1933), show him responding

> To that stern colour and that delicate line
> That are our secret discipline

in landscape and life. He has turned from books to men;
though at times he feels 'That the heart grows old' and
'The living beauty is for younger men', he has reached a
maturity of vision from which an astringent, athletic
quality emerges, and he may properly hope to

> Dine at journey's end
> With Landor and with Donne,   ('To A Young Beauty')

for he has written many a

> Poem maybe as cold
> And passionate as the dawn.   ('The Fisherman')

Cold passion; that is the clue to his new use of words.
Previously they had been symbols with a penumbra of indefinite associations; now they were chastened and
defined, their excrescent tendrils lopped. Small wonder
that Yeats influenced, and was influenced by, the Imagists.
A 'Thought from Propertius' might almost have been written
by H.D. Under the stress of this new severity the suave
rhythms gave place to more broken, freer measures, owing
something to free verse as well as to Georgian experiments
in 'substitution'.

His old interests survived, love of dream ('Presences'),
the memory of beautiful women ('Memory', His Phœnix'),
admiration of simple joy ('Tom O'Roughley'), of the ballad
of youth ('To a Young Girl'), of the lost civilisation;
but these were expressed with a new decisiveness, per-
meated with reflection. Symbolism recurs obscurely in
'The Double Vision of Michael Robartes', but in the main
any difficulties encountered in the later poems are due
to terseness rather than to indirection.

He withdrew more and more to the solitude of the mind,
but this does not mean that he wished to escape the complexities of the last twenty years. In 'The Second
Coming' he saw the time as ripe for a new advent:

> Things fall apart; the centre cannot hold. . . .
> The best lack all conviction, while the worst
> Are full of passionate intensity.

But the 'Second Coming' did not necessarily mean peace
and purification.

> And what rough beast, its hour come round at last,
> Slouches towards Bethlehem to be born?

It is a 'terrible beauty' that he discovers in 'Easter
1916', and, in 'A Political Prisoner', a sense of human
suffering.
Because his heart is torn by the struggles of

> That crafty demon and that loud beast
> That plague me day and night,

he seizes the more unerringly on his moments of respite,
and, in his wishes for his daughter, bestows on her all

those gracious and quiet qualities that he sees as most
difficult of attainment to-day. 'The Tower' (1928),
with its symbolism of retirement and study, brings peace
after unrest as he frees himself from the world. Not
without hatred of 'Decrepit age that has been tied to me',
he announces his renunciation of active life, but

>   Never had I more
>   Excited, passionate, fantastical
>   Imagination, nor an ear and eye
>   That more expected the impossible.

The sonnet 'Leda and the Swan' has all his early pre-
Raphaelite colour, while 'The Tower' itself is a col-
location of 'images in the great Memory stored', that
gives the lie to his surrender. This volume indeed
shows a new richness of feeling and diction after the
acidity and asceticism of the previous years. 'A Prayer
for my Son' heralds a Jacobean grace seen also in the
series 'A Man Young and Old'. Regrets remain, but with
the weakening of the passions comes an inner balance
consolidated in the 1933 volume, 'The Winding Stair'.
    Here still in

>   A storm-beaten old watch-tower,
>   A blind hermit rings the hour,   ('Symbols')

but the sould has found that age need not mean a living
death or abstraction.
    He can contemplate outer events, the state of poetry,
his own past, the passions of the young, seeing them all
sub specie æternitatis: 'Everything that is not God consumed with intellectual fire.' In early life his subjectivity was purely emotional; now the insistence is
on intellect. Epigrams, gnomic verses, now recalling
Blake, now the Greek anthology, prove the completeness
of his mastery. He can face the spectacle of the artist
at odds with life coolly ('The Choice'), while death
seems no longer a triumphant victor.
    The freeing of his spirit is revealed in the many
songs of young love, as in 'Words for Music Perhaps'. In
'A Woman Young and Old' the thin music of Housman swells
to a richer cadence. His pilgrimage has been a long one,
but he has at last conquered the craving for a mystical
experience; in a brief dialogue expressing the victory
of the Heart over the Soul, he announces both the conflict of his life and its resolution:

THE SOUL.   Seek out reality, leave things that seem. . .
            Look on that fire, salvation walks within.

THE HEART.   What theme had Homer but original sin?

It is as untrue to conclude (with Mr Herbert Read) that
Mr Yeats 'remains in the end faithful to the spirit of
another age' as to declare (with Mr F.R. Leavis) that
his poetic career is a warning. Both statements, by their
antithetical opposition of age to age and romantic to
classical or modern, neglect the fine gradations by which
one may, and indeed must, pass into the other.

'We were the last romantics' the poet declares, looking back to his youth; but though he has never sold that
birthright, his poetry has, by an inner compulsion, 'moved
with the times', and the symbolical stair of his tower is
as typical of our age, as 'modern' and at the same time
as eternal, as is the winding stair of Mr T.S. Eliot's
'Ash Wednesday'. . . . .

Note

1 See note to item 83.

90. DENIS JOHNSTON GIVES A DUBLINESQUE VIEW OF 'WHEELS
AND BUTTERFLIES'

1934

This is a review of 'Wheels and Butterflies' (1934) by
Denis Johnston, Mr Yeats as Dramatist, 'The Spectator',
30 November 1934.

William Denis Johnston (b. 1901), playwright and biographer, was born in Dublin, educated at Christ's
College, Cambridge, and Harvard University. He directed
the Gate Theatre, Dublin (1931-6) and was a BBC war
correspondent (1942-5) and director of programmes (1945-7).
He has held academic posts in the USA including the Head-
ship of the Theatre Department at Smith College, Massa-
chusetts. His plays include 'The Old Lady Says No' (1929);
'The Moon on the Yellow River' (1931); 'A Bride for the
Unicorn' (1933); and 'The Scythe and the Sunset' (1958).
His autobiography 'Nine Rivers from Jordan' (1953) was
followed by a biography, 'In Search of Swift' (1959).

A few years ago, it is told of Mr. Yeats that he was
deputed by his fellow Directors to explain to one of Dublin's many garret dramatists what was wrong with a play
that had had to be rejected by the Abbey Theatre. He did
it in this way. 'We liked your play,' he said, 'but it
has one or two faults. The first is that the scenes are
too long.' He considered deeply for a while before continuing. 'Then, there are too many scenes,' he concluded.
This shattering criticism is so succinct and yet so comprehensive that it is worthy of being preserved to the
honour of Mr. Yeats.

In the dedication of the present volume and in the
several prefaces to the individual plays, Mr. Yeats
throws out yet another challenge to the garrets and cellars
of his home town in a couplet from which the book derives
its cryptic title:

> To Garret or Cellar a wheel I send,
> But every butterfly to a friend.

Such a prefix is both apt and fitting for a collection of
plays: most of which, he is careful to tell us, have been
specifically written for performance on the first floor
only, or, in other words, in the drawing rooms of large
country houses. Fortunately, indeed, these Noh Plays
of Mr. Yeats have not been so confined in their presentation, and each has been successfully performed in the
theatre, to which they are all eminently suited.

Mr. Yeats has a characteristic capacity for appearing to take us into his confidence. He allows us the
privilege of hearing him think aloud, whether in prose or
in verse, and in turning over the pages of his book we
come across in turn most of the loves of his more recent
years — Dean Swift, the Classical Stage of Japan, Celtic
muthology, psychical research, and just a touch of politics. For notwithstanding his admonition from the witness
box to Mr. Peadar O'Donnell to 'stick to literature and
keep politics as a recreation for his old age', it is well
recognized that Mr. Yeats, when he chooses, is one of the
ablest politicians in Ireland and has on more than one
occasion beaten the professionals to the ropes.

'The Words Upon the Window Pane' is an interesting
addition to the growing mass of Swift literature. Mr.
Yeats is right when he says that Swift haunts. Whether
he is as right in his prefatory speculations is, like
everything else connected with the terrible Dean, a matter
for argument. It is a common practice these days to
enlist Swift in the ranks of the great Irish patriots as
the inventor of those shopkeepers' slogans that pass for

national economics today. But Swift's love for Erin is
more problematical than his hatred of the Whigs. After
all, he was only the first generation of his family to
belong to the Middle Nation, that gay race of conquering
freebooters whose mild-mannered descendants seem nowadays
to be born only to be lectured. What was the liberty
for which Swift fought and for the vindication of which
he so eloquently congratulates himself in his own epitaph?
Mr. Yeats suggests that it was Vox Populi, or the National
Bent or Current. Possibly this is the same thing that
Mr. De Valera refers to when he says, 'When I wish to
know what the Irish people want I look into my own heart.'
    The play itself, like the Séance which it portrays, is
only haunted by Swift, his extraordinary mistress and
still more extraordinary wife, and it provides what must
be one of the most difficult playing parts ever written
for a woman. As in Lord Longford's 'Yahoo', the author
attempts to invent an imaginary conversation between the
Dean and Vanessa on the occasion of his ferocious final
visit to Celbridge — a conversation which of its very
nature can never surpass the actual reported facts — the
arrival, the letter flung down, and the silent departure.
With Stella he is on firmer ground. It is one of her
verses, written to the Dean in honour of a birthday, that
forms the words from which the play derives its title, and
Mr. Yeats goes so far in his admiration of these as to
call her a better poet than her friend. He is not one of
those to give countenance to the ungallant, and characteristically Dublin suggestion that she had the benefit of
the assistance of Dr. Delany.
    It appears that a Japanese friend during one of his
visits to this part of the world presented Mr. Yeats with
a sword. How this was received does not appear, or to
what purpose it has been turned, and it is interesting to
speculate what Mr. Yeats may have done with a sword.
However, as this may be, Mr. Yeats, in return for this
rather unusual gift, wrote a play of impeccable orthodoxy about the Resurrection and dedicated it to his
Oriental friend, almost as effective and entertaining
a response as the original gesture. This play is the
least interesting part of his book. The discussions of
Ebionite and Sabellian are on a well-worn battleground and
the dialogue is not particularly revealing. In its spoken
sentiments this play is stainless. In the implications to
be drawn from the Dionysian goings-on in the street
outside, the play is one over which the late J.W. Robertson
would have chuckled and rubbed his hands. Luckily,
theatre audiences do not usually exert themselves to the
extent of considering implications, which probably ex-

plains why this play, if not receiving the advisable
Imprimatur from Gardiner Street, has, at any rate,
escaped pious violence. Nobody can ever doubt or deny
Mr. Yeats' courage, and perhaps a sword was not so bad
a present after all. Has not Mr. Yeats himself, whether
intentionally or not, given one to his country in his
time? — a sword that has been heard rattling ever since,
for good or ill.

'Fighting the Waves' — once known by the excellent
title of 'The Only Jealousy of Emer' — and 'The Cat and
the Moon', are first-rate examples of Mr. Yeats' later
vein in the Theatre and of the surprising fact that the
classic Irish drama is taking its technique from Japan.
Both plays suffer to some extent from this Noh influence.
The Prologues and Epilogues, chanted by black-clad figures,
their faces lined to represent masks and dressed in costumes that must inevitably evoke a smile from any ordinary
playgoer, the 'difficult and irrelevant words', to quote
his own criticism, and his insistence upon the use of such
infantile musical instruments as drums, rattles and
whistles, must inevitably create a barrier between the
audience and a proper enjoyment of the real core of Mr.
Yeats' work. These things might be introduced to divert
attention from the jejune material of intellectual young
men who write for experimental theatres. But both these
plays are good in themselves. In conception, imagination
and treatment they are not only superb pieces of writing,
but very excellent stories, consummately expressed in
terms of the stage. The Antheil music for 'Fighting the
Waves', originally scored for a full orchestra, is here
added as an appendix rescored for piano alone. It is an
exciting and fascinating piece of work. At the first
rehearsal it is said that Dr. Larchet's orchestra, unacquainted with the work of this young American *protégé*
of Ezra Pound, involuntarily stopped after the first few
bars, full of profuse apologies for having, as they thought,
got the parts mixed up. Such, however, was not the case,
and they were eventually persuaded to resume. On better
acquaintance it proves to be a fitting accompaniment for
the discordant grandeur of this tale of Fand and Cuchulain.

91. A PERSONAL APPRECIATION OF YEATS'S WORK BY F.P.
STURM

1934

These comments were written to Yeats in a letter dated
21 December 1934 by F.P. Sturm. The letter is included
in F.P. Sturm, 'His Life, Letters and Collected Work'
(1969), edited by Richard Taylor.
   For note on F.P. Sturm see p. 273.

My dear Yeats,
You should have omitted the word 'Putrid'(1) from the
preface to your new Cuala book. And yet I dont know.
The fool who said it may be sure that at least one word
he has uttered will be read, in your preface, when all
he has written is on the penny bookstall. . . .
   If you really believe the time has come for you to stop
writing verse you should consult a physician, because there
must be something wrong with your liver. It must be thirty-
five years since I was asked to review THE SHADOWY WATERS.
I was at the time a young and cock-sure undergraduate,
quite ready to take over the command of the Fleet, give
a few condescending lesson in theology to the Roman
Colleges, and was filled with the modest conviction that
my Latin verse put Propertius to shame. But I had not
the cheek to write a review of THE SHADOWY WATERS. It
flabbergasted me. I read nothing else for at least a year.
I remember taking it to bed with me every night, filled with
despair by a technical perfection that I knew was forever
beyond me. Now I am an ageing man (no, an old man), and
still faithful to the one great poet that my time has
produced.
   There is more in your verse now than ever. I am sure
there is more in it than you yourself suspect. Even
when you try to write carelessly a supernatural light
shines through your indolence and irritability. In the
words of your so American friend Ezra Pound 'the mist
clings to the lacquer'.
   And where is your new version of THE VISION? Surely
you have not scrapped it because of a few Latin howlers(2)
that the publisher's reader should have corrected. It is
a great book and it must reappear. But I hope without any
grease-droppings from the dull tallow-candle of Theosophy.
   I meant this to be a letter of thanks for all you have
published since I last heard from you, but it seems I am
beginning to criticise. Well, I have the right. If it

had not been for you I might have been a writer myself,
but your work poisoned by anaemic Muse with envy, so that
she has become a scholar who translates Macrobius and
writes her scrannel verses on such thin paper that it is
fit only for . . . but for that facet of literature
read the Cantoes of (no name no pack drill)
    I suppose we are both too old to do anything very
energetic, but if you have a spot of youthful fury to
spare do tell in what publisher's cellar you have left
THE VISION. If I am unfortunate enough to survive you
I may at some future time be able to rescue it.
    I have carefully read Pounds HOMMAGE TO SEXTUS PRO-
PERTIUS. I know Propertius fairly well. Why in God's
name should a fragmentary, inaccurate, perverse though
occasionally amusing American paraphrase of a Latin poet
be published as though it were an original work? I dont
say it isnt worth the money. It is quite worth the half-
crown it costs. And that is my opinion of it.
    I am going to say what has been on my mind for years.
In its original version THE SHADOWY WATERS is a great and
beautiful work. Every alteration you have since made is
an outrage. Great poetry makes poor pantomime. It is
the fault of that cursed Abbey Theatre.

F.P. Sturm

Personally typed, & typed v. badly.

Notes

1 Yeats was quoting Ezra Pound's comments on the verse in
  Yeats's 'The King of the Great Clock Tower', Dublin
  (1934).
2 On 26 August 1929 Sturm advised Yeats to 'get some
  friend who knows Latin to read the proofs to you this
  time. I know that I am a pedant, but pedants read
  you. We cough in ink till the world's end, as you
  cruelly said, but the least of us would save you from
  the errors which spoil 'The Vision' as it is now.
  Personally, I think your philosophy smells of the fagot.'
  (For full text of this letter see Item 68.)

92. J.H. POLLOCK ON THE EMOTIONS OF AN EXILE

1935

This comment is taken from J.H. Pollock, 'William Butler Yeats' (1935).

John Hackett Pollock (1887-1964), educated at the Royal, later the National University of Ireland, was a pathologist and a founder member of the Gate Theatre, Dublin. He wrote novels, poems and plays under the pseudonym 'An Philibin'. His plays include 'The Fourth Wise Man', a nativity play; his latest poetry appeared in 'Lost Nightingale' (1951). His novels include 'The Valley of the Wild Swans' (1932) and 'Mount Kestrel' (1945).

Some, even among those acquainted with his writing, may learn with surprise that Dr. Yeats possesses a novel to his credit: let me rather say, a novelette, the diminutive being justified upon the score of length. I possess a copy of the second edition of this little book, published originally in the Pseudonym Library under the pen-name of 'Ganconagh'; I regard it as of prime importance in connexion with the origins of Dr. Yeats's work; it shows that preoccupation with Sligo which characterises the early poetry of his objective period, and has for a central *motif* the homesickness of Sherman, temporarily exiled in London, in the employment of an uncle, whom I suspect of being a Pollexfen family portrait; in point of fact I am persuaded that John Sherman himself is but the projection upon paper of the youthful William Butler Yeats, resident, like Sherman, in Hammersmith, fretting for Sligo town, thinly veiled under the name of Ballah. The autobiographical element, always implicit, becomes explicit upon one occasion which compels quotation:

> The grey corner of a cloud slanting its rain upon
> Cheapside called to mind by some remote suggestion
> the clouds rushing and falling in cloven surf on the
> seaward steep of a mountain north of Ballah. . . .
> Delayed by a crush in the Strand, he heard a faint
> trickling of water near by; it came from a shop-
> window, where a little water-jet balanced a wooden
> ball upon its point. The sound suggested a cataract
> with a long Gaelic name, that leaped crying into the
> Gate of the Winds at Ballah. . . . He was set dreaming
> a whole day by walking down . . . to the border of the
> Thames. . . . It made him remember an old day-dream

of his. . . . a certain wood-bordered and islanded lake,
whither in childhood he had often gone blackberry
gathering. At the further end was a little island
called Inniscrewin. . . . Often when life and its
difficulties had seemed to him like the lessons of
some elder boy given to a younger by mistake, it had
seemed good to dream of going away to that islet and
building a wooden hut there, and burning a few years
out, rowing to and fro, fishing, or lying on the island
slopes. . . .

I venture to think that reasonable imaginative intuition would divine in this passage the emotional foundation of 'The Lake Isle of Innisfree', even in the absence
of Dr. Yeats's confirmation provided in 'The Trembling of
the Veil', the autobiography of his adolescence:

I had still the ambition, formed in Sligo in my teens,
of living in imitation of Thoreau on Innisfree, a little
island in Lough Gill, and when walking through Fleet
Street very home-sick I heard a little tinkle of water,
and saw a fountain in a shop-window which balanced a
little ball upon the jet, and began to remember lake
water. From the sudden remembrance came my poem
'Innisfree'.

The power to evoke Irish landscape, the capacity to
produce *atmosphere* is also present in the germ in 'John
Sherman', although this immature method is less elaborate,
less deliberate, less sophisticated, one may say, than it
subsequently became under the influence of literary self-
consciousness.

The town was dripping, but the rain was almost over.
The large drops fell seldomer and seldomer into the
puddles. It was the hour of ducks. . . . The water
slid noiselessly, and one or two of the larger stars
made little roadways of fire into the darkness. . .
once or twice a fish leaped. Along the banks were the
vague shadows of houses, seeming like phantoms
gathering to drink.

Those who are acquainted with Sligo, or any West of
Ireland town upon a wet evening, must admit the adequacy
of this representation, and also of a subsequent description:

The woman selling gooseberries; the river bridge; the
high walls of the garden where it was said the gardener

used to see the ghost of a former owner in the shape
of a rabbit . . . the deserted flour store; the
wharves covered with grass . . . grey clouds covering the town with flying shadows rushed by like the
old and dishevelled eagles that Maeldune saw hurrying
towards the waters of life.

The most important quality, however, in this tentative
little excursion into fiction, properly so called, consists in a degree of simplicity, of human sympathy, of
sentiment, not to say of sentimentality, which does not
appear again in any subsequent work. There is nothing
abstract in the group of characters, nothing, might one
even say, distinguished; yet although ordinary, the
author succeeds in making them essentially alive and
interesting: while the reflections upon everyday life
which occasionally emerge, display a practical acumen
which one would not expect from Dr. Yeats, merely upon a
survey of his more representative work. The mood which
produced 'John Sherman' never returned. . . .

A Full Moon in March (1935)

93. THE MYTHOLOGY OF HIS OWN PERSONALITY

1935

An unsigned review of 'A Full Moon in March' (1935), The
Mind of Mr Yeats in Verse, 'Times Literary Supplement',
7 December 1935.

Mr. Yeats now gives us two more versions of his short play,
'The King of the Great Clock Tower', which previously
appeared in prose. Of the revisions one is in verse,
because he came to the conclusion that 'prose dialogue
is as unpopular among my studious friends as dialogue
in verse among actors and playgoers'. The other version omits a character, the King, for the sake of greater
intensity. This preoccupation with a rather Ninety-ish
fable evidently has importance. The theme is of a lover
treated by a queen with 'virgin cruelty' (his head is cut
off). In his destruction, however, he wins her: the
head sings, the queen sinks down embracing it. Since
the beginning Mr. Yeats has poeticized the aloof woman,
and it still seems in this book that the obsession is
not yet exorcized. The play in its ballet form is
apparently telling on the stage.
 Other poems show a greater public interest than
hitherto exhibited. His lines to Parnell are in the bare
yet resounding accents we call 'the later Yeats' and
admire:

   Through Jonathan Swift's dark grove he passed, and there
   Plucked bitter wisdom that enriched his blood.

At one time, it seems, Mr. Yeats thought of writing a
marching song for Irishmen — even for the Blueshirts,
but his enthusiasm for these dwindled — and here are
given his attempts, to the tune of O'Donnell Abu.
Certain lines reveal tendencies of his mind: 'But a
good strong cause and blows are delight';   'Down the
fanatic, down the clown';   and the following:

> When nations are empty up there at the top,
> When order has weakened or faction is strong,
> Time for us all to pick out a good tune,
> Take to the roads and go marching along.
> March, march — How does it run? —
> O any old words to a tune.

This is as near to Fascism as Mr. Yeats can go.   In another
song he calls on living Irishmen to be worthy of their
great ancestors: 'Justify all those renowned generations.'
    A number of 'Supernatural Songs' close the book: they
are put in the mouth of one Ribh, a hermit, an imaginary
critic of St. Patrick, whose 'Christianity, come perhaps
from Egypt like much early Irish Christianity, echoes
pre-Christian thought'.   It is not easy to discover the
purport of this creation.   There is praise of passion
ever seeking its highest state:

> For the intercourse of angels is a light
> Where for its moment both seem lost, consumed.

And as on earth so in heaven:

> As man, as beast, as an ephemeral fly begets,
>   Godhead begets Godhead,
> For things below are copies, the Great Smaragdine
>   Tablet said.

But Ribh finds Christian love insufficient, and studies
hatred:

> For that's a passion in my own control,
> A sort of besom that can clear the soul
> Of everything that is not mind or sense.

And adds:

> Hatred of God may bring the soul to God.

In conclusion Ribh sees man

> Ravening, raging, and uprooting that he may come
> Into the desolation of reality.

So does Mr. Yeats make a stark mythology of his own personality, more bleak than the old Celtic mythology in
which he first dressed himself, more bleak but better.
Perhaps it has a tone that Heraclitus himself would not
have found displeasing. And who can sum it up but Mr.
Yeats in his 'Prayer for Old Age', from which state he
has squeezed more music than most poets:

> God guard me from those thoughts men think
> In the mind alone;
> He that sings a lasting song
> Thinks in a marrow-bone. . . .

> I pray— for fashion's word is out
> And prayer comes round again—
> That I may seem, though I die old,
> A foolish, passionate man.

It is a small book, heavy with the accustomed and
personal use of words, speaking an ever-young longing and
an ageing anguish.

94.   MEDIATING BETWEEN THE EXTERNAL WORLD AND THE ANCESTRAL
HABIT

1935

A review of 'A Full Moon in March' (1935) by Michael
Roberts, The Moon and the Savage, Sunlit Heart, 'The
Spectator', 27 December 1935.

   Michael Roberts (1902-48) was educated at King's
College, London and Trinity College, Cambridge. He
taught science at the Royal Grammar School, Newcastle,
and became Principal of the College of St Mark and St
John, Chelsea. His works included 'Critique of Poetry'
(1934); 'Newton and the Origin of Colours' (1934);
'T.E. Hulme' (1938). His 'Poems' were published in 1936,
and he edited the Faber Books of Modern and Comic Verse
and a selection of Elizabethan Prose.

Some of us who are now thirty read Yeats ten years ago,
and we were fascinated and troubled by all his talk of
images and symbols. There was something hostile to our
own conception of poetry in his work, an element which
in the hands of lesser men could so easily become clap-
trap that we avoided it and turned to more astringent
poets. Mr. Yeats, it seemed, was toying with the verbiage
of Theosophy and Madame Blavatsky, a self-contained
philosophy and language that made no contact with the
thought and language of science and of ordinary speech.
There seemed, in spite of obvious exceptions, to be a
danger that Mr. Yeats was falling into A.E.'s way of
thinking of a specific mystical experience as the only
true subject of poetry. Since then, Mr. Yeats has
written poems which have reoriented our whole view of
his work: the early enthusiasm is justified, the suspicion dispelled. 'The Tower' and 'The Winding Stair'
showed that Mr. Yeats could create his own symbols:
'That dolphin-torn, that gong-tormented sea', and stamp
them by varied repetition with a special meaning. The
symbolism may be narrower in scope than the Christian
symbols, but within its chosen field it is intensely
effective, and though Mr. Yeats has learned something
from Neo-Platonism and is still fascinated by the vision
of the naked hermit upon Mount Meru or Everest, over
against that Eastern ideal of passive contemplation he
sets the passion for love and action.

His new book includes two plays upon that theme: one
of them, 'The King of the Great Clock Tower', was published in a prose version last October. Mr. Yeats has
rewritten it in verse because 'prose dialogue is as unpopular among my studious friends as dialogue in verse
among actors and playgoers'. The new version has greater
intensity than any of Mr. Yeats' earlier poetic dramas:
it turns wholly upon one theme, the severed bleeding head
of the wild, half-crazy, wandering poet singing to the
Queen the song which the living man had come to sing. 'A
Full Moon in March' is still more concentrated: the
King is eliminated; the Queen and the Stroller are the
only characters, and the Queen herself, a masked figure,
orders the killing of the Stroller. The Queen, the symbol of that romantic inhumanity which haunts so much of
the earlier poetry of Yeats, succumbs to the dead man's
song; and the attendant who represents the spirit of the
Stroller asks from his 'savage sunlit heart': 'What can
she lack whose emblem is the moon?' and the other answers
for the Queen: 'But desecration and the lover's night.'

The shorter poems have the same poetic intensity as
the plays. The feeling is tempered to the theme, and the

pitch is not raised to sentimental melodrama. Phrases
as simple as ordinary speech are marked with a singing
rhythm, and chosen so well that, in thinking of the same
subject, the reader is henceforward compelled to quote
them. Mr. Yeats can make poetry of abstractions, a thing
which only two other living poets, Mr. Richard Eberhart
and Mr. Herbert Read can do, and through it he can express
his yearning for an aristocratic tradition and his passionate belief in dedication to a cause, in the power of
born leaders, and in the value of the life of the emotions:

> God guard me from those thoughts men think
> In the mind alone;
> He that sings a lasting song
> Thinks in a marrow-bone.

These poems play upon habits of thought and emotion which
are so deeply ingrained in us that they appear to be part
of the structure of our mind, and they mediate between
the external world and the ancestral habit. The poems
in this small book of seventy pages are among the best
that Mr. Yeats has written.

95. A WRITER OF VERSE DRAMA SEES THE POET'S WORKSHOP

1936

A review of 'A Full Moon in March' (1935) by Austin Clarke,
Mr Yeats Contrasts in Verse and Prose, 'London Mercury',
January 1936.
    For note on Austin Clarke see p. 282.

The last reward of fame is to please all or few. As a
political prophet Mr. Bernard Shaw is claimed at present
both by Fascists and Communists. As a great poet, Mr.
Yeats pleases those who regard him as the last of the self-
named romantics as well as those who hail him as the first
considerable convert to modernism. The two versions of
the one dance-play which appear in this volume indicate
that Mr. Yeats is unable, except by violent exclusion, to
solve his own antinomies.
    'The King of the Great Clock Tower' is yet another
parable of that romantic extravagance and waste which have
had a lifelong fascination for Mr. Yeats except in his art.

Mr. Yeats borrows the theme of the Singing Head from one
of his own early Celtic Twilight tales, and the Salome
plot brings us back to the 'nineties. We do not find
here, however, the viciousness of Wilde but only that
dream-cruelty which is a *sine qua non* of the fairytale
world. The romantic Stroller has his head chopped off
for his pains, but why should the beautiful queen appear
thereafter in a costume which suggests a woman surgeon?
In the second version called 'A Full Moon in March', all
is changed, utterly changed. The image-seeking Stroller
is transformed into a Swineherd, in foul rags, who makes
an impudent proposal to Her Majesty:

>   A song—the night of love,
>   An ignorant forest and the dung of swine.

The rude fellow is promptly despatched and his lousy head
sings a mocking song of Jack and Jill which recalls the
lighter metaphysical moods of Mr. W.J. Turner and Mr.
Eliot. We must admit, however, that the iconoclastic
mood changes again:

>   Why must those holy, haughty feet descend
>   From emblematic niches, and what hand
>   Ran that delicate raddle through their white?

With these lovely lines Mr. Yeats takes sanctuary once more.
    But this volume has another and exciting interest. 'The
King of the Great Clock Tower' was originally published
a year ago in a private edition as a prose play. To
compare prose and verse is to discover oneself in the
poet's workshop. Here is an example of the prose version:

THE KING.   What do you want?

STROLLER.   A year ago somebody told me that you had
            married the most beautiful woman in the
            world, and from that moment I have had her
            image in my head, and month by month, it has
            grown more and more beautiful. I have made
            poems about her and sung them everywhere, but
            I have never seen her.

In the new version this becomes:

THE KING.   What do you want?

STROLLER.   A year ago I heard a brawler say
            That you had married with a woman called

> Most beautiful of her sex. I am a poet.
> From that day out I put her in my songs,
> And day by day she grew more beautiful.
> Hard-hearted men that plough the earth and sea
> Sing what I sing, yet I that sang her first
> Have never seen her face.

It would be interesting to speculate how far the Abbey
prose with its deliberate simplicity and insistence springs
from the same eloquent impulse as the poetry with its
external effects.

Of the shorter poems in this volume the three marching
songs, apparently inspired by the short-lived Blue Shirt
movement in Ireland, are poetically limited by their
popular (or rather unpopular) intention. But the grand
style is evident in such lines as these:

> Whence had they come,
> The hand and lash that beat down frigid Rome?
> What sacred drama through her body heaved
> When world-transforming Charlemagne was conceived?

Here indeed Mr. Yeats proves himself master of that eloquence which he spent half a lifetime eradicating from
his own literary movement.

96. R.P. BLACKMUR ON YEATS'S MAGIC AS A MACHINERY OF MEANING

1936

This criticism by R.P. Blackmur of Yeats's use of magic
first appeared as The Later Poetry of W.B. Yeats, 'The
Southern Review', Autumn 1936. It was subsequently included in 'The Expense of Greatness' (1940).

Richard Palmer Blackmur (b. 1904) has been a professor
of English at Princeton University since 1951. His pub-
lications include 'The Double Agent' (1935); 'The Good
European' (1947); 'Language as Gesture' (1952); 'The
Lion and the Honeycomb' (1955); and 'Form and Value in
Modern Poetry' (1957).

The later poetry of William Butler Yeats is certainly
great enough in its kind, and varied enough within its

kind, to warrant a special approach, deliberately not the
only approach, and deliberately not a complete approach.
A body of great poetry will awaken and exemplify different interests on different occasions, or even on the
same occasions, as we may see in the contrasting and often
contesting literatures about Dante and Shakespeare: even
a relation to the poetry is not common to them all.   I
propose here to examine Yeats's later poetry with a special
regard to his own approach to the making of it;   and to
explore a little what I conceive to be the dominant mode
of his insight, the relations between it and the printed
poems, and — a different thing — the relations between
it and the readers of his poems.
   The major facts I hope to illustrate are these: that
Yeats has, if you accept his mode, a consistent extraordinary grasp of the reality of emotion, character, and
aspiration;   and that his chief resort and weapon for the
grasping of the reality is magic;   and that if we would
make use of that reality for ourselves we must also make
some use of the magic that inspirits it.   What is important is that the nexus of reality and magic is not by
paradox or sleight of hand, but is logical and represents,
for Yeats in his poetry, a full use of intelligence.   Magic
performs for Yeats the same fructifying function that
Christianity does for Eliot, or that ironic fatalism did
for Thomas Hardy;   it makes a connection between the poem
and its subject matter and provides an adequate mechanics
of meaning and value.   If it happens that we discard more
of Hardy than we do of Yeats and more of Yeats than we do
of Eliot, it is not because Christianity provides better
machinery for the movement of poetry than fatalism or
magic, but simply because Eliot is a more cautious craftsman.   Besides, Eliot's poetry has not even comparatively
worn long enough to show what parts are permanent and
what merely temporary.   The point here is that fatalism,
Christianity, and magic are none of them disciplines to
which many minds can consciously appeal today, as Hardy,
Eliot, and Yeats do, for emotional strength and moral
authority.   The supernatural is simply not part of our
mental furniture, and when we meet it in our reading we
say: Here is debris to be swept away.   But if we sweep
it away without first making sure what it is, we are
likely to lose the poetry as well as the debris.   It is
the very purpose of a supernaturally derived discipline,
as used in poetry, to set the substance of natural life
apart, to give it a form, a meaning, and a value which
cannot be evaded.   What is excessive and unwarranted in
the discipline we indeed ought to dismiss;   but that can
be determined only when what is integrating and illumi-

nating is known first. The discipline will in the end turn
out to have only a secondary importance for the reader;
but its effect will remain active when he no longer
considers it. That is because for the poet the discipline,
far from seeming secondary, had an extraordinary structural,
seminal, and substantial importance to the degree that
without it he could hardly have written at all.

Poetry does not flow from thin air but requires always
either a literal faith, an imaginative faith, or, as in
Shakespeare, a mind full of many provisional faiths. The
life we all live is not alone enough of a subject for the
serious artist; it must be life with a leaning, life with
a tendency to shape itself only in certain forms, to afford
its most lucid revelations only in certain lights. If our
final interest, either as poets or as readers, is in the
reality declared when the forms have been removed and the
lights taken away, yet we can never come to the reality at
all without the first advantage of the form and lights.
Without them we should *see* nothing but only glimpse
something unstable. We glimpse the fleeting but do not
see what it is that fleets.

So it was with Yeats; his early poems are fleeting,
some of them beautiful and some that sicken, as you read
them, to their own extinction. But as he acquired for
himself a discipline, however unacceptable to the bulk of
his readers, his poetry obtained an access to reality.
So it is with most of our serious poets. It is almost
the mark of the poet of genuine merit in our time — the
poet who writes serious works with an intellectual aspect which are nonetheless poetry — that he performs his
work in the light of an insight, a group of ideas, and
a faith, with the discipline that flows from them, which
taken together form a view of life most readers cannot
share, and which, furthermore, most readers feel as
repugnant, or sterile, or simply inconsequential.

All this is to say generally — and we shall say it
particularly for Yeats later — that our culture is incomplete with regard to poetry; and the poet has to provide for himself in that quarter where authority and value
are derived. It may be that no poet ever found a culture
complete for his purpose; it was a welcome and arduous
part of his business to make it so. Dante, we may say,
completed for poetry the Christian culture of his time,
which was itself the completion of centuries. But there
was at hand for Dante, and as a rule in the great ages
of poetry, a fundamental agreement or convention between
the poet and his audience about the validity of the view
of life of which the poet deepened the reality and spread
the scope. There is no such agreement today. We find

poets either using the small conventions of the individual
life as if they were great conventions, or attempting to
resurrect some great convention of the past, or finally,
attempting to discover the great convention that must
lie, willy-nilly, hidden in the life about them.   This
is a labor, whichever form it takes, which leads as
often to subterfuge, substitution, confusion, and failure,
as to success;   and it puts the abnormal burden upon the
reader of determining what the beliefs of the poet are
and how much to credit them before he can satisfy himself of the reality which those beliefs envisage.   The
alternative is to put poetry at a discount — which is
what has happened.

   This the poet cannot do who is aware of the possibilities of his trade: the possibilities of arresting,
enacting, and committing to the language through his
poems the expressed value of the life otherwise only
lived or evaded.   The poet so aware knows, in the phrasing
of that prose-addict Henry James, both the sacred rage
of writing and the muffled majesty of authorship;   and
knows, as Eliot knows, that once to have been visited by
the muses is ever afterwards to be haunted.   These are
qualities that once apprehended may not be discounted
without complete surrender, when the poet is no more than
a haunt haunted.   Yeats has never put his poetry at a
discount.   But he has made it easy for his readers to
do so — as Eliot has in his way — because the price he
has paid for it, the expense he has himself been to in
getting it on paper, have been a price most readers
simply do not know how to pay and an expense, in time
and labor and willingness to understand, beyond any
initial notion of adequate reward.

   The price is the price of a fundamental and deliberate
surrender to magic as the ultimate mode for the apprehension of reality.   The expense is the double expense of,
on the one hand, implementing magic with a consistent
symbolism, and on the other hand, the greatly multiplied
expense of restoring, through the *craft* of poetry, both
the reality and its symbols to that plane where alone
their experience becomes actual — the plane of the
quickened senses and the concrete emotions.   That is to
say, the poet (and, as always, the reader) has to combine, to fuse inextricably into something like an organic
unity the constructed or derived symbolism of his special
insight with the symbolism animating the language itself.
It is, on the poet's plane, the labor of bringing the
representative forms of knowledge home to the experience
which stirred them: the labor of keeping in mind *what*
our knowledge is of: the labor of craft.   With the

poetry of Yeats this labor is, as I say, doubly hard,
because the forms of knowledge, being magical, do not
fit naturally with the forms of knowledge that ordinarily
preoccupy us. But it is possible, and I hope to show it,
that the difficulty is, in a sense, superficial and
may be overcome with familiarity, and that the mode of
magic itself, once familiar, will even seem rational for
the purposes of poetry — although it will not thereby
seem inevitable. Judged by its works in the representation of emotional reality — and that is all that can be
asked in our context — magic and its burden of symbols
may be a major tool of the imagination. A tool has
often a double function; it performs feats for which it
was designed, and it is heuristic, it discovers and performs new feats which could not have been anticipated
without it, which it indeed seems to instigate for itself and in the most unlikely quarters. . . .

[The critic goes on to discuss 'The Second Coming' and
'The Magi'.]

We ought now to have enough material to name the two
radical defects of magic as a tool for poetry. One
defect, which we have just been illustrating, is that
it has no available edifice of reason reared upon it
conventionally independent of its inspiration. There
is little that the uninspired reader can naturally refer
to for authority outside the poem, and if he does make a
natural reference he is likely to turn out to be at least
partly wrong. The poet is thus in the opposite predicament; he is under the constant necessity of erecting his
beliefs into doctrines at the same time that he represents their emotional or dramatic equivalents. He is,
in fact, in much the same position that Dante would have
been had he had to construct his Christian doctrine while
he was composing 'The Divine Comedy': an impossible
labor. The Christian supernaturalism, the Christian
magic (no less magical than that of Yeats), had the
great advantage for Dante, and imaginatively for ourselves, of centuries of reason and criticism and elaboration: It was within reason a consistent whole; and its
supernatural element had grown so consistent with experience as to seem supremely *natural* — as indeed it may
again. Christianity has an objective form, whatever the
mysteries at its heart and its termini, in which all the
phenomena of human life may find place and meaning. Magic
is none of these things for any large fraction of contemporary society. Magic has a tradition, but it is secret,
not public. It has not only central and terminal mysteries

but has also peripheral mysteries, which require not only the priest to celebrate but also the adept to manipulate. Magic has never been made 'natural'. The practical knowledge and power which its beliefs lead to can neither be generally shared nor overtly rationalized. It is in fact held to be dangerous to reveal openly the details of magical experience: they may be revealed, if at all, only in arbitrary symbols and equivocal statements. Thus we find Yeats, in his early and innocuous essay on magic, believing his life to have been imperiled for revealing too much. Again, the spirits or voices through whom magical knowledge is gained are often themselves equivocal and are sometimes deliberately confusing. Yeats was told to remember, 'We will deceive you if we can,' and on another occasion was forbidden to record anything that was said, only to be scolded later because he had failed to record every word. In short, it is of the essence of magical faith that the supernatural cannot be brought into the natural world except through symbol. The distinction between natural and supernatural is held to be substantial instead of verbal. Hence magic may neither be criticized nor institutionalized; nor can it ever reach a full expression of its own intention. This is perhaps the justification of Stephen Spender's remark that there is more magic in Eliot's 'The Hollow Men' than in any poem of Yeats; because of Eliot's Christianity, his magic has a rational base as well as a supernatural source: it is the magic of an orthodox, authoritative faith. The dogmas of magic, we may say, are all heresies which cannot be expounded except each on its own authority as a fragmentary insight; and its unity can be only the momentary unity of association. Put another way, magic is in one respect in the state of Byzantine Christianity, when miracles were quotidian and the universal frame of experience, when life itself was held to be supernatural and reason was mainly a kind of willful sophistication.

Neither Yeats nor ourselves dwell in Byzantium. At a certain level, though not at all levels, we conceive life, and even its nonrational features, in rational terms. Certainly there is a rational bias and a rational structure in the poetry we mainly agree to hold great — though the content may be what it will; and it is the irrational bias and the confused structure that we are mainly concerned to disavow, to apologize or allow for. It was just to provide himself with the equivalent of a rational religious insight and a predictable rational structure for the rational imagination that in his book, 'A Vision' (published, in 1925, in a limited edition only, and then

withdrawn), he attempted to convert his magical experience
into a systematic philosophy. 'I wished,' he writes in
the Dedication to that work, 'for a system of thought
that would leave my imagination free to create as it
chose and yet make all that it created, or could
create, part of the one history, and that the soul's.'
That is, Yeats hoped by systematizing it to escape from
the burden of confusion and abstraction which his
magical experience had imposed upon him. 'I can now,' he
declares in this same Dedication, 'if I have the energy,
find the simplicity I have sought in vain. I need no
longer write poems like "The Phases of the Moon" nor
"Ego Dominus Tuus", nor spend barren years, as I have
done three or four times, striving with abstractions
that substitute themselves for the play that I had
planned.'

'Having inherited,' as he says in one of his poems, 'a
vigorous mind,' he could not help seeing, once he had
got it all down, that his system was something to
disgorge if he could. Its truth as experience would be
all the stronger if its abstractions could be expunged.
But it could not be disgorged; its thirty-five years of
growth was an intimate part of his own growth, and its
abstractions were all of a piece with his most objective
experience. And perhaps we, as readers, can see that
better from outside than Yeats could from within. I
suspect that no amount of will could have rid him of his
magical conception of the soul; it was by magic that
he knew the soul; and the conception had been too
closely associated with his profound sense of his race
and personal ancestry. He has never been able to
retract his system, only to take up different attitudes
towards it. He has alternated between granting his speculations only the validity of poetic myth and planning
to announce a new deity. In his vacillation — there
is a poem by that title — the rational defect remains,
and the reader must deal with it sometimes as an intrusion upon the poetry of indeterminate value and sometimes
as itself the subject of dramatic reverie or lyric
statement. At least once he tried to force the issue
home, and in a section of 'A Packet for Ezra Pound' called
'Introduction to the Great Wheel' he meets the issue by
transforming it, for the moment, into wholly poetic terms.
Because it reveals a fundamental honesty and clarity of
purpose in the midst of confusion and uncertainty the
section is quoted entire.

Some will ask if I believe all that this book contains, and I will not know how to answer. Does the

word belief, as they will use it, belong to our age,
can I think of the world as there and I here judging
it? I will never think any thoughts but these, or
some modification or extension of these; when I
write prose or verse they must be somewhere present
though it may not be in the words; they must affect
my judgment of friends and events; but then there
are many symbolisms and none exactly resembles mine.
What Leopardi in Ezra Pound's translation calls that
'concord' wherein 'the arcane spirit of the whole
mankind turns hardy pilot' — how much better it
would be without that word 'hardy' which slackens
speed and adds nothing — persuades me that he has
best imagined reality who has best imagined justice.

The rational defect, then, remains; the thought is not
always in the words; and we must do with it as we can.
There is another defect of Yeats' magical system which
is especially apparent to the reader but which may not
be apparent at all to Yeats. Magic promises precisely
matters which it cannot perform — at least in poetry. It
promises, as in 'The Second Coming', exact prediction of
events in the natural world; and it promises again and
again, in different poems, exact revelations of the supernatural, and of this we have an example in what has to
many seemed a great poem, 'All Souls' Night', which
had its first publication as an epilogue to 'A Vision'.
Near the beginning of the poem we have the explicit
declaration: 'I have a marvelous thing to say'; and
near the end another: 'I have mummy truths to tell.'
'Mummy truths' is an admirable phrase, suggestive as it
is of the truths in which the dead are wrapped, ancient
truths as old as Egypt perhaps, whence mummies commonly
come, and truths, too, that may be unwound. But there,
with the suggestion, the truths stop short; there is,
for the reader, no unwinding, no revelation of the dead.
What Yeats actually does is to summon into the poem
various of his dead friends as 'characters' — and this
is the greatness, and only this, of the poem: the summary,
excited, even exalted presentation of character. Perhaps
the rhetoric is the marvel and the evasion the truth.
We get an impact as from behind, from the speed and
weight of the words, and are left with an ominous or
terrified frame of mind, the revelation still to come.
The revelation, the magic, was in Yeats' mind; hence
the exaltation in his language; but it was not and could
not be given in the words of the poem.
   It may be that for Yeats there was a similar exaltation
and a similar self-deceit in certain other poems, but

as the promise of revelation was not made, the reader
feels no failure of fulfillment. Such poems as 'Easter,
1916', 'In Memory of Major Robert Gregory', and 'Upon a
Dying Lady' may have buried in them a conviction of
invocation and revelation; but if so it is no concern
of ours: we are concerned only, as the case may be,
with the dramatic presentations of the Irish patriots and
poets, Yeats' personal friends, and Aubrey Beardsley's
dying sister, and with, in addition, for minor pleasure,
the technical means — the spare and delicate language,
the lucid images, and quickening rhymes — whereby the
characters are presented as intensely felt. There is no
problem in such poems but the problem of reaching, through
a gradual access of intimacy, full appreciation; here
the magic and everything else are in the words. It is the
same, for bare emotion apart from character, in such
poems as 'A Deep-Sworn Vow', where the words accumulate
by the simplest means an intolerable excitement, where the
words are, called as they may be from whatever source, in
an ultimate sense their own meaning.

> Others because you did not keep
> That deep-sworn vow have been friends of mine;
> Yet always when I look death in the face,
> When I clamber to the heights of sleep,
> Or when I grow excited with wine,
> Suddenly I meet your face.

Possibly all poetry should be read as this poem is
read, and no poetry greatly valued that cannot be so
read. Such is one ideal towards which reading tends;
but to apply it as a standard of judgment we should first
have to assume for the poetic intelligence absolute autonomy and self-perfection for all its works. Actually,
autonomy and self-perfection are relative and depend upon
a series of agreements or conventions between the poet and
his readers, which alter continually, as to what must be
represented by the fundamental power of language (itself
a relatively stable convention) and what, on the other
hand, may be adequately represented by mere reference,
sign, symbol, or blue print indication. Poetry is so
little autonomous from the technical point of view that
the greater part of a given work must be conceived as
the manipulation of conventions that the reader will, or
will not, take for granted; these being crowned, or
animated, emotionally transformed, by what the poet
actually represents, original or not, through his mastery
of poetic language. Success is provisional, seldom
complete, and never permanently complete. The vitality

or letter of a convention may perish although the form
persists. 'Romeo and Juliet' is less successful today
than when produced because the conventions of honor,
family authority, and blood-feud no longer animate and
justify the action; and if the play survives it is
partly because certain other conventions of human character do remain vital, but more because Shakespeare is the
supreme master of representation through the reality of
language alone. Similarly with Dante; with the cumu-
lative disintegration, even for Catholics, of medieval
Christianity as the ultimate convention of human life,
the success of 'The Divine Comedy' comes more and more
to depend on the exhibition of character and the virtue
of language alone — which may make it a greater, not a
lesser poem. On the other hand, it often happens that a
poet's ambition is such that, in order to get his work
done at all, he must set up new conventions or radically
modify old ones which fatally lack that benefit of form
which can be conferred only by public recognition. The
form which made his poems available was only gradually
conferred upon the convention of evil in Baudelaire and,
as we may see in translations with contrasting emphases,
its limits are still subject to debate; in his case the
more so because the life of his language depended more
than usual on the viability of the convention.
     Let us apply those notions, which ought so far to be
commonplace, to the later work of Yeats, relating them
especially to the predominant magical convention therein.
When Yeats came of poetic age he found himself, as Blake
had before him, and even Wordsworth, but to a worse
extent, in a society whose conventions extended neither
intellectual nor moral authority to poetry; he found
himself in a rational but deliberately incomplete,
because progressive, society. The *emotion* of thought,
for poetry, was gone, along with the emotion of religion
and the emotion of race — the three sources and the three
aims of the great poetry of the past. Tyndall and Huxley
are the villains, Yeats records in his Autobiographies,
as Blake recorded Newton; there were other causes, but
no matter, these names may serve as symbols. And the
dominant aesthetics of the time were as rootless in the
realm of poetic import and authority as the dominant
conventions. Art for Art's sake was the cry, the Ivory
Tower the retreat, and Walter Pater's luminous languor
and weak Platonism the exposition. One could say anything but it would mean nothing. The poets and society
both, for opposite reasons, expected the poet to produce
either exotic and ornamental mysteries or lyrics of mood;
the real world and its significance were reserved mainly

to the newer sciences, though the novelists and the playwrights might poach if they could. For a time Yeats
succumbed, as may be seen in his early work, even while
he attempted to escape; and of his poetic generation he
was the only one to survive and grow in stature. He
came under the influence of the French Symbolists, who
gave him the clue and the hint of an external structure
but nothing much to put in it. He read, with a dictionary, Villiers de L'Isle-Adam's 'Axel's Castle', and
so came to be included in Edmund Wilson's book of that
name — although not, as Wilson himself shows, altogether
correctly. For he began in the late 'nineties, as it were
upon his own account, to quench his thirst for reality
by creating authority and significance and reference in
the three fields where they were lacking. He worked
into his poetry the substance of Irish mythology and
Irish politics and gave them a symbolism, and he developed
his experiences with Theosophy and Rosicrucianism into a
body of conventions adequate, for him, to animate the
concrete poetry of the soul that he wished to write. He
did not do these things separately; the mythology, the
politics, and the magic are conceived, through the personalities that reflected them, with an increasing unity
of apprehension. Thus more than any poet of our time he
has restored to poetry the actual emotions of race and
religion and what we call abstract thought. Whether we
follow him in any particular or not, the general poetic
energy which he liberated is ours to use if we can. If
the edifice that he constructed seems persónal, it is
because he had largely to build it for himself, and that
makes it difficult to understand in detail except in
reference to the peculiar unity which comes from their
mere association in his life and work. Some of the
mythology and much of the politics, being dramatized and
turned into emotion, are part of our common possessions.
But where the emphasis has been magical, whether successfully or not, the poems have been misunderstood,
ignored, and the actual emotion in them which is relevant to us all decried and underestimated, merely because
the magical mode of thinking is foreign to our own and
when known at all is largely associated with quackery and
fraud.

We do not make that mistake — which is the mistake of
unwillingness — with Dante or the later Eliot, because,
although the substance of their modes of thinking is
equally foreign and magical, it has the advantage of a
rational superstructure that persists and which we can
convert to our own modes if we will. Yeats lacks, as
we have said, the historical advantage and with it much

else; and the conclusion cannot be avoided that this
lack prevents his poetry from reaching the first magnitude. But there are two remedies we may apply, which
will make up, not for the defect of magnitude, but for
the defect of structure. We can read the magical
philosophy in his verse *as if* it were converted into the
contemporary psychology with which its doctrines have so
much in common. We find little difficulty in seeing
Freud's preconscious as a fertile myth and none at all in
the general myth of extroverted and introverted personality; and these may be compared with, respectively,
Yeats's myth of *Spiritus Mundi* and the Phases of the
Moon: the intention and the scope of the meaning are
identical. So much for a secular conversion. The
other readily available remedy is this: to accept
Yeats's magic literally as a machinery of meaning, to
search out the prose parallels and reconstruct the symbols he uses on their own terms in order to come on the
emotional reality, if it is there, actually in the
poems — when the machinery may be dispensed with. This
method has the prime advantage over secular conversion
of keeping judgment in poetic terms, with the corresponding disadvantage that it requires more time and
patience, more 'willing suspension of disbelief,' and a
stiffer intellectual exercise all around. But exegesis
is to be preferred to conversion on still another ground,
which may seem repellent: that magic, in the sense that
we all experience it, is nearer the represented emotions
that concern us in poetry than psychology, as a generalized science, can ever be. We are all, without
conscience, magicians in the dark.

97. STEPHEN GWYNN ON THE EFFECT OF 'CATHLEEN NI HOULIHAN'

1936

This comment is from Stephen Gwynn, 'Irish Literature
and Drama in the English Language: A Short Story'
(1936).
    Stephen Lucius Gwynn (1864-1950), novelist, political
historian and biographer, was born in Co. Donegal and
educated at the University of Oxford. He was Nationalist
MP for Galway from 1906-19. His novels include 'The Old
Knowledge' (1901); 'John Maxwell's Marriage' (1903);
and 'Robert Emmet' (1909). His 'Collected Poems' were

published in 1923; his studies of 'Dean Swift' (1933)
and 'Goldsmith' (1935) were followed by 'Aftermath'
(1946). His article, An Uncommercial Theatre, 'Fortnightly Review', 1 December 1902, recorded enthusiastically the effect of 'Cathleen ni Houlihan' on him — he
had never known what drama might be before — and the
passage quoted below returns to his memories of that performance. He was more critical of 'On Baile's Strand'
(for avoidance of the obvious), 'The King's Threshold'
and 'The Shadowy Waters' (for not being in touch with
ordinary humanity), and 'Deirdre' (for being too short
for its theme) in an article on Poetry and the Stage,
'Fortnightly Review', 1 February 1909.

The style of acting identified with the Abbey Theatre
is due to the genius of the Fays — and of W.G. Fay
especially. Frank Fay had much to do with the speaking
of words: but in both these directions, the instinct
of the actors got full support from Yeats, who was the
central figure and true driving force of the movement.
Such a force attracts other forces; it is a rallying
point; and up to this no one but Yeats had given the
Irish players anything of account to play. A.E.'s
'Deirdre' did not raise more than curiosity in me; and
my reactions had a certain importance, as I suggested and
organized the London visit. But the effect of 'Cathleen
ni Houlihan' on me was that I went home asking myself
if such plays should be produced unless one was prepared
for people to go out to shoot and be shot. Yeats was
not alone responsible; no doubt but Lady Gregory helped
him to get the peasant speech so perfect; but above all,
Miss Gonne's impersonation had stirred the audience as
I have never seen another audience stirred. At the
height of her beauty, she transformed herself there into
one of the half-mad old crones whom we were accustomed
to see by Irish roadsides, and she spoke, as they spoke,
in a half-crazy chant. But the voice in which she
spoke, a voice that matched her superb stature and
carriage, had rich flexibility and power to stir and to
stimulate; and the words which she spoke were the words
of a masterpiece. Yeats has said somewhere that his
defect as a dramatist is that normal men do not interest
him; but here in one brief theme he had expressed what
a hundred others have tried to do, the very spirit of a
race for ever defeated and for ever insurgent against
defeat. He had linked this expression with the picture
of a perfectly normal Irish household group; the small farmer, greedy for more land, his wife even more set on gain

than he, their son who is about to marry, and the girl who
is to bring her portion with herself. The old wandering woman who comes in, welcomed to the hearth because it would
not be lucky to turn her away at such a time, speaks at
first in riddling words, yet the meaning of them is plain
to any Irish audience. The name that she gives herself belongs to a past half-faded out of memory, the past in which
Irish poets wrote songs in Irish; yet it wakens an echo in
the present. 'Some have called me Cathleen the daughter of
Houlihan.' 'I think I knew some one of that name once,' says
Peter Gillane. 'It must be some one I knew when I was a
boy.' The audience was quick to catch the implication: memory of a nation's youth, memory of a man's youthful generosity, half-forgotten later. But the song that rebel Ireland had made for itself when Ireland was grown English-
speaking was a song about 'The Poor Old Woman', and all Ireland knew the 'Shan van Vocht'. 'Oh, the French are in the
bay, says the Shan van Vocht.' What bay? Killala Bay, where
Humbert landed in 1798. A bay, half of whose shores belong
to Yeats's own county of Sligo: and there and then he set
his scene. The old woman had been talking to the young
bridegroom, saying to him such things as indeed the one who
spoke the words has spent her life saying to the young men
and young women of Ireland: 'They that have red cheeks shall
have pale cheeks for my sake: and yet they will think themselves well paid.' As she speaks, a far-off noise of cheer-
ing is heard; the old woman rises, still bent and weighed
down with years or centuries; but for one instant, before
she went out at the half-door, she drew herself up to her
superb height; change was manifest; *patuit dea*.(1) Then in
an instant the younger son of the house rushes in crying
out: 'The French are in the bay! they are landing at
Killala!' and such a thrill went through the audience as I
have never known in any other theatre. Such a thrill these
words could waken only in an Irish audience — and indeed
that audience was largely composed of Miss Gonne's ultra-
nationalist following. Only one thing was needed to drive
home the symbolism. 'Did you meet an old woman and you coming up the road?' the mother says. 'No,' the boy answers,
'but I met a young woman and she had the walk of a queen.'
   Many performances in many countries have shown that this
little masterpiece can produce its effect even to strangers;
but the original creation of the part and the original
creator of it gave a singular impulse. They made a live
thing, a true expression of the life of Ireland, out of
what had been a literary experiment.

Note

1 The goddess was revealed.

The Oxford Book of Modern Verse, 1892-1935 (1936)

98. ONE OF THE MOST WIDELY DISCUSSED BOOKS OF THE YEAR

1936

The review of 'The Oxford Book of Modern Verse, 1892-1935' (1936) by John Hayward, Mr Yeats's Book of Modern Verse, 'The Spectator', 20 November 1936.

John Hayward (1905-65) was educated at Gresham's School, in France, and King's College, Cambridge. He was editorial advisor to the Cresset Press, Vice-President of the Bibliography Society and Editorial Director to the 'Book Collector'. He edited 'The Collected Works of the Earl of Rochester' (1926); 'Poetry and Prose of Donne' (1929); 'Letters of St Evremond' (1932); Swift's Gulliver's Travels, etc.' (1932); and 'Swift's Selected Prose' (1949). His anthologies included 'Nineteenth Century Poetry' (1932); 'Seventeenth Century Poetry' (1948); 'Donne' (Penguin Poets, 1950); 'Penguin Book of English Verse' (1956), and 'The Oxford Book of Nineteenth Century Verse' (1964).

'The Oxford Book of Modern Verse' will surprise and bewilder a great many people. It will, I believe, shock some of its editor's friends, admirers and disciples, particularly the youngest of them, and it will certainly be, to the envy of more commercially minded publishers, 'one of the most widely discussed books of the year'. This is all to the good. Poetry draws strength and encouragement from debate, and the debate promises to be a lively one, since the selection Mr. Yeats has made is unlikely to meet with approval from experienced critics. But before going any further it is important that the

ordinary reader, or, more precisely, the reader who finds
all the poetry he needs in the Oxford Books of Verse,
should understand clearly that 'The Oxford Book of Modern
Verse', though it has been chosen by Mr. Yeats, assumes,
by virtue of its title, an authority it would not possess
if it had been called, as I think it should have been,
'Mr. Yeats's Book of Modern Verse'. For the implication
is that the Delegates of the Clarendon Press, having given
their imprint to the book, and having included it in a
series which, for better or for worse, is commonly accepted
as authoritative, and permanent, offer it as a definitive
anthology of modern poetry. This it most certainly is not.

No one is going to deny the attraction of Mr. Yeats's
name on the title page; no one can fail to be curious
about the attitude to contemporary poetry of its most
eminent living exponent. But, in selecting him to edit the
last of the Oxford Books for many years to come, the Delegates of the Clarendon Press may not unreasonably be
accused of opportunism of a kind that tempts newspaper
editors to print the opinions of the Church on the Modern
Novel and of Modern Novelists on the Church. Mr. Yeats
is a poet. It does not follow, it very·rarely follows
that the creator is also a critic. (Dryden implied as
much when he observed that 'the corruption of a poet is
the generation of a critic'.) It is the nature of an
artist that he cannot, as a critic can, be detached and
impersonal in his relations with art. No better confirmation of this could be found than in the extremely personal introduction Mr. Yeats has written to introduce his
extremely personal choice of modern verse by poets 'who
have lived or died from three years before the death of
Tennyson to the present moment'.

Some statistics may help the reader to realise the scope
of his anthology. Ninety-five poets are represented by
438 poems — figures which justify, at least arithmetically,
Mr. Yeats's contention that 'England has had more good
poets since 1900 to the present day than during any period
of the same length since the early seventeenth century'.
Pride of place (estimated in pages) is given to Miss
Sitwell(18), followed by Herbert Read(17) and W.J.
Turner(16); Binyon and Lady Gerald Wellesley(15); Eliot,
Yeats, Gogarty(12); Sturge Moore(10); O'Connor, Arthur
Waley, Sacheverell Sitwell(9); Wilde, Francis Thompson,
Abercrombie, MacNeice(8); Hopkins, Bridges, Monro, Robert
Nichols, Day Lewis(7); Dowson, Synge, Blunden, Higgins,
Masefield, A.E., Pound(6); Blunt, Davies, Lawrence, De la
Mare(5); Stephens, Housman, Tagore, Lady Gregory,
Flecker, Auden(4); Hardy, Margot Ruddock, Henley, George
Barker(3). Twenty-two poets are represented by a single

short poem apiece. Apart from Eliot and Pound, no
American poets are included; on the other hand, 41 of
the poems are translations, chiefly from the Irish.
Robert Graves and the executors of Sir William Watson
refused permission to print. Kipling and Pound are poorly
represented because the Clarendon Press would not pay for
their work. The following omissions will probably be
regretted, and perhaps resented, in some quarters:
Wilfred Owen, T.E. Hulme, Charles Sorley, Edwin Muir,
Isaac Rosenberg, and Dylan Thomas.

Unfortunately, Mr. Yeats's fragmentary introduction
throws very little light on his method of selection. It
is a curious, tantalising and unintegrated piece of work,
too perfunctory and shapeless to satisfy the reader who
expects a critical survey of modern verse and not sufficiently conclusive to explain or justify Mr. Yeats's
predilections. There are, however, hints and implications. Thus, the disproportionate amount of space given
to Herbert Read's long poem 'The End of a War' can be
accounted for by Mr. Yeats's 'distaste' for war poems and
his decision to print, as an example, one that has not
found its way into anthologies and was, in fact, written
long after the armistice. Yet I cannot agree that Mr.
Yeats's contention that 'passive suffering is not a theme
for poetry' — surely a very questionable assertion — is
a reason for excluding from his anthology Wilfred Owen,
who, technically at least, has been an influence, second
only to Hopkins, on the young poets of today whom Mr.
Yeats pretends to admire.

I find it far more difficult to understand Mr. Yeats's
abounding admiration for the verse of Lady Gerald Wellesley
and W.J. Turner. 'I have read,' he says, 'certain poems
by them with more than all the excitement that came upon
me when, a very young man, I heard somebody read out in a
London tavern the poems of Ernest Dowson.' And later he
adds the puzzling remark that he would 'but for a failure
of talent have been in [the school] of Turner and Dorothy
Wellesley.' I am at a loss to understand what the author
of 'The Tower' and 'The Winding Stair' implies by 'a
failure of talent' or why, a major poet, he should aspire
to be of the 'school' of two minor poets. It would be more
reasonable, I feel, to attribute his pleasure in Lady
Gerald Wellesley's verses, which were unknown to him 'until
a few months ago', to the fact that at their best they
echo his own.

The preponderance of poems by Irish writers, like
Gogarty, Higgins and O'Connor, and of poems which can be
classed as ballads, songs and folk-legend is not unexpected,
though many of them would be more appropriate to an Oxford

Book of Irish Verse than to the present volume. This
Irish bias, I suspect, accounts for Mr. Yeats's preference for Louis MacNeice amongst the youngest of the
moderns. Auden and Spender, oddly enough, are very weakly
represented. Still, many people will probably feel that
it is premature to include in an Oxford Book poets born
little more than twenty years ago who have only just begun
to find their pens.

The scope, however, of Mr. Yeats's anthology was,
presumably, fixed by its sponsors, so that the Delegates of the Clarendon Press will have only themselves
to blame if they find that their new book is in part
unrepresentative, in part out of date, in a few years
time. Meanwhile they and their technical staff, whom I
had always supposed and have, indeed, claimed to be
accurate beyond reproach, must find somebody to blame
for slovenly proof-reading. The misprints, omissions
and inconsistencies in the indexes are an insult to the
reputation of a great press.

99. THE WELTER OUT OF WHICH GREAT POETRY HAS EMERGED

1936

An unsigned review of 'The Oxford Book of Modern Verse,
1892-1936, Chosen by W.B. Yeats' [by John Sparrow], Mr
Yeats selects the Modern Poets, 'Times Literary Supplement', 21 November 1936.

John Sparrow (b. 1906) critic and barrister, was
educated at New College, Oxford and has been Warden of
All Souls College since 1952. He commanded the Cold-
stream Guards in 1940. Some of his essays are collected
in 'Independent Essays' (1963) and 'Controversial Essays'
(1966.

Even those who find fault with the choice of poems or
quarrel with what is said in the introductory essay,
must accept this book with gratitude for what it is: the
judgment of one who is for many the greatest poet and the
greatest critic of his age upon something which has
mattered to him intensely throughout his life, and to
which he himself has contributed as much as any other man
— the poetry of his own generation and the generations
which have succeeded it. Let us be grateful to the Oxford

Press for giving Mr. Yeats and ourselves this opportunity
instead of committing the task to someone who would have
chosen a more objectively 'representative' selection, and
would have made his introduction a mere register of the
poetry included.

Mr. Yeats's is an anthology which reflects its maker.
That it will provoke criticism there is no doubt, for Mr.
Yeats is an adept at trailing his coat: in the field of
verse he trailed in days past a coat 'covered with em-
broideries out of old mythologies'; he has since then discovered that there is no lack of 'enterprise in walking
naked'; and in the field of criticism also he is provo-
cative as he traces the influences at work in the poetry
of the last half-century and pronounces judgment on tendencies and men, and on the work which is the outcome of
their interaction.

His main theses are not unfamiliar: he has written
more fully elsewhere of the first wave of 'modernism'
recorded in this book: the effort of his own contemporaries
to 'purify poetry of all that is not poetry', of the 'impurities' of politics and morality; he has elsewhere
defended traditionalism and 'good manners' in writing, and
insisted on the necessity of discipline, and on the banish-
ment from poetry of what he somewhat capriciously calls
'science'. In composing this book Mr. Yeats has allowed
these doctrines full play; indeed, he has nowhere else
given so extended an account, so continuous an analysis,
of modern poetical tendencies, and nowhere else has he
been able so to illustrate it by a choice from the works of
contemporary poets.

Those first modernists, still under the spell of Pater's
doctrine (and Mr. Yeats places Pater, somewhat tendentiously,
on the threshold of this anthology), seem hardly modern
to-day, so many modernisms have supervened. There has
come over us, first of all, a change in sensibility, in
'awareness'; a change which enables us to accept metaphors
and images which forty years ago — to the generation
which hung a Whistler upside down at the Tate — would have
seemed meaningless, impossible. There has occurred also
a change, due to the transfusion into literature of an
element which began to colour life after the War — an
element first realized and conveyed by Mr. T.S. Eliot.
There has been an attempt to banish intellect even more
completely, by abandoning the element of meaning, an attempt
carried to extremes by James Joyce and Gertrude Stein.
There has been, finally, a movement which makes Miss
Sitwell, Mr. Pound, even Mr. Eliot, 'too romantic to seem
modern', and which, for all its modernity, has driven the
wheel full circle, so as to restore the intellect to some

measure of its old importance. The verse of the poets who
fill the closing pages of this book, philosophical, intro-
spective, satirical and often, in a way, religious, is
'modern' in the latest sense of the word; while taking
full advantage — some might say more than full advantage — of recent innovations in technique and theory,
they have restored to literature the 'impurities' which
earlier modernists had banished. To those who feel a
hankering after the doctrine of art for art's sake, or,
indeed, even a hankering after art, their work may prove
as uncongenial as Browning's did to Mr. Yeats's generation; but even with them Mr. Yeats finds himself in
sympathy: 'In this moment of sympathy,' he declares, 'I
prefer them to Eliot, to myself — I too have tried to
be modern.'

There is then no lack of breadth, either in the selection, or in the sympathies displayed in Mr. Yeats's introduction. We range from Dowson to Mr. Herbert Read, from
Henley to Mr. T.S. Eliot, from Michael Field to Miss
Sitwell. Some exclusions will be deplored indignantly
(that for instance of Wilfred Owen), others perhaps less
so (Mr. Humbert Wolfe is not represented, nor is Mr.
Alfred Noyes). The whole tribe of 'War' poets is scarcely
noticed — Rupert Brooke has but a single poem, and that
not a 'War' poem; 'passive suffering,' says Mr. Yeats, 'is
not a theme for poetry,' and they are accordingly excluded. Perhaps a sounder observation would have been
that poets whose inspiration comes from some overwhelming
catastrophe like the War, and who are caught by it before
they have evolved a definite style or attitude, are likely
to produce poetry which not having in it the seeds of
influence or change is but a dead-end in the history of
literature. That, however, would be no reason for excluding them if their poetry was of merit; and one cannot
but suspect that Mr. Yeats's dogmatic utterance (which
could surely be disproved by other examples) only masks a
personal distaste for the particular poetry in question.

Mr. Yeats's personal predilections show themselves as
much in his inclusions as in his refusals. He allots a
surprising number of pages, for instance, to Gogarty and
to Dorothy Wellesley. It is easy to see what it is that
he finds congenial in the former pair: Gogarty is a
lyrical poet of great and in England we fancy unsuspected
merit, very closely resembling Mr. Yeats himself in his
middle period; Dorothy Wellesley's work, we surmise,
appeals chiefly to Mr. Yeats because it is free from
'science', from any dependence on specifically 'modern'
sources of inspiration, because it is austere and aristocratic in its tone, and returns to the old sources of

poetry; it is significant that the most ambitious poem
by that author here included is a meditation of the element
of fire. It has, in short, so much that appeals to the
theoretic critic in Mr. Yeats that he may, we think, have
over-rated its poetic value.

The personal character of this selection, however, does
not upset its balance; it provides a fair, if not a full,
conspectus of the poetry of the last half-century — a
conspectus which provokes a variety of reflections. No
one will accuse Mr. Yeats of unfairness to the post-Eliot
school of poetry: here they are in full force, Auden,
Spender, Day Lewis, with Madge, Empson, Barker and
MacNeice in attendance. It is an aid to judgment to see
them in the setting provided by their contemporaries and
immediate predecessors; and it is surprising how little
of the weight of the book they carry: it ends, not with
a trumpet-call, but on a quiet, not wholly discordant,
but wholly indecisive note. Seen in this purely literary
setting, their work stands revealed most clearly as a
social, not a literary, phenomenon. Sensitiveness is
theirs, and sincerity; an unlimited receptivity of impressions from without and from within; but too many of them
provide the dreary spectacle of men born clever trying to
be poets, and a few the still sadder spectacle of born
poets trying, all too successfully, to be clever (that is
the fatal path into which Mr. Day Lewis, one of the few
potentially great poets of our time, runs the risk of being
seduced).

In a confusion of poetic theory the natural impulse
of the poet is easily drowned or diverted; the different
waves of modernism alluded to above have swept over literature in such quick succession that their implications have
not been understood or assimilated, and the younger poets
of to-day seem proudly conscious that Pound and Joyce,
Rimbaud and Eliot, Miss Sitwell and Gerard Manley Hopkins
stood sponsors at their christening, and to be unaware of
how discordant a bevy of godparents they are and what ir-
reconcilable gifts they have bestowed upon their children.
It is for this reason that the most memorable, if not the
most interesting, poetry in this book is to be found in
its earlier and its middle pages.

'I think England has had more good poets from 1900 to
the present day than during any period of the same length
since the early seventeenth century,' says Mr. Yeats. His
anthology goes far to justify the claim: he shows himself,
we think, the finest poet in the book; by his side stand
Bridges, Francis Thompson, Mr. Ralph Hodgson, Mr. W.H.
Davies, Mr. de la Mare, Miss Sitwell, Mr. Eliot, Mr. F.R.
Higgins, Mr. Day Lewis. These — and not a few others

might be mentioned — are poets;   when they write one
lends them an ear forgetful of their literary or political
tendencies, of what wave of theory they may represent.
There are differences, in all conscience, between them;
but that which unites them is stronger than that which
divides.   Austin Dobson and Mr. Empson, on the other hand,
are not poets: when we read such work as theirs we are
too conscious of differing idioms, successive waves of
fashion;   and any reader can without difficulty place
each in the social or historical setting to which he
belongs   and which he reflects.

This anthology is peculiarly interesting because it
not only affords specimens of great poetry but also reveals
the welter out of which great poetry, in a time of literary
confusion, has emerged.   In his introduction Mr. Yeats,
eloquent without allowing his cadences (as they do occasionally in his prose) to run away with his thought,
reduces that confusion to an intelligible order — a
task only possible to one who is both sympathetic and
acute.   His own greatness in poetry of several very different kinds is due to his power of understanding and
assimilating the influences of which he writes — gifts
which, standing alone, would make him a great critic, but
which, fortunately for the world, have been conferred upon
one who was born a poet and has made himself an artist.

100.   YEATS AND THE 'SCRUTINY' TRADITION

1937

A review of 'The Oxford Book of Modern Verse, 1892-1935',
by H.A. Mason, Yeats and the English Tradition, 'Scrutiny',
March 1937.
    H.A. Mason (b. 1911), a Fellow of Clare Hall, Cambridge,
was educated at the universities of London, Oxford and
Cambridge.   He was senior lecturer in the University of
Exeter, and F.R. Leavis Lecturer in the University of
Cambridge.   His publications include 'Humanism and Poetry
in the Early Tudor Period' (1959);   'Shakespeare's Tragedies
of Love' (1970);   and 'To Homer through Pope' (1972).

Someone in 'Country Life' writes that 'the Oxford Book of-
Anything- has come to stand happily in our minds for the
profit and pleasure of accuracy, scholarship and fine

taste'. And without wishing to endorse everything in the other Oxford Books of Verse, one can say that they have a high representative value. It is therefore astounding that the present selection should appear in this series. Although, as recent anthologies have made distressingly clear, there seems no longer to be a general consensus of opinion as to which are the better modern poems, so that every choice must seem unduly personal, it does appear a counsel of despair to entrust the selection to one whose taste is merely eccentric. And if the word should appear too severe for the selection, the perverse 'introduction' fully deserves it.

Any observations upon the book bear consequently more on the interests of Mr. Yeats than on the problem of an adequate anthology of modern poetry. First of all, it seems probable that the greater part of what has been written between the years 1892 and 1935 just hasn't interested him at all. At any rate, he has reprinted the standard anthology favourites of, for instance, Ralph Hodgson, Gordon Bottomley, Flecker, Newbolt and Julian Grenfell. Wilfred Owen, T.E. Hulme and Isaac Rosenberg do not appear, though they may have been excluded as being 'War Poets'. For 'certain poems written in the midst of the great war' are dismissed on the grounds that 'passive suffering is not a theme for poetry'. At the other end his choice of the younger poets seems to follow the current values (against which various protests have been made in these pages) so closely that it is only charitable to suppose that his interest in them is recent and slight.

Some of his positive preferences remain to me frankly inexplicable. 'I think England has had more good poets from 1900 to the present day than during any period of the same length since the early seventeenth century,' he says in his Introduction. If the number of pages allotted to each poet counts for anything Edith Sitwell with eighteen and Walter James Turner with seventeen are our most important poets. And that their eminent position in the anthology is not accidental is made clear by the claims made for them in the Introduction. Loyalty to his friends no doubt explains the favourable treatment of Johnson, Dowson and Sturge Moore. But as for the Irish brigade, which is given such prominence, one can only quote against Yeats his own lines 'to a poet who would have me praise certain bad poets, imitators of his and mine' —

You say, as I have often given tongue
In praise of what another's said or sung,
'Twere politic to do the like by these;
But was there ever dog that praised his fleas?

Nothing so much marks the distinction between the ability
to criticize in the act of writing a poem and the power of
criticizing the poems of others, as his remarks on Eliot
and Hopkins. It is almost as though he did not understand the tradition of which he is a part. At any rate,
he speaks of Eliot's 'rhythmical flatness', and says 'nor
can I put the Eliot of 'The Waste Land' among those that
descend from Shakespeare and the translators of the Bible.
I think of him as satirist rather than poet.' Against
Hopkins he seems to hold a temperamental aversion. 'I
suspect a bias born when I began to think.' Yeats gives a
ludicrous account of 'sprung verse' and prints the lesser
poems. The selections from Hardy and Pound (though
monetary considerations may have entered here) point the
same way. Only one poem of Edward Thomas is given.

Yeats's self-depreciatory remarks on his own position
('I, too, have tried to be modern') recall forcibly what
Lawrence had to say about 'art-speech'. His own poems,
chosen from his later work, coming between his contemporaries,
Arthur Symons

> (And the mandolins and they,
> Faintlier breathing, swoon
> Into the rose and grey
> Ecstasy of the moon)

and Ernest Dowson

> (Wind and woman and song,
>   Three things garnish our way:
> Yet is day over long),

accentuate the deficiencies of the chronological method,
and provide a criticism (or, at least, another selection
could), of the whole period covered by this anthology.
Mr. Yeats towers over so many schools, or, as he prefers
to put it, 'writing through fifty years I have been now of
the same school with John Synge and James Stephens, now
in that of Sturge Moore and the younger "Michael Field":
and though the concentration of philosophy and social
passion of the school of Day Lewis and in MacNeice lay
beyond my desire, I would, but for a failure of talent
have been in that of Turner and Dorothy Wellesley.'
American Poetry is not represented.

101. PRIVATE MEANINGS IN AN OLD SCRIPTURE

1937

An unsigned review of 'The Ten Principal Upanishads', Myths
for the Poets, 'Times Literary Supplement', 22 May 1937.

It seems probable that the Upanishads, like most scriptures
of the distant past, cannot be understood by the modern
reader without a great apparatus of learning, linguistic,
anthropological and archaeological. The jumble of magic,
metaphysics and mythology in the ten Upanishads translated
here will cause the average reader to lose his way at
once. In one and the same composition he will find subtle
abstractions, fine-spun and lacking any apparent connexion
with reality, and he will also learn that merely to recite
this work will bring him 'good luck, good luck beyond
measure'. It is almost as though the writings of Hegel
were used as a charm or an incantation, which when suitably
repeated would ensure a good harvest.
     This attitude of mind is hard to understand, and through-
out these compositions there is the same baffling mixture
of the concrete and the abstract. The mysterious word
'Om' or 'Aum' seems at once to have a metaphysical import,
though perhaps not even as definite as the meaning given
to such a notion as that of the Absolute in European
thought, and at the same time to have a magical importance
purely as a word. Thus, though indivisible, it can be
divided into its component letters, and

> the waking condition, called the material condition,
> corresponds to the letter A, which leads the alphabet
> and breathes in all the other letters. He who under-
> stands, gets all he wants, becomes a leader among men.

But there is much else which one may be sure cannot be
interpreted without knowledge of Indian folk-lore in the
remote past, and of the philosophical notions that obtained
at the time. And, as with other scriptures, one may suspect
that much which appears simple and obvious in translation
had a different and much less obvious meaning originally.
     Mr. Yeats is evidently unconcerned with whatever mean-
ing the Upanishads might have to a scholar or an anthro-
pologist. No commentary and scarcely any notes are provided; and it seems that he intends these compositions to
be read as scriptures are commonly read by the faithful and
for the sake of the meaning that the modern reader can put

into them from his own background of thought or feeling.
Such works, as Mr. Waley pointed out in his account of the
writings of Lao Tse, are extremely elastic and can have a
different meaning to each generation; indeed, it is only
in recent years that the difficult art of not understanding
the mystical or philosophical works of the past has been
acquired. It is easy to see how the Upanishads could be
stretched to give inspiration to a religious inquirer of
the present day; but in Mr. Yeats's hands they prove even
more elastic and are put forward to be of service to the
poet.

It was under the influence of George Russell that Mr.
Yeats, as he tells us in his preface, first approached
these Sanskrit scriptures, only to be repulsed by 'poly-
glot phrases, sedentary distortions of unnatural Engligh
. . . muddles, muddied by "Lo Verily" and "Forsooth".' It
was necessary for him, before he could believe or disbelieve, to put their thought into 'a language wherein we
are accustomed to express love and hate and all the shades
between.' This he and Shree Purohit Swāmi have done
superlatively well, and we may well be grateful for the
beautiful prose that results; but if Mr. Yeats has been
intent on using his own language in his own way it can
hardly be that all his fine shades of meaning coincide
with those of the original. Whether the result has been
to make him believe or disbelieve, he scarcely tells us.
He explains that he undertook this work 'to confound
something in myself', and then writes rather obscurely
of a connexion between the doctrine of the Upanishads and
modern psychical research.

But his recommendation of the Upanishads to the modern
poet seems to be more important. He observes that many
modern poets have attempted to create a mythology for
themselves and have perhaps reached 'a neighbourhood
where some new Upanishad, some new half-asiatic masterpiece,
may start up before our averted eyes.' The present translation is therefore offered 'to some young man seeking,
like Shakespeare, Dante, Milton, vast sentiments and
generalizations.' One may suspect that it is meant to be
read in much the same spirit as certain modern poems have
to be read, without any exact comprehension. Myths can
have their effect in poetry without being understood; they
provide, as little else can, a sequence of powerful and
moving images which are to be valued for their own sake.
But the modern poet cannot find, like Dante or Milton,
his inspiration in a lucid and intelligible mythology in
which he believes; his inventions must be private, subjective and therefore obscure. Thus an old scripture,
into which any private meaning can be read, may well be
exactly the kind of inspiration he needs.

102. DOROTHY M. HOARE ON YEATS'S USE OF IRISH SOURCES

1937

This extract is from Dorothy M. Hoare, 'The Works of Morris
and Yeats in relation to Early Saga Literature' (1937;
1971).

Agnes Dorothea MacKenzie Hoare (Mrs de Navarro) was
educated at the Universities of Aberdeen and Cambridge.
She was a Fellow, Lecturer in English and Associate of
Newnham College, Cambridge, and Cambridge University
Lecturer in Anglo-Saxon. Her publications include 'Some
Studies in the Modern Novel' (1938; 1940; 1955).

The direction towards vagueness and inaction which the
Irish tales afforded is seen again in some poems published along with 'The Countess Cathleen' in 1892. 'Fergus
the Druid'(1) is a short poem dealing with the story of
Fergus' abdication in favour of Conor, a theme matter-of-
fact enough. Yeats, however, changes it to a kind of
mystic utterance:

> I would be no more a king
> But learn the dreaming wisdom that is yours. . . .
>
> I see my life go dripping like a stream
> From change to change; I have been many things. . . .
>
> But now I have grown nothing, being all,
> And the whole world weighs down upon my heart.

This inactive contemplation is at once typical of Yeats,
and needless to say utterly divorced from the saga reality.

Another Irish poem in the same volume, 'The Death of
Cuchulain' (a versification of the oral form of the story
given by Yeats later in 'On Baile's Strand' from the saga
source), is remarkable only in its perfect catching of the
Morris tone, with its static, weighted, yet curiously
empty effect:

> In three days' time he stood up with a moan
> And he went down to the long sands alone.
> For four days warred he with the bitter tide
> And the waves flowed above him and he died.

Nowhere yet does the Irish story appear in its own
light. And nowhere is Yeats' poetry enriched by the Irish

subject, although it affords him opportunity for reverie.
This is a curious fact and indicates that these Irish
poems were possibly artistic exercises rather than freshly
felt and freshly communicated amotion.   This view seems
to be reinforced by the fact that the influence of Morris
is nowhere more distinct and evident, as we have seen,
than in the poems based on Irish saga or legend.   This
significant piece of evidence serves to indicate that to
Yeats the world of Irish saga must have meant essentially
the same thing as the wonder-world of Morris' imaginings.

   This 'romanticising' influence is seen again very
markedly in the poem 'Baile and Aillinn', published in
'Poems, 1899-1905'.   Here the story is taken from the
'Scél Baili Binnbérlaig',(2) the story of Baile the Sweet-
spoken.   Even as we have it in the Irish, the tale is a
curious one, a mixture of romance with what may have been
a real or remembered event.   To turn it into modern verse
and yet keep the flavour of the original is almost
impossible — it needs a childlike freshness, together with
a certain amount of courtly sophistication.   Chaucer might
have managed it;   the tale has something of the sweetness
and grace of the typical medieval legend, being outside the
characteristic Irish manner.   But Yeats has not attempted
to give the saga-story in its curiosity and attraction.
He has given us what his imagination, set off by the idea
of the central event in the story, makes of it — a
jewelled expression of a languid emotion.   A curious but
unexplained occurrence in the Irish story — the coming of
the strange messenger to the lovers in turn with the lying
tale of the other's death — is changed by Yeats to a deed
brought about by the Master of Love: 'Baile and Aillinn
were lovers but Aengus, the Master of Love, *wishing them
to be happy in his own land among the dead,* told to each
a story of the other's death so that their hearts were
broken and they died.'(3)   The italicised phrase indicates
from what point of view the story is regarded — the typical
Yeatsian acquiescence in death.   Significantly, the verse
is again reminiscent of 'The Earthly Paradise':

      That old man climbed;   the day grew dim;
      Two swans came flying up to him,
      Linked by a gold chain each to each,
      And with low murmuring laughing speech
      Alighted on the windy grass.
      They knew him;   his changed body was
      Tall, proud and ruddy, and light wings
      Were hovering over the harp-strings
      That Etain, Midhir's wife, had wove
      In the hid place, being crazed with love.

The kind of metamorphosis which takes place here, by
which Aengus discards the disguise of the old man and is
seen in his youthful beauty, is much more akin, in tone,
to the wonder-workings of Morris' romance than to the Irish
saga, although Yeats has here borrowed a *motif* which can
be found in specific Irish tales. The languid air of the
last two lines could have come only from the atmosphere
of the Pre-Raphaelites.

The second half of the tale becomes much more authentically Yeats', and yet even here there are lines which owe
their movement and atmosphere to Morris:

> They know all wonders, for they pass
> The towery gates of Gorias,
> And Findrias and Falias,
> And long-forgotten Murias,
> Among the giant kings whose hoard,
> Cauldron and spear and stone and sword,
> Was robbed before earth gave the wheat;
> Wandering from broken street to street
> They come where some huge watcher is.

In the first four lines Yeats clearly is using the names
and legends of Ireland purely for their sound-value, and
is stirred by them to depart into the vaguely large and
romantic atmosphere of the Morris world; observe the force
of 'broken' and 'huge' in the last two lines, used entirely
to build up the impression begun by 'giant kings', the
kind of self-conscious romantic situation which the sagas
cannot supply.

Another poem in this volume, 'The Old Age of Queen
Maeve', shows more specifically the alterations which Yeats
makes in his material. The episode is derived from the
'Aislinge Œnguso', a tale which is nothing if not matter-
of-fact. Whatever significance lies behind the Síd of
Uaman incident, it is thought of as on a plane with, and
essentially similar to, the happenings in everyday life.
The tone is not one of surprise or strangeness, but of the
plainness of fact. But in Yeats' poem any comparison with
the original is practically impossible. He has abstracted
from the story the fact that Maeve (with Ailill) helps
Angus to obtain Caer, and makes this the basis for an
excursion into the fantastic:

> She told them of the many-changing ones;
> And all that night, and all through the next day
> To middle night, they dug into the hill.
> At middle night, great cats with silver claws,
> Bodies of shadow, and blind eyes like pearls,

> Came up out of the hole, and red-eared hounds
> With long white bodies, came out of the air
> Suddenly, and ran at them and harried them.

Yeats' imagination has obviously been drugged by the images
gathered from the reading of Welsh and Irish story, and
he has here re-cast them in a pattern.   Though the lines
describe movement, there is no sense of motion in them.
The poem has the effect of tapestry, or of the figures on
a curtain which hold one's attention before the play
begins. Unfortunately, the play never does begin.   The
dual form of the poem, combining this still embroidery with
the personal note which is heard before and after the tale
is told, is not very successful.   But it is noteworthy
that the personal passages come with a curious freshness
and sincerity after this not very convincing rhetoric:

> O unquiet heart,
> Why do you praise another, praising her,
> As if there were no tale but your own tale
> Worth knitting to a measure of sweet sound?

. . . In speaking of the Yeats of the Irish Movement,
I have necessarily been unjust, because silent, to the later
Yeats. . . where to a changed and graver music the poet has
given us expression of a stern contact with life. We are
no longer in the coloured land of dreams, but in the harshness of actuality . . . . [These] poems have obviously
come from an imagination which has suffered and whose
dreams have been invaded by thought.

Notes

1 See 'Scéla Conchobair maic Nessa', translated by Whitley
  Stokes (from L.L.) in 'Ériu', iv, p. 22.   The tale is a
  simple straightforward account of how Conor obtained
  Fergus' power in the kingdom, through his mother Nessa's
  diplomacy.
2 See 'Rev.Celt'. xiii, p. 220.
3 So Yeats in an introductory phrase to the poem.   The
  italics are mine.

The Herne's Egg (1938)

·103. YEATS'S EXTRAVAGANT AND AUDACIOUS FANTASIES

1938

An unsigned review of 'The Herne's Egg, A Stage Play'
(1938) and 'Essays 1931 to 1936' (1937), Yeatsian Fantasy,
'Times Literary Supplement', 22 January 1938.

The fantastic element which Mr. Yeats has managed to hold
in check for many years has returned with full force in
much of his recent work. His new play, to which tattered
scraps of the Nō form still cling, is well calculated to
displease the reverend and to delight the irreverent because of its extravagant and audacious fancies. The
symbolic action begins amid 'mist and rocks'; Celtic
Twilight kings from the poet's ever-present past appear in
dumb show, waging an endless magic battle complete with
swords and shields. They pause among blows to exchange
a merry anecdote concerning Mr. Yeats's favourite poetic
insect, the flea. More serious occasion for heroic dis-
pute is caused by the robbery of the sacred heron's egg
from the banquet-hall at Tara. The holy egg, though
boiled, had been rescued by Attracta, the priestess and
bride of the Great Herne. 'There is no reality but the
Great Herne,' declares Attracta. But King Congal is better
acquainted with modern psychology than Leda's sister in the
western world:

> Women thrown into despair
> By the winter of their virginity
> Take its abominable snow,
> As boys take common snow, and make

An image of god or bird or beast
To feed their sensuality.

Reeling from the banquet-hall with his rough followers,
Mike, Pat, and others with similar Abbey Theatre names,
Congal, in a drunken whim, commands that the priestess
be delivered over to the lusts of seven men. As the seven
stand in a row casting lots, Attracta sings in mystical
antinomianism:

When I take a beast to my joyful breast,
Though beak and claw I must endure,
Sang the bride of the Herne, and the Great Herne's bride,
No lesser life, man, bird or beast,
Can make unblessed what a beast made blessed,
Can make impure what a beast made pure.

In the last scene, which takes place effectively in moonshine, Congal, a Fool, Attracta, the rustic Corney, and
a real Irish donkey are the principal performers. Congal
is slain, whereupon Mr. Yeats produces a dramatic artifice
in order to resolve his central theme of animal vigour and
reincarnation. The new reincarnation of Congal is indicated by Attracta:

I thought that I
Could give a human form to Congal,
But now he must be born a donkey.

Written in loose, rough-and-ready measures, as the
quotations show, this brief extravaganza reads at times like
a hotch-potch of quotations from Mr. Yeats's own work. The
poet's impulse is as strong as ever, but signs of flagging
inspiration are apparent to be disquieting. Were it not for
these signs one might suspect that Mr. Yeats was deliberately
parodying the author of 'Shadowy Waters' and, with malice
aforethought, finding in his own mystical philosophy an
unavoidable *reductio ad absurdum.*
    The collected essays are mainly composed of introduc-
tions to various books. But they also include Mr. Yeats's
talk on modern poetry which was broadcast from the London
BBC in October of the year before last. 'Nothing in this
book is journalism,' declared Mr. Yeats,

nothing was written to please a friend or satisfy an
editor, or even to earn money. When I introduced a
book it was some book I had awaited with excitement;
nor was anything written out of the fulness of knowledge;
why should I write what I knew? I wrote always that when

I laid down my pen I might be less ignorant than when
I took it up. I think my head has grown clearer.

Readers who are acquainted with the 'Autobiographies'
will be already familiar with many of the themes on which
Mr. Yeats discourses in a prose still rich and dreamful
in movement, and will share with him the pleasures which he
takes in self-discovery. Here, once more, he discusses
Berkeley's idealism at length, and Dunne's 'Experiment
with Time' continues to excite his imaginative curiosity.
'Only where the mind partakes of a pure activity can art or
life attain swiftness, volume, unity,' declares Mr. Yeats,
but this and similar pronouncements do not leave the reader's
head much clearer. In the detail of changing opinion or
literary anecdote Mr. Yeats is always more enlivening. One
of the most interesting essays is that on Shelley, for it
is a pendant to the two well-known essays which Mr. Yeats
wrote on Shelley's poetry many years ago, and he revises
here to some extent his opinion of the poet's form of symbolism. He makes, too, an interesting confession:

When in middle life I looked back I found that he and
not Blake, whom I had studied more and with more approval,
had shaped my life, and when I thought of the tumultuous
and often tragic lives of friends or acquaintances I
attributed to his direct or indirect influence their
Jacobin frenzies, their brown demons.

The last three essays consist of introductions to 'An
Indian Monk', 'The Holy Mountain', and 'Mandukya Upanishad'.
Here, in the vagueness and romantic remoteness of Asiatic
thought, Mr. Yeats finds the excitement of spiritual sur-
mise and imaginative novelty. He quotes admiringly from
Urdu:

A miracle indeed!
Thou art Lord of all Power.
I asked a little power,
Thou gavest me a begging-bowl.

Mr. Yeats, who dislikes the Christian restriction of
thought, fails to perceive in this quatrain an eminently
Christian platitude.

104. A NEW EXTRAVAGANZA

1938

A review of 'The Herne's Egg' (1938) by Austin Clarke,
Irish Poets, 'New Statesman and Nation', 29 January 1938.
For note on Austin Clarke see p. 282.

Mr. Yeats's almost successful attempt to escape completely
from the Celtic Twilight won the admiration of all who
like a good fight. Applause greeted his resolution to
'Hurl helmets, crowns, and swords into the pit'. But
mists of his own past have defeated Mr. Yeats at last.
His new extravaganza begins with a couple of Celtic kings
fighting an endless magic battle with bronze weapons.
When we meet them again they are blind drunk and fighting
with less heroic implements to the accompaniment of drum
and concertina:

> To arms, to arms! Connaught to arms!
> Insulted and betrayed, betrayed and insulted.
> Who has insulted me? Tara has insulted.
> To arms, to arms! Connaught to arms!
> To arms — but if you have not got any
> Take a table-leg or a candlestick,
> A boot or a stool or any odd thing.
> Who has betrayed me? Tara has betrayed!
> To arms, to arms! Connaught to arms!

Supported by the bibulous Pat, Mike, James and 'The
boys', King Congal decides that Attracta, the priestess,
must be raped by seven men in succession. Attracta, we
may explain, had been leading an immoral life with a bird,
to wit, a heron. The play ends on a pantomimic note on
a mountain at moonrise: 'the moon of comic tradition,
a round smiling face.' Accompanied by one of Mr. Yeats's
Fools, Congal enters. As an immolation to the Great
Herne, he permits himself to be killed with a kitchen
spit by the Fool. Meanwhile, Attracta and Corney, her
servant, come on the scene, the latter bringing his
pet donkey.
  Attracta, who knows all about the ways of transmigration,
attempts to thwart the Great Herne by offering herself to
Corney. But the conspirators are anticipated by the
donkey, who has retired off-stage in pursuit of a female
of his species. The spirit of King Congal is doomed to
re-appear on earth in a humiliating shape. As the
dejected Corney remarks:

All that trouble and nothing to show for it,
Nothing but just another donkey.

Mr. Yeats has attempted to capture the madcap spirit
of the old mock-heroic tales of Gaelic tradition.   But
exuberance of spirits requires exuberance of language
as in those tales: Rabelaisian mysticism without the
necessary torrent of vocabulary is surely an unnatural,
if not monstrous, product.   Synge might have succeeded,
but it seems to me that Mr. Yeats succeeds merely in
parodying himself rather unpleasantly.   His last play
rewarded us with a magnificent lyrical ballad.   Here
the verse remains thin and sourish — small beer, in fact.

105.   JANET ADAM SMITH ON 'THE HERNE'S EGG'

1938

A review of 'The Herne's Egg' by Janet Adam Smith, 'The
Criterion', April 1938.
    Janet Adam Smith (Mrs John Carleton) was Assistant
Editor of 'The Listener' (1930-5), Assistant Editor (1949-
52) and Editor (1952-60) of the 'New Statesman and Nation'.
Her books include 'R.L. Stevenson' (1937) and 'John
Buchan: A Biography' (1965).   She edited the 'Collected
Poems of R.L. Stevenson' (1950);   the 'Faber Book of
Children's Verse' (1953) and the 'Collected Poems
of Michael Roberts' (1958).   Michael Roberts was her first
husband (see note p. 360).

Mr. Yeats has always made it quite clear for what audience
he would like to write his plays, and for what audience
he does actually write them.   'They should be written,'
he said in his note to 'The Only Jealousy of Emer' (1919),
'for some country where all classes share in a half-
mythological, half-philosophical folk-belief which the
writer and his small audience lift into a new subtlety.'
And again, in a note to 'At the Hawk's Well' (1916):
'Shakespeare's art was public, now resounding and de-
clamatory, now lyrical and subtle, but always public,
because poetry was a part of the general life of a people
who had been trained by the Church to listen to difficult
words, and who sang, instead of the songs of the music-
halls, many songs that are still beautiful. . . . We must

recognize the change as the painters did when, finding
no longer palaces and churches to decorate, they made
framed pictures to hang upon a wall. Whatever we lose
in mass and in power we should recover in elegance and in
subtlety.'
Since these words were written, other poets have tried
to build up a public poetic drama. They know as well as
Mr. Yeats that there is no 'half-mythological, half-
philosophical folk-belief' shared by all classes; but
they find a story or a situation which is familiar to
at any rate a number of people in all classes, and make
a start with that. O'Casey takes football and the War,
Auden and Isherwood the lost heir or an Everest expedi-
tion, Eliot a story found in every school history-book.
In the attempt to make a public drama they may get into
queer company, and they are often mocked by those who are
still busy with 'framed pictures to hang upon a wall'.
They are not too proud to make use of rhythms that the
audience knows already, the dance tune, the Salvation
Army hymn. They exploit some things with which the
theatre public is familiar in order to lead it on to the
unfamiliar. Their plays have lines and passages that are
hard to grasp at a first meaning, but the spectator can
usually negotiate these with the help of the life-line
provided by the well-known story.
Mr. Yeats has all the technique for writing public
plays. The language of his recent work is bare and
simple; he writes nothing as complicated in syntax as
some of the sentences in the soliloquy with which 'The
Ascent of F6' opens; the words never draw attention to
themselves, but always point to the action; there are no
extraneous rhetorical passages which could be cut away
without affecting the structure. Yet his plays remain
private and difficult, for Mr. Yeats is a proud and solitary man. He goes to church, but not at service time; and
he will not stoop to look for his stories. His subjects
come from a mythology which is not common even to the
friendly audiences which see his plays acted in the Abbey
Theatre. They come from his own private Celtic-classical-
cabbalistic-Buddhist amalgam; and anyone who is not of
Mr. Yeats's circle must be prepared to work hard, not
only to enjoy the plays, but even to discover what
they are all about.
There are two possible approaches for the outsider.
He can visualize the action as a kind of dance, and enjoy
the changing patterns made by the stiff, inhuman figures.
Several of the stage directions for 'The Herne's Egg' —
'Many men fighting with swords and shields, but sword
and sword, shield and sword, never meet' — recall

passages in Ninette de Valois's ballet 'Checkmate'. Or
he can make himself so familiar with the rest of Yeats's
writings that the images of the moon, the sword, the egg,
and the rest, may come to have for him something of the
value that they have for Yeats. Such a reader will find
himself in familiar country with 'The Herne's Egg'.
Here is the implicit belief in the eternal circuit and
recurrent phases; the usual figures of king, woman, fool;
the images of the moon, great birds, etc. But even so
the reader is always likely to be stumped in the end by
some new addition to the private mythology. I doubt if
all the point of the ending to 'The Herne's Egg' — the
death of the king and conception of a donkey — would be
grasped by anyone who had not heard of the belief held by
certain Lamaists that the living can influence the shape
into which the dead are re-born, and had not read such an
account of it as Mrs. David-Neel gives in 'With Mystics
and Magicians of Tibet', where a Lama is reborn as a
donkey. This is not a question of pedantically 'explaining' a myth, but of knowing that the myth exists, and has
been believed by thousands of people, and is not only a
bright idea of the poet's. Without that knowledge, the
story can be understood, but the tension of the situation
cannot be felt. It is hard to judge of this from a reading only; the priestess in 'The Herne's Egg' appears
'walking in her sleep', and the whole play might be made
so dream-like on the stage that we should accept anything
as right.

106.   A DICTIONARY OF THE SYMBOLS AND METAPHORS

1938

A review of 'A Vision' (1937) by Stephen Spender, 'The
Criterion', April 1938.
    Stephen Harold Spender (b. 1909) was educated at
University College, Oxford, and he has been a poet,
critic, editor, novelist and short-story writer. He is
now a Professor of English at University College, London.
His autobiography, 'World Within World' (1951) and his
'Collected Poems' (1955) have been followed by 'Love-Hate
Relations: A Study of Anglo-American Sensibilities' (1974).
The reference to Fascism in this review reminds us that
Spender and Auden were prominent members of a group of
left-wing, anti-Fascist poets which included C. Day Lewis

and Louis MacNeice.

Four days after his marriage, Mr. Yeats's wife surprised
him by attempting automatic writing. The attempt was soon
very successful and the unknown writer, on receiving an
offer from Mr. Yeats that he should spend the rest of
his life putting together these disjoined phrases, replied, 'No, we have come to give you metaphors for poetry.'
    The spirit which made this remark deserves a literary
prize, for not only is it responsible for some of the
greatest poetry in the English language, but also it has
provided a valuable hint towards the critical attitude
which the reader may perhaps — fortified by that voice
from the 'other world' — take up towards 'A Vision'.
For, whatever the merits of Mr. Yeats's philosophy, here
we have a valuable and illuminating dictionary of the
symbols and metaphors in his later poems. Here we are
able to discover what precisely is the significance of
symbols such as the mask, the gyre, the lunar phases;
what are the uses in Yeats's poetry of his ideas of
Fate and the Will. Many readers will also find that this
dictionary, in common with all definitions of words for
that matter, is not only an explanation and an end of
inquiry, it is also a starting off point in a search
for new meanings and a stimulus to poetry as yet unwritten.
For example, I myself am stimulated by the idea in Yeats
of the Mask-, which I take to be the fixed character
which the will, like a chisel, sculpts on the face of
man; just as in books on economics I am stimulated by
the images suggested by the Law of Marginal Productivity.
    Later on, Mr. Yeats's 'instructors' dropped their
secondary role of giving him metaphors and supplied him
with what one can only call an Encyclopedia of knowledge,
life, death, the universe, history, etc. — an 'Encyclopedia Fascista', edited by Spengler, would perhaps be the
best account of it, had not Spengler written his own.
Here, I am unable to follow Mr. Yeats in anything like his
entirety. I can only echo the tactful words pf A.E. on
the wrapper: 'I am unable in a brief space' (this goes
for me as well) 'to give the slightest idea of its packed
pages, its division of the faculties of man, the Will,
the Creative Genius, the Mask and the Body of Fate and
their lunar gyrations, or of its division of the transcendental man, the daimonic nature and its cycles and
their relation to our being, or of the doctrines of the
after-life. Almost any of its crammed pages would need a
volume to elucidate its meanings. It is possible it may
be discussed feverishly by commentators a century hence,
as Blake, . . .' etc.

The name of Blake pulls me up, for I should have thought
that anyone desiring to make himself ultimately understood
beyond the mere ferment of 'feverish discussion' would
beware of falling into the jungles of the Prophetic Books.
Like Blake, Mr. Yeats is prodigiously systematic, often
illuminating, clear and even precise. The difficulty is,
though, to discover on what plane he is being clear and
to what he is consistent — where, in fact, his system,
with its extensive philosophic claims, actually links
up with reality. It is perhaps typical of Mr. Yeats's
whole method, that although the nature of his spiritualist
experiences is described, no serious attempt is made to
prove to the reader that the creaking of boards in his
house, the sudden appearance of smells and so on, have
really the significance which Mr. Yeats attributes to
them. It is a pity that people who have Mr. Yeats's
experiences do not attempt to establish them with proofs
which are acceptable to the sceptical, because if such
experiences are real they are vastly important. On the
other hand, if the physical universe has a special kind of
behaviour which it hoards up for Mr. Yeats, it is difficult to see how to relate this to the rest of human
experience.

Mr. Yeats's diagrams and tables are extremely logical
and clear, in their mediaeval way; it is when I come to
his summing up of the history of civilization that everything is so generalized as either to seem meaningless or
else to be matter which could only assume shape and significance in Mr. Yeats's poetry. However, occasionally
the puzzle clears up, and we recognize behind the lulling
self-loving fervour of Mr. Yeats's prose a voice which,
whether from this world or the next, is after all not so
unfamiliar. For example, in the Examination of the Wheel,
the voice appears in an illuminating footnote: 'A
similar circular movement fundamental in the works of
Giovanni Gentile is, I read somewhere, the half-conscious
foundation of the political thought of modern Italy. . . .
It is the old saying of Heraclitus, "War is God of all,
and Father of all, some it has made Gods and some men,
some bond and some free," and the converse of Marxian
socialism.' It did not altogether surprise me to read
that when Yeats read Spengler, he discovered so many
parallels with both the ideas and the sources of his own
instruction as to suggest a common 'instructor'.

Spengler, Stefan George, D'Annunzio, Yeats: is it
really so impossible to guess at the 'instructors' who
speak behind these mystic veils? It is interesting, too,
to speculate whether Fascism may not work out through
writers such as these a mystery which fills its present

yawning void of any myth, religion, law or even legal
constitution, which are not improvised.

107.   ARCHIBALD MACLEISH ON PUBLIC REALITY AND YEATS'S
POETRY

1938

Archibald MacLeish's description of Yeats as a poet of pub-
lic speech was welcomed by Yeats in a letter to Dorothy
Wellesley. It appeared in an article on Public Speech and
Private Speech in Poetry, 'The Yale Review', Spring 1938.
The excerpt which is included here is from a later version,
The Public World: Poems of Yeats, from MacLeish's book
'Poetry and Experience' (1961).
    Archibald MacLeish (1892-1973) was educated at Yale and
Harvard Universities, served in the US Army, practised law,
edited 'Fortune' (1929-38), was Librarian of Congress (1939-
44) and Boylston Professor, Harvard University (1949-62).
His volume of 'Collected Poems' was published in 1952; and
'The Wild Old Wicked Men and other poems' in 1968'. His
prose includes 'Poetry and Opinion' (1950) and 'Poetry
and Experience' (1961).

No, the problem is real and has been real in every country in the
West, Russia included, Russia particularly included, ever
since the industrial revolution and its consequences turned
the old personal world in which the arts could live in public as well as in private into the impersonal world of the mass
society, and it was not resolved for Yeats by his dream of
a pre-Christian Ireland. Twenty years later in 1913 'romantic Ireland' was 'dead and gone': it was 'with O'Leary in
the grave' and he was face to face with an actual Ireland, an
Ireland with a middle class like any other, an Ireland with
its fair share of the hatred, the lying, the greed and the
hypocrisy which afflict us all. And face to face with that
public reality he found himself face to face also with the
problem of art he had dodged before - the problem most contemporary poets continue to dodge - the problem of the place
of poetry in this unpleasant prospect. Being the man he was
he faced it squarely, and faced it, moreover, in a poem,
and published his poem ('The Grey Rock') precisely where it
belonged, at the beginning of 'Responsibilities', with 'September 1913' and the rest of those political poems beside it.

Purgatory: first performance (1938)

108.   UNA ELLIS FERMOR ON THE FIRST PERFORMANCE OF
'PURGATORY'

1938

Extract from Una Ellis Fermor, The Abbey Theatre Festival
(7-20 August 1938), 'English', Autumn 1938.
    Una Ellis Fermor (1894-1958) held the Hildred Carlile
Chair of English Literature at Bedford College, London.
Her books included 'Christopher Marlowe' (1927); 'The
Jacobean Drama' (1936); and 'The Irish Dramatic Movement'
(1939).

The discussion of 'Purgatory' in the press was long,
tedious, and ultimately irrelevant; a play is a play.
This seemed to me, from the impression of a single performance, to be a study of the experience of two minds,
one dead, one living, in face of the consequences of a
deed of criminal irresponsibility amounting almost to a
crime. It was informed all through by the author's view
of expiation, that sin cannot be wiped out by violence,
evil by another kind of evil, but only by that form of
understanding which is sometimes called repentance. It
was a grim and interesting play, finely set and produced,
and well acted. It left the audience puzzled because
the implications were more than skin deep, but it did
not give me, at any rate, the impression that its main
purpose was a discussion of the technical nature of purgatory. It was a play; and, coming from Mr. Yeats, should
best be considered as a piece of dramatic poetry and understood and appreciated in those terms.

109. F.R. HIGGINS ON YEATS'S TWO COMMINGLING STATES OF
VERSE

1938/1939

From 'The Irish Theatre: Lectures delivered during the
Abbey Theatre Festival held in Dublin in August 1938'
(1939), edited by Lennox Robinson.
  Frederick Robert Higgins (1896-1941) became an office
boy in Dublin at fourteen, later a trades union official,
and an editor of various Irish journals. He became
Managing Director of the Abbey Theatre and wrote a play
'A Deuce of Jacks' (1955) as well as several volumes of
poetry, which include 'Salt Air' (1924); 'The Dark Breed'
(1927); 'Arable Holdings' (1933), and 'The Gap of Bright-
ness' (1940). His Rabelaisian conversation appealed
to Yeats.

There is a fascination in what is difficult. And in his
next verse play, 'The King's Threshold', we find the pre-
eminence of poetry not only recognised in the offices of
state — which is the theme — but also in his own immediate achievement on the stage. With this play Yeats
had left his peasant-folk. The first phase — that of
themes from simple country beliefs — was ended. His
second, his most important phase, had begun. Kings and
their contenders, their lovers and their poets, became
his heroic figures; and such figures in his plays have
the remoteness of powers passionately warring on the peaks
of unhuman isolation. Their tragic splendours are more in
harmony with the aristocratic dignity of his speech, and
that speech is heard in mounting triumph throughout this
cycle of heroic plays — in 'On Baile's Strand', in
'Deirdre', and in 'The Green Helmet'. In these plays
spirit and intellect are clinched in utterances of power,
wisdom and nobility. Here the union of verse and action
is also an excellent welding. There is nothing unwieldy.
Solid poetry — direct as prose — is nimble to the
players' mouths and movements. Yes, that dexterity in
dialogue is evident in all his plays of this period — in
all except maybe in the earlier 'Shadowy Waters', where
every line seems drugged with drowsy beauty. Yet one's
attempt to criticise the apparent lack of action in that
play is numbed. You are reduced into silence by its full
poetry, and soon you find yourself with the players murmuring towards the final curtain:

O flower of the branch, O bird among the leaves,
O silver fish that my two hands have taken
Out of the running stream, O morning star,
Trembling in the blue heavens like a white fawn
Upon the misty border of the wood,
Bend lower, that I may cover you with my hair,
For we will gaze upon the world no longer.

The story, the plot in Yeats's plays, is never very
dramatic. All his themes are exceedingly simple, trivial
in many cases; he shows little power of inventing a
story, but he discovers in the trivial dramatic possibilities — for his intellect in many respects is ingenious
rather than imaginative. You are rarely held by the intensity of the story; instead you are held spellbound by the
intensity of thought and passion and by the consistent
loveliness of apt speech, by the poetry. His plays have
'poetry hid in thought or passion', as Coleridge says, 'not
thought or passion disguised in the dress of poetry'. The
outward sensuousness of his language is consumed by fiery
thoughts or passions. Take away these and little is left
to enrich the stage — it is, as I have said, bare of plot.
    In this craft of play-writing, as in his lyric verse,
beauty is taut and passion precise. The speech cadence is
hesitant, yet full of verve and altogether impudently
sweet. Yeats had no melodic ear; he could not measure
words to musical stresses — he realised their significance, sought hard to employ them; but they were not at
his command. In my opinion, that very lack of musical
ear offered remarkable compensation. It saved him, at
worst, from an easy jingle of softly flowing sounds; from
a monotony of regularity in well timed stresses. Indeed,
his innocent offences against the laws of musical gram-
marians, his unconscious flaws in conventional melody,
are responsible maybe for his curiously haunting harmonics
in rhythm. These unexpected gaps staying his music, these
hesitations in verbal sureness, altogether dramatise his
cadence. His carefully poised verse is tuned, as it were,
slightly off the note. Throughout one listens as to a
folk-singer, in a constant fear that the thin run of
melody will break on the perilous top note — altogether
a tantalising music and a very personal music. Indeed,
the very complex personality of this poet gives distinction to everything he writes. His most formal lines, the
most prosaic statement of his, stick in the mind, due
possibly to some twist of syntax. Every quaint experience,
passionate phrase, or queer thought becomes grist to
his creative mill; while his own brooding on character
gives an almost passionate importance to the commonplace.

And through all appears the clear image of himself,
impressionable — even gullible — in his momentary
fierceness or foible.

In the beginning of the century, Yeats's cry was the
cry of the awaking Russian Intellectuals: 'Return to
the simple folk, to the heroic folk'. On the strength
of that cry he hoped to stimulate a heaven-storming
imagination and to establish a fine literature. That
cry of his found echoes in many a sincere and lonely
heart. The wild riders had gone forth working their will,
fulfilling the fears of Standish O'Grady and the hopes of
A.E.; and through them the pagan Cuchulain stands foremost today in the Irish pantheon. Did not Pearse accept
Cuchulain as the inspiration of heroic young Ireland —
only to triumph ? Ah, but 'Up, Saint Patrick!' was
the cry of the shop-keeping politicians, those defenders
of the Faith, and they also triumphed in their time when
danger was past. In Dublin today we have two statues.
One to the Irishman, Cuchulain; and it stands in the
General Post Office, where the spiritual fight was won.
The other to Saint Patrick, the foreigner; and it stands
in the street — 'a future symbol of our past', as Gogarty
says of the Hay Hotel. Ireland, the land of Two Myths!
The voice of that man in the street was heard against the
new literary forces. Synge succumbed before it; Yeats
furiously contended against it; but in 1910 'The Green
Helmet', the last of Yeats's heroic plays in the manner of
the second phase, was produced. After it Yeats discarded
the embroidered coat, made of old mythologies. Younger
forces were shaping the Theatre; these forces received
greater response from the audience, and that audience was
not to Yeats's liking. Intense agitation appears in his
mind — not exactly with the theatre, but with the mid-
dling-minded. He admired the prose realists; he appreciated the rise of their work; but their work showed
tendencies not in keeping with his purpose, the purpose
for which he laboured. Their common carpentry was creaky
beside the pliable branch of verse. Would he renounce
what he had begun?

> The fascination of what's difficult
> Has dried the sap out of my veins and rent
> Spontaneous joy and natural content
> Out of my heart . . . .

>   My curse on plays
> That have to be set up in fifty ways,
> On the day's war with knave and dolt,
> Theatre business, management of men.

> I swear before the dawn comes round again.
> I'll find the stable and pull out the bolt.

Was he dissatisfied with vain endeavours to create a great peasant art — a 'popular' poetry? Did the world of his imagination revolt from the limp imagination of Main Street? His own poetry never saw eye to eye with the middle classes. The bloodlessness, the loose sentiment of middle-minded verse was to him an abhorrence. There were, for him, only two commingling states of verse. One, simple, bucolic, or rabelaisian; the other, intellectual, exotic, or visionary. The middle minds lacked distinction, poise; their excursion into these states were the affectations of hikers — so he had little interest or patience with them. To them his poetry may seem a beautiful secretion from a mind of aristocratic pedantry in which the insignificant is given an absurdly pontifical importance. Yeats, however, nobly asserted his aloofness, striking home with a more telling and naked enterprise in song; and so declined for years his interest in the theatre. He retired, as it were, into his own shell; but from there we gradually hear the almost imperceptible music of a lost Kingdom.

After fifteen years of silence, Yeats again showed renewed enthusiasm in verse play-writing, but from a very different viewpoint — a viewpoint for which one may call his third and final phase. He demanded a very intimate stage for a most selective audience. His 'Four Plays for Dancers' were, let me say, a chamber poetic drama for the delight of a few, sufficiently learned or imaginative to enjoy the absence of scenery and facial expression. In them one avoids the realistic intrusion of the actor, who under a mask becomes an impersonal, abstract symbol. His voice is intensified by the employment of complex music, or by drum-taps; and between speeches, the tension of silence is likewise intensified by the controlled movements of a sympathetic dancer. In such an esoteric and unhuman medium, Yeats believed that he had 'found out the only way the subtler forms of literature can find dramatic expression'; and he rejoiced in what he called his 'freedom from the stupidity of an audience'. . . .

The poetic plays of Yeats, those of his three phases, all spring from a lyrical impulse. That impulse never leaps beyond one act, and these one-act plays have all the attributes in content and in style of a lyric poem. They are sparse in substance and economical in speech, from his earlier wistfulness of loveliness to his later wispiness of power; for subject, there always appears the

same conflict of spirit or intellect. In these plays
majesty descends on threadbare speech; we gaze upon the
sinewy thigh; through his invigoration, poetry on the
stage again becomes sovereign. He had dreamed of a poetic
stage, as I have said, with himself as main occupant;
and that is what he has achieved.

110. LOUISE BOGAN ON THE UNDEVIATING COURSE OF AN
INSPIRED MAN

1938

This extract is from Louise Bogan's article on William
Butler Yeats, 'Atlantic Monthly', CLXI, 5, May 1938. This
was reprinted in Louise Bogan, 'A Poet's Alphabet' (1970).
    Louise Bogan (1897-1970) was educated at Boston Uni-
versity. She won various poetry awards including the
Bollingen Prize (1955) and held various visiting Profes-
sorships. Her 'Collected Poems, 1923-1953' was published
in 1954, 'The Blue Estuaries: Poems 1923-1968' in 1968.
A poetry editor of the 'New Yorker', her 'Achievement in
American Poetry 1900-1950' was published in 1951, her
'Selected Criticism' in 1955.

'We should write out our thoughts,' Yeats has said, 'in
as nearly as possible the language we thought them in,
as though in a letter to an intimate friend.' And again:
'If I can be sincere and make my language natural, and
without becoming discursive, like a novelist, and so
indiscreet and prosaic, I shall, if good or bad luck make
my life interesting, be a great poet; for it will no
longer be a question of literature at all.'
    If we grant naturalness, sincerity, and vigor to Yeats's
late style, we still have not approached its secret. Technical simplicity may produce, instead of effects of tension and power, effects of bleakness and poorness. What
impresses us most strongly in Yeats's late work is that
here a whole personality is involved. A complex temperament (capable of anger and harshness, as well as of
tenderness), and a powerful intellect, come through;
and every part of the nature is released, developed, and
rounded in the later books. The early Yeats was, in
many ways, a youth of his time: a romantic exile seeking,
away from reality, the landscape of his dreams. By

degrees — for the development took place over a long
period of years — this partial personality was absorbed
into a man whose power to act in the real world and endure the results of action (responsibility the romantic
hesitates to assume) was immense. Yeats advanced into
the world he once shunned, but in dealing with it he
did not yield to its standards. That difficult balance,
almost impossible to strike, between the artist's
austerity and 'the reveries of the common heart' — between
the proud passions, the proud intellect, and consuming
action — Yeats finally attained and held to. It is
this balance which gives the poems written from (roughtly)
1914 on (from 'Responsibilities', published in that year,
to poems published at present) their noble resonance.
'I have had to learn how hard is that purification from
insincerity, vanity, malignance, arrogance, which is the
discovery of style.'
    Technically, the later style is almost lacking in
adverbs — built on the noun, verb, and adjective. Its
structure is kept clear and level, so that emotionally
weighted words, when they appear, stand out with poignant
emphasis. 'The Wild Swans at Coole' (1919) opens:

    The trees are in their autumn beauty,
    The woodland paths are dry,
    Under the October twilight the water
    Mirrors a still sky;
    Upon the brimming water among the stones
    Are nine and fifty swans.

Equipped with this instrument, Yeats could put down, with
full scorn, his irritation with the middle-class ideals
he had hated from youth:

    What need you, being come to sense,
    But fumble in a greasy till
    And add the halfpence to the pence
    And prayer to shivering prayer, until
    You have dried the marrow from the bone;
    For men were born to pray and save:
    Romantic Ireland's dead and gone,
    It's with O'Leary in the grave.
    . . . .

    Was it for this the wild geese spread
    The grey wing upon every tide;
    For this that all that blood was shed,
    For this that Edward Fitzgerald died,
    And Robert Emmet and Wolfe Tone,

All that delirium of the brave?
Romantic Ireland's dead and gone,
It's with O'Leary in the grave.

On the other hand he could celebrate Irish *salus, virtus,*
as in the poem 'An Irish Airman Foresees His Death', and
in the fine elegies on the leaders of the 1916 Easter
Rebellion.

And Yeats came to be expert at the dramatic presentation of thoughts concerning love, death, the transcience
and hidden meaning of all things, not only in the form of
a philosopher's speculation, a mystic's speech, or a
scholar's lonely brooding, but also (and this has come to
be a major Yeatsian effect) in the cracked and rowdy
measures of a fool's, an old man's, an old woman's song.
'The Tower' (1928) and 'The Winding Stair' (1929) contain
long meditations — some 'in time of Civil War' — upon
his life, his times, his ancestors, his descendants; upon
the friends and enemies of youth.

111. CLEANTH BROOKS ON YEATS'S CREATION OF A MYTH

1938

This extract is taken from Cleanth Brooks, Yeats: the
Poet as Myth-Maker, 'The Southern Review', Summer 1938;
it was included in 'Modern Poetry and the Tradition'
(1939).

Cleanth Brooks (b. 1906) was educated at the Universities of Vanderbilt, Tulane and Oxford. He was Pro-
fessor at Louisiana State University before becoming
Gray Professor of Rhetoric, Yale University. He has been
a visiting professor at several universities and from
1964-6 was Cultural Attaché at the American Embassy in
London. He edited 'The Southern Review' with Robert Penn
Warren from 1935-42. His books include 'Modern Poetry
and the Tradition' (1939); 'The Well Wrought Urn' (1947);
'Studies in the Structure of Poetry' (1947); 'The Hidden
God' (1963); and 'William Faulkner: The Yoknapatawpha
County' (1963).

William Butler Yeats has produced in his 'Vision' one of
the most remarkable books of the last hundred years. It
is the most ambitious attempt made by any poet of our

time to set up a 'myth'. The framework is elaborate and
complex; the concrete detail constitutes some of the
finest prose and poetry of our time. But the very act
of boldly setting up a myth will be regarded by most
critics as an impertinence, or, at the least, as a
fantastic vagary. And the latter view will be reinforced
by Yeats's account of how he received the system from
the spirits through the mediumship of his wife.

The privately printed edition of 'A Vision' appeared
so long ago as 1925, but it has been almost completely
ignored by the critics even though there has been, since
the publication of 'The Tower' in 1928, a remarkable
resurgence of interest in Yeats's poetry. Indeed, Edmund
Wilson has been the only critic thus far to deal with
'A Vision' in any detail. His treating it in any detail
is all the more admirable in view of his general interpretation of the significance of Yeats's system. For Wilson,
as we have already seen, considers the symbolist movement
as a retreat from science and reality; and Yeats's system,
with its unscientific paraphernalia, its gyres and cones,
its strange psychology described in terms of Masks and
Bodies of Fate, and most of all its frank acceptance of
the supernatural, is enough to try the patience of any
scientific modernist. A very real regard for the fineness
of Yeats's later poetry has prevented him from carrying
too far the view of Yeats as an escapist. But to regard
the magical system as merely a piece of romantic furniture is to miss completely the function which it has
performed for Yeats.

The central matter is science, truly enough, and Edmund
Wilson is right in interpreting the symbolist movement as
an antiscientific tendency. But the really important
matter to determine is the grounds for Yeats's hostility
to science. The refusal to accept the scientific account
in matters where the scientific method is valid and relevant is unrealistic, but there is nothing 'escapist' about
a hostility to science which orders science off the pre-
mises as a trespasser when science has taken up a position where it has no business to be. For example,
Victorian poetry will illustrate the illegitimate intrusion
of science, and Yeats in his frequent reprehension of the
'impurities' in such poetry — far from being a romantic
escapist — is taking a thoroughly realistic position. The
formulas which Edmund Wilson tends to take up —
scientific = hard-headed, realistic; antiscientific =
romantic, escapist — are far too simple.

We have argued in earlier chapters that all poetry
since the middle of the seventeenth century has been
characterized by the impingement of science upon the poet's

world. Yeats, after a brief enthusiasm for natural science
as a boy, came, he tells us, to hate science 'with a
monkish hate'. 'I am,' Yeats tells us, 'very religious,
and deprived by Huxley and Tyndall. . . of the simple-
minded religion of my childhood, I had made a new religion, almost an infallible church of poetic tradition,
of a fardel of stories and of personages, and of emotions,
inseparable from their first expression, passed on from
generation to generation by poets and painters with some
help from philosophers and theologians.' Here is the
beginning of Yeats's system.

It is easy, when one considers the system as expressed
in 'A Vision', to argue that Yeats's quarrel with science
was largely that the system of science allowed no place
for the supernatural — visions, trances, and incredible
happenings — which began to manifest itself to Yeats at
a very early period in his life. Undoubtedly Yeats
wished for an account of experience which would make room
for such happenings. But if we insist on this aspect of
the matter, as most critics have done, we neglect elements
which are far more important. Granting that Yeats had
never had a single supernatural manifestation, many of
his objections to science would have remained. The
account given by science is still abstract, concerned
with values, and affording to interpretations. Yeats
wished for an account of experience which would surmount
such defects: as he once put it, a philosophy which was
at once 'logical and boundless'. The phrase is an important one. Had Yeats merely been content to indulge himself in fairy tales and random superstitions, he would
never, presumably, have bothered with a system of beliefs
at all. A philosophy which was merely 'boundless' would
allow a person to live in a pleasant enough anarchy. The
'logical' quality demands a systematization, though in
Yeats's case one which would not violate and oversimplify
experience.

The whole point is highly important. If Yeats had
merely been anxious to indulge his fancy, not caring
whether the superstition accepted for the moment had any
relation to the world about him — had he been merely an
escapist, no system would have been required at all. For
the system is an attempt to make a coherent formulation
of the natural and the supernatural. The very existence
of the system set forth in 'A Vision' therefore indicates
that Yeats refused to run away from life.

But if he refused to run away from life he also refused
to play the game with the counters of science. For the
abstract, meaningless, valueless system of science, he
proposed to substitute a concrete, meaningful system,

substituting symbol for concept. As he states in the
introduction to 'A Vision', 'I wished for a system of
thought that would leave my imagination free to create
as it chose and yet make all it created, or could create,
part of the one history, and that the soul's.'(1) Or if
we prefer Mr. Eliot's terms, Yeats set out to build a
system of references which would allow for a unification
of sensibility. Yeats wanted to give the authority of the
intellect to attitudes and the intensity of emotion to
judgments. The counsel of I.A. Richards is to break
science and the emotions cleanly apart — to recognize
the separate validity and relevance of 'statements'
(scientific propositions) on the one hand and of 'pseudo-
statements' (unscientific but emotionally valid statements)
on the other.

Yeats, on the contrary, instead of breaking science and
poetry completely apart, has preferred to reunite these
elements in something of the manner in which they are
fused in a religion. His system has for him, consequently,
the authority and meaning of a religion, combining intellect and emotion as they were combined before the great
analytic and abstracting process of modern science broke
them apart. In short, Yeats has created for himself a
myth. He says so frankly in the closing paragraphs of
'A Vision' (1925 edition): 'A book of modern philosophy
may prove to our logical capacity that there is a transcendental portion of our being that is timeless and space-
less . . . and yet our imagination remains subjected to
nature as before. . . . It was not with ancient philosophy because the ancient philosopher has something to
reinforce his thought — the Gods, the Sacred Dead,
Egyptian Theurgy, the Priestess Diotime. . . . I would restore to the philosopher his mythology.'

It is because most of us misunderstand and distrust the
myth and because we too often trust science even when it
has been extended into contexts where it is no longer
science that most of us misunderstand the function of
Yeats's mythology. A further caution is in order. Yeats
has called his system 'magical', and the term may mislead
us. Yeats even claims for the system a capacity for prediction. In 1917, in his 'Anima Hominis', he wrote: 'I
do not doubt those heaving circles, those winding arcs,
whether in one man's life or in that of an age, are mathematical, and that some in the world, or beyond the world,
have foreknown the event and pricked upon the calendar
the life-span of a Christ, a Buddha, a Napoleon'; and
in the earlier edition of 'A Vision', there actually
occurs a prophecy of the next two hundred years. But
the system does not serve the ends of 'vulgar magic'.

Yeats obviously does not propose to use his system to
forecast the movements of the stock market, or to pick
the winner of the Grand National. The relation of the
system to science and the precise nature of Yeats's
belief in it will be discussed later. For the present,
the positive qualities of the myth may be best discussed
by pointing out its relation to Yeats's poetry.

The system may be conveniently broken up into three
parts: a picture of history, an account of human psychology, and an account of the life of the soul after death.
The theory of history is the easiest aspect of the system.
It bears a close resemblance to Spengler's cyclic theory.
(Yeats takes notice of this, but he points out that his
system was complete before he had read Spengler.)
Civilizations run through cycles of two thousand-odd years,
periods of growth, of maturity, and lastly, of decline;
but instead of Spengler's metaphor of the seasons, spring-
summer--autumn-winter, Yeats uses a symbolism drawn from
the twenty-eight phases of the moon. For example, whereas
Spengler speaks of the springtime of a culture, Yeats
speaks of phases 1 to 8 (the first quarter of the moon).
A civilization reaches its zenith at the full moon (phase
15) and then gradually declines, passing through phases
16 to 28 (the dark of the moon) again. Yeats further
complicates his scheme by dividing his cycle into two
subcycles of twenty-eight phases and of one thousand-
odd years each. The phases 15 of these two subcycles
which make up the two thousand years of Christian civilization are, for example, Byzantine civilization under
Justinian and the Renaissance. Our own period is at
phase 23 of the second subcycle; the moon is rapidly
rounding toward the dark when the new civilization to
dominate the next two thousand years will announce itself — 'The Second Coming'.

The full moon (phase 15) symbolizes pure subjectivity,
the height of what Yeats calls the 'antithetical' which
predominates from phase 8 (the half moon of the first
quarter) to the full moon and on to phase 22 (the half
moon of the last quarter). The dark of the moon ('full
sun') symbolizes pure objectivity, the height of what
Yeats calls the 'primary', which dominates from phase 22
to phase 8. The critical phases themselves, 8 and 22,
since they represent equal mixtures of primary and antithetical, are periods of great stress and change. So
much for the four cardinal phases. Each of the various
twenty-eight phases, indeed, is assigned a special
character in like manner.

An account of phase 23 will be sufficient illustration
— all the more since this phase is the subject of several

of Yeats's poems.   Yeats regards phase 22 as always a
period of abstraction.   Synthesis is carried to its
furthest lengths and there comes 'synthesis for its own
sake, organization where there is no masterful director,
books where the author has disappeared, painting where
some accomplished brush paints with an equal pleasure, or
with a bored impartiality, the human form or an old bottle,
dirty weather and clean sunshine' ('A Vision').   In
the next phase, phase 23, which the present world has
already entered upon (Yeats gives the year of transition
as 1927) 'in practical life one expects the same technical
inspiration, the doing of this or that not because one
would, or should, but because one can, consequent license,
and with those 'out of phase' anarchic violence with no
sanction in general principles.'(2)
    It is a vision of this period which Yeats gives us in
what is perhaps the best known of his historical poems,
'The Second Coming':

> Turning and turning in the widening gyre
> The falcon cannot hear the falconer;
> Things fall apart;   the centre cannot hold;
> Mere anarchy is loosed upon the world.

In 'Meditations in Time of Civil War' Yeats gives
another vision of the same period, one which employs
again the symbol of the hawk but this time joined with
the symbol of the darkening moon itself.   In Section VII
of this poem the poet has a vision of abstract rage,
'The rage-driven . . . troop' crying out for vengeance
for Jacques Molay, followed by a vision of perfect loveliness — ladies riding magical unicorns.   But both visions
fade out and

> Give place to an indifferent multitude, give place
> To brazen hawks.   Nor self-delighting reverie,
> Nor hate of what's to come, nor pity for what's gone,
> Nothing but grip of claw, and the eye's complacency,
> The innumerable clanging wings that have put out the
>   moon.

The moon is used as a symbol of the imagination in its
purity, of the completely subjective intellect.   It has
this general meaning in many of Yeats's poems — for
example, in the poem, 'Blood and the Moon', where it is
played off against blood (which is comparable to the sun,
or the dark of the moon) as a symbol of active force — of
the objective, or the primary.
    An examination of the various meanings of blood in this

poem will indicate how flexible and subtle the 'meanings'
attached to one of Yeats's concrete images can be. The
symbol first occurs in the phrase, 'A bloody, arrogant
power'. The tower on which the poet stands has been
built by such a force and the symbolic meaning of the
term is partially indicated by the characterization of the
power as 'bloody', shedding blood. But the meaning is
extended and altered somewhat in the reference to Swift's
heart: 'in his blood-sodden breast' which 'dragged
him down into mankind'. Blood here is associated with
elemental sympathy, though the reference to Swift's
particular quality of sympathy qualifies it properly —
a sympathy grounded in one's elemental humanity which
cannot be escaped and which — from the standpoint of the
pure intellect — may be said to drag one down. The
third reference to blood occurs in the phrase 'blood and
state', and a third connection emerges — the connection
of blood with nobility and tradition.

These references, it is important to notice, do not
so much define the meaning of the symbol as indicate the
limits within which the meaning (or manifold of meanings)
is to be located. That meaning emerges fully only when
we reach the last two sections of the poem where the
symbols of blood and moon enter into active contrast:
action contrasted with contemplation, power with wisdom,
the youth of a civilization with its age.

> The purity of the unclouded moon
> Has flung its arrowy shaft upon the floor.
> Seven centuries have passed and it is pure,
> The blood of innocence has left no stain.
> There, on blood-saturated ground, have stood
> Soldier, assassin, executioner,
> Whether for daily pittance or in blind fear
> Or out of abstract hatred, and shed blood,
> But could not cast a single jet thereon.
> Odour of blood on the ancestral stair!
> And we that have shed none must gather there
> And clamour in drunken frenzy for the moon.
>
> Upon the dusty, glittering windows cling,
> And seem to cling upon the moonlit skies,
> Tortoiseshell butterflies, peacock butterflies,
> A couple of night-moths are on the wing.
> Is every modern nation like the tower,
> Half dead at the top? No matter what I said,
> For wisdom is the property of the dead,
> A something incompatible with life; and power,
> Like everything that has the stain of blood,

> A property of the living; but no stain
> Can come upon the visage of the moon
> When it has looked in glory from a cloud.

The development is very rich, and even though the poet in
the last stanza has apparently reduced his meaning to
abstract statement, the meaning is fuller than the statement taken as mere statement. We must read the lines in
their full context to see how their meaning is made more
complex, and, if one likes, more 'precise' by the development of the symbols already made.

The tower itself, it is probably unnecessary to add, is
the symbol of the poet's own old age and the old age of the
civilization to which he belongs —

> Is every modern nation like the tower,
> Half dead at the top?

The poem itself is a very fine example of the unification of sensibility. As we have said, the poem refuses to
be reduced to allegory — allegory which is perhaps the
first attempt which man makes to unite the intellect and
the emotions when they begin to fall apart — Spenser's
'Faerie Queene', for example. Moreover, the poet has
repudiated that other refuge of a divided sensibility,
moralization following on a piece of description —
Tennyson's 'Princess', for instance. One can imagine how
the poem would probably have been written by a Victorian;
the old man standing upon the tower surveys from its
vantage point the scene about him; then the poet, having
disposed of the concrete detail, moralizes abstractly on
the scene to the effect that wisdom and power are incom-
patibles. Instead, Yeats has confidence in his symbols;
the concrete and the abstract, thought and feeling, coincide. The poet refuses to define the moralization except
in terms of the specific symbols and the specific situation given.

A more special and concentrated example of Yeats's
contemplation of the cyclic movement of history is revealed
in his 'Two Songs from a Play'. These poems really represent his account of 'the first Coming', the annunciation
to Mary of the birth of Christ, the dynamic force which
was to motivate the two thousand year cycle of Christian
civilization. The first stanza of the second song will
further illustrate the close dependence of Yeats's
poetry on his system.

> In pity for man's darkening thought
> He walked that room and issued thence

In Galilean turbulence;
The Babylonian starlight brought
A fabulous, formless darkness in;
Odour of blood when Christ was slain
Made all Platonic tolerance vain
And vain all Doric discipline.

We have already commented on the fact that, according
to Yeats's system, new civilizations are born at the dark
of the moon — at the first phase. When the moon is dark,
the stars alone are to be seen — hence the 'Babylonian
starlight' may be said to have brought the new force in.
But the phrase is used not merely to indicate that the
time is that of the first phase of a civilization. Baby-
lon is associated by Yeats with the early study of the
stars, and more than this, with a mathematical, historyless
measurement of events. The Babylonian starlight, then,
is not only eastern starlight but the starlight as associated with the objective and the 'primary'. (In his
system Yeats indicates that he considers the West as
dominantly antithetical, the East as dominantly primary;
moreover, the two thousand years of Graeco-Roman civilization is dominantly antithetical; the cycle of Christian
civilization, dominantly primary.) The phrase' fabulous,
formless darkness', one finds (in 'A Vision') to come from
a pagan philosopher of the fourth century who described
Christianity as 'a fabulous, formless darkness' that
blotted out 'every beautiful thing'. The conception of
the advent of Christianity on the rational ordered classic
world as a black cloud boiling up out of the ancient East
is further developed in the last three lines of the stanza.
'Blood', we have already seen, is another one of the primary symbols, and it is the odor of this blood which
breaks up the order of classic thought and the classic
discipline of action. The implied image, very powerful
in its effect, is that of men made frantic and irrational
by the smell of blood.
    Examination of 'A Vision' will also throw light on the
first lines of the stanza. Yeats is describing man just
before the advent of Christianity:

    Night will fall upon man's wisdom now that man has
    been taught that he is nothing. He had discovered,
    or half-discovered, that the world is round and one
    of many like it, but now he must believe that the sky
    is but a tent spread above a level floor, and . . .
    blot out the knowledge or half-knowledge that he has
    lived many times.
        The mind that brought the change [that of Christ],

if considered as man only, is a climax of whatever
Greek and Roman thought was most a contradiction to
its age;   but considered as more than man He controlled
what Neo-Pythagorean and Stoic could not — irrational
force.   He could announce the new age, all that had
not been thought of or touched or seen, because He
could substitute for reason, miracle.

We say of Him because His sacrifice was voluntary
that He was love itself, and yet that part of him
which made Christendom was not love but pity, and
not pity for intellectual despair, though the man in
Him, being *antithetical* like His age, knew it in the
Garden, but *primary* pity, that for the common lot, man's
death, seeing that He raised Lazarus, sickness, seeing
that He healed many, sin, seeing that He died.

The celebrated poem, 'Leda and the Swan', is of course
related to the same general theme, for the annunciation
to Leda is felt by the poet to have ushered in the cycle
of classic civilization.   Leda and her swan are thus felt
to be parallel to Mary and her dove.   The power with which
Yeats handles the old myth resides in part in the fact
that his own myth allows him to take the older one in
terms of *myth*, reincorporating it into itself.   'Leda and
the Swan', far from being merely a pretty cameo, a stray
objet d'art picked up from the ruins of the older civilization, has a vital relation to Yeats in his own civilization of the twentieth century.

Notes

1 This statement occurs in the privately printed edition
  of 'A Vision' which appeared in 1925.   The new edition
  does not differ from the earlier fundamentally in the
  system that it sets forth, though it has many omissions
  and revisions of statement, and some extensions.
2 From the earlier edition.   The account of history in
  the 1938 edition breaks off after the discussion of
  phase 22.

112. L.A.G. STRONG'S APPRECIATION OF YEATS'S ACHIEVEMENT

1938

This is an article by L.A.G. Strong, W.B. Yeats, 'The
Spectator', 18 November 1938.
   Leonard Alfred George Strong (1896-1958) was born of
Irish parents in Plymouth and was educated at the Uni-
versity of Oxford. He wrote poems, short stories, novels,
biography and criticism and local history, and he broad-
cast on the BBC frequently. His poetry includes 'Dublin
Days' (1921); 'Northern Light' (1930); and 'Call to the
Swans' (1936); and his novels include 'The Garden' (1931)
and 'Sea Wall' (1933), both located in Dublin.

Achievement in art alone need not make a man great: many
great artists have been less than great men. Though he
has been all his life a poet, and has made all his
energies and interests serve his art, William Butler
Yeats is the greatest poet writing English today because
those energies and interests have the range and intensity
that mean greatness in the man. No one of our time has
written a poetry which touches life at so many points,
and so nobly.
   A tremendous vitality, physical as well as mental, has
enabled Yeats to exercise himself in manifold activities.
His country and his upbringing provided them, and they
came naturally to his genius. Most Irishmen who have done
their country service fall into one of two classes. There
are those whose service has been direct, who have expressed
their patriotism in politics, in warfare, in philanthropy,
or what you please: and there are those who have shed
upon Ireland the lustre of their achievements. Yeats can
be confined to neither class. He has done his country
incalculable direct service, and shed upon her the lustre
of the greatest reputation in contemporary poetry. And
he has done it without any splitting of his powers, simply
by being himself.
   Of Anglo-Irish Protestant stock, he received from his
father, John Butler Yeats, the portrait painter, a ready
encouragement not to be afraid of ideas, and to think for
himself. The country round Sligo where his earliest years
were spent, gave him the first impulse of patriotism.
The images impressed there upon his quick senses have remained with him and coloured his thought. When he and
his sister were exiled in London, they stood in angry
misery by the drinking fountain near Holland Park, longing

for a sod of Sligo turf to hold in their hands. The sod
of turf has never been forgotten. From that childish
longing grew a fierce desire to serve Ireland. The
young man strove to affirm the Irish character in all he
saw, to rouse a national consciousness in literature as
well as in politics, to create an art in which Ireland
could speak with her own voice.

His incandescent mind drew heat from many fires. He
learned all he could of Irish legend and folklore. He
studied painting and drawing, listened to Dowden and
Henley, heard Florence Farr speak verse, and met Maud
Gonne. Oscar Wilde showed him the possibilities of perfect speech, William Morris, whom he deeply admired, suggested ideas which have been fundamental to his thought.
He mortified his flesh, travelled about Ireland lecturing, and poured out his personality in an impassioned
effort to awaken his countrymen. From these activities he
discovered the need for a public as distinct from a private personality. If the poet was to be saved from the
mere vulgar attrition of causal contacts, he must have a
defence.

'I had sat late talking in public bars, had talked
late into the night at many men's houses, showing all my
convictions to men that were but ready for one, and used
conversation to explore and discover among men who looked
for authority.'

For greatness, in this imperfect world, depends not
only on the possession of great qualities, but on the
peculiar craft and toughness needed to guard them. Many
brilliant promises are never fulfilled through failure
to learn this.

Yeats learnt it. He learnt something about poetry
too. At first, his mystical beliefs had urged him to
keep his poems impersonal, to weave the personal emotion
(and there was plenty of it) into 'a general pattern of
myth and symbol'. Now his expression became more objective
and direct: and he found for his external activities
exactly the right channel. Some amateur actors had started
a theatre. Yeats saw its possibilities, collected his
friends, and the Irish National Theatre was born. This,
and the literary revival of which it was part, did Ireland
a service which we cannot calculate. Here was a national
movement: books written by Irishmen who lived in Ireland,
plays acted by Irish actors for an Irish audience, work
which spoke to the Irishman first and to the rest of the
world afterwards. Yeats was its central figure, and,
in addition to his own plays, gave it its greatest
dramatistdramatist. Meeting Synge in Paris, where he was
working, disappointed and obscure, Yeats divined his powers,

and sent him back to Ireland, to write plays which enriched
the world.   Yeats supervised the business of the theatre,
helped to train the actors, built up a technique for the
speaking of verse, attended to a hundred things, and, by
his inspiration and his growing prestige, delivered the
movement from provincialism and secured for it an international repute.   Plays and players travelled, achieved
new standards of acting, and forced sophisticated audiences
to realise that Ireland had a theatre which, on its own
ground, could compare with any.

Into this project, of which he was the first to perceive the political significance — his sense of reality
has always been terrifying — he poured all his skill in
debate, his knowledge of men, his cunning in manoeuvre,
his prowess in combat.   It saved him from his ability to
meet the world with its own weapons;   it gave scope for
energies which could perhaps have made him less a poet.

In open politics, Yeats's activities have been subsidiary
but continuous.   A Senator in his later years, he has done
much valuable work behind the scenes, as an unofficial
negotiator: work for which he is peculiarly fitted.

But the greatest achievement of his life is his poetry.
The early poetry was something of an escape, from a world
'too full of weeping' to be understood, to the land of the
free imagination, that Land of Heart's desire to which, in
his play, the fairy beckons the newly married bride.   Then,
in his middle years, he made a complete break, put off
'the embroidered cloak', and resolved

    To write for my own race
    And for the reality.

The new poetry, bare, 'withered into truth', proved capable
of including without loss of dignity almost the full range
of modern life.   Yeats has not only written the perfect
political poem;   he has made noble poetry of the most un-
promising subjects, with a power of phrase recalling that
of Swift.

The mysticism and interest in magic that occupy the
religious side of his mind have been regarded by many
critics as the detritus of his poetic activity.   It is
significant, however, that the voices which guided the
writing in 'A Vision' said their purpose was to give him
'metaphors for poetry':   and that it is in the earlier
book on magic, 'Per Amica Silentia Lunae', that the key to
his whole outlook is given:

    We must not make a false faith by hiding from our
    thoughts the causes of doubt, for faith is the highest

achievement of the human intellect, the only gift
man can make to God, and therefore it must be offered
in sincerity.   Neither must we create, by hiding ugliness, a false beauty as our offering to the world.

A sociable man, a wit, and a brilliant talker, Yeats
never swamps his company.   He is vividly interested in
anyone who has a mind of his or her own, and as eager to
find out what they think as to speak himself.   What is
more, he brings out the best in those who meet him,
enabling them to talk at a level of which they would
never have thought themselves capable.   The only people
who fail with him are the foolish, the arrogant, and
those who treat him with reverence.   This he cannot
abide.   It arouses his dislike at once, and his dislikes
are vigorous: yet he never lets them influence his
literary judgement.   Thus, turning in disgust from a
writer who sought to interest him in literary gossip, he
came out a few days later with a magnificent tribute to
the writer's work.

This integrity, this aristocracy of mind, never fails
him.   He can be mischievous on occasion: there is nothing
forbidding about him, and he loves a good story.   Kind
to the timid, he will dismiss a bore with exemplary
sharpness.   He has helped and encouraged scores of young
writers: and he never swerves in art, in faith, or in
friendship.

113.   PHILIP HENDERSON ON THE VIOLENCE IN YEATS'S LATER
WORK

1939

This extract is from Philip Henderson, 'The Poet and
Society', (1939).

Philip Henderson (b. 1906) was educated at Bradfield
College;   he has written and edited several books, and
worked for the British Council and Dent.   His 'First
Poems' appeared in 1930, his novel 'Events in the Early
Life of Anthony Price: A Novel' in 1935, and his studies
'The Novel Today' in 1936 and 'The Poet and Society' in
1939.   He edited Emily Brontë's poems in 1951.

The weary, disillusioned, intellectualist mood of 'The
Tower' has completely disappeared by the time we come to
'The Winding Stair' (1933). As he grows older Yeats
grows also increasingly more violent. 'The Winding Stair'
is not the work of an old man at all; it is the work of
a man whose blood is still teeming with the vigour of
life. His tower no longer puts him in mind of 'Il
Penseroso's' Platonist toiling by the midnight candle: it
has now become for him an emblem of the 'bloody, arrogant
power' of the Middle Ages. It is, he declares, his
emblem.

> In mockery I have set
> A powerful emblem up,
> And sing it rhyme upon rhyme
> In mockery of a time
> Half dead at the top.

Meditating upon the barbarous deeds done in his tower in
the days that are gone, he laments his own inactivity:

> Odour of blood on the ancestral stair !
> And we that have shed none must gather there
> And clamour in drunken frenzy for the moon.

Is he telling us after all that action is better than a
contemplative life, better than 'this sedentary trade',
than self-searching and the pursuit of wisdom? He leaves
us in no doubt that this is what he does mean. But what
kind of action is it that he has in mind? Angrily he
demands:

> Is every modern nation like this tower,
> Half dead at the top? No matter what I said,
> For wisdom is the property of the dead,
> A something incompatible with life: and power,
> Like everything that has the stain of blood,
> A property of the living.

But by this time Yeats had already given his support to
O'Duffy, who had appeared on the scene as a Cosgravite,
strengthened by an organization of Blue Shirts — a patriot,
Yeats felt, who would keep the rebellious workers and
peasants down, a man who could be depended upon to defend
ancestral houses and the inherited glory of the rich and
save Ireland both from revolution and the shop-keeping
values of the new middle class. In 'A Full Moon in
March' (1935), Yeats comes forward as the champion of the
Blue Shirts and Irish Fascism:

> Money is good and a girl might be better,
> But good strong blows are delights to the mind.

His 'Three Songs to the Same Tune' were adapted as their
marching song, with the refrain:

> Down the fanatic, down the clown,
> Down, down, hammer them down,
> Down to the tune of O'Donnell Abu.
> When nations are empty up there at the top,
> When order has weakened and faction is strong,
> Time for us all, boys, to hit on a tune, boys,
> Take to the roads and go marching along.

This is a very long way indeed from the mediums of
Soho, the Japanese poets and lay brothers dreaming in
some medieval monastery. It looks as though Yeats himself has become an old bellows full of angry wind, fallen
a prey to the political hatred he so much deplored in his
friends — but in this case, I am afraid, it is merely
hatred generated by threatened privilege, the 'traditional sanctity and loveliness' of his Tory mysticism.
'What's Whiggery?' he cries in 'The Winding Stair':

> A levelling, rancorous, rational sort of mind
> That never looked out of the eye of a saint
> Or out of a drunkard's eye.
>   All's Whiggery now,
> But we old men are massed against the world.

But what sort of mind looks out of the eye of W.B.
Yeats at the age of seventy-three? Last year saw the
appearance of the revised 'A Vision', a small collection
of essays and a play, 'The Herne's Egg'. From 'A
Vision' we learn that he attributes his development as a
poet to certain 'Instructors', whose messages came to him
through the mediumistic activities and the automatic
writings of his wife. The magical view of experience that
he here attempts to rationalize into a system has, he
says, helped him 'to hold in a single thought reality
and justice'. But what reality and what sort of justice?
There is, first of all, the reality of his personal
emotions — his 'barren passion' for the women he has
loved, who, from his point of view, have so tragically
wasted their lives in politics.

> Dear shadows, now you know it all,
> All the folly of a fight
> With a common wrong or right.

> The innocent and the beautiful
> Have no enemy but time.

Then there are the men he has known, whose ghosts he
invites to supper in his ancestral tower — Synge, Dowson,
Lionel Johnson, the old astrologer, George Pollexfen,
Major Robert Gregory, soldier, scholar, horseman, 'our
Sidney and our perfect man': there is the Connemara
fisherman who goes to a grey place on a hill to cast his
flies at dawn, 'that wise and simple man' who had made
him want to 'write for my race and the reality' — all
these have become part of his life and mind, and he has
woven them into a personal legend to fill his loneliness.
There are the things that he has observed outside himself,
from nature, which he has made into symbols of emotion
and imagination — the wild swans at Coole, the cold and
rook-delighting heaven, the moor-hens that build by the
stream below his tower, sea-birds, the hawk in proud
loneliness. Secondly, there is the reality of social and
political events — the race-meetings, and hunts in Galway
and Mayo, the outbreak of civil war in 1913, the repression of the Easter rising in 1916, followed by the execution and imprisonment of his friends, his scorn of the
small middle class, his uneasiness and finally his fury
in the face of a possible working-class revolution — his
whole anti-democratic, anti-rational, individualist attitude finally coming to a head in a rebellious truculence
and the marching songs for Irish Fascism. And in the
background there is the melancholy dreamy beauty of the
Irish landscape, the rather tumbledown grandeur of the
estates of the rich, the old Anglo-Irish families, and the
fine eighteenth-century houses on Merion Square, Dublin.
This is the material, the 'reality' of Yeats's mature
poetry.

But what of its 'justice'? His Instructors, he says,
forced him to a more severe meditation, they strengthened
his self-possession and integrity as a poet, and apparently
they have lately suggested to him that he could best
write for his race and the reality by exalting the bloody,
arrogant power of the middle ages and writing for General
O'Duffy. But then the spiritual world is always notoriously
reactionary in political matters, and mysticism and the
supernatural, whatever form they take, and however they
are approached, seldom lead their devotees to anything
like social justice. As for his last play, 'The Herne's
Egg', it is even more fantastic and remote from reality
than anything he has ever written in his most bemused
romantic days. By this time Yeats should be doing something better than listening to spirit messages and

hatching out fabulous eggs.   After all, the test of a poet
in the last analysis is how much reality he dare put into
his poetry — and by reality we mean the world of his
time, the world in which he actually lives.

It may be objected that this is to over-simplify the
issue, because for the poet there will always be at the
heart of experience an essential incompatibility between
the imaginative life and the claims of actuality;   that for
him reality must always be far more in the world of the
imagination than the actual world of daily life.   But the
peculiar interest of Yeats's poetry is precisely this:
starting from a conception of the imagination as something
almost entirely divorced from the actual world, his whole
development has been an heroic effort to reconcile these
two worlds, to abolish the false distinction between them,
and to see them as one.   At times he has succeeded magnificently.   But he has also, and to a much larger extent,
failed altogether because of his refusal to come to terms
with the most significant thought and the most vital historical movements of his day.   And the fact that he now
recognizes this failure himself has only made him in his
last years the more bitter and violent.   This is the quarrel with himself out of which he has made poetry of an
angry splendour and which has led him to assert, with a
certain weary self-contempt, that the half-read wisdom of
dæmonic images suffice the ageing man as once the growing
boy.

114.   DESMOND MacCARTHY ON YEATS'S LOFTY SINGLENESS OF
PURPOSE

1939

This is Desmond MacCarthy's summing up of Yeats's achievement on hearing of his death.   It appeared under the title
of W.B. Yeats in 'The Sunday Times', 5 February 1939.
    For a note on Sir Desmond MacCarthy see p. 317.

In the judgment of not only my generation but of his
younger contemporaries (though we differ about poetry on
so many points), Yeats was the greatest of all living
poets, and it is impossible not to believe his work will
last.   We claim that he possessed those qualities which
in the past have ensured repeated resurrections: per-

fection of diction at once personal and characteristic of
his race (an element which enters into the complete expression of any personality);   and a most delicate balance in
what he wrote between the claims of thought (sincerity)
and of poetic intuition which need not necessarily be
based upon convictions.

This is how Dr. Day Lewis, a representative younger poet,
speaks of him in 'A Hope for Poetry':

> Yeats, the last in the aristocratic tradition of poets,
> remains the most admired of living writers: none of
> us can touch his later work, and it is too personal in
> idiom, too insulated to allow easy communication of
> its powers.   He stands, a lesson to us in intensity,
> demanding from us a complete subjection to the poetry
> that occupies us, yet never asking of poetry more than
> lies within its proper jurisdiction.

That is a little difficult to understand, but what, I
take it, Mr. Day Lewis means is that although Yeats is
aristocratic in temper and even averse to such themes
as move poets like himself to write verse, nevertheless
from his example, they, too, can learn the true relation
of a poet to subject-matter: that the poet should yield
himself completely to the emotion it inspires, but never
attempt to make his verse the vehicle of all he may think
about it.   Only in so far as thought has become emotion
and emotion thought are ideas capable of poetic expression.   Such was the practice of the great poet who has
just died.   He put artistic values first, even if he had
to speak through 'a mask' to do so, and he would pause,
as it were, while climbing the hill of his own thought, at
the point where the poetic view was clearest.   He allowed
(in spite of strong temptation at moments to write only
as an Irish patriot) the genius of poetry in him to work
out its salvation, knowing that it could only be matured
by self-watchfulness: 'That which is creative must
create itself.'   Yeats constantly 'curbed his magnanimity'
(as Keats counselled Shelley to do) in order to be the
more an artist, whose preoccupations will, of necessity,
be different from ours.

There is a well-known passage in one of Keats's letters
on what he calls 'negative capability', which, he says,
Shakespeare 'possessed so enormously'.   A poet exhibits
this when he shows himself

> capable of being in uncertainties, mysteries, doubts,
> without any irritable reaching after fact and reason.
> Coleridge, for instance, would let go a fine isolated

verisimilitude caught from the penetralium of mystery,
from being incapable of remaining content with half-
knowledge. . . . With a great poet the sense of
beauty overcomes every other consideration.

And this was true of Yeats.

HIS ULTIMATE FAITH
He was conscious all his days of an antagonism between
the imaginative life and the world of industry, politics,
and science. His 'Autobiographies' reveal this, and also
the steps he took to prevent being dominated by that world.
His early efforts to acquire a living faith in Irish
mythology and fairies, his frequentation of spiritualists,
necromancers, and astrologers, and his continued preoccupation with Theosophy and Eastern thought, were certainly in part devices for protecting his imagination.
    It was puzzling sometimes to guess from his talk how
much he really believed in what he spoke of as certainties.
But in whatever degree conviction was due to a wilful
suspension of critical judgment, those experiences certainly left a residuum of genuine philosophic faith behind.
He believed in a great common mind and memory — that
of Nature herself, which in varying degrees all men share;
also that the common contents of this deeper mind could be
evoked in individuals by symbols and by poetry. It was
a philosophy nourishing to a poet, dignifying his task and
distinguishing it from that of the mere purveyor of
literary amusement.
    Yeats will strike posterity as he strikes us, namely,
as a writer strangely aloof from the enlightened thought
of his age. But that will be no drawback. Enlightenment
is not stable, and the uninteresting part of the works of
past poets who were also thinkers is apt to be that which
reflected the most directly the thought of their age.
It is not the theological scholasticism of Dante, or the
philosophic orthodoxy of Lucretius, or the orthodox nineteenth-century doubt of Tennyson that keep their poetry
alive.

THE TURNING POINT
There are two phases in the work of Yeats, and the earlier
glides into the latter. The first, the Celtic-twilight
period, is also the most intensely subjective. A poet
may be great who lives in a world of his own into which we
can only pass ourselves in certain moods: Spenser is such
a poet, and perhaps if his work is taken as a whole, so,
too, is Yeats. But in his later work, which shows a vivid
apprehension of realities, he becomes also a poet who, so

to speak, invades our common experience and expresses it
dramatically or in his own person. This is the greater
Yeats, though his first phase produced his most popular
poetry, and poetry, too, of the first order.

To it belong the deservedly renowned Innisfree poem
and the poem with its last well-known line, 'Tread
softly because you tread on my dreams', and the lovely song
'All things uncomely and broken', and the sweet fanciful,
traditional song with its refrain, 'O that none ever loved
but you and I!' and

> A pity beyond all telling
>   Is hid in the heart of love.

The ancient myths of Ireland, the mysteries of
Rosicrucians, amorous idealism, these were his themes,
and he clothed these themes, remote from actual life, in
rich literary language. There is no doubt that some (but
not most) of the most beautiful things he wrote belong to
this period. But as time went on his manner changed.
This was partly due to the influence of Synge, the Irish
peasant dramatist, but also to some change in the poet's
mind. He remained the exquisite craftsman he had been,
but he became a craftsman of a different kind. In the
last but one volume of collected verse which he published
there is a short poem which expresses the nature of this
new direction in technique. It is called 'A Coat', and
it runs thus:

[Quotes 'A Coat', 'Collected Poems', p. 142; see
text, p. 240.]

During his first period he had aimed at founding an
Irish theatre which should produce drama that was 'remote,
spiritual, and ideal'. He wrote for it 'The Land of
Heart's Desire', 'The Countess Cathleen', and 'The King's
Threshold', etc., and that moving little play of national
aspiration, 'Cathleen Ni Houlihan'. As 'John Eglinton'
points out in his admirable 'Irish Literary Portraits'
(Macmillan), in defending Synge's drama, in preaching a
doctrine of the imaginative arts from the ambiguous text
of 'The Playboy', which he did with admirable self-for-
getfulness, Yeats was in effect breaking the mould of
Irish drama as it had existed hitherto in his mind: and
henceforth in his own poems also he began to turn from
the abstract to the personal and concrete.

THE NATURE OF HIS LATER POETRY
The French Symbolists had been one of the discoveries of
the nineties, but Yeats had been the only major poet to
be deeply influenced by them — though Sturge Moore
translated admirably two of Rimbaud's poems. In Yeats's
early work there are often 'magic' lines like those which
glimmer in the cloudy opals of Mallarmé — lines with a
long, vague echo, such as, 'O sweet everlasting voices be
still!' The influence of the Symbolists persists in his
second period, but with a difference. It is another kind
of abstruseness, springing sometimes from a divided aim:

    THE SOUL: Seek out reality, leave things that seem.

    THE HEART: What, be a singer born and lack a theme?

    THE SOUL: Isaiah's coal, what more can man desire?

    THE HEART: Struck dumb in the simplicity of fire!

    THE SOUL: Look on that fire, salvation walks within.

    THE HEART: What theme had Homer but original sin?

In his later poems he took his inspiration from 'the
heart'.
    The characteristics of these later poems are the most
subtle use of spoken as opposed to literary language;
a far great variety of mood; and a new intellectual
hardness.
    Among the moods he has expressed with a unique enduring
charm in this later verse are a cold and beautiful melancholy, associated chiefly with old age and an exultant
poetic arrogance:

    I would be ignorant as the dawn,
    That merely stood, rocking the glittering coach
    Above the cloudy shoulders of the horses;
    I would be - for no knowledge is worth a straw -
    Ignorant and wanton as the dawn.

I quote these lines also as an example of that miracle he
often achieved of evoking a vision without direct description. These lines are not a description of dawn, any
more than:

    But look; the morn in russet mantle clad
    Walks o'er the dew of yon high eastern hill.

What they convey is a *sensation* which has the power to
create different pictures in different minds.   To write
thus is the sign of a true poet.

PERSONAL RECOLLECTIONS
To me, as a critic, it was natural thus to attempt,
however sketchily, a review of his work on hearing of his
death.   My acquaintance with him, though of many years'
standing, does not permit me to draw a pen-portrait of
Yeats himself.   I can only note down what those who met
him casually might have observed.   He was the only poet
I ever talked with whose talk and attitude (pose, if you
like to call it) never allowed you to forget for a moment
that he was a poet.   His conversation was full of flour-
ishes.   I remember him crying once in the midst of an
argument: 'The music of heaven is full of the clashing
of swords';   and I remember the relish with which these
words rippled from his mouth.   'I ought to spend ten years
in a library, and Lionel Johnson - ten years in a wilderness without a book.'   That is still as distinct to the
ear of my memory, though it was uttered nearly forty years
ago, as his protest when I pointed out that he had contra-
dicted himself.   'Oh, you're putting tin-tacks in the
soup!'   I visited him twice in his dark rooms near King's
Cross, but both occasions were wasted.   I could not get
him to talk about literature or poetry, topics on which,
as his exquisite criticism shows, his comments were those
of a profoundly ardent, meditative mind.   He insisted
then, as often again afterwards, on talking about ghosts
and magic.

On such themes his sense of fun, which illuminated his
comments on human beings, was in abeyance.   I remember
Edmund Gosse telling me that Yeats had told him how he
had noticed that a man who was pacing the room was followed by a 'small green elephant'.   'And then,' the poet
added, 'I knew he was a very *wicked* man.'   Gosse observed
that it was hardly fair to condemn anyone for a little
thing like that.

In young manhood his dark abstruse air was immediately
striking.   Your first impression of him was that he took
little interest in life outside his imagination, while his
extreme shortness of sight often made him seem oblivious
of those he was with.   It was not really so: nor was
there self-assertion in his hieratic pose.   As he grew
older, the dignity of his life and his impersonal pride as
poet lent a more enigmatic impressiveness to his romantic
appearance.   And now, when I think of him as a man, what
remains with me is his dignity;   the lofty singleness of
purpose with which he affronted the long humiliation of
life.

115.   W.H. AUDEN ON A JUST MAN

1939

This poem by W.H. Auden, In Memory of W.B. Yeats, was
originally published in 'New Republic', 8 March 1939.
Part 2 was added to the version published in 'Collected
Poetry of W.H. Auden' (1945).

Wystan Hugh Auden (1907-73) was included in Yeats's
'Oxford Book of Modern Verse' (1936). Yeats wrote in
his Introduction to that anthology of MacNeice, Auden and
Day Lewis handling traditional metres with a new freedom,
and talked of their 'social passion, their sense of suffering'. He wrote to Mrs Llewelyn Davies on 19 March
1937 to say he admired Auden more than he had said in
the Anthology. And in this poem Auden shows his own
regard for the older poet.

1

He disappeared in the dead of winter:
The brooks were frozen, the airports almost deserted,
And snow disfigured the public statues;
The mercury sank in the mouth of the dying day.
O all the instruments agree
The day of his death was a dark cold day.

Far from his illness
The wolves ran on through the evergreen forests,
The peasant river was untempted by the fashionable quays;
By mourning tongues
The death of the poet was kept from his poems.

But for him it was his last afternoon as himself,
An afternoon of nurses and rumours;
The provinces of his body revolted,
The squares of his mind were empty,
Silence invaded the suburbs,
The current of his feeling failed: he became his
    admirers.

Now he is scattered among a hundred cities
And wholly given over to unfamiliar affections;
To find his happiness in another kind of wood
And be punished under a foreign code of conscience.
The words of a dead man
Are modified in the guts of the living.

But in the importance and noise of tomorrow
When the brokers are roaring like beasts on the floor
    of the Bourse,
And the poor have the sufferings to which they are
    fairly accustomed,
And each in the cell of himself is almost convinced
    of his freedom;
A few thousand will think of this day
As one thinks of a day when one did something slightly
    unusual.

O all the instruments agree(1)
The day of his death was a dark cold day.

2

You were silly like us: your gift survived it all —
The parish of rich women, physical decay,
Yourself; mad Ireland hurt you into poetry.
Now Ireland has her madness and her weather still,
For poetry makes nothing happen: it survives
In the valley of its saying where executives
Would never want to tamper; it flows south(2)
From ranches of isolation and the busy griefs,
Raw towns that we believe and die in; it survives,
A way of happening, a mouth.

3

Earth, receive an honoured guest;
William Yeats is laid to rest:
Let the Irish vessel lie
Emptied of its poetry.

Time that is intolerant
Of the brave and innocent,
And indifferent in a week
To a beautiful physique,

Worships language and forgives
Everyone by whom it lives;
Pardons cowardice, conceit,
Lays its honours at their feet.

Time that with this strange excuse
Pardoned Kipling and his views,
And will pardon Paul Claudel,
Pardons him for writing well.

In the nightmare of the dark
All the dogs of Europe bark,
And the living nations wait,
Each sequestered in its hate;

Intellectual disgrace
Stares from every human face,
And the seas of pity lie
Locked and frozen in each eye.

Follow, poet, follow right
To the bottom of the night,
With your unconstraining voice
Still persuade us to rejoice;

With the farming of a verse
Make a vineyard of the curse,
Sing of human unsuccess
In a rapture of distress;

In the deserts of the heart
Let the healing fountain start,
In the prison of his days
Teach the free man how to praise.

Notes

1 The latest version reads 'What instruments we have
  agree'.
2 The latest version reads 'Would never want to tamper,/
  Flows on South'.

Select bibliography

WORKS LISTING SOME OF THE CRITICISM OF YEATS

COWELL, Raymond (ed.), 'Critics on Yeats', London, Allen
& Unwin, 1971.
Contains two sections, the first includes 17 pieces
written between 1886 and 1939, the second 16 grouped
under the heading 'Modern Critics on Yeats'.
CROSS, K.G.W., The Fascination of What's Difficult, 'In
Excited Reverie: A Centenary Tribute to W.B. Yeats 1865-
1939', ed. A. Norman Jeffares and K.G.W. Cross, London,
Macmillan, 1965, pp. 315-37.
This is a balanced survey of Yeats criticism and research
up to 1965, by the co-editor (with R.T. Dunlop) of 'A
Bibliography of Yeats Criticism 1887-1965', London, Mac-
millan, 1971. It lists some previous surveys (in article
form) on p. 322.
KEANE, Patrick J. (ed.), 'William Butler Yeats. A
Collection of Criticism', Chicago, McGraw-Hill, 1973.
This collection reprints twelve essays or extracts from
books.
PRITCHARD, William H. (ed.), 'W.B. Yeats: A Critical
Anthology', Harmondsworth, Penguin, 1972.
This anthology contains a useful selection of critical
material grouped under 'Early Criticism' (to 1940) containing 39 pieces, and 'Later Criticism' (after 1939)
containing 24 pieces. The Select Bibliography has some
surprising omissions, the Cross and Dunlop 'Bibliography
of Yeats Criticism', for instance, and the books by T.R.
Henn, Giorgio Melchiori, A.G. Stock and Peter Ure.
Such omissions indicate the personal nature of the anthologist's choice of examples.

BIOGRAPHIES

ELLMANN, RICHARD, 'Yeats: The Man and the Masks', London, Macmillan, 1948.
HONE, JOSEPH, 'W.B. Yeats', London, Macmillan, 1943.
JEFFARES, A. NORMAN, 'W.B. Yeats: Man and Poet', London, Routledge & Kegan Paul, 1949; rev. edn, 1962.
These three books are based upon studies of Yeats's MSS, unpublished material, letters, diaries, etc., and upon discussions with Yeats's family and friends.
TUOHY, FRANK, 'Yeats', London, Macmillan, 1976.

CRITICAL STUDIES

BRADFORD, CURTIS, 'Yeats at Work', Urbana, Southern Illinois University Press, 1965.
This study is based upon examination of selected MSS. and shows how the poems were shaped as a result of much rewriting.
ELLMANN, RICHARD, 'The Identity of Yeats', London, Oxford University Press, 1954.
A useful critical study.
HENN, T.R., 'The Lonely Tower: Studies in the Poetry of W.B. Yeats', London, Methuen, 1950; 2nd edn, 1965.
A general study which gives a good account of Yeats's Irish background and also deals well with his interest in art.
JEFFARES, A. NORMAN, 'A Commentary on the Collected Poems of W.B. Yeats', London, Macmillan, 1968.
An account of the poems' dates and sources, with comments on their meanings.
JEFFARES, A. NORMAN and KNOWLAND, A.S., 'A Commentary on the Collected Plays of W.B. Yeats', London, Macmillan, 1975.
An account of the plays' dates of composition, production and publication, with comments on their meanings.
MacLIAMMÓIR, MICHÁEL and BOLAND, EAVAN, 'W.B. Yeats and his World', London, Thames & Hudson, 1971.
A general presentation of Yeats's background which is well illustrated.
STALLWORTHY, J., 'Between the Lines', London, Oxford University Press, 1963.
An examination of Yeats's methods of writing verse, illustrated by reference to several poems.
STOCK, A.G., 'W.B. Yeats: His Poetry and Thought', Cambridge University Press, 1961.
A useful general introduction to Yeats.

TORCHIANA, DONALD T., 'Yeats and Georgian Ireland',
Evanston, North Western University Press, 1966.
Deals largely with Yeats's interest in eighteenth-century
Anglo-Irish writers.
URE, PETER, 'Yeats the Playwright', London, Routledge &
Kegan Paul, 1963.
A careful discussion of Yeats's dramatic work.
WILSON, F.A.C., 'Yeats and Tradition', London, Gollancz,
1958.
A study drawing particular attention to Yeats's interest
in occultism, Neo-Platonic tradition, etc.
YEATS, J.B., 'Letters to his son W.B. Yeats and others',
London, Faber & Faber, 1944.
These letters illustrate the close friendship between
father and son and show their continuing interchange of
ideas.

Index

The Index is arranged in three parts: 1, Works of W.B. Yeats; 2, People and Places mentioned in Yeats's Work; 3, General Index.

1 WORKS OF W.B. YEATS

2   PEOPLE AND PLACES MENTIONED IN YEATS'S WORK

3   GENERAL INDEX

PR
5907
.W2
136228

W. B. Yeats : the critical heritage /
   edited by A. Norman Jeffares. London
   ; Boston : Routledge and Kegan Paul,
   1977.
   xvi, 483 p. ; 23 cm. (The Critical
heritage series)

   1. Yeats, William Butler, 1865-1939--
Criticism and interpretation--
Addresses, essays, lectures.
I. Jeffares, Alexander Norman.

InGo   09 MAY 79   3469618   IGCGbp   77-30043

THE CRITICAL HERITAGE SERIES

GENERAL EDITOR: B. C. SOUTHAM

Volumes published and forthcoming

Continued